AUTO RESTORATION TIPS & TECHNIQUES

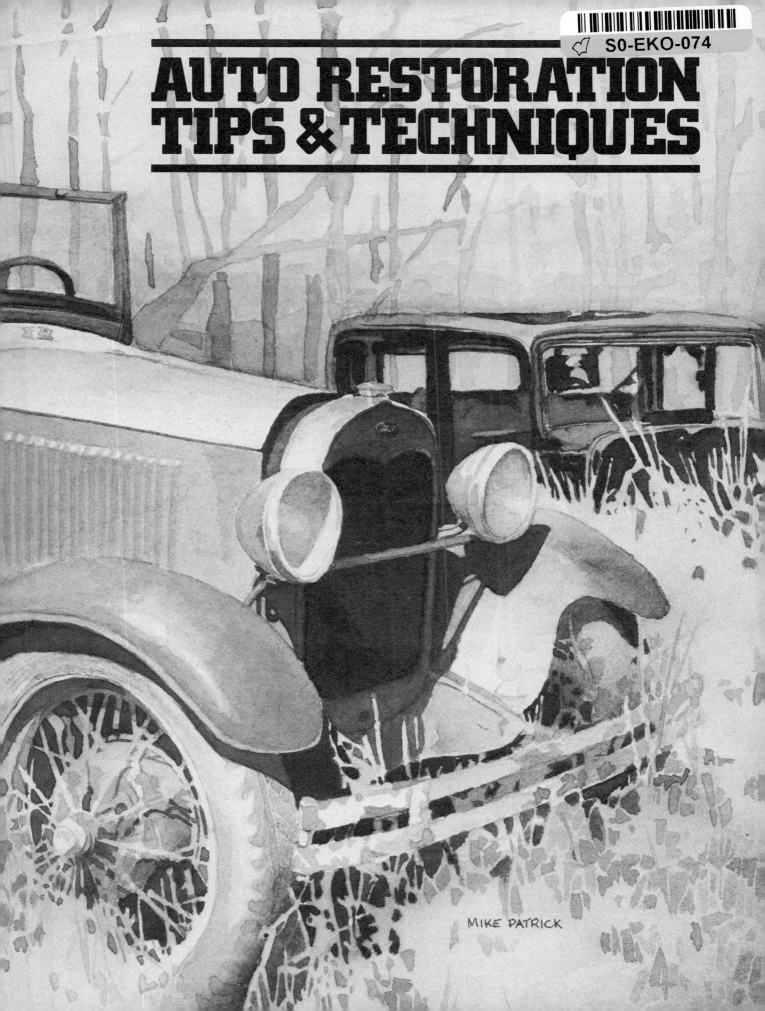

MIKE PATRICK

INTRODUCTION

Every "old car nut" has, upon towing or trailering his latest project car home, been greeted with a variety of reactions from friends, family and neighbors, not the least common of which is the question, "Why did you spend perfectly good money for a piece of junk like that?" Why indeed, when for the cost of just the engine rebuild on your '37 DeSoto you could have bought, say, a microwave oven?

People being people, the reasons for buying and restoring an old car are as varied as the vehicles themselves. Some, perhaps tempted by the "brokers" and "financial counselors" who have today trespassed into what was once simply a hobby, are interested in the inflation-fighting *investment* potential of old cars. Like antique furniture and other collectables, the prices of vintage cars have been lately rising faster than the national debt, property taxes and a Saturn V rocket put together, at least if we are to believe what we read in classified ads and auction results.

Others restore old cars for sentimental reasons. It may be a car they once owned in high school, or more often, the car they always *wanted* in high school. Perhaps it was just the long-gone shape of the radiator that intrigued them, the sweep of the fenders, the cut of the windshield or the nostalgia of such anachronisms as running boards and fender-mounted spare tires. Few projects can afford the satisfaction of a restored car, whether in the pride of ownership boosted continually by car meets and admiring bystanders, or the simple joy of rediscovering pleasure driving on a spring jaunt through a pungent country morning.

The diverse processes of alchemy that transform junk into pride and pleasure are loosely grouped under the title of the book before you. We could have filled 1000 pages or more pursuing the same subjects and still not have covered every refurbishment on every car, but most of the common problem areas are covered. Restoration has several definitions, from "cleaned up" to "rebuilt" to "fully restored." The latter is the most thorough, generally involving removal of the body from the frame and complete overhaul of all mechanical and cosmetic features. We've seen Model A Fords, for example, restored for a cost of $3000—and the same model restored for $12,000. The direct correlation in restoration between time and money means that the more work you can do yourself, the less the restoration will cost overall. Like the rest of our line of automotive books, this publication is designed for the do-it-yourselfer who can't afford to turn his entire project over to a professional shop with a carte blanche attitude. It's for this same reason, directing our editorial approach to the hobbyist of average means, that we don't cover the restoration of the classics, those gleaming behemoths whose Tiffany prices make them toys for the wealthy alone.

Obviously, there are obstacles to the restoration process which you and I in our home garages cannot overcome. Even the hobbyist multi-talented in the mechanical areas seldom has the skill/experience or shop tools to perform his own machine work, plating or upholstery. We cover these subjects hoping to pre-warn you of problems, equip you with the knowledge of what needs to be done and illustrate how it's done when done correctly. Our appendices advise you of where to get parts and services, locations of museums where restored cars can be examined, and most important, where to join the club relating to the marque you've chosen. This can be the single most important move before beginning your restoration.

Ideally, you are reading this book *before* buying that rusty relic of the Thirties, Forties or Fifties. The advice herein on how to obtain a car will be worth the cover price even if it scares you away from your dream car and onto something a bit more practical. If the proverbial basket case of potential automobile is already crowding the lawnmower and bicycles to the rear of your garage, this book will have served its purpose if it shortens the time between those first "old junk" comments and the inevitable post-restoration ones of "When can we get a ride in your *neat* car?"

JAY D. STORER

COVER: Photographer Eric Rickman catches Linn Davis in the act of refinishing the wood on his 1948 Chrysler Town & Country convertible to match his already-restored 1947 T&C 4-door. Tender loving care—that's the name of the restorer's game, and these two fine examples of the nearly lost art of wooden body building deserve all of it that they can get. Cover design by Dick Fischer.

AUTO RESTORATION TIPS & TECHNIQUES

Edited by Spence Murray. Copyright © 1976 by Petersen Publishing Co., 8490 Sunset Blvd., Los Angeles, Calif. 90069. Phone: (213) 657-5100. All rights reserved. No part of this book may be reproduced without written permission. Printed in U.S.A.

ISBN 0-8227-0657-1

Library of Congress Catalog Card No. 76-7170

CONTENTS

RESTORATION: EMOTION OR INVESTMENT?
HOW TO EAT YOUR CAKE WITHOUT TAKING A VERY COLD BATH

BY JIM NORRIS

There would be no market for restored cars if you could go into a new car dealer and buy one off the showroom floor. But that is not possible. A new car dealer sells only new cars from his showroom floor. He is in the business of making money from brand-new, mass-produced vehicles.

If you wish to own an out-of-date, worn-out, derelict automobile that has been separated from its frame and has been laboriously put back together, you will not be able to go to your friendly dealer—not even to his used car lot. He will gladly sell you a worn-out, nearly new car, or if you wonder about reconditioning one of his "rock-bottom specials," he will gladly unload one of the asthmatic dogs hiding in the back row by the fence.

This is not good. Stop such inclinations before they start. You don't just buy an old car and start repairing it. Restoring a car demands sophisticated thinking—at almost every bend in the road. It's a pursuit where you don't consciously make any mistakes. The reason for that is that the people who pioneered the restoration game were perfectionists, and on the whole were sick and tired of involving themselves in cars with mistakes. Those are the people in this field. You had better get used to it.

TOWARD PERFECTION

There are many things that make attractive the fine art of restoring a car. One could write a book on nothing but psychological analysis of why people restore cars, and still run out of room to include every last reason. What is it? A good value? Pride? Identity? Deep satisfaction at your own labor? The list goes on and on.

There's another attractive thing about restoring a car of the Twenties, Thirties, or Forties, too, a thing that's not easy to express. It's an awareness that once America was a pretty good place after all, and our cars, even though narrow and underpowered, were reliable machines, in spite of their Spartan attributes. But, like lemmings in a headlong rush to the sea, we forgot those things in the middle Fifties under the deluge of fins, width, and gadgetry. All but blinded to our automotive past, we soon tired of our conspicuous consumption and gladly submitted to the chiropractic terror of the economy car.

These tiny lifeboats, chiefly of foreign manufacture, wheezed and strained across the land and gave hope to our diminishing pocketbooks. But as we wheezed and bounced about, sardine-like, some of us began to wonder what caused all this. Why was motoring—the most passionate of American pursuits—no longer exciting? And then we remembered the narrow, underpowered, sturdy cars we had left behind...the cars from an age when we were still young and naive, and perhaps even happy, too. Well, how about those gracefully curved fenders—when each wheel had one? What about those high, majestic hoods? They were narrow, too. But at least you had room to wiggle your toes, or room to cross your knees without dislocating a kneecap. The more we thought about those days of uninhibited American motoring, the better it sounded. The only thing is, the more we think about it, the more others are into restored cars, too.

In the industrialized countries today, of which America has once

again taken the lead, there's no human being made who at one time won't have at least some concept of the old car that he'd like to own. And when it comes to shelling out hard cash, the personal images of preference begin multiplying through the various stages of condition and style all the way up to the highly personalized customs.

Another way to begin our sophisticated approach to auto restoration is to understand the profit advantage of a true restoration versus the lessened profit advantage of a hot rod. As far as an investment is concerned, a hot rod is nice; and as a group they are lots of fun. There are few identity builders of more standout impact than a creative expression with your own automobile—especially with a powerful engine in a light body, and so on. But unlike the last generation, the push now is toward faithful restorations. It is rather a shock when a custom-car perfectionist finds that his creative flair has turned a good-looking Ford of the Thirties into something that is worth about half the amount of money of a properly restored original car. This is especially true in the open cars, and with others that, because of lower production figures, would qualify as rare body styles. Forget what you've heard about convertibles having no protection against air pollution, having no defense against roll-overs, and other practical nonsense. The fact is that open-top cars are the top of the heap when it comes to the ultimate in a beautiful and highly desired restoration. Whether or not to shoot for a hot rod or a full restoration can be a definite problem, and one that affects the end result with varying degrees of emotionalism. A calculated, cold-blooded investment approach would come to another conclusion—especially when it comes to the immense popularity of the Fords of the Thirties, a thing largely related to the fact that you can buy any part you need for them.

It's as attractive as it is important.

If, on the other hand, you have a hankering for a car with largely nonavailable parts, and you really want to drive and enjoy it daily, even use it for a home-to-work car, there is definite reason to seek engine conversions and driveline modifications so that you can preserve its same, original outward appearance. This result is actually a different category than a hot rod—although usually the engine conversion is one with a great deal more horsepower.

I. AN EMOTIONAL APPROACH

What has caused the beauty of the engine swap to evolve into the restoration ethic? Today, they are no longer the same. There are probably more swaps than ever, but they're off in their own ballpark. While once the engine swap cult acted as the catalyst to get the restoration people going, now they are considered separate entities. A sophisticated restorer can pause at this point, where once the rivers were one, and can look about him at the automotive scene until he picks up the trail of the essentially emotional approach. He can examine its beginnings. He can watch it come together again at the high end of the scale—the auction block where the good restorations are now sold. Having traced the emotionalism and the investment ethic, each in its own way, he is in a better position to watch them intertwine. Subject to less confusion, he is therefore more sophisticated.

To begin our discussion of a purely emotional approach to auto restoration, let us take a look at the first stirrings of the game that began back in the early Fifties. For it was then that the modern, mass-produced, overhead-valve V-8 first took shape in the public's mind. During the war, with a freeze on new cars, a man would go for a rebuild on his own or an identical engine when

forced to decide. It's what was expected. But then, in 1949, the ohv Cadillac V-8 hit the country. In 1951, the Chrysler Hemi V-8 followed, later adding scaled-down Dodge and DeSoto versions of the same engine. Ford and Merc said goodby to the venerable flathead with their own ohv V-8's in '54, Lincoln's having premiered 2 years earlier.

The public, by that time deeply rooted in commonplace designs for a favorite warhorse, looked hungrily at the plethora of smaller, more powerful, cooler-running engines, as a bleary-eyed maiden after the charge of the Light Brigade.

Mechanics, who early in the game had not cooperated ("Ooh—you can't do that—wrong width, wrong length —engine mounts—adaptor plates, and so on—horrors!"), now began to change their tune. People were starting to demand engine swaps.

At that point, Detroit got into the act. As engines got better, designs took advantage of some vague Detroitese mutation policy and got progressively worse. People began putting two and two together and taking matters into their own hands. When you had a Lincoln Continental owner, for example, who wasn't anxious to part with his absolutely beautiful body shape for want of a reliable engine, the outcome was easy to predict.

In the late Fifties the epidemic was in full swing—literally creating a new American subculture. Swaps were keen. The better and more exotic the job, the more the suspender-pulling pride of the owner. The movement toward exotica continued unabated until the middle Sixties.

At this point, we had another, more finely chiseled direction coming out of all this. The name was money. The game was inflation. The player was the automobile restorer.

Millions of Twenties, Thirties and Forties cars that had gone to the junkyard during and shortly after the war had provided the scrap iron that was good for munitions people and developing or war-torn nations. That left a dearth of cars for home use. Right away the value of such scarce cars went up. Oh, there were plenty of new cars rolling off Detroit lines, all right. Engines were super, but bodies by and large weren't all that much better than what had come before. They were costing more and were more intricate and led to more owner woe when they broke. They weren't as simple any more. But they were faster, didn't overheat as easily, and people bought them in record numbers. More chrome—to rust. More weight—to dissolve your gas budget. Lower didn't necessarily mean supersonic speeds. Usually it just meant less headroom, and seating postures that gradually aimed at the prone position. Somewhere in all of this, cars began taking on a mind of their own. It was as if the driver was a puppet, a hired hand who merely had to sit still and push a variety of buttons—most of which didn't work anyway after a few months of ownership. People, good citizens that they were, went forward bravely in droves, cash in hand. The trouble is they couldn't pay for them, and a gigantic credit reservoir came into sprawling proportions.

Backtracking with our emotionalism to 1958, still sucking up the residue of history, the restoration bug started walking under its own power after the failure of the Edsel. "Let them eat cake!" was the Madison Avenue war cry. But people no longer wanted to eat cake. They were choking on cake.

Predictably, there was a decline into the Sixties. Less chrome. Smaller size. The Larks, the Valiants, the Falcons, the Corvairs. Economy. Damn if you feel like a sardine. "Join with us!" the public was told. Economy cars are a new national pastime. Tighten your belts. Hard times in the market place. After all, here come the small, cramped foreign cars that get all kinds of good gas mileage. These were the new insects—strange, bug-like autos in relation to what we had known, little more than velocipedes crawling over the nation's highways. Roller skates on wheels.

And on we go, still emotionalizing. Into the recession of 1969. Detroit's dying gasp with the muscle cars. Brutes that were low-flying aircraft more than they were cars of the earth. A few people were now looking dead center at the perfect size and horsepower ratings of the Fords

in the Thirties, but most people didn't notice—yet.

People started looking backwards when the unleaded darkness fell across the land. Forget what Sam's gas station tells you in the radio commercials. Sure, unleaded gas is cleaner. But is it clean enough to turn the smog problem around? Especially in light of hotter-running radiators? What about metals? How much torture can they stand? What about the guy down the block who can't afford 7 grand for a new "midsized luxury compact?" Detroit, however, fights back. In typical fashion. Stronger valves, gaskets that will resist more heat, Detroit says. But how much more—and for how many more miles? We aren't told. Where are the steam cars, the electrics, or the gas turbines? Where are the new concepts? "We're not ready," Detroit says—for the umpteenth time. "We're only ready to charge you $6000 for the same car for which we once charged you $2700—prices and the cost of living has gone up, you know." And we question more—through committees, through articles, through stories, through anguish. Detroit won't allow themselves to be taken to the mat. "New fabrics, new vinyls, the dash of tomorrow!" they say. If we don't like it we can lump it. At least one auto manufacturer has said that if the government gets unreasonable in making him do what he doesn't want to do, he will simply take his football and go home, and then there won't be any game anymore. How about that for progress?

And there you have it. Most people who are into the emotional side of restoration are convinced that

there is no longer any automotive progress coming out of Detroit.

At such periods of postulation, it is easy to remember American cars as they once were. In all probability, you or your father or someone you know has an unshakable memory of those days in the Depression when maybe the only pair of pants you owned was held up by a belt that was two sizes too big; and something like music from "The Sting" bounced around inside your head along with the pangs of a desire to get enough to eat; and when "All in the Family" was something you lived through, not something that came at you from a 16-in. box of glass. Maybe at the time you didn't think much of your car, either. Maybe it was an old Ford, or a Chevy, a Plymouth, or an old, comfortable Hudson 8. Something to get around in, to take for granted. But guess now where it hurts, when you scratch your head and wonder why you ever got rid of it. Sure, it was high, and maybe ungainly, with wide running boards and narrow seats, but to you it was all there was, and what's more, you probably owned it, lock, stock and barrel.

The more you concentrate on that old car, the more it comes to life, with all the original sparkle. For want of a momentary example, let's say you had a '39 Ford. Remember those 24 studs on the cylinder heads? That familiar, twin-hose radiator, cute in spite of itself? Or the high carburetor bowl and its round casting circle with the numbers "97"? They were the happy moments—because you knew where everything was, and you did it all yourself.

Maybe it all started when men moved off the farms, and were forced to relinquish their horse. But he didn't give up the affection, he merely transferred it to his car. When food and jobs were scarce, about the only thing of value to a struggling young adult was his car. But now it is different, even though the human spirit won't change, and even though a man may ressurrect the car he once loved. Yet who is to say that restoring a car is not the truest form of devotion?

That, then, is the emotional side of the issue. No matter how calculating a man may become, the emotional view of a restored car can not be destroyed—it can only be altered. A man who is blind to it, or won't admit that it exists, is a fool.

II. THE INVESTMENT

So with that in mind, let us proceed to the practical side of things. The investment. Now that we acknowledge that a marriage has taken place, let us prepare the wedding bed. This notion is not as funny as it sounds. Many a restorer will tell you that he has inadvertently sub-

1. No, it's not a basketball championship at this big-city arena, but full of winners, anyway. This pre-1925 Packard Twin Six is a good example.

2. Most other thoughts stop when a Ford of the Thirties eases through the auction block. This '35 Fordor is now worth six times its new car price.

3. Don't think for a minute that a high-dollar auto auction is not also a supreme moment in emotionalism. This is a skilled auctioneer.

stituted his church marriage for his garage marriage—not always it may be added—with happy results for the former.

To get to any superb fishing hole, there are usually tangled vines, rough water, and unpredictable ground between you and the hole. And why not? The most accessible are fished out first. It's a rule of thumb that can apply to auto restoration as well.

While it is true that certain models of Duesenbergs have appreciated nearly 1000% over the last decade, and one in particular that sold for $5000 in 1960 was sold for close to $60,000 in 1970, it is also true that there are infinite broken restorer hearts littering misinformed suburbia today. That particular Duesie that was worth an astounding $70,000 in 1972, sold later for $90,000; recently selling a fourth time for $165,000 in Florida.

On the other hand, there are plenty of people who have sunk thousands into a particular Ferrari or similar exotica, only to discover that their particular example is not rare after all—this on top of the ructions that restoring a car can introduce into family life.

Take the harrowing experience of trying to compare the three following examples. One, that we might call the "most exotic," recently sold at a Scottsdale, Ariz. auction for $160,000. The unrestored excellent example was a 1926 Daimler Phaeton State Tourer, built by Windovers for the Maharaja of Rewe. Called the "Gray Star of India," the car was expressly designed for hunting the white tiger and for transporting his highness around for a

week of religious activities. The "most astounding" could be called the 1948 Dodge Club Coupe that surfaced at a Southwest auto auction after spending *all* its life in a Texas barn. While the '46 through '48 Dodges are considered in some investment circles as lead sleds, this unrestored mint example sold for $10,000 the first time out, primarily because it had been driven a confirmed grand *total of 3.2 miles* since leaving the production line, lo those many years ago.

Lastly, the "least loved" of the lot might be considered to be the metallic bronze 1939 Dodge Luxury Liner 6 that went through a 1976 auction in Santa Monica, Calif. at the ungodly sneeze of $100, primarily because the interior was shot. But if the writer had owned that Dodge—which was essentially a straight piece of machinery—he would now be confined to a white coat, singing la-la to a chimney sweep. Maybe it was the design. Who knows? But the sad fact is that many people will put up with a car with mechanical faults if they like the design. Detroit loves that train of thought, of course, restyling its offerings every year in order to compensate.

For years, one powerful man stood in the face of this nearly conspiratorial scheme—and that man was Henry Ford. As Paul Woudenberg's 1976 analysis *Ford in the Thirties* has pointed out—a book of value to any restorer: "History appears to be vindicating Mr. Ford. His unique car with its uncompromising quality and technical eccentricities is the one mass-produced car of that turbulent decade which arouses the loyalties and passions of devoted followers 40

years later. Perhaps it is because we still see the man so clearly in the car."

We have only to look to the current auctions to understand. But before we do look at the auction scene, let's put into perspective something that every cold-blooded investor would like to know: namely the nature of the ballgame, and where the boundaries are.

At present, the top of the inflated cycle is not yet in sight for the car that you are about to restore—providing that you do it right. There are certain cars that you'll want to stay away from, and others that you'll be wise to seek out.

THREE POINTS OF VIEW

Assuming that you are serious about the patience, the money, and the excellence demanded in the auto restoration game, we are presenting here three points of view. One was prepared by Mike Lamm for *Motor Trend,* the second, also for *Motor Trend* by Robert J. Gottlieb, and the third is a concentrated look at the auction block—concentrated because often the clearest picture of a used car or restored car market can be gleaned from cramming lots of cars into a short period of time.

If we were all emotional buyers, there would be no need for such a cold-blooded look. If we all bought rusted hulks for the sheer joy of restoration, there would be no need for knowing what the rest of the world was doing. They could be damned, and we wouldn't care. (Some restorers still operate on this principle, of course.) But not to know the difference is just plain stupidity. Stupid because of the cost involved, in both time and money; and stupid because of the great, I repeat great, potential for monetary gain. That's because with each passing year there are more interested people, but fewer restorable cars.

Dealing in automobiles is like trying to slay the many-headed Hydra from Greek mythology. Each head cut off would be replaced by two others. If you can't watch both heads at the same time, your chances of getting what you want are, safe to say, reduced. But since the emotional buyer and seller and the cold-blooded investor are in the same game, it is a situation that causes both approaches to spill over their boundaries and become one, only to invariably break out into their separate ways, leaving a little residue behind each time the pas-

sions are pronounced. The emotional people, however, usually get the shorter end of the stick, while the cold-blooded investor is frequently hoodwinked when it comes to the finer points of restoration. The latter danger we will cover in our article, "Amateur vs. Professional Restorer," to follow later in this book. For now, however, it is important to take the logical approach. We must first know the nature of the most likely cars to restore; secondly, we must know what they are worth, and lastly but most important, we must know how to restore them. For therein lies the secret to the whole restoration scene. We must know how to do the work that will enable us to make the profit. If we can't, we must find somebody reputable who will do it for us, but it is by all odds better if we do it ourselves. Not only will our profit be greater if and when we sell our labor of love, but the satisfaction will be in knowing how we did it, and why. It will be a satisfaction unmatched—and *that* revelation is very nearly the literal truth. Ask any wife of a serious restorer. But first, to the logical start: the words of two highly respected automotive writers. These are the more recent cars from which you may wish to choose in order to start a restoration.

Mike Lamm writes: "I want to mention that any car, if you keep it long enough, will eventually appreciate—become more valuable. If you hang onto your 1966 Valiant 6 sedan for 50 years, for example, you'll eventually get more than you paid for it initially. But not too

many people want to hang onto that sort of car for so long. What I've tried to do in my list of appreciators is to include those cars that are on their way up now, or will be in the near future. Today, for instance, you can probably pick up a pretty decent Plymouth Superbird for less than $2000. It's not a tremendously practical car, but I mention it because I see Superbirds becoming the Auburn speedsters of tomorrow. In 10 years or so, a cherry Superbird might well be bringing $10,000."

See List of Restorable Cars—Page 10.

Lamm's list is restricted to roughly the decade following 1949. However, what it has going for it is to indicate the enormous supply of cars from which to choose. What are bringing high dollars on the auction block are without doubt the older cars, but when they become exhausted—and recent examples are beginning to point in that direction—then eyes will turn to the cars in his list. Also, he is talking about *unrestored* examples. Such a list is useful because it lets the serious restorer know how much he might have to shell out just to buy the car in the first place.

What is now happening is that certain buyers are acquiring junk examples of an old car and are getting in over their heads in the cost of restoration. Lots of such half-finished examples are being unloaded on the auction blocks, where they will bear the title of "Reconditioned" cars. A reconditioned car is one that has been put in driving

condition, without regard to the meticulous, exact care that must accompany a true restoration.

Other buyers will go for the unrestored cars in good or excellent condition. It is hard to find these pampered or long-garaged old cars. But certain buyers want them for either: A) lower-priced, reliable, "conversation-piece" transporation (in lieu of an expensive de-smogged etc. new car), or B) a speculation investment that they can unload to a private party or at the auction block for a healthy profit.

Lamm continues: "The rules of thumb for cars that become appreciators most quickly (and this has applied to antiques and classics) are: 1) Sporty body styles are more desirable than prosaic ones—convertibles, roadsters, some wagons. 2) Impressive, expensive cars tend to bottom-out quickly and then rebound quickly and to greater heights. 3) Cars that were popular to begin with often tend to remain popular."

Granted that you're now aware of a few desirable makes, and granted that you are prepared to restore a particular choice. What about the future of the restoration scene? Restorations by nature can be long-term projects. It is not unusual for any investment market to have changed when finally you are ready to "cash in."

While it is true that many automobile men will tell you that a value of any car is only proportional to what people are willing to pay for it, such a definition becomes painfully simplistic for the reason that cars are always prisoners of the law of supply and demand. It's always a case that such and such is worth so much "IF." There are a few more "IF's" to consider for the restorer, and the biggest is the state of the market for the current skyrocketing prices. Such a state can only result in an adjustment downturn arising from a runaway situation. It is a pattern that always attracts the devious restoration man (see the "Amateur vs. Professional Restorer" article). Suffering from other pressures, too, the prices eventually will drop when the word finally sinks in that many so-called true restorations are merely skillfully reconditioned cars. Things would hold it a lot longer if it weren't for this potential powder keg. Does that mean that the old car hobby will, as a defense, degenerate into a hobby only for the rich?

Some soothing words on skyrocketing prices were delivered in *Motor Trend* by Robert J. Gottlieb, a lawyer and an extremely knowledgeable writer on the automotive scene. Gottlieb's words were prompted by a letter he had received from one anxious observer. To find an example, the observer mentioned a near-mint original Chevrolet Nomad that was sold for $8500, and wailed that because it's only a car, how can anyone with any sense pay that kind of money for transportation merely to relive history?

Gottlieb wrote, "If a buyer is willing to pay $8500, then that's its value. If no one is willing to pay more than $300 for the same car, then its value is $300."

But times have indeed changed.

That's the important thing. Such a similar letter, repeated many times recently, is indicative of a mutual astonishment at the price spiral for an excellent-condition old car.

Of the early Forties (and Fifties, too), Gottlieb wrote, "A good used car could be purchased for $250. Used luxury cars were in the $1000 to $1500 range. Horseless carriages and cars which we now call "classics" averaged $150 to $200, which was just slightly under the established price for late-model used cars.

"Since that period, the dollar has decreased in value, interest in old cars has intensified and the prices of contemporary cars have increased. The ratios are still constant."

The ratio that Gottlieb is talking about is the price of a new car, say from $6000 to $9000, and the money that can be commanded from the average unrestored special interest or antique. That money is less—an aid for maintaining that "new car aura." There is, as Gottlieb writes, a "direct ratio to the present cost of a good used car."

The exceptions, of course, are what bring the shock. Gottlieb writes, "At the extreme upper end of the scale, the contemporary Stutz ($100,000), Rolls Royce Camargue ($90,000) and a few other modern exotics are in the same price range as the true classics which were their counterparts when new. While the intense interest in our hobby has spawned what appears to be a drastic increase in the value of the cars, that increase has really been consistent with increases caused by inflation, although I do recognize a few exceptions."

The exceptions, of course, are the main attraction for those who would like to induce some of the cream to rub off on them, and so we've had an enormous proliferation of the auto makes now being restored.

Gottlieb puts more perspective to this phenomena:

"For centuries, man has considered certain forms of painting, sculpture and design as art. Today, in the minds of many people, the automo-

2

1. **Excitement reigns on high as a '33 Auburn Boattail Speedster has its turn. With a Lycoming V-12, one just sold for $42,000; blown 8's are also hot.**

2. **Now the bad news. To the amateur, most auction cars exploit blind faith. Many '61-'65 Continentals go through—seldom bring over $3800. (Arrow shows one reason.)**

LIST OF RESTORABLE LATE-MODEL CARS

MAKE & YEAR	CURRENT NORMAL PRICE RANGE*†	PREDICTED RATE OF APPRECIATION	COMMENT
FORD MOTOR CO. PRODUCTS			
Ford V-8, 1949-57	$100-800	medium	Go for conv, hdtp, Crestliner.
Ford retractable hardtop, 1957-59	300-1800	medium	Complicated roof mechanism.
Ford plexi-roof hardtops, 1954-56	300-1200	slow	Try for Crown Victoria.
Ford Mustang, 1965 conv	400-2500 +	fast	Fastback might come along later.
Shelby Mustang 350 GT	1200-1800	fast	Shy away from Shelby 500-GT.
Thunderbird, 1955-57	1000-4500 +	slow	Peaked several years ago.
Thunderbird, 1958-60	150-1000	slow	Try for conv or rare sunroof.
Edsel, 1958-60	150-5000	slow	Beware fake convs made from Fords.
Mercury, 1949-50	200-1200	medium	Go for Tpk Cruiser, big V-8s.
Lincoln, 1949-57	400-3000	fast	Cosmos, Capris, convs good bets.
Continental Mk II, 1956-57	2000-4000	medium	No age onus, still prestigious.
Lincoln, 1958-60	100-2000	slow	Mk III, IV, V convs going up.
Lincoln, 1961-66 conv sedans	600-2000	slow	Parts & repairs expensive.
Continental Mk III & IV, 1966-up	2300-4000	slow	Haven't bottomed out yet, but will soon.
GENERAL MOTORS PRODUCTS			
Chevrolet, 1949-54	100-1000	slow	Go for convs & hardtops.
Chevrolet, 1955-57	250-4000	medium	Nomads, convs high, may have peaked.
Corvette, all	2000-6000	medium	Late models haven't hit bottom yet.
Corvair, all	150-2000	slow	Spyders, convs most desirable.
Pontiac, 1949-65	150-900	slow	Bonnes, GP, convs, f.i. good bets.
Pontiac GTO, 1964-69	650-1500	medium	Convs going up fast.
Oldsmobile 88 & 98, 1949-59	150-3500	medium	1949-54s now in demand.
Oldsmobile Vista Cruiser, all	300-1500	slow	Sporty wagons due to spurt soon.
Oldsmobile Toronado, 1966-67	500-1500	medium	Good ones to hang onto.
Olds F-85 and 4-4-2	150-1500	slow	Turbocharged F-85, conv will go up.
Buick, 1946-52	300-2700	slow	Open bodies & fbks in demand.
Buick Skylark, 1953-54	800-3500	medium	1953 more sought after than '54.
Buick Riviera, 1963/4-66	200-900	slow	Long-term investments.
Buick Special, 1961/62	150-400	slow	Get conv or Skylark w/aluminum V-8.
Cadillac, 1949-64	250-3500	fast	Eldo Brougham has peaked, watch '49-'50s.
Cadillac Eldorado, all	1200-4500	slow	Fleetwoods to go up fast; Eldo convs hot.
CHRYSLER CORP. PRODUCTS			
Plymouth 6, 1949-54	150-800	slow	Belvedere & conv desirable.
Plymouth V-8, 1955-59	150-1400	slow	1956 Fury most desirable.
Superbirds	1800-2400	fast	Might be tomorrow's Auburn speedsters.
Dodge, 1949-60	100-900	slow	D-500s & muscle V-8s good bets.
DeSoto, 1949-61	250-1800	medium	Adventurers, 1955s, 1961s best.
Chrysler Town & Country, 1946-50	1500-5000	medium	Wood-trimmed.
Chrysler V-8, 1951-60	150-1200	medium	Convs & wagons in good demand.
Chrysler 300-letter, 1955-61	500-3500	fast	Later 300s less desirable (post '58).
Chrysler Imperial, 1949-64	250-2000	fast	LeBarons coming up fast.
AMERICAN MOTORS & FOREBEARS			
Hudson stepdowns, 1948-54	100-2500	medium	Hornets, hdtps, convs in demand.
Hudson, post-1654 (Nash)	100-600	slow	Demand may increase in a few years.
Nash, 1949-57	100-1500	medium	Airflytes, Farinas coming up.
Nash Rambler, 1950-60 (American)	250-900	fast	Economical everyday wheels.
Nash Metropolitan, 1954-62	150-600	fast	Good commuter transportation.
Hudson Jet, 1953-54	150-1200	medium	Economical, parts hard to find.
Nash-Healey, 1951-54	1800-3600	medium	Earlier ones more in demand.
Rambler Martin, 1965-66	400-800	slow	Might catch on later.
AMX, 1968	1200-2400	slow	Should catch on soon.
INDEPENDENT MAKES			
Studebaker coupe, 1953-54	250-1900	medium	Becoming rare.
Studebaker Hawks & GTs	600-2500	medium	Shy away from lesser Hawks.
Studebaker Avanti, 1962-64	2300-3500	slow	They're high already.
Packard, 1948-56	350-2000	slow	Many well cared for.
Packard Caribbean, 1953-56	850-2800	medium	1953 is most desirable.
Packard Hawk, 1958	600-1200	slow	Studebaker derivative; last Packard.
Kaiser & Frazer, 1946-55	150-2500	slow	Look for exotic body types.
Kaiser Darrin conv., 1954	2400-4000	fast	Values have shot up lately.
Henry J, 1951-54	150-900	slow	Economical.
Willys Jeep, military	800-1400	slow	You can sell them for what you pay.
Willys Jeepster, 1948-51	300-1800	slow	Look for Six with o.d.
Willys Aero, 1952-55	300-1300	slow	Well engineered, economical.
Muntz Jet, 1950-55	1200-3000	medium	Hard to find, powerful.
Dual Ghia, 1955-63	2500-5000	slow	Might take downturn.

*Low figure denotes "unrestored-poor condition"
High figure denotes "unrestored-excellent condition"
†Please note: market prices are now higher.

bile in certain forms has joined that traditional Big Three. Why is it that one oil painting won't bring $50 while another will command $100,000? The reason is obvious. Why won't one car bring $50 and another will command $100,000? The reason should be just as obvious.

"For years many art collectors have considered their collections as much a hedge against inflation as a joy forever. Now, automobiles have been discovered as an equally good hedge. That means an even greater demand than simple popularity might decree, and as demand goes up, so does price. One advantage the automobile collector has over his painting counterpart: Try driving your Rembrandt around the block on a warm spring afternoon!"

Yet to sum up the true perspective of the great benefits of restoring a car to enjoy or to sell, as Gottlieb maintains, the "entire discussion boils down to a couple of fine points: The man who could rather easily buy a new car 30 or 40 years ago could probably have extended himself a little and gotten into one of the specialty or classics of the day. The man who can afford a new car today can probably afford to extend himself a little and get into a good collector car ... The fact that someone has an overabundance of money to invest in something special shouldn't be discouraging to the rest of us.

"People who don't have a half million dollars won't give up their interest in and desire to own art because someone pays $1 million for a Renoir.

"The lucky few who can afford extravagances should neither be criticized nor envied. The extravagances raise the prices for particular vehicles only and not necessarily for all vehicles of the same year and make ... I assure you that the old car hobby will *never* degenerate into a hobby only for the rich."

Of particular concern to Gottlieb and others in the face of the astounding new field of automotive investment is the question that investors always ask: "How much, how fast, and how long?" Gottlieb's prediction is clearly stated:

"We are about to experience a general decline in prices. The reason is that they have risen too rapidly. It will take about a year before equalization occurs and prices start going up.

"The leveling period will take its toll of ... established antique and classic car dealers ... but by the same token, look for expansion into the hobby by your local new and used car dealers. It's only a matter of time before most of them will carry one or two hobby cars as an accessory to their usual offerings.

"In relation to the coin, stamp, stock or art markets, old car prices will reflect relatively few up and down cycles. The long-range prediction is certainly optimistic for those who have the cars."

NOW IT'S UP TO YOU

It then comes down to getting the cars. An investor, at this point, whether he likes it or not, will have to know something about where to look and what to consider.

Mike Lamm's chart will go a long way toward sifting the flyspecks from the pepper for the beginner, while Gottlieb has been helpful to the investor in clearing away the cobwebs of speculation and doubt. The auction price chart will let you know what it's like when your hard restoration work meets someone else's money. We're not assuming that it will be your mouth and your money.

You're the guy who not only has to know *more* than the man with the money, but you're the guy who will do the work, and last but not least, you're the guy who will *get* his money. And you know why? Because you're the guy who knew what he was doing, why he was doing it, and you're the guy who had all the *fun* watching your baby grow. Now can you begin to see why some of the more passionate auto men devote their whole lives to the restoration scene?

As you seek the old car of your dreams, you will soon uncover a couple of alternate paths. You will locate other vintage tin devotees, who would part with their car for a price; and then there is the "discovery," or more rewarding derelict. There's nothing like being the *first* to locate and really appreciate an impressive old automobile. Whether you buy from a farmer (see the article in this book on that) or from a city slicker, you'll have to ask yourself a few relatively pointed questions before parting with your hard-earned lettuce. (After all, we're all farmers in our own way, aren't we?)

How much time are you planning to allow? That is, are you willing to spend 13 years of sorting and sweating and trial and error? Are you more willing to put that restored car on the road as quickly as possible? Are you willing to follow any leads you may encounter—and maybe devise a few creative ones of your own? Or do you plan to take the easy way out—and follow the well-worn path?

What you might do is to swap a rare classic in derelict condition for an older model—but not a classic—in mint condition. It is a fact that there are many owners who have been able to swap their way to more expensive cars that they were unable to buy in the first place.

Next, you must a take a long, hard look at your capabilities. If you don't know how to restore a car, then we'll show you, or tell you where it can be done. That's the purpose of this book. But going in, it will help, for example, if you're an enthusiastic mechanic. What are your particular skills? Do you have factory experience in machine shops or in automobile production? Even aircraft factory experience would help. Can you rebuild a carburetor, or do you just *talk* about it? And while you're at it, just exactly *where* do you expect to work on your car? Obviously you'll have to have the space to do the work. You should plan on extra space to store extra parts, or in which to remove some of the bulkier body panels. A two-car garage would be nice, if you're lucky.

Then there comes the onus of cold hard cash, and the time you'll have to devote to what you've bought. In the first place, you'll soon discover that what you're into is a long-term project. If you don't plan on turning into a social hermit, that will delay the restoration just that much further. If you count on at least a year of work, figuring that you'll have one night free a week, you're already in trouble. What happens if you spend 5 months looking for a long out of date but vital part? All right, try thinking about buying a parts car. One that is very bad in the areas that yours is strong in, but is rich in good accessories and body parts, for example. That's one strong solution. Just ask any successful or serious restorer.

And while we're on your associations with other restorers, it's an absolute necessity. You've got to get involved with others who are sharing your discipline, self-denial, and concentration. You will keep one another going. First, write to all the major clubs of your car's make in

RESTORATION: EMOTION OR INVESTMENT?

ACTUAL MARKET PRICES FOR POPULAR OLD CARS

Year/ Engine	Model	Category/Condition	Bid	Sold	Date	Where
BUICK						
1931/8	91C/4-dr.	Unrestored-Good	$4250		2/76	Ga.
1936/8	Spec./4-dr.	Unrestored-Fair	$900		2/76	N.J.
1936/8	40/4-dr.	Unrestored-Good		$1800	3/76	La.
1937/6	4-dr.	Reconditioned-Good		$2500	1/76	Ariz.
1940/8	Spec./4-dr.	Unrestored-Excellent Sidemounts-12,789 mi.		$9000	1/76	Ariz.
1940/8	Spec./4-dr.	Reconditioned-Good	$3100		2/76	Fla.
1941/8	Super/Convt.	RESTORED-Excellent	$8000		2/76	N.J.
1963/V-8	Riviera	RESTORED-Good		$1850	1/76	Ariz.
1963/V-8	Riviera	Unrestored-Good		$1100	2/76	N.J.
1964/V-8	Riviera	Unrestored-Fair		$500	2/76	N.J.
CADILLAC						
1931/V-12	Convt.Cpe.	RESTORED-Excellent		$38,000	1/76	Ariz.
1931/V-12	Dual Cowl Phaeton	RESTORED-Excellent		$67,000	1/76	Ariz.
1931/V-12	Convt.Cpe.	RESTORED-Excellent Prev. owned by film star Tom Mix	$47,500		1/76	Ariz.
1932/V-8	Sport Phaeton	RESTORED-Excellent Used by F.D.R. in 1932 Campaign		$45,000	1/76	Ariz.
1937/V-8	4-dr. Sedan	RESTORED-Good		$2550	1/76	Ariz.
1941/V-8	4-dr. Sedan Fleetwood	Unrestored-Good	$2250		2/76	Fla.
1947/V-8	4-dr. Sedan Fleetwood	Unrestored-Fair	$500		2/76	Fla.
1949/V-8	Convt.	Reconditioned-Excellent		$4500	4/76	Ga.
1951/V-8	4-dr. Sedan Fleetwood	Unrestored-Good		$2000	1/76	Ariz.
1954/V-8	Eldorado	RESTORED-Excellent		$8000	3/76	La.
1962/V-8	Eldorado	Unrestored-Poor	$300		2/76	Fla.
CHEVROLET						
1929/6	Roadster	RESTORED-Excellent 5-time Nat'l Winner		$11,500	4/76	Ohio
1930/6	Coupe	Reconditioned-Good In storage-30 years	$4000		1/76	Ariz.
1938/6	Coupe	Reconditioned-Good		$3900	2/76	N.J.
1938/6	Bus. Cpe.	RESTORED-Fair		$800	2/76	N.J.
1939/6	Bus. Cpe.	Reconditioned-Good		$2750	3/76	La.
1940/6	Master Town Sedan	Unrestored-Good		$1900	4/76	Ga.
1947/6	Fleetline 2-dr. Fastback	Unrestored-Excellent	$2900		1/76	Ariz.
1954/6	Corvette	RESTORED-Excellent		$9000	4/76	Ga.
1957/V-8	Corvette	RESTORED-Excellent Fuel-Injection		$10,700	4/76	Ga.
1957/V-8	Bel Air	Unrestored-Poor		$550	4/76	Ohio
1957/V-8	Bel Air Convt.	Reconditioned-Excellent		$3100	4/76	Ga.
1960/V-8	Impala 2-dr. H.T.	Reconditioned-Good		$1150	4/76	Ga.
CHRYSLER						
1934/8	Imperial Convt. Sedan	RESTORED-Excellent	$53,000		2/76	N.J.
1947/8	Town&Country Convertible	RESTORED-Excellent		$7800	1/76	Ariz.
1947/6	Town&Country Sta. Wagon	Unrestored-Excellent		$6500	1/76	Ariz.
1948/8	New Yorker 4-dr.	Unrestored-Good		$3000	1/76	Ariz.
1954/6	Windsor Del. 4-dr.	Unrestored-Excellent		$4200	4/76	Ohio
1962/V-8	Imperial LeBaron 4-dr.	Unrestored-Fair	$1050		1/76	Ariz.
1962/V-8	Imperial Crown Convt.	Unrestored-Good		$2100	4/76	Ga.
DE SOTO						
1949/6	Custom 4-dr.Sedan	Unrestored-Fair		$850	2/76	Fla.
1952/V-8	Sportsman 2-dr. H.T.	Unrestored-Excellent		$2200	2/76	N.J.
1956/V-8	2-dr.Convt.	Unrestored-Excellent		$3450	1/76	Ariz.
DODGE						
1941/6	Del.Cpe.	Unrestored-Good		$2700	2/76	N.J.
1948/6	4-dr.Sedan	Reconditioned-Fair		$550	4/76	Ga.
1955/V-8	Custom Royal	Unrestored-Fair		$700	2/76	N.J.

your area. Find out what's going on. Participate. Talk to those who love or who are concerned about your particular make. One advantage of being a member of the Ford V-8 Owner's Club, or the Lincoln-Zephyr Club, or whatever, is that you can plant the word of what you're looking for, and the word gets passed around that you're looking for a such and such, and pretty soon it will come back to you that so and so has a such and such, and so on.

Also, if you wind up by having a whole lot of friends working for you, your chances are increased in finding just what you're looking for. Don't stick around home when seeking your find, either. Visit places that "people would never stop in." Use your imagination. Up in the woods, near the tiny country hamlets. Check real estate offices out in the boonies. They frequently see old cars out in the back of some house somewhere. Leave several self-addressed envelopes or a business card or something. And don't forget, the big-money people frequently employ agents to beat the bushes for them. So there's nothing wrong with you doing it. The only thing is, you'll have to consider paying a finder's fee only if a lead that he or she has given you actually results in the purchase of a car. If you don't make this clear, you'll find your mailbox stuffed full of "suggestions," many from people who might also ask for some kind of fee. Of course, what you do is up to you. Old country garages, or even city ones, who have been in business a long time frequently know who's got an old car. Farmers and the people who work for them, such as boondock machine operators and well diggers—people who are out on the range—can sometimes unearth surprising finds. That's another reason, of course, to check with the farmer. And be prepared to go far and wide to do it, too.

You'll also want to cultivate the habit of checking probate sales and estate auctions when the long-time resident dies. Often, in these large residence neighborhoods, the original family will still occupy the big house, with an equally stupendous find lurking in the garage or under cover by the old favorite apple tree or something. This is not a wild shot. The writer is frequently haunted by a huge old house he knew long ago. The place was overgrown with weeds for years. Inside, there was a poor, decrepit old soul who had lived high off the hog for at least a generation. She used to ask, "Want to buy the old car for $300?" "Now, *where* would I get $300?" the writer would answer.

In the corner of a brick arbor, fronted with vine-covered Roman columns, there was a massive fountain pool, where long water streams came out of a sculpted gargoyle's nose. Behind this 6-ft. edifice, there was an old car from the Twenties. With very few miles on it, the car had been covered for 22 years, and then when the cover finally rotted away, it was left to rust in the elements. When the writer was very young, he remembers that someone had said it was a Rolls-Royce. Later he found out from an old gardenner that the car was a 1931 Phantom II Sport Phaeton, and when he went back in horror in an effort to talk with the old woman on what he had not understood until it was too late, he found that the woman had died, the probate sale had already been consummated, and the big 6-cyl. classic had gone to some auction outfit in the Southwest. It's the type of story to make any good restorer cringe.

When it comes to the end result of all this—knowing that you've done a good job in selecting the car of your dreams, around which to lavish your love—there will also come a time known as the moment of truth. How much is it all worth? Thanks due primarily to the Lord and our founding fathers, how much your car is worth is never an out and out certainty. What your car is worth will be primarily what you are willing to show that it's worth. If you care enough, the world will more than return the compliment. If you don't, then nothing will more surely reveal itself.

There are those who say that the demonstrated value of a particular make, in a particular condition, is secondary to the emotionalism of watching a full restoration take shape. If automobiles were sound investments, there would be few cars of a vintage nature still available. Everybody would own one. It is precisely because of the financial hazards that a restorer must justify his commitment. Only a fool, for example, would spend years seeking out a Whippet, or Viking, or 1917 Apperson Jackrabbit, and then pay vast sums of time and money to complete a grand restoration, hoping that a hungry public would rush headlong to the marque's exalted throne.

ACTUAL MARKET PRICES FOR POPULAR OLD CARS

Year/ Engine	Model	Category/Condition	Bid	Sold	Date	Where
EDSEL						
1958/V-8	Citation 2-dr.Sedan	Reconditioned-Fair		$450	1/76	Ariz.
1959/V-8	Ranger 2-dr.H.T.	Unrestored-Excellent		$2100	1/76	Ariz.
1959/V-8	Ranger 4-dr.	Reconditioned-Fair	$500		3/76	La.
FORD						
1918	Model T/4	Unrestored-Fair		$2400	1/76	Ariz.
1922	Model T/4 Sedan	Unrestored-Good		$4400	1/76	Ariz.
1928	Model A/4 Roadster Pick Up	RESTORED-Good		$6500	2/76	Fla.
1929	Model A/4 Phaeton	RESTORED-Excellent		$10,200	4/76	Ga.
1931	Model A/4 Phaeton	RESTORED-Excellent		$12,300	1/76	Ariz.
1930	Model A/4 Cabriolet	RESTORED-Excellent		$13,500	4/76	Ohio
1931	Model A/4 2-dr.Sedan	Reconditioned-Fair		$2500	2/76	Fla.
1932	Model 18/V-8 Roadster	RESTORED-Excellent		$23,500	4/76	Ga.
1934	Model 40A V-8 Phaeton	RESTORED-Excellent		$26,000	1/76	Ariz.
1934	Model 40A V-8 Phaeton	RESTORED-Excellent		$28,000	2/76	Fla.
1935	Model 48 V-8 Convt.	RESTORED-Excellent		$10,100	2/76	Fla.
1934	Model 40A 2-dr.Sedan Chev 350/V-8 Disc Brakes	Reconditioned-Excellent	$7900		2/76	Fla.
1936	Fordor/V-8 Touring	RESTORED-Good		$13,750	2/76	Fla.
1937	Convt./V-8	RESTORED-Good		$9700	4/76	Ga.
1938	Convt./V-8	RESTORED-Excellent		$10,250	2/76	N.J.
1939	Conv/Sed./V-8	RESTORED-Excellent		$16,750	4/76	Ga.
1940	Convt./V-8	RESTORED-Excellent		$11,100	3/76	La.
1956	T-Bird/V-8	RESTORED-Excellent		$11,100	1/76	Ariz.
1957	T-Bird/V-8	RESTORED-Excellent		$9500	4/76	Ohio
HUDSON						
1941/8	4-dr. Commodore	Unrestored-Good		$1550	2/76	N.J.
1936/6	2-dr.Sedan	Unrestored-Excellent	$3500		1/76	Ariz.
1938	4-dr. Terraplane	Reconditioned-Good	$2000		1/76	Ariz.
1952	4-dr. Hornet Twin H.P.	Unrestored-Good		$1000	1/76	Ariz.
1954	4-dr. Hornet	Unrestored-Good		$1450	2/76	Fla.
1954	4-dr. Jet	Unrestored-Good		$975	3/76	La.
LA SALLE						
1930/V-8	Roadster	RESTORED-Excellent Originally owned by actor Errol Flynn	$20,000		1/76	Ariz.
1930/V-8	Convt./Sed.	RESTORED-Excellent		$39,500	4/76	Ga.
1939/V-8	4-dr./V-8 Model 50	Unrestored-Good		$3250	2/76	N.J.
LINCOLN						
1932/V-12	KB Sedan	RESTORED-Excellent		$24,000	1/76	Ariz.
1937/V-12	Zephyr Cpe.	Reconditioned-Good		$6600	1/76	Ariz.
1939/V-12	Zephyr 4-dr.	Reconditioned-Good		$7500	1/76	Ariz.
1946/V-12	Continental	Reconditioned-Good		$5300	4/76	Ohio
1948/V-12	Continental	RESTORED-Excellent		$11,000	1/76	Ariz.
MERCURY						
1940/V-8	2-dr.Convt.	Unrestored-Excellent		$5000	1/76	Ariz.
1940/V-8	2-dr.Convt.	RESTORED-Excellent	$11,500		4/76	Ohio
1948/V-8	Sta.Wagon	RESTORED-Good		$4300	1/76	Ariz.
1951/V-8	Sta.Wagon	RESTORED-Excellent		$9000	2/76	Fla.

RESTORATION: EMOTION OR INVESTMENT?

What we are dealing with is the particular pursuit of long-dead machines, and with the people who barter for them under the aegis of guidelines that don't exist.

More than most pursuits, therefore, it takes strong savvy to know what the old car market will bear.

Because a car can be *both* an emotional and objective purchase, one can never be sure of exactly how the fires of popularity will spread or subside.

It is with these things in mind, therefore, that the prudent restorer, or old car investor, realizes that any list, guide, chart, or survey is merely suggestive, never definitive.

The following value reports are of interest only as far as they go. They help the restorer place an approximate figure on a particular make and year. Since they contain a record of cars sold at auctions for the first 5 months of 1976, they can be said to be fairly well insulated against cyclical interference, since the market as a whole was on the up side during that period.

What does a close look at these reports tell us? First, it tells us that not all makes are included, certainly no foreign cars. The reason for that is not that foreign cars are bad investments, only that this book is aimed at people with more desire than money, and that includes an aversion to a trip to England for parts. More often than not, the person with carefully budgeted funds will have to do much of the restoration work himself. It is to that person that this book is aimed.

Secondly, one finds that the ultra-expensive cars most normally unaffordable are lacking from this report. One would be surprised at the *few* Duesenbergs that actually go through the average auto auction—an average of three per auction. Some will push $165,000 for a perfectly restored example. Most Duesenbergs will not go that high. One was reported to sell at a special auction for some $345,000. Some of the more wild predictions are looking at a day when that figure could turn into a half-million dollars. Predictions are easy to make. Nazi Reichsmarshal Herman Goering's 1944 armor-plated Mercedes sold for $160,000. Few of us attend those special auctions. Most of us will visit one of the three or four established full-time professional auctioneers that deal in old cars and rotate from city to city around the country—wherever the willing buyers for such things reside. There are several auctioneers. One company, the Kruse Classic Auction Co. of Auburn, Ind., has developed a fast-moving regimen that will put them in 40 or 50 cities a year. Many of the people who gain an interest in restored cars say that somewhere along the line they remember visiting a Kruse auction.

The reports here presented are a compilation from Kruse and other auctions, arranged to show, by make, the most likely cross-section of year and model to be offered for sale. Many were not included due to

ACTUAL MARKET PRICES FOR POPULAR OLD CARS

Year/Engine	Model	Category/Condition	Bid	Sold	Date	Where
NASH						
1932/8	998/7-pass. Touring	Unrestored-Fair		$8500	4/76	Ohio
1936/6	4-dr.Sedan Ambassador	RESTORED-Fair Twin Ignition		$1800	4/76	Ohio
1951/6	4-dr.Sedan Ambassador	Unrestored-Excellent		$1500	1/76	Ariz.
1953/6	Healey Convt.	Reconditioned-Good		$6250	2/76	Fla.
OLDSMOBILE						
1947/8	Convertible	Reconditioned-Good		$3800	1/76	Ariz.
1948/8	Sta.Wagon	RESTORED-Excellent		$7600	4/76	Ga.
1951/V-8	4-dr.88	Unrestored-Excellent 390 Original mi.		$5000	4/76	Ohio
1950/V-8	4-dr.88	Unrestored-Good		$2100	2/76	Fla.
1963/V-8	Convertible Starfire	Unrestored-Good		$1400	4/76	Ga.
1966/V-8	Toronado	Unrestored-Excellent		$3200	2/76	Fla.
PACKARD						
1932/8	4-dr.Convt. Super 8	RESTORED-Excellent		$33,000	1/76	Ariz.
1934/8	4-dr.Convt. Dietrich body	RESTORED-Good		$18,500	2/76	N.J.
1936/8	2-dr.Coupe Rumble Seat	RESTORED-Good		$18,250	3/76	La.
1937/6	115C/Convt. 2-dr.	Reconditioned-Good		$6450	4/76	Ohio
1939/8	Super 8 Club Coupe	Reconditioned-Good		$7500	4/76	Ga.
1953/8	Convertible Caribbean	RESTORED-Excellent		$6500	4/76	Ga.
1956/V-8	400 H.T.Cpe.	Unrestored-Poor		$600	1/76	Ariz.
1956/V-8	Executive	Unrestored-Poor	$200		2/76	N.J.
PLYMOUTH						
1933/6	4-dr.Sedan	RESTORED-Good		$2400	3/76	La.
1933/6	4-dr.Sedan	Unrestored-Good		$2200	4/76	Ga.
1936/6	2-dr.Bus.Cpe.	Unrestored-Good		$1550	2/76	Fla.
1936/6	4-dr.Sedan	Reconditioned-Fair		$500	2/76	Fla.
1939/6	2-dr.Coupe	Unrestored-Good		$2900	2/76	N.J.
1941/6	4-dr.Sta.Wgn.	Reconditioned-Good		$4600	1/76	Ariz.
1948/6	2-dr.Clb.Cpe.	Reconditioned-Good		$1000	4/76	Ohio
1948/6	2-dr.Sedan	Unrestored-Good		$2100	2/76	N.J.
1957/V-8	Fury/2-dr. Hardtop	Unrestored-Good		$1300	1/76	Ariz.
PONTIAC						
1936/6	2-dr.Sedan	Unrestored-Fair		$1000	4/76	Ga.
1940/6	Sta.Wagon.	Reconditioned-Good		$5200	1/76	Ariz.
1941/6	2-dr.Sedan Streamliner	Reconditioned-Good		$1800	1/76	Ariz.
1948/6	Deluxe Sed.	Unrestored-Poor		$350	4/76	Ohio
1951/8	2-dr.Sedan Fastback	Reconditioned-Good		$1000	2/76	Fla.
1965/V-8	2-dr.Sedan Grand Prix	Reconditioned-Excellent		$3500	2/76	Fla.
STUDEBAKER						
1951/6	Champion	Unrestored-Fair	$700		2/76	Fla.
1952/V-8	Commander 3-spd.w/O.D.	Reconditioned-Good		$2500	4/76	Ohio
1959/6	Silver Hawk	Reconditioned-Good	$1300		2/76	Fla.
1961/V-8	Lark 4-dr.	Unrestored-Excellent		$1300	4/76	Ohio
1963/V-8	R-1 Avanti	Reconditioned-Good		$3000	3/76	La.
1963/V-8	R-2 Avanti	RESTORED-Excellent		$5000	1/76	Ariz.
1963/V-8	G.T. Hawk	Unrestored-Excellent		$3000	3/76	La.
1964/V-8	Coupe	Unrestored-Good		$1500	2/76	N.J.

space limitations, but the ones that appear more often than not are the cars that will come through the block time in and time out. They are, in short, what the buyers are going for. If a particular report does not include your particular favorite, it would be a relatively simple matter to deduce an approximate value by looking at the years on either side. As a guide this report can be useful. Take this book with you to an auto auction, as an indication of what you can expect. If you are to begin the restoration game in earnest, you will no doubt discover the following ten points:

TEN POINTS TO CONSIDER

1. Some makes are more popular than others. It is not a figment of someone's imagination. It is a fact.

2. Cadillacs, Packards, and Lincolns of the early Thirties can command awesome amounts of money—if they are full restorations.

3. A full restoration is far and away the most sought-after prize. This is especially true with the cars that were expensive to begin with.

4. The only thing worse than a full restoration that is not done properly is an unrestored car in poor condition. If you can't complete a faithful restoration, then shoot for the reconditioned category. But by all means, be honest about it. If there is any danger to the restoration business today, it is from the people who try to (and sometimes do) pass slipshod jobs off as full restorations.

5. Old Chevrolets, because they are relatively inexpensive, are rapidly increasing in popularity as restorations.

6. Some makes, not particularly sexy or popular to begin with, do not command high prices—no matter how faithful the restoration. However, if you have one of the really rare finds: a 1929 Stutz Blackhawk Roadster, a 1912 Simplex Shaft Drive Phaeton, or a 1933 Auburn V-12 Boattail Speedster, to name but three, do not despair. Heaven awaits.

7. On the other hand, some makes are becoming *notorious* for showing up for sale at the auctions having side-stepped a full restoration. Many owners of such material are hesitant, and for good reason, of investing time and material if their car's popularity is in doubt. If more owners could find the dedication to overcome this situation, it would do a lot to keep the restoration game from becoming too restrictive.

8. An unrestored car of excellent condition is next in popularity to a fully restored example—but the hardest of all to find. Again, it's the law of supply and demand.

9. If you insist on getting into foreign car restorations, be advised: You probably won't get your money out. There's not the demand among restorers for contending with a plethora of body styles and types among individual makes. This is particularly true of Rolls-Royce—you really have to know your beans to avoid getting cleaned. It's a rare Rolls that will bring more than $25,000, even fully restored, even though one or two examples have brought in excess of $70,000. You won't see any of these cars on our report. What you will see, on the other hand, are the most frequently auctioned makes, and in a culling of hundreds of prices, you'll find the most representative values for each.

Not unexpectedly, they're all American makes—and are further presented in correct proportion to their popularity. If you don't see your particular year among this list, take heart; you may have a diamond in the rough, a rare find, or another one of the years of the makes currently popular. It might be just the thing to spark a new tributary of interest on the fast-running river of the restoration game—a river that is rising nearly as fast as it is moving.

10. If you have a chance to buy a Ford—especially an open-top model built in the Thirties—think long and hard before turning it down. To this point at least, a Ford, first, last, and always, has remained the most popular car to restore. On any given day at an auto auction, more Fords than any other make will appear—often at the rate of four or five to one. The reason? Parts. Millions were stockpiled due to the philosophy of the company's founder. These NOS (New Old Stock) parts are still in relatively plentiful supply. There are also many companies across the country manufacturing exact replicas of original parts. Not only available, but inexpensive. But a Ford's popularity is more than that. A Ford was always defiantly different. It is an ideal to which many of us now wish to return. Restoring one properly can be very nearly a magical experience.

A final note—on the chart, Ariz. means Arizona, Fla. is Florida, N.J., New Jersey; La., Louisiana; Ga., Georgia.

So there you have it: how to evaluate the emotion versus the investment potential of it all. If you have stayed with us this far, you *must* have patience. For restoration is the *epitome* of patience. By presenting an article to you in this way, we've already helped you take two giant leaps forward: you've gained insight and you've demonstrated patience. Next, you'll want to get that favorite car. Have fun, because that, too, is what it's all about. The odds are that you—the one who's reading this—are in a much better position to accomplish your dream than you think you are. Why? Because you care! In the restoration game, those who *care* seem to attract more than their share of good fortune. ⚙

1

1. Perspiring with chrome and class, no finer restoration exists than the chic wood- and steel-bodied '48 Chrysler Town and Country 4-door sedan.

RESTORATION: AMATEUR VS. PROFESSIONAL

WHAT YOU DO, LIKE WHAT YOU KNOW, CAN DIFFER FROM WHAT YOU ARE

BY JIM NORRIS

There are a lot of deep pits that you, as a restorer, can fall into, but the biggest revolves around the choice of the car itself. Professional thinking starts by knowing the difference between the winners and the losers. Once you know that, you're thinking like a professional. Once you forget that, you're thinking like an amateur. However, in the car restoration business, a professional is also someone who is dedicated to perfection and who charges money for his efforts. An amateur is someone who does not carry the same degree of dedication, nor does he charge the same kind of money for his efforts, chiefly because he does not devote full time to that activity. Also, a professional is someone who learns quickly to tell the difference between good cars and bad cars. So, for you, between these two approaches rests the fine art of auto restoration.

In addition to the basic difference between final car appearances and work habits of an amateur and a professional, and the type of thinking that teaches you to watch for increasingly subtle differences between the two, there is another index by which to distinguish the truth—an index perhaps more important than any other. And that is, very obviously, the end product.

Today, there are several amateurs who are turning out finer and more dazzling restorations than many professionals. These are people who have a great reservoir of knowledge about their craft, yet they are not interested in an overwhelming profit for their labors; indeed, sometimes they are not interested in any profit—at least not at the beginning.

They work slowly and very carefully, and their work is nearly perfect. Usually they have a long background in automobiles and individual commercial experience in the separate parts of an automobile. They are as familiar with compression, heat and combustion as they are with frame and body alignment, trim, fit and applying finish materials. Their desire and affection for their work is high, and their immediate desire for money is low. They are willing to postpone a profit until their labors are completed. Such men are ideally suited to the demands of auto restoration.

How do you find these brilliant amateurs who can think and act like professionals? The answer is, you don't. Unless you stumble onto one, by chance or through a club, you are likely to face an agonizing deci-

sion that leads only one way: *You are going to have to be that person.* The first thing you can do is to read this book from cover to cover. The second thing is to find and talk to others who have restored or who are restoring cars of their own. From those two actions, all the others will evolve. You will travel to meets and to auctions. You will learn what's popular and what's not. You will get a car and start to work on it. You will budget your time, your money and your searches for parts. You will gain enthusiasm for working with your own hands. Most of all, you will begin to realize that the one you were seeking all along . . . *is you.*

It is very desirable, therefore, to become an amateur with a professional's thinking. Unfortunately, there are many so-called professionals who think like amateurs. The only real difference is the fact that professionals charge lots of money for working on your car, and you may or may not be able to see just exactly what they did or did not do. Only a completely naive owner would permit this sort of thing to happen. A truly professional owner would know the condition of every bolt and every strand of wire on his car. So it appears that the definition has a lot to do with which side of the fence you're on, doesn't it? Since you're going to do much of your work anyway, why not decide for yourself? Why not come with us on

1. A professional would be careful here. This '29 Model A has fender and running bboards beyond repair. Reason? Serious rust. Moreover, headlights are not Ford. They're too large.

2. An amateur wouldn't want this car. Only five were built. He'd be in impossibly far over his head—even if he could come up with the $60,000-plus that it would take to buy this unrestored example. Car is a 1933 Pierce Silver Arrow.

3. A hot little number and still somewhat of a sleeper is this '47 Ford convertible V-8. How sharp are your eyes on this car? See caption No. 1 on page 22 for explanation.

4. An example of a desirable restoration taking shape is this 1936 Ford Cabriolet in new coat of blue.

3

4

a tale of intrigue to the hallowed environs of one professional restorer, and then decide what is the professional and what is the amateur approach to the art of automobile restoration.

YOU BE THE JUDGE

First, be advised: there is now a plethora of fast-buck artists in the auto restoration business. Consequently, this one tale of intrigue comes from a big-city Model A shop, or more specifically, an example of a Southern California rip-off. Every big city has them, simply because the men with money who are into restorations as an investment or as a hedge against inflation are often not aware of the tricks that may be pulled in order to fleece some $8000 to $10,000 from their very busy bank accounts.

Taken from the beginning, this is a chronology of a hypothetical Model A owner, who visits "Mr. X's" shop after looking through the yellow pages, an oft-repeated hazard, because Mr. X may be the closest Model A restoration "specialist" within the physical reach of a busy executive, doctor or some similar professional man. These are prime candidates for seeking a variety of hedges against inflation.

In this case, such a man is taking his beloved Model A to an amateur who advertises himself as a professional. It is a terrible mistake, because the car owner is unprepared for what he gets. The trouble is, this is patterned after a true story, and there are many people doing the same thing and getting away with it. The only way to stop it is to make people aware of the tricks that are sometimes practiced. In the restoration business, exacting care is supposed to be something you can take for granted, a *sine qua non*. But it is not safe to take it for granted, because some shops only pretend to the perfectionism practiced by genuine restorers. Hopefully, we have now made that point clear.

Let's start with the owner, bringing his Model A to Mr. X. The latter, an intrepid soul with more talk than scruples, tells the owner that his Model A will be completely restored, and that at least a 90-point car will result.

After the agreement is made, the shop workers, who dutifully labor for Mr. X, work at flank speed to tear the car down. Working 8 hours a day for 2 days solid, the boys reduce the Model A to its component parts.

All bolts are placed in a bucket—used bolts, used washers, everything; used lock washers, even cotter pins. Everything that comes off the car, in the condition in which it's found, gets thrown into the bucket, which is then sent to the platers to get cadmium-plated. Even electrical components such as starter relays, switches and cutouts and things like throttle linkages and the like are put into the bucket for cadmium plating.

The parts then return to Mr. X's shop, looking like new in their coats of cad plate. Mr. X immediately tells the customer, "Everything has been rebuilt and cad plated." The Model A owner lets down a trifle on any apprehension he may have had and begins to spread the word to his associates that an expert, a highly efficient professional is restoring his Model A. Relieved, he then goes about his own business and looks for the day when his 90-point Model A can become a showpiece and a beautiful hedge against inflation.

Meanwhile, Mr. X's operation swings into high gear. All lock washers, which by now have been cad plated, are reused. Now unless the customer wishes to undo every bolt on the chassis, any verification of this act will be fruitless. A lock washer, of course, must *never* be reused. The customer does not know what has happened, of course. If by chance a lock washer has split, it will be replaced, but *only* then—not a frequent occurrence.

Mr. X, having once stripped a frame, has now abandoned the practice, because he has decided that it costs too much money. The customer was told, however, that his frame would be stripped. In typical rip-off character, the frame was sent to be sandblasted, and Mr. X produced five or six spray cans in lieu of proper repainting, which our shop hero also decided would be "too much." As to what kind of spray paint was selected for this chore, naturally it

was the cheapest possible brand.

The shop help then sprayed the frame, and Mr. X reported to the customer that, marvel of marvels, he had "put a beautiful lacquer job on the chassis." This further enhanced the customer's pride. He could hardly contain himself at hearing such good news. What was *not* revealed was that the spray cans covered up all spun rivets, bad joints and the like on the A's 46-year-old chassis. Regarding cracks, the philosophy was: "Unless it's entirely obvious or is in immediate danger of breaking something, the customer can't see it, so why fix it?" That was the theory. Any shop worker who by this time knew enough to question what was going on was fired, and a new man, expressly selected for his willing back and insufficient knowledge, was picked up to replace him. In such an

operation, it is never hard to find replacements.

Mr. X did not believe in replacing loose rivets, nor in tightening running board brackets. If the running board was ready to fall off because bolts and not original rivets were used, the more expensive riveting operation was omitted and the bolts were merely tightened, rusted condition or not.

At this point in the well-orchestrated ruse, it's time for the Model A owner to know what a professional job he is paying for, and so the painted chassis is presented for his inspection—great, assuming he knows nothing about cars. The customer comes down. Everything looks good. The frame is painted, he sees a whole box of cadmium-plated bolts, and Mr. X is the beneficiary of many good wishes from the cus-

tomer. The customer pleasantly shakes Mr. X's hand before bidding adieu and going about his business.

SPRINGING THE RIP-OFF

Now it's time for the spring work. Mr. X barks an order and his employees take apart each of the A's transverse springs. Each of the leaves is then painted.

They were not deburred, nor were their ends chamfered. They were hit quickly with the buffing wheel to remove rust; sometimes were skinosed, although at what Mr. X called "extra cost," and they were painted. Then they went back under the car, and Mr. X told the customer that he had completely rebuilt the springs. The truth was, of course, that neither spring had been re-arched or heat-treated. Each was merely an old spring that had been

1. Body welt on this canvas-topped Model A has been drilled for screws, one of which has fallen out. The original welt wasn't drilled; an amateur might miss this flaw.

2. One of the drawbacks of the early wire wheels was their proneness to cracking across the hub face. Arrow reveals crack here; something not pointed out to the man who bought it on this otherwise clean '31 Model A.

3. More in-depth inspection by a professional has turned up something else its amateur owner missed. Ford factory used only one manifold gasket. Someone installed an extra here (arrow) to compensate for warped manifold.

4. Another Model A nicety shows up in a crack across the valve seat. It could progress to the water jackets if not taken care of right away.

5. Here's the culprit. Thumb is over the warped portion of the A's exhaust manifold. Black, looped portion is intake manifold from updraft carb.

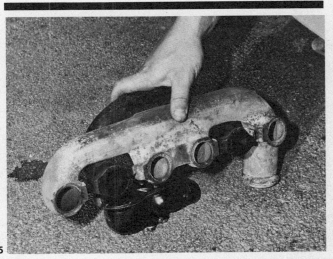

taken apart, cleaned and put back together. The owner didn't know this.

Regarding the Model A's spring shackles, if the bushing looked okay, Mr. X would order it put back together. His reasoning was, "The new bushings are too hard for the shackles to fit. One has to ream them out, and because of the time required, I'll leave the old bushings to mate with the new shackle bolt." Predictably, if the old shackle bolt was not literally in pieces, chances are it would make a return trip via the cad plating route. (A new shackle bolt would stay black.)

Throughout all of this, the customer would be advised that his Model A was being restored according to what Mr. X termed "show quality." The trouble is, you could take any six Model A chassis after his efforts and not find any two of them the same. Heretofore Mr. X has been saved by the fact that many of his customers have simply not shown their cars in competition. But when they do, and judges begin some very hard looks, the Mr. X's in this world invariably change their acts to fit the temper of the times. From an amateur, Mr. X will always inherit his pound of flesh.

Among the most flagrant of his methods concerns the running gear, traditionally a sore spot for the novice—and for the novice owner. It's a sore spot because few take them apart to check.

Many Model A ring and pinion sets, when taken apart, are discovered to be loaded with pits from excessive usage. What wouldn't be after nearly half a century of wear? Our hypothetical A was heavy with pits on the acceleration side. Traditionally, if a gear has pits you must change it, or if a ring and pinion has obvious wear patterns, you should change it.

Mr. X, on the other hand, holds that if it didn't howl when the owner brought it in, let's reinstall the gears (even though they could be ready to break). Bear in mind that with Mr. X's operation doing the honors, none of these gears have been magnafluxed; his is simply a method of reinstalling worn-out gears, and calling them brand new. No carrier bearings were replaced, only given new seals. Again, his theory is, "If no weird noise was made on the way in, *that* rear end will be there to stay." (Of course, the gear housing was cleaned up to look presentable.)

Brakes are the same. He never puts new brake springs on a car. He always sends them out to get cad plated (even though cad plating normally weakens the tension on springs).

Many former customers wonder about their brake pedals not returning all the way. Mr. X normally assuages them with a wink, a shoulder shrug or some other well-patented gesture. The sad truth is, however, that with a weak return spring, a serious or even fatal accident becomes a definite possibility should locked-up brakes occur. Our intrepid Mr. X, fearless with someone else's life, counters these trepidations with, "It looks good to me. I've never had any trouble before."

Moving to the front of the car, Mr. X leaves the bushings in the kingpins and leaves the same kingpins—after nothing more than glass beading and a coat of spray paint. The owner is then told, "You've got new kingpins, new bearings...you name it!" If the owner asks for the information in writing, Mr. X will refuse. If the owner insists, Mr. X will develop diarrhea of the fingers on the work order: "New bearings, new seals"—whatever. Now he is taking a calculated chance. But Mr. X is gambling that our owner is an amateur, a gamble that is to pay off.

After delays, followed by months of "work," followed by more delays, our Model A finally is ready to go, and even though the customer has actually received less than a fourth of that sum in parts and labor, he gets a bill for nearly $10,000.

A GOOD OBSERVER

It's a brief sketch of what's going on in the restoration field today. Such shoddy results are getting passed off as true restorations. Being forewarned, however, is being forearmed, and if enough restorers rise to the defense of perfection, there will be no danger of this becoming only a hobby for the rich. Still, if enough of these counterfeit jobs grace the auction blocks across the country, it won't be too long before a backlash starts in, and the vaunted hedge against inflation now enjoyed by the well-restored car will

all but disintegrate.

The man who wants to learn to think like a professional, therefore, must cultivate the art of perceptive observation. It is a fact that many of the so-called club runs and rallies are promoted by the fast-buck shop owners, whose "skill" in producing the Model A just described have reached such proportions that most restorers are nearly convinced that a Mr. X knows what he's doing, and has a right, therefore, to justify a good reputation. You must begin to cultivate your art of observation by using your own brain rather than his. Don't just listen to his words. Go down to his shop. What operation does he have? Look especially at his tools—their completeness, how they're used, how they're arranged.

If a man has a $50 set of tools and a big mouth, it tells you something. You can't work on old cars unless you have equipment—the proper tools to do the job. And you're kidding yourself if you think otherwise.

If a man has the tools, there is always the hope that he can do the job. But if he doesn't have the tools, no matter how honest he is, that man flat can't do the work, period.

What you'll probably find true of most so-called restoration people is that the front of a shop is graced by lots of shiny objects: painted wheels and new tires, lots of cadmium-painted bolts, neatly stacked and painted chassis frames. Those people who are getting into auto restoration as novice customers are invariably attracted by this show of expertise and glitter. But you are entitled to more than that.

1. Called by some "the reigning queen of the Thirties' Ford open cars," this is not the Roadster, but brother Cabriolet. Graceful lines everywhere are evident. If you're planning to restore it, you'd better be graceful.

2. To an early Ford flathead freak, this is worth a thousand words—whether you're a professional or amateur.

3. A few months earlier, this '47 Ford convertible had $1100 worth of new cream paint. What's wrong? Plenty. We'll show you a few of the problems. If you're an amateur, you might miss them.

4. Even though this '36 Cabriolet has concealed horns and other first-time classy touches, restorer has to watch for cracks on headlight mounts.

5. In photo No. 3, you'll notice that the inside of the trunk is not the same color as the outside paint; it's dark brown. Should match. Also, door weather stripping wasn't painted.

6. Inside door panel, not clipped tight, came loose and picked up paint spray. Just plain sloppy work.

3

4

5

6

As Shakespeare once said: "There are none so blind as those who will not see." It is important that your eyes remain open every step of the way. This is not a regulated enterprise you're in, and as such, there is no other widespread automotive operation containing as much thievery. "Let the buyer beware" should be your guiding motto. It will keep your eyes open and will save you time, money and perhaps sanity. Once you know what can happen to those who have bought restorable cars, it only makes your personal selection process that much more intelligent. You, as a truly professional owner, will need to avoid the costly arrogance of the amateur. Several examples should suffice to help screw your own head on straight.

PROFESSIONAL SECRETS

One of the first things to consider, of course, is the purchase of the car that you want to build to the best-of-show or 90-plus points category. But forget these goals if at the start of your work you don't have what is basically a good car! A true professional will not buy a car that is loaded with body filler. This represents sheetmetal damage that has been repaired so that it is easily detectable; in other words, it has to be redone or the panels must be replaced. Why throw good time and money after bad?

The professional has one advantage over the amateur at the outset, as a rule, and that is that he has probably already researched the car. He understands what the factory has built into the car. An amateur, on the other hand, will buy a car and do the required research while he is working on it.

This is bad. Too many things can crop up to slow or even halt precious progress. A novice should spend whatever time is necessary to research what he is about to buy. Some of the more successful restorers have spent a good year or two in looking at newspaper ads or in formulating a private opinion of what is needed in order to buy and restore intelligently. Others, more enlightened to begin with, don't need that much time. Research would include attending auctions, car meets and talking to people who know the answers, or who have "been there" with the almost religious process of restoring a model of your eventual choice.

Research points out what the car was like when new. It helps you

spot what parts might be authentic and what parts are not. It is not uncommon for an owner to represent a car as completely authentic when in fact it might have the wrong headlights, hubcaps, dash knobs or a long list of such things. This is of concern in light of Detroit's ability to make do in styling with a part that may be 1 or 2 years old, and even with retro-fit or replica parts in some cases. Without this type of research to know what you're truly dealing with, you could wind up buying a car that looks very pretty to you when in fact you have just bought a car that is a terrible mess due to its limited authenticity.

A good example is Ford, because so much has been done to Ford over the years that several things can become instant drawbacks. The most famous example is the engine. Since any of the flathead V-8's could be

made to fit any of the bodies from '32 to '48, it can be difficult to be on your toes. But in order to receive top points and value for a laboriously restored Ford, you need the exact matching year on both body and engine.

It will be to your disadvantage, for example, to produce a magnificent '35 Roadster with a '37 engine. An amateur will see the V-8, but he cannot tell you the difference between the two engines. To him they look the same, but the difference between them is substantial. Cylinder heads, water outlets, combustion chambers, pistons, forged crankshaft mains and the famous Stromberg "97" carburetor represented major engine changes for '37. An amateur would probably not know this.

Research will enlighten you, also, on particular unseen problem areas. Certain Chevys, for example, had weak axles; certain other makes

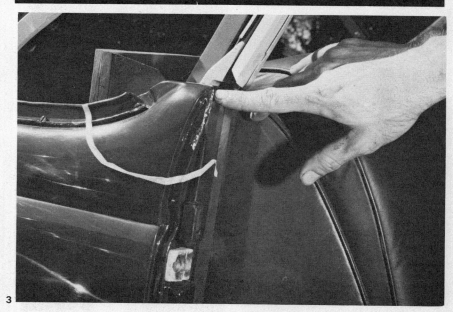

were notoriously subject to rust spots. Overheating was an early Ford V-8 trait for those who failed to consider some maintenance and driving practices. Choices like these would certainly affect any heavy use to which your restored car would be put. Rust, of course, can often be disguised, especially under a coat of paint. *Learning* the car is important to the novice, as is *learning the value of the car,* but only if he is willing to truly learn values. Sadly, many people are now paying highly inflated prices for cars that simply have facelifts.

---

1. Still on the '47 Ford convertible, the upholsterer, happy with his work on neat, pleated brown front seat, inadvertently drove a carpet nail through main top hydraulic line, ruining paint.

2. Worse, painter didn't take pains to put the '47's frame in correct alignment. A modern lift used for a pre-'49 Ford convertible can flex the frame and cause door chipping. Car should have been raised by the axles.

3. Open cars are always prone to more body flex, and as such, the amateur has to be diligent in his search for cracks. This area on the Cabriolet's door frame was rewelded.

4. Effects of time, hard cornering, bad roads, etc., produce stress cracks on certain areas. On rumble seat cars, this was a well-known place.

5. On this '32 Chevrolet, the crack is along a seam line, where factory joined the body. Leading has cracked. Considering the Chevy's wooden body frame, about the only way to go is with Alum-A-lead, a trademarked product, but it's no picnic to restore such a Chevy, and not for an amateur.

BATHS CAN BE COLD

It can be sad indeed for the man who falls in love with a shiny restoration if he is not aware that the sheetmetal is very rough or that the primer is ready to pop loose from a body that is loaded with bondo. There are too many people today who are hoodwinked into paying extra amounts of money for a shiny car of this type, as opposed to those who pass up a rough-looking machine whose only fault is paint that has faded to a red haze and a few football-sized, though easily repairable, body dents.

While on this subject, let it be said that unscrupulous body men can wreck an entire project before it really starts. Improper bondo, leading to cracks on primer that is uneven and poorly applied, is really inexcusable. If you're not doing this kind of work yourself, be sure to get all repair estimates in writing. Only an amateur will think it's not necessary and fall victim to the old snare-all: "Let's be friends. I'll give you a verbal quote for all bodywork, and I'll take care of all the things you want. Trust me." Then when you pick up the car for a fender work job, you find primer spray all over an improperly masked hood, parts of your removed chrome missing or lost and some things not done as promised, because it won't take you much time to get them done at a later date. At least that's what the body man tells you, assuming you can get any exact information from him at all.

When you realize, for example,

that metal finishing—the final step of metalworking—could ruin an expertly straightened panel, it is not a pretty picture to buy an expensive old car and then realize that such slipshod work will have to be redone. Poor craftsmanship in the metal-finishing stage means that expert painting cannot cover up the defects. In fact, a professional painter following the work of a body-working amateur may hesitate to do his best work on such a panel, and the total job will be unsatisfactory.

For example, after the roughing-out, straightening, shrinking and welding have been completed, the metal finishing must take care of any low spots or surface irregularities. It must roughen the metal surface to permit better paint adhesion, with a good transition from the base metal to the adjoining paint. If at this point any low spots are detected, only an amateur would try to grind out a depression. The result would be a thin and weakened area. Nothing is worse than a repaired panel with visible low spots or deep scratches. Professional thinking, in short, would not allow these defects to occur. They never just happen. An amateur allows them to.

When it comes to engine and driveline repair, it should be obvious that an amateur will be content if the engine produces barely noticeable knocks or doesn't smoke too badly. The professional, on the other hand, is concerned with putting the entire car back together in such a way that all mechanical components work as well as they did originally, if not in some cases a bit better.

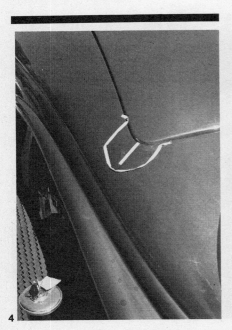

4   5

A professional, upon buying a car, will not attempt to start an engine that hasn't operated in 30 years! There might be some cylinder rust or one of a number of age-caused debilitations. He will not attempt to get that car running just to move it around. He knows that just perhaps it might be an engine that could be dismantled. He just might be able to have the cylinders honed—in case there is some cylinder rust in it—and have a good running engine.

The amateur, on the other hand, will attempt to start the engine—with perhaps a half-seized condition—and wind up cracking a piston, perhaps breaking a rod and totally destroying the engine!

The same things are true of transmissions and their related situations. The professional will dismantle one, perhaps find that the trans is in perfect condition, then reassemble it, using all new seals. This means that he can get into his car and drive it. He's not going to have a seal break in 100 miles, suffering dumped oil and a seized condition. An amateur, however, would not care (or know) what precautions were needed and would suffer the latter fate.

A professional will not attempt to get a car running for the time being, just for the sake of getting it started. An amateur—trickster that he thinks he is—will follow a series of patchwork operations, and wind up doing more damage to the eventual condition of the car than had he left it alone. Nothing is worse than breaking the $50 parts because the connected 20¢ parts were overlooked.

Let's go back to the last example, regarding the transmission seals. A lot of amateurs will take an old car with bad seals and find themselves rolling along at a breezy 70 mph before seizing an overdrive because its attendant seal—not attended to in 30 years—similarly failed. Another example is the amateur who won't put a crankshaft seal in a car that has been sitting for years, on the theory that he can see only a *minor* leak emanating from the seal's general area when the engine is started. He is the man who will take off on a trip of 200 or 300 miles and will lose the seal entirely, to become the unwilling possessor of a seized engine, stranded along a lonely road somewhere.

These are acts of sheer stupidity. There are probably as many examples as there are seals that can hold lubricants and parts that can rust. A professional will make it his busi-ness to become aware of them. An amateur ignores them.

SPEAK THE TRUTH

Another big difference between the amateur and the professional is that a professional will do only the work for which he is qualified. If a man is good with engines and body-work but not on instruments, for example, he will seek knowledge on instrument repair before blindly jumping into an area of which he knows nothing. Or he will take such a part to a specialist. Only an amateur would take a rare $200 clock out of a car and try to fix it himself. A professional will take it to a watchmaker and spend the extra money. An amateur would probably yank it out of the dashboard, flip some oil on it, and then wonder why it doesn't work.

Most of the professionals in the restoration business admit that they cannot themselves take care of an entire car and produce a 90-plus points result. Some can *approach* a complete restoration, but few have the *total* necessary skills. It takes a lot in one package to do so. You, by reading and following this book, can become highly proficient. But only an amateur will boast that he can be skilled in every phase. Likewise, he is the same person who, as owner of one of the older bodies with wood framing, now rotted, will not, as he should, replace it board for board, but will load it with plastic wood, put screws in it and then a year lat-

1. Another area to watch if you plan to restore a Ford of the Thirties is the simple check of felt-backed door handle; it's an anti-rattle secret.

2. Banjo steering wheel was prized Ford accessory. This is stock, but check underside of steering wheel hub for part numbers. Also note early '36 fuel gauge in hand. This dash, a restored gem, proves car is late '36.

3. Oak framing is a definite must for checking. Rest of the car is steel, a definite plus over wood-framed Chevys of the period. Ford's movable seat back opened up huge rear storage area, and this in a basic 2-seat car. Amateur should know these things; it's valuable research.

4. Embedded knife means rotted wood, not a cheery thought in this otherwise cosmetically okay '32 Chevy. Amateurs might miss; professionals won't.

er wonder why the body is squeaking and the doors are falling open!

The big difference is, very simply, that the professional goes over the car from one end to the other. He starts at the front bumper and he ends up at the rear, after he has personally unfastened and refastened every bolt and fastener in that car and has examined every part. The ones he personally doesn't do, he takes out and has done. When he gets through with all this, he has a car that he is proud to own and to pass on. It is a car whose value he is proud to acknowledge and receive when the moment finally comes that he and his favorite car part company, if indeed they ever do.

The amateur will start at the front bumper, wash the car, then start with a spray can and paint over everything he can hide. He'll get it looking pretty, and then he's satisfied with the car.

The difference might as well put the final judging on two different planets, however, because in no way are the two cars comparable. ♟

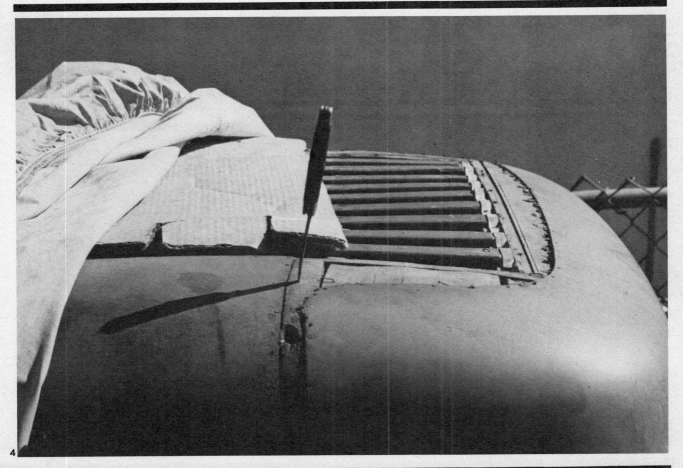

BUYING THE FARMER'S CAR BE COOL 'BOUT THAT CHOICE VT; BOONDOCK FOLK AREN'T DUMMIES

Once upon a time there was a nice farmer who sold his car to an automotive writer. The story of that transaction was published in a magazine that is no longer in business. The two events have absolutely nothing in common, but serve to illustrate a point. The point is that dealing with a farmer is something that sneaks up on you, and once the deal is made or lost, there's no backtracking—something like a magazine that goes out of business. They are both iron-clad situations. Once they both get into the groove for a method of operating, they both become extremely difficult to change—even if that similarity leads only one way—to the grave.

Some farmers are brilliant people. They have been educated at prominent universities; some have advanced degrees in agriculture or related disciplines. Experiences teaches, however, that such farmers would not normally permit hundreds of rusted hulks to permeate their carefully planned farm establishments.

Across the United States, the acres of outstanding Vintage Tin are not hard to find. But a naive farmer is, indeed, hard to find. What we're dealing with is an ability to communicate. That's your job. Don't leave it up to the farmer. He will do it only one way—his. Finding an owner of the VT that you've been able to spot, on your auto trip across country is the big test, of course. There are many tales of eager young Bucks hopping across the barren desert to grab likely looking VT prospects, only to retreat rapidly with a hind-end full of buckshot, or with a similiar inconvenience. You don't just pull up next to a likely looking hulk and start loading up. Someone, somewhere, has proprietary rights to a particular VT—even if it's the state. It's not that difficult, really, to find out what coun-

ty you're in, and go to the county office to inquire who has the map for such and such area and take it from there. More times than not, an owner will give you far more courtesy than you've bargained for. He—or whatever entity it is—will probably think you're doing him a favor for removing the eyesore. So, again, it's a simple matter of using your head.

The most likely prospect—the most complete VT examples—normally are protected within the confines of someone's yard, or adjacent field. In that case, you'll have to read on. For that's what we're talking about.

One case that comes to mind at the outset, is the story of the Model A prize winner that was found at the bottom of a junk heap, after one of the disastrous Topanga Canyon, Calif., fires. The eager young restorer was inquiring around, when he was told that the big heap existed, but that he "wouldn't find anything worthwhile," because the conflagra-

tion had just ended after a 2-week rampage. It wasn't the first time a fire had struck the tinder-dry area, nor will it be the last. For some reason, the wind patterns at certain times of the year blow down the canyon like wind through a flint box. Sage brush makes good tinder.

Rummaging around through the mess, the intrepid lad found the charred A chassis and body remains. Using an ingenious method of rope and a makeshift trailer, he removed the corpus delecti to the sanctity of his backyard. The boy's father later explained that "We wanted to show the world what a complete restoration was."

You won't have to go to such length to prove that you can restore faithfully a derelict automobile. But you should know that others have blazed the trail (even fires, too,) and you should have no fear when confronting an absolute zero that you are about to become the Lone Ranger. It's more likely that you

PHOTOS BY JIM NORRIS, JOHN THAWLEY AND BUD LANG

won't give a damn about the work ahead of you, but will care about recognizing the pitfalls in acquiring it in the first place. Alright, here are a few tips.

Rule No. 1—Be Looking For It.

It's a funny thing, but many people can motor down a country road and completely miss what is pointing its rusted nose right at them. There are many finds that are nearly hidden from view, but by far the biggest hurdle is to be alert for the roadside VT that has been embraced by 20 years of devil grass or oak tree deposits. In the mountains, it's the same, only with pine needles and rocks. The desert? Sand, mesquite bushes and creepy crawlies.

You've got to remain alert to what you're seeking. But if you ask any restorer, he'll tell you that some of the best times of his life were spent looking for undiscovered Vintage Tin—the further from home you wander, the more exciting the find. For the simple reason that, by definition, nobody in your immediate locale will have ever seen your discovery, and it immediately becomes identifiable with you and you alone. To be blunt, it's one of the

1. Don't be surprised if dealing with a farmer for his hulk of Vintage Tin leads you to this. Notice general overall condition of this 1930 Ford AA truck. Once, it was a C-cab.

2. Hunting for VT in the farm country can be a test of your patience. The farmers won't be pushed.

3. Neither will they throw anything away. Farm country can be a bonanza for VT sleuths. But it's no place for an automotive tenderfoot.

4. A close look at the farmer's derelict C-cab chassis reveals its gravestone appearance. The farmer said he couldn't remember how long the beer can had been there. The writer never drank that brand.

joys of life. Okay, so where do you look?

Rule No. 2—Look in the Right Places.

It stands to reason that you don't go moping around because no abandoned VT in excellent condition smiles at you and pokes its eager high cowl from behind a tree alongside a major and well-traveled highway. While there's enough VT around this country, there are certain spots where it's not. Certainly not for long. You've got to *dig* hitting the back country. There are a few well-known examples in every city (everybody knows about them, of course) but the name of the game is boondock city. You've got to realize that people have to eat something, other than hot dogs and beer, and in all probability, the stuff will have to be grown or fed until it's butchered. There are more people in the cities than a hundred years ago, that's for sure, but without vast farmlands, this nation would collapse. How about that? Automobiles are to a healthy economy what farm products are to a healthy human being. Not a bad thought to hold in your craw while you try to remember where that article on the farmer's car was suggesting that you look. If nothing else, it will call for a beer. Cheer up—looking for the farmer's car is a fun thing—as you will soon see by reading on.

The first thing you have going for you will be a knowledge that people in farm or agricultural areas rarely throw anything away. This is especially true of machinery. There's always a belief to a farmer that: "Someday that durn blasted contraption will get fixed." Because it might not work at the time, and because the farmer's livelihood depends on things that work, there's only one way for his mind to adjust to the situation. He will often figure: "If it's put somewhere still in view, then it won't be forgotten, and someday someone can fix it." If the broken machine represents farm equipment that has been updated, he will, if he can afford it, purchase the new machine, and be only too glad to let the old one sit under the oak tree and acquire its lovely suntan of brown. Unfortunately, the tan is only of one kind, and pretty soon his machinery is rusted together, and is no more use than a glob of modern art.

When the discarded machine is the farmer's car, chances are that its fate will be the same as any of his discarded machinery. Nevertheless, somewhere in the recesses of his agricultural mind, there's the notion that "someday we'll get it to run."

When you meet such a man, and spot what may be a delectible find out in his pasture, all is therefore not as easy a picking as you might think. You won't be fooling anybody but yourself if you confront the farmer with a holier-than-thou lie that is calculated to blow him out of the saddle. If you say what the farmer wants to hear, you're in luck. If you don't, forget it. For out in the great windy spaces of Nebraska, Kansas, Wyoming, Oklahoma, or up in the Texas panhandle, farm folk proceed at pretty much their own pace. So, baby, you'd better look like one of them when you hove into view. Remember, a lot of farmers who have tilled the soil of an area, after his father, and his father before him, and who have worked the same ground, are of the unshakable opinion that it's *his* ground, over which fly *his* birds, in the adjacent streams of which swim *his* fish, and through the nearby woods of which run *his* game. If you don't accept this fact going in, then, brother, forget about the whole scene, and get your car someplace else. At least dress the part, for cripes sakes! That brings us to rule No. 3.

Rule No. 3—Dress the Part.

That goes for not only you, but

the car you drive when you come into town loaded for bear—in other words with the cash in your pockets to buy some decent VT. What if you're in Nebraska with your Rolls Royce Camargue and New York plates. Or how about pulling up into parts of Iowa with your California Continental? There you go. Or you might try the northern reaches of the Dakotas, in your '76 Cad Eldorado Convertible, and then tell the farmer all about the fact that it was the last one sold in San Francisco or something, while you finally get around to informing him that you "won't pay one nickle more than $100 for the forlorn '31 A Roadster Pickup over there by the barn." It's the same in northern California if your license plate says "Los Angeles" proudly displayed at the top. Some of those places up around Burney or up near the Oregon border dearly "love" hot-shot dudes from L.A. Or while we're at it, try hunting Vintage Tin from the God-fearing folk in Oregon's Willamette Valley, with your Jensen Interceptor Convertible bearing California plates, and your well-manicured nails clutching a wad a new C-notes inside the pocket of your James Oviatt suit. Fine, if *all* that new money is going to the farmer (although he would probably be suspicious of such a tactic and refuse on the spot), but don't try to talk like the second coming and expect to get to first base. Enough said? Obviously.

Not only do you have to watch your dress and your wheels, but you'll have to guard your loose mouth, and the tendency to "get it over with." Farmers don't do business that way. If he sizes you up as a cityslicker, you're dead from the start.

What you want to do is to play the part of the earthy, low-buck hobbyist who would like to "get an old car to tinker around with." Wear your *old* Jeans, an old shirt and some beat-up boots. You might even try the coveralls that many farmers like to wear. But don't over-do it, unless you can really play the part. He might be suspicious of that, too. If you've got a drawl, and a leathery face, and roll your own, however, don't worry, everything will come naturally, and you'll probably have a friend for life, once you and the farmer agree on a price for the VT. That, then, leads into the next point of importance.

Rule No. 4—Handle the Approach with Proper Psychology.

First of all, the farmer won't know you from a load of hay, if you play your cards right. That means: Watch your language. Talk his language. Don't overdo it, however. He can tell when you're acting up a storm. Just be down to earth. Listen more than you talk. Don't act dumb, either. Just act sufficiently broke, but eager. It was well put in

Walter Tevis' book, "The Hustler," as Minnesota Fats said: "Play a little *under-speed,* 'till you get down to talking real money." Great advice.

One automotive writer of established prominence put it this way, while reporting on dickering for a 1927 Buick in a Nebraska cow pasture:

"We pulled into the farmer's yard. Right away I knew this was going to be a toughie. Our jaws hit the floor-mats of the late-model Olds when we saw this guy's yard. It was VT heaven, a veritable rodder's dream, with many T's, A's, and other neat early cars. The farmer looked like he had all the wisdom of Solomon written into the hard lines of his old face.

"It was a real test of a bargaining poker face to even talk intelligibly, with all that mouth-watering VT around. But I steeled myself to the

1. Original floor board piece is propped over the chassis rails. Do you think a termite inspector would recommend fumigating? Notice the farmer's GT-40 near the tractor. Be careful of such farmers.

2. Here's a 1938 Packard, Series 120, 4-door sedan. The farmer will sell it to you. Several small details, including: how much you can buy it for, and how do you get it out, are your problem. Don't forget your tetanus shots, either.

3. This '42 to '48 Ford looks to be in relatively good shape. The Model A, stacked up next to it, wasn't as lucky.

4. Many farmers will procrastinate doing business until they've shown you around the place. Often, a farmer has surprises lurking. This is his '29 Franklin Speedster with a Dietrich body—a rare body style even when new—now a mind-blower.

task—hoping that my partners could conceal their enthusiasm. I didn't even bat an eye when he showed us the cherry C-cab; the perfect '29 A Roadster or the three T-tubs. Of course, I started the conversation by saying that we had seen the old Buick and *might* be interested in buying an old thing like that to work on."

The writer then went on to say that the procedure was: a) not to press the issue, and b) to offer the farmer a smoke. Predictably, the farmer preferred to roll his own, but the offer was sufficient to get him to talk about farming, the weather, Nebraska, and taxes. It was not known in what order those subjects were of interest to the farmer.

Anyway, after the farmer rolled his own cigarette (the writer remembered that they were Old Bugle Brand), there was an impromtu tour of the farmer's spread, while the fellow went about his chores. This routine consisted of: a) feeding the sheep, b) not saying anything about the Buick, and c) throwing a question or two "off the head" about some of the cars he had stashed around the place "to show him we were genuine old cars fans."

This particular farmer had certain examples of long-forgotten makes, but seemed rather unconcerned about the whole thing. One of the cars was a 1919 Gardner—*running.* Apparently, the farmer was only too happy to demonstrate.

There was also discovered a taboo against hot rodders—a predictable thing since most farmers aren't overjoyed at the thought of someone cutting up his beloved VT. This thought was driven home in the following exchange:

"The farmer had made his feelings plain when he drawled to us about some missing doors on a '29 Roadster. The writer listened intently.

'Well sir,' the farmer said, 'some hot rodder from California came in here about a year ago tryin' to buy that A, and when I told him I'd never sell that car to someone who wasn't going to treat it proper, he went away. But 'lo and behold, he came back later *at night,* and just as he was carting off the doors to my A, I let him have it with my 12 gauge. Now, I keep the doors in my house.'

The part about the shotgun unnerved us all, but we sympathized with him, and agreed that people with no respect for property were a disgrace. Of course, I had from the start, made it clear that we were only interested in cars to *restore,* not to hot-rod."

After several hours with the farmer, it was thought that there had been sufficient introductions and so on to ask the farmer if he would drive over—so that one could take another look at the Buick. The car was some 6 miles away, in a distant field, and the automotive restorer/writer made sure to mention that he

needed at least one more look because, as he said, "When we first saw the car we didn't want to trespass on the other farmer's property," and by so doing, the first farmer could be impressed by the enthusiasts' respect for law and order. The Buick had been obviously stored on a neighbor farmer's land.

During the trip over to see the Buick, the farmer ram-rodded his new Ford LTD like Walker Evans over dirt, sending explosions of dust in all directions, and prairie dogs scurrying for their holes in panic.

As the writer put it, "He drove like a madman—90 mph over dirt roads. We had a hard time keeping up with the old devil—and when we finally got to the old Buick, there he was, with the dust settling slowly, leaning against his LTD, rolling another Bugle." If the writer of the second report doesn't get sued, let me say, of the farmer's method of checking out his derelict '27 Buick: "That's poetry in moving!"

To make a long and intriguing story short, the dealings finally began, and the eager restorer told the farmer that he could only give him what he had on him, which, he said, amounted to $100. He mentioned that there was an awful lot of woodwork to be replaced on the car, a true assessment. The farmer—an experienced trader himself, then said, in his peculiar down-home rasp: "What've ye got to trade here, any gold coins, tools, guns—hell, I'll take anything in trade I can use."

Now the negotiations were in full swing—and juices on both sides were flowing. (It should be obvious that the farmer we're talking about is *not* an example of Grant Wood's immortal "Farm Folk," but a man, whose behavior might indicate a liking for the bottle variety. That's *not* the juice we're talking about here—nor is it O.J. Simpson."

"All I have on is a Mickey Mouse Watch," the writer said. The watch had come from Disneyland for $20.

"Let me see that watch you're wearin'," the farmer bellowed, good naturedly.

The farmer almost ripped it off the writer's wrist, and held it up close to his eye.

"That's a deal! Give me $100 and this here watch!"

Drawing up a bill of sale, and signing off all his traveler's checks, the writer had therefore purchased one 1927 Buick, in need of restoring.

4

BUYING THE FARMER'S CAR

Then the fun began; as it will for you, when and if you're in a similar position. (Not exactly the *same* position, however!)

Rule No. 5—What to Do After You've Bought It.

Now you've succeeded. You are to be congratulated in carrying out a good transaction. The farmer is happy, and you are happy. That's as it should be. One-half the battle is over. The other half is about to begin cheers.

Naturally you'll try to get a title from the owner or get him to file for a duplicate and have him mail it to you. It will alleviate some problems if you're bringing it home to a title state. Some states don't have titles, in which case you should get a bill of sale and have it notarized by a local notary public. The fee is usually only a few dollars.

It's nice if you can get the frame or similar into the bed of your El Camino, F-100, or whatever, but for most purchases you'll have to tow or trailer it home. That will present a whole new set of problems. In almost every state it's not legal to flat-tow a car on the pavement—unless it's currently registered, and unless all the lights and directional signals work. Most VT finds, however, are not even this lucky. Flat-towing, therefore, is normally out.

Most of the big, national trailer rental outfits don't rent car-hauling trailers, and the utility trailers that they do rent, aren't usually capable of handling the weight of a complete car—not when the weight is concentrated in the contact of the four wheels. They might be okay for carrying a body or a bunch of parts, but not for hauling a complete car.

Smaller, local trailer-renting outfits in most cities will probably have what you need. The trouble is, most of them won't rent one to go out of state. And this bit of trivia happens to be stenciled all over the trailer—so don't get any ideas.

What, then, is left? Well, there are a few people who specialize in hauling cars around the country, but it's a service that is usually expensive. They prefer to pick up cars that are easy to get to. The price goes way up if they have to spend time trying to get the car out of a ditch of something.

If you use their services, be sure to accurately describe the car's condition, location and approximate size and weight, and set a firm price before the deal is made.

You might even know someone who has a trailer. Be careful, though about renting a car-carrying trailer from a racer. Such trailers are often not as heavy as you need.

If you do, find out what his race car weighs. If it's a full bodied stocker, the trailer should be strong enough for any VT. It should have good lights, surge brakes, and preferrably springs and tandem axles, if you're hauling a complete car. Another alternative could be for all the guys in your local club, to chip in together on buying or building a trailer that everyone could use. Rule No. 5 is not to be taken lightly, either.

Rule No. 6—Come Prepared.

The best thing, of course, is to be prepared to haul the VT home on

1. The first impression was that this rare Franklin, emerging unceremoniously from a farmer's barn, was every bit the apparition as the Titanic slamming into its iceberg.

2. Once outside, in the light of a prairie afternoon, the rare Franklin Speedster came across like Cinderella's coach—with the broke photographer only a pumpkin.

3. You never know exactly what a farmer will sell, and what he won't. This one, he won't. For their day, the air-cooled Franklins were some kind of engineering!

4. Alright, the talk's over, and you've bought a derelict car. Don't just stand there—gaping at it. Move your buns and grab the wrenches. It's your ball game from now on, baby.

the spot. That means: Do some homework in gear and logistics before you start out expressly to get your VT. Sideline trips normally have you unprepared. The best thing is to go out there with some trusted friends and go expressly for the tin.

It would be advisable to take along a big hoist, cutting and welding equipment, and maybe a crane for those hard-to-liberate pieces.

Some tools that you really *should* bring with you are:

1) a winch
2) hacksaw and extra blades.
3) heavy hammer and chisel.
4) nut-cracker, wrenches, and breaker bar.
5) Liquid Wrench, and WD40 in the *spray can*.

6) impact screwdriver (the kind you hit with a hammer).

7) electric drill (if you have an extension cord and a 110-volt power-tap for your car.)

8) don't forget your favorite brand of bailing wire and rope (coat hangers help, too).

It is very true that nothing is worse than finding something you really want but can't get home because you didn't bring the tools to get it with. Often, too, the VT you've bought is buried underneath a stack of washing machines, bed springs and bits of other cars, or whatever. You'd be surprised at how much junk will sometimes be in the way.

It's good to be able to use your winch or just a plain old block and

tackle. Sometimes, too, the only way to remove a car from its long-time resting place is to *dismantle it*. It sounds like a drastic move, but early cars are pretty simply built. With the right tools and with a little patience to cope with the rusted nuts and bolts, the job won't take as long as you think. That last bit of assurance naturally leads into the last point to remember:

Rule No. 7—Learn to Accept Disappointment.

Sometimes the hardest of all rules to accept is that nevertheless, you must have to expect a loss now and then. For example, when you've carefully planned a trip; have used all your guile, and then the farmer won't sell it.

A lot of farmers are of the opinion that there will be another "crazy war," and that the situation will drive prices sky high for scrap iron. Worse, is the farmer who says: "I'll just sit on my old car, because one of these days (years) I'm going to restore it."

Lastly, some humor. If you meet a farmer who says the following things, beware. He's a farmer, alright, but not the kind you think. Watch out. *He's farming you,* and you're about to be harvested. Don't, therefore, pay too much money!

3

4

IF THE FARMER SAYS THIS	HE MEANS THIS
Motor quiet.	Using 60-weight oil
Needs minor overhaul	Needs new engine
Needs major overhaul	Ready for the junkyard
Burns no oil	Just throws it out
Gone over and checked out	Sandblasted the plugs
Body fair	No visible dry rot
Body good	Puttied holes
Parts car	Beyond repair
Immaculate	Had it washed
Concours	Had it waxed
Drive it away	I'm on a hill
Deliver—for expenses	I like caviar
Drive anywhere	Within 10 miles of home
Fine old classic	His car
Bowlegged old dog	Your car
Has classic lines	Box on wheels
Desireable classic	Nobody likes it
Modern classic	1960 Plymouth
Rare classic	Nobody liked it new
Stored 20 years	Engine froze when new
Completed Glidden Tour	On a trailer
Extensive rechroming	Polished one bumper
Other interests conflict	Wife said ditch it
Call any time	It's hard to sell it
No time to restore	Parts don't exist
Good investment	Has hit rock bottom
Rough	Too bad to lie about
Sharp	Whitewall tires
Need money	Found a better car
Must sacrifice	Can't give it away
Firm	$300 off for cash
Asking	$1000 off for cash
Leaving for the Army	Bank is going to repo it
New top	Only 4-years old
Solid as a rock	Everything rusted together

There, you see? You didn't think the farmer had it in him, did you? Cheers again!

HOW HARRAH'S DOES IT
INSIDE THE RESTORATION SHOPS OF THE FAMOUS HARRAH'S AUTOMOBILE COLLECTION

BY PAUL DEXLER

As of this writing, the Bugatti Type 57SC coupe belonging to Harrah's Automobile Collection has just taken the "Best In Show" trophy at the Pebble Beach Concours d'Elégance.

Pebble Beach is the most prestigious concours in the country, and Best In Show there doesn't come easy. "Of course," you might say, "all it takes is plenty of money." Not so. William Harrah has money, and the corporation that runs Harrah's Automobile Collection has money, but it takes more than money to come up with a 100-point car. Harrah's shop isn't the only one that can do it, but with over 90 full-time employees, it is probably the biggest shop devoted specifically to car restoration in the world. The techniques used there are certainly valid anywhere else.

Several trips to Harrah's Automobile Collection over a period of three years showed us the way, and even the backyard restorer can benefit from the Harrah method.

During these trips, we were able to watch the process take shape on a 1924 Brooks steam sedan. Three years? For one car? In that shop? Right. Done properly, these things can't be hurried.

You've never heard of a Brooks steamer? Neither had we. It was a product of a small company in Canada that flashed in and out of the automotive scene just before the Great Depression. They produced only about 170 cars in four years of operation. The car is based on the Stanley patents and is the very model of a modern condensing steamer... inefficient, underpowered and short-ranged. In level country, it had a range of about 150 miles, providing it was kept below its maximum speed of 40 mph. The one in the Collection may very well be the

only one in existence, and as the song goes, "...they'll none of them be missed."

The Stanley design, even with the condenser in front to increase the range between water stops, is a technological dead end. The heavy, 2-cyl. steam engine, built in a unit with the back axle, contributes massively to the weight of the car, sprung and unsprung. The equally heavy boiler and condenser in front, plus the 21-gal. water tank under the floor, mean that weight must be eliminated from every possible place

to produce a vehicle that can even get out of its own way.

The body is a Weymann patent fabric-covered body, a great favorite of builders of the Twenties and Thirties who were out to reduce vehicle weight. Despite that, the car weighs a whopping 3800 lbs., and with only 18 bhp to move it. Needless to say, performance is far from sparkling.

Why restore a *rara avis* (turkey) like this? Just because it is that rare and unusual. Also, how far should it be restored? Harrah's Automobile Collection performs two types of

2

3

4

5

1. We couldn't resist this graphic before-and-after shot of the Brooks.

2. The 1924 Brooks Steamer looked like this when it entered the restoration shops of Harrah's Automobile Collection. Flapping fenders, dry rot and lots of rust tell of neglect.

3. Here's what the Brooks looks like now and what you would have seen on the showroom floor of your Brooks dealer. It runs as well as it looks. And it only took 3 years.

4. Success really starts here in the Collection's automotive library. The filing cabinets hold literature on just about every make of automobile ever produced anywhere in the world.

5. Glass cases along the walls hold bound copies of virtually every automotive magazine ever published, going back to the 19th Century.

6. An item like this 1939 Hupp Skylark brochure is considered commonplace in the Collection's library.

6

restoration. First and much easier is the cosmetic restoration. This is done on cars that have been well restored before they come to the collection and on cars that have been preserved unrestored. A cosmetic restoration can be relatively quick, but the car has to be in pretty good mechanical condition before it can be performed.

The second type of restoration is the complete or "ground up" restoration. As you can see from the "before" photo, the Brooks was in a condition that required this type of restoration. Years of rust and dry rot had taken their toll. Whichever type of restoration is performed, the result must be the same: The car must be in original condition. That's not "near original" or "almost original" condition, but *exactly* the way the car would have looked had it been driven out of the showroom this morning instead of so many years ago.

This means no substitutions, such as using chrome instead of nickel plating or plating wheels or other parts because "it looks better that way." Original means just that: *original.* So far, we have come across only one instance in the entire Collection where a modification was allowed. It was on another steam car, one of the great Dobles. These suffered a weakness in the gear case that eventually caused it to crack in half. A special brace has been installed, and now the case will never crack. The brace isn't original, but Abner Doble designed it when he became aware of the problem. That kind of non-originality is allowed.

A car brought into the Collection is first cleaned of all the grime and bird droppings it may have accumulated through the years, and then it is photographed. Thoroughly photographed. Our "before" shot of the Brooks is from one of these photo sessions. A series of detailed—and we mean really detailed—black and white photos is taken. Every possible area of the car is photographed from every possible angle. Close-ups of every unusual detail are shot. Once the car is in the shop and fully disassembled, these photos are the only record left to show exactly how that little molding met the panels and where those funny-shaped, nickel-plated gismos were used. While all this cleaning and photographing is going on down in the shops, the researchers in the library on the second floor of the main restoration building are doing their

thing too. The collectors who work for Harrah's Automobile Collection don't just purchase cars, although much time is spent chasing down rumors of a rare and unusual vehicle hidden in some barn somewhere. They also buy for the Collection catalogs, accessory catalogs, parts books, service manuals, owner's manuals, back issues of automotive magazines and anything else automotive that you or they can think of. All this material is carefully cataloged by the library staff and made available to bona fide automotive researchers. As a point of interest, no matter who the researcher is and no matter who he represents, even the Collection itself, he is not allowed to remove any actual material from the library. Photocopies, yes. Xeroxes, yes. But an actual catalog or manual, no.

1927 BROOKS STEAMER
FIVE PASSENGER SEDAN
EQUIPMENT NO. 436
RESEARCH AND RESTORATION MANUAL

MECHANIC'S COPY

Next, the car to be restored is attacked by the researchers from two directions at once. First, all the printed material pertaining to the car is assembled in a folder. This includes catalogs, manuals, parts books, original builder's photos, magazine photos and anything else that shows or describes how the car looked when it was new. Photos and articles about someone else's spiffy restoration or modernization attempt long after the car was first built are either ignored or used with several grains of salt. The objective of the Collection is to present the car as it was when it was new, not as someone years later thought it should be.

The second direction of approach by the research team starts by carefully scraping down the paint to find out what the original color was. Then little samples of paint, upholstery cloth, wind cord and anything else that has deteriorated over the years are assembled.

From all this material about the car, 3-hole binders are prepared. In them are put prints of all the "before" photographs, along with xerox copies of all the catalogs, manuals and contemporary press materials. Another section of the binders has samples of all the materials used in the car, accompanied by samples of the new replacement materials, if they are in stock in the Collection's parts department, or by an indica-

tion that they will be or have been ordered.

One copy of the binder is turned over to the shop foreman with the car when the process is to physically begin. Other copies, with slightly different contents, are retained for parts and other purposes. The car is assigned to a master restorer and to a bay in the workshop, where, except for brief excursions to other parts of the main shop or to some of the specialty shops, it will remain during the restoration.

In the main shop, the car will be disassembled down to the frame and its parts will be cleaned, sandblasted if required and inspected. If needed, new parts will be ordered from the necessary suppliers. The researchers in the library have found sources all over the world for some of the exotic materials and parts needed in old cars. Cloth for upholstery may be woven in England, a mechanical part may come from Germany.

At the rear of the Collection's present home, there is a large, airplane hangar-like building that is not open to the public. This houses

6

1. The end product of the research is the mechanic's copy of the restoration binder on a given car.

2. At the beginning of the restoration book are exterior photos of the car as received by the Collection.

3. Following the exterior shots are complete interior details that show how everything goes together.

4. Xerox copies of the owner's manual and/or shop and service manuals are included in the restoration binders.

5. Final section of the restoration book includes samples of all the materials needed to complete the restoration. Photos indicate placement of materials on the actual car.

6. For the final part of its restoration, the Brooks was placed in the immaculate work bay of the Collection's steam car specialist.

7. Steam expert Cal Tinkham saw to it that the engine and running gear were in showroom new condition. Specialists like Tinkham are one reason the "Harrah Method" works so well.

8. A 2-cyl. steam engine is combined with the Brooks rear axle, contributing massively to unsprung weight.

9. Underhood area of the Brooks is filled with boiler and burner. The radiator-like unit that will live in front is actually a condenser.

7

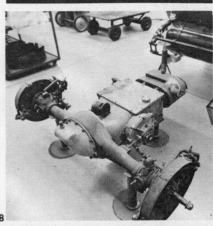

8

9

the woodworking shop, and it was to this shop that the body of the Brooks was sent after it was removed from the chassis. Two of the side panels had been caved in, and the rest of the wooden frame of the body was full of dry rot. Using the original pieces as patterns, a new frame was fabricated. The car was at this stage when we first saw it in 1974.

The mechanical end of the restoration of the Brooks was turned over to Mr. Cal Tinkham, the Harrah's Automobile Collection's specialist in steam-powered vehicles. He removed the mechanical parts from the chassis and started to work on them at his workbench. The car was ultimately to be reassembled in his work bay.

Besides the main restoration shop and the woodworking shop mentioned above, the Collection has a paint shop, an upholstery shop and a foundry. In addition, there is a wash rack/steam clean shop, to which cars make many visits in various stages of dress and undress.

It was almost a year before we saw the Brooks again. Then it was sitting on stands in Tinkham's work bay, reflected slightly in the immaculately clean floor. Body and chassis had been mated again, with the interior in place, but the engine/rear axle assembly was sitting on the floor behind the car, and the boiler and burner unit stood in the open in front of the firewall. Tinkham was painstakingly getting all the working parts togther again.

During the course of a restoration, often parts are needed that are just not available from any source, anywhere. Then drawings are carefully made, and the resulting prints are sent out to manufacturers who can fabricate the part. In other cases, the prints are taken down to the Collection's own fully equipped machine shop or foundry, and the parts are made in-house. The Collection is as cost-conscious as any other restorer, and sometimes making parts in-house is cheaper than having them made elsewhere. It just takes more time.

In some cases, the Collection's shops have had to resurrect whole skills in order to obtain the parts needed. The art of the wheelwright, for example, has just about died out. While some of the Collection's specialists are men who learned their trade in Detroit or other auto centers when the industry was young, their wheelwright hadn't even been

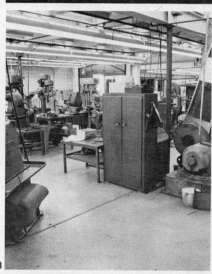

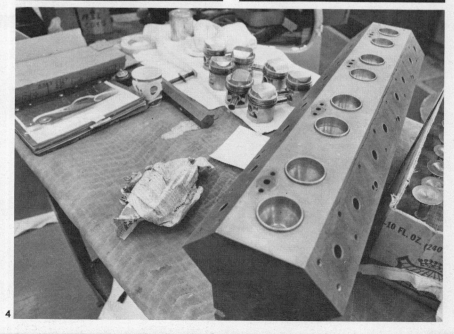

born when most of the cars in the Collection were built. A young man in his 20's, he has become a true artist at an almost forgotten craft. The Brooks needed his services, too, since each of its wheels has 12 lacquered oak spokes.

This is only one example, but the Collection's staff includes specialists and artisans in every one of the myriad skills required in the trade of carriage maker.

The results of all this tender loving care, artistry and patience can be seen in the "after" photos of the Brooks.

Here are cars that look—and perform—exactly as they did when they were new. Each of them is a unique example of the car builder's art, important for some special reason of design or engineering, and preserved to perfection.

Sure, it takes a lot of money to restore a car this way. It takes a lot of money to restore any car, any way. But the research is what makes restorations done in Harrah's Automobile Collection's shops the 100-point winners in concours. The cars are right, absolutely right, down to the last detail of trim and accessories. They are also perfectly drivable, and it is nice to know that the Harrah's Automobile Collection people will exercise them to maintain their perfection.

5

6

1. At the same time that the Brooks' engine was being rebuilt, the Bugatti that took "Best in Show" at Pebble Beach in 1976 was getting its going-over.

2. Sometimes a restoration may require stripping a car down to the bare frame. This prewar Datsun, along with the Brooks and the Bugatti, got this type of restoration.

3. If a needed part can't be purchased or farmed out to a specialist, it can be made in this completely equipped machine shop.

4. The Bugatti's engine was spread out over a tabletop, with the restoration binder for the car very much in evidence.

5. Many times a complete, ground-up restoration is not required. This Cadillac V-16 required only a cosmetic restoration.

6. A Packard 12 phaeton receives the final finishing touches of a full restoration.

7. This miniscule 1910 model was the first to carry Ettore Bugatti's own name. The aluminum-bodied 2-seater is being detailed.

7

FACING A BASKET CASE

THE ART OF TAKING IT APART, AND SOME HINTS ON FINDING THOSE MISSING BITS AND PIECES

A basket case can quite properly be described as a car whose parts are best toted home in a basket. That is, if you can locate a basket sufficiently large. It might just as well be a snow shovel job, or maybe the gathering of parts is best left to a rake. But whatever the condition of the car you plan on restoring, basket case is as good a term as any if the car doesn't run and it has to be carted off bodily.

We've already looked at car-seeking, car-obtaining, and car-identifying chapters. Now it's time to get into car dismantling, which, believe it or not, is an art unto itself. Not a science, since no two derelict automobiles are absolutely identical and will therefore require somewhat differing techniques, but an art. But even with art there's a wrong way and a right way to take a car apart—as well as there is to taking

anything mechanical apart. Permit us to run through the basics of disassembling a derelict 1936 Ford roadster and see if we can learn anything.

GETTING STARTED

Getting your basket case home is your problem, and each of us can tell a different story. Ours was trailered. So much for that. The real first step in redoing any car is, once

1

you get it home, to photograph it from every possible angle; overall shots as well as close-ups of the details. The snaps will be invaluable when it comes time to put it all back together. If you could strip and completely rebuild a car in, say, a week. or less, you could remember where all the doo-dads went. But be aware that you'll be spending a year or more, especially if you're all thumbs, and it's easy to forget which hinge or bracket went where.

Gather up as many photos or old ads of your car as you can. They'll help you identify missing parts or show you the curve of the body or proper relation of this-to-that in the event yours has come a cropper with a gravel truck in the past.

Our '36, when acquired, consisted of a bare body and that's about all; but, nevertheless, there were a number of gizmos that had to be removed. The cowl vent and attaching hardware, for example, some remaining dashboard pieces, some parts of the door latches, and so forth, were taken off and relegated to properly marked coffee cans or boxes. Hinges, bolts, pins, etc., from the left door went into a can plainly labeled "Left Door." Ditto for the right door, the dash, and so on. Also put into its respective container was a written list of parts either missing entirely or broken or worn beyond fix-ation. These slips will become your *wants* when the next swap meet comes along. Even screws, bolts, etc., that were stripped or badly rusted were stored with their related parts. When the time finally rolled around to screw all this stuff back together, *then* replacement screws and bolts were fetched, the hardware freshened up, and so forth. Had we simply dismantled the relic into a jimongous pile on the garage floor, we'd still be dreaming about our machine instead of driving it around. Get the idea?

PARTS LOCATION

Quite apart from acquiring the basic car itself—and basic is the right word since this particular car was a bare body with doors and a front axle—there was an obvious need for the stupendous number of individual parts and components that make up a '36 Ford roadster. Unfortunately, for us anyway, much of the roadster's makeup is akin to nothing else in Ford's '36 lineup from the cowl aft—except some parts interchangeability with the almost as equally rare phaeton (built to a 5555 number). The cowl, windshield assembly, doors and door hardware, seat framing and cushion springs, body quarter panels and rear fenders (to name just a few items) were all peculiar to the roadster. This kind of problem could apply to you, too. The rear fenders you need for your Ajax town car *may* not be the same as those for an Ajax coupe.

Shagging missing parts for our project car took us off in many directions—some blind alleys, too. Swap meets, naturally, turned up some original roadster hardware as well as some repro parts. The glovebox, for example, was a repro. But the glovebox door itself, complete with locking latch, came from a swap meet vendor. (These minor but necessary pieces are not interchangeable between the roadster/phaeton and the other 14 body styles.)

The real point of all this, regardless of the make and model of your restoration project, is to emphasize the need to make a careful list of everything you think you'll need to finish your car. A complete list of *parts wanted* will come from the smaller lists you've already put in the individual cans and boxes for Left Door, Rumble Seat, and so forth.

As experience will eventually show—that, if this is your first built-up car, and as you already know if it's your second or third, an important aspect of parts scrounging is the availability of the hardware; if they're for a very common model (some idea of what's common can be decided by checking facyory-production figures) most pieces will be easy to come by. Our 3862 roadsters were augmented by some 160,000 Fordor Touring Sedans, 14,000 convertibles, etc. Parts common to all 16 models will naturally be far easier to locate than roadster-only components. If your missing part is a common one then you can shop prices and condition between swap meets, or even between different vendors at the same meet. But if it's a rarity, you'd best throw caution to the winds and get that scarce wiper motor arm while the getting's good. Even if you later find another one, or a better one, for a lesser price, buy it and pride yourself in having an extra that you can peddle yourself.

Don't let the swap meet-er tell you what year, make and model the

1. Seeking a project can be half the fun, but the real work lies ahead. This fellow doesn't need a basket to put parts in, for this is all there is, there ain't no more. Model TT truck like this one would be a good first-time project for a novice.

2. The buyer of this '40 Pontiac will face his first acid test when getting the derelict out of the junkyard.

part is for. I've been as gullible here as the next guy. At a Ford meet in Dearborn last year I passed up a rare '36 roadster windshield wiper motor for $60 for the simple reason that I couldn't afford it. Three tables away was another one for $10—and the guy said it was indeed for a '36. Naturally, I grabbed the cheaper one, only to find it was for a '34 closed car. To me, at least, they looked alike, and I came away 10 clams to the poor. If you don't know what you're looking at for certain, don't tip your hand (and lack of certainty) and ask, "Is that for a '38 Ford convertible sedan?" Instead, simply ask, "Whatzat fit?"

BITS AND PIECES SOURCES

One-make car clubs abound, and there is surely one somewhere dedicated to your make of car (and sometimes model, too). Check the newsstand publications like *Hemmings Motor News* and *Special Interest Autos,* for example, for notices or membership-pulling ads from single-make clubs. Write to them as a potential member (which you'll surely be at this point) and ask for a recent copy of their newsletter. Most of them run sell-or-trade ads and maybe you can track down that evasive part by mail. In our own case a membership in the Early Ford V-8 Club of America brings us their very fine V-8 Times every other month. From an ad in one issue I acquired my right-hand running board—but it does pay to be wary, for one man's statement "Very Fine Condition" may, to you, mean the piece is pure junk. Ask for a concise description of the part, whether the price includes mailing or shipping, and ask if crating (if it's a big piece) is included.

While NOS is the purist restorer's byword (that means New Old Stock, indicating an original part never installed on a car), there are many things to shy away from. One is wiring—either individual strands or complete harnesses. Others are the many assorted rubber parts: glass moldings, anti-squeak buttons, body/frame webbing, door stops, grommets, etc. Materials of this nature deteriorate with age, whether in the factory box or not. Nothing short of hermetically sealing a firewall grommet will have saved it over the years. Items like this are best if they're in repro. Besides, they're readily available from dozens of sources. The same thing goes for dash and handle knobs of early-day

plastics, felt-like window channeling, and on and on.

From the firewall forward all '36 Ford passenger-car models are the same. This means front fenders from a phaeton, sedan delivery, Tudor or whatever, will interchange with a station wagon, 3-window coupe, roadster or whatever. Front fenders, then, along with inner splash panels, the grille assembly, all four hood panels, trim moldings, radiator and assorted air baffles, headlight assemblies, bumper, bracketing, and so forth, are all interchangeable and

thus very common at swap meets. This is where you can shop prices, compare condition against cost, or even swap off an extra hard-to-find part you might have for a more common one you still need. What's important is to learn if this applies to all the various models of your particular car.

HASTE IS A NO-NO

Let us expound a bit on trying to intermix haste with restoration. A nameless purist restorer was busily salvaging—and this is the purest of

coincidence—a '36 Ford roadster and found he needed a complete floor-pan. Luckily, all '36 (and '35, for that matter) passenger-model floors are identical. But, unluckily, the hasty Eastern restorer glommed the first floor he found advertised—by a Western car wrecker. The order was to fly it, cost no object. It wasn't until after the crate was built, costing more than the floor and the labor to cut it out of a body, that it was discovered the box wouldn't fit through the cargo hatch of a 707. In the end it was shipped by rail—which wouldn't have required so expensive a packaging job. Our Easterner should have taken the time to seek a floor closer to home.

---

1. Trailers can be purchased or rented, but having one of your own is a good investment. During most at-home restorations, the car has to be moved countless times. Handy attachment is some sort of winch for loading and unloading.

2. At swap meets or junkyards, make certain of the parts you need before buying. Car parts from different models may look alike, but you can rest assured the wrong ones won't fit when you get them home.

3. Search out any literature regarding your car, the illustrations will be of value when looking for missing parts and when reassembling your restoration. Swap meets are good sources for brochures and other printed matter.

4. Photograph your prize as soon as you find it, the pictures will help immeasurably later on. Take more pictures as your dismantling proceeds, for later cars consist of thousands of parts and you'll want to remember where everything goes, and how it all fits back together.

One final parts source. Consider buying a *second* car as an aid in restoring the first one. The parts car needn't be complete, and while it should be the same year as your first love, it needn't necessarily be the same body style. If the price is right, there are all manner of things you can make use of. In my own case, I needed a complete '36 frame—'35's and '36's are interchangeable between all passenger models. Local sources were asking $100 and up. After some searching I discovered a derelict '35 5-window coupe—for $100. After the frame was eyeball-checked for square and pulled out from under, I began stripping off what few bits and pieces were intact and showed potential reuse. Dash instruments, glovebox door, window mechanism, rumble lid, metal spare tire cover, and so on

3

and so forth. Even though many of the parts were not compatible with the roadster, they became good swap meet material. I didn't keep a close record on this aspect of the car—although it's a very good idea to do so—but I came out about even in the end. In other words, by the time everything was swapped off, the replacement frame cost next to nil—to say nothing of the dollars saved in the few parts I did keep that were usable on the project roadster.

Now, a full 7 years after starting on the basket case, I have a nearly completed roadster. There are yet a few oddments lacking, but they're not important to its runability, and I know they'll turn up eventually. It has taken perseverance and time—plus knowledge acquired along the way. When commencing, for example, I didn't know only 3862 roadsters were produced. This meant that parts I'd eventually need wouldn't be available at every bend in the road. (Knowing this going in, I'd have been better off with a Fordor sedan.) With the toll the passing 38 years have taken on the roadsters, I'll hazard a guess that less than 200 exist in the U.S., Canada and Mexico. This means the repro parts producers aren't going to undertake a lot of expensive tooling to reproduce an item for which there is virtually no demand—making the genuine pieces virtually impossible to find, with prices to match.

SPACED OUT

It may not immediately occur to the novice restorer that he'll need room to perform his magic—lots of room. It may seem that one car needs only occupy a one-car garage stall. But, dear readers, this is hard-

ly the case. At-home rejuvenators find themselves overly crowded in even a two-car garage, while three only *may* suffice. If you're faced with complete dismantling, figure that the body will take a one-car stall, the chassis a one-car stall, and the bits and pieces—to say nothing of space for yourself to move around in—yet another one-car stall. Outside storage of the car or its major components might be alright temporarily, but as the pieces are restored you'll want to get them under-roof, especially if you're subjected to inclement weather part of the year. Too, you're already faced with severe deterioration of your car—or you wouldn't be restoring it—and you don't want to keep the downgrading of the wood, metal, upholstery, etc., to continue.

Then there's the very likely possibility that later along the road to restoration you'll acquire a "parts car," one not necessarily of the identical body style to your own, but at least one of the same year. The interchange of parts between body styles will turn out to go further than even your fondest hopes, so make a mental note that you'll need additional room for that extra car.

If you start a first-time restoration project with the usual small assortment of basic hand tools, keep in mind that you'll have to acquire additional hand and power tools as you go along. And they take space, plus the space needed to use them. Unless you're only going to dismantle the car then send its components out to professionals for finishing, then reunite the parts when you get them back, you won't need much more than a full set of wrenches, screwdrivers, and so forth. But if you're the true do-it-yourself type, then plan on outfitting yourself with far more than this. Besides the normal full complement of mechanic's hand tools, you'll need woodworking equipment (if your project contains any wood at all), a hefty floor jack (plus 2 jackstands as a minimum, or better yet, four), welders, power tools such as a body grinder, drill motor, an air compressor, bench grinder, big and little bench vises, and so on ad infinitum. There is no end of equipment available for working on cars—be they old or new—and we've seen people new at the restoring game who outfitted themselves with tools that outstrip even the cost of the car undergoing work.

Regardless of the work you're

planning to do yourself, there are some areas where you'll probably be calling on professionals, or at least firms and services set up to handle the specialized fields of plating, upholstery and maybe painting. But even in these areas there is much the do-it-yourselfer can do to stave off high professional cost. In painting, for example, you may not have, or want to acquire, the techniques of finish spray painting, but if you're going to do any metal work at all, you'll need to know how to lay on primer and other undercoats. These materials are very forgiving and it doesn't take much practice to shoot on a coat of primer, but it will take a compressor, spray gun and enough hose to reach around the car. There is much more on painting elsewhere in this book, but these are merely words of warning of what lies ahead for you in bringing that old Ajax coupe, or whatever, back to life, and a hint of why no restorer ever considers himself as having enough room to work.

In this same vein (if you are faced with even temporary outside storage of, say, the body), don't overlook the fact that primer paint is usually very porous and that moisture can and will seep through the coating you've so carefully laid on and begin the rusting process all over again—the one you've worked so hard to eliminate. Don't, for heaven's sake, take a body down to bare metal (or even a portion of it), prime it, then set the body outside while you work on the chassis in the garage. It won't take long for all that work to disappear down the drain and the body winds up looking as bad—or worse—than when you started on it. Once a part or major piece has been restored, keep it indoors from that time on.

A three-car garage did we say a while ago? Better make that four!

AND MORE SPACE

During the scouting our staffers did while this book was being prepared, we were in and out of literally dozens of garages, from the one-car size (shudder!) to a 10-car unit—the latter not a commercial restorer's shop, but on private property yet! The owner prefers to remain anonymous, but as long as he was house shopping, he kept his eyes open for what would ideally suit his space-needing hobby of auto restoration. He found it, in the form of the servants' and chauffeurs quarters of what had long ago been a magnificent estate but which now had been sub-divided down into manageable-sized lots. The estate had once required 40 servants for upkeep and maintenance, and the builders (back in 1912) had erected a 10-car garage as an ell to the servants' house. Now, 10-car garages are not all that rare in areas of affluence, but this one had only double doors leading into it, then it widened out to a huge "T" shape. But the thing that

struck us about this particular set-up, was that it harbored a *turntable* so that cars could be headed inside, then headed out again; no reason for backing out and presumably risking rear-end damage against walls or fountains.

A personal acquaintenance of ours is building a new house for himself and his wife—the kids long since having been raised and sent out into the world on their own. This guy is a car nut, too, and his completed home will consist of a one-bedroom house with an adjoining 10-car garage. Instead of a turntable, though, this garage will have 10 stalls, each with its own door. But to upstage the man with the turntable, our friend is currently shopping for a pair of electrically operated car hoists—like are commonly used at muffler shops. They are sometimes seen at equipment auctions in the larger cities, are available at very reasonable prices, and do not required an underground hydraulic ram for raising and lowering.

Now, we certainly don't expect any of our readership to rush out and start searching for unusual houses for what is admittedly an unusual hobby, but again we're merely pointing out that space—roofed-over space!—is what the restorer will need.

If having done one restoration job already has whetted your appetite for doing another—and another, and another, etc.,—it might pay you to look into the purchase of a car trailer. Somewhere along the line it seems that the car undergoing a rebirth has to be trailered somewhere—either intact or at least sizeable portions of it—and the cost of several rental trailer trips can add up. The trailer can be either new or used, but if it isn't equipped with a winch for urging a running-less car up and down the ramps, try a marine supply store where you'll find all manner of hand and electrically operated winches available. Land-bound sailors use them for launching and retrieving trailered boats, and one will become among your more frequently used apurtenances. (Don't overlook the need for trailer storage at home, too).

AND FINALLY

Picking through the foregoing brings to focus the more important steps and techniques required for dismantling any car—be it a 1936 Ford roadster or not—so a brief review of the highlights is in order.

Photograph the car from all angles the moment you acquire it—before you touch *anything*. Take detail shots of the debris that may be lying inside—one restorer didn't know he had a particular part until a friend identified it for him from a photo taken of the mess in the back seat area.

Seek photos, brochures, ads—anything pertaining to your particular make. The model or body style isn't all that important, but it's helpful of course. Compare these photos to your derelict before unbolting things, for original factory literature will show the car as it used to appear, and you may find something to unbolt which isn't stock so you can just throw it away or save it for swap meet fodder.

Sort related components into labeled boxes, identifying each piece in turn with a piece of masking tape or a stringed tag for later identification by box.

Make lists of parts as you go that are beyond salvation, thus beginning to build your *parts wanted* lists for later swap meets.

Find out, if you can, the general availability of parts for your car, considering both the factory production numbers and what you see at swap meets. Most Ford parts are fairly common, depending of course upon age of the car, since they were made in staggering quantities. But goodies for, say, a Model 77 Willys will be tougher to find.

Haunt the swap meets once your particular needs are known, especially—if you can find them—meets concentrating on the car(s) of your choice. I've been to many Ford-only meets and Chrysler-only meets, but even so, each still had vendors offering hard-to-find jewels for just about everything else.

Make *sure* the part you need is the part the swap meeter is selling. Don't rely on him, rely only on yourself after having *thoroughly* acquainted yourself with every single aspect of your parts-needing car.

Don't hurry. Most restorers don't set themselves a completion deadline. Haste makes waste, and in restoring a basketcase, this can be a serious waste of money. Remember, that the longer you take restoring your car, the more valuable it should be since the intervening time, alas, has probably taken its toll of other cars exactly like yours. ⚙

1. Wait a minute. Get your purchase home and study it carefully before beginning to strip it down or you'll end up with a mountain of parts and not remember where everything goes.

2. Valuable sources of information are original factory service manuals, and they're becoming more prominent at swap meets. Older automotive books and magazines, as at lower left, are valuable not only for their ads which picture cars brand new, but for occasional detail articles on a "new" engineering advancement—which may be on the car you're restoring. Consider a set of date-matched license plates (upper right) for your car, too.

3. Scan swap meet displays closely. Here is an assortment, for example, of Model T chassis parts, but for some reason there's also a vintage push-button radio there, too.

4. Don't overlook the lowly commercial vehicles in your quest for a restorable veteran, they're becoming more popular (reflected in asking prices!) as passenger cars become increasingly scarce.

4

FREEING FROZEN FASTENERS EVEN THOUGH YOU MAY HAVE THAT VINTAGE PIECE SAFELY HOME, YOU STILL HAVE TO GET IT ALL APART

Vintage tin? Great. Trouble is, it's always held together by about 50 lbs. of vintage nuts and bolts covered with an almost equal quantity of vintage rust and corrosion. Obviously, if that Overland Bluebird touring car you've just acquired is going to form the basis of a points-winning concours restoration, or even if your plans call for nothing more than driving it on special occasions, you've got to dismantle it with a minimal amount of damage and destruction.

After you've had the experience of stripping down one automotive relic things are likely to be a bit easier on your second effort, if for no other reason than you know what to expect. Anyone who sets about building a car with the idea that it's going to come apart and go together like a plastic model is in for a really big surprise. What's guaranteed to send even strong men weeping on their way to the loony bin is when their ordinary "brute force" approach to taking things apart results in the breakage of some irreplaceable piece of machinery.

The key to salvaging important parts intact is in thoroughly analyzing the entire situation before you attempt any disassembly work at all. Three factors are of greatest importance: (1) What are the materials used in the parts and in the fasteners holding them together? (2) What conditions are likely to be locking the fasteners in place? (3) What is the best no-slip way of gripping and applying force to the fasteners in question?

Iron, steel, brass, aluminum, and zinc or white metal castings constitute the large majority of all automotive parts. Techniques that may free the threads of a steel screw threaded into a cast iron part may

have just the opposite effect if the screw is of brass or aluminum, due to different expansion rates. Additionally, a brass screw in a steel part is a whole different snooker game from a steel screw in a brass part. Also, the corrosion which affects ferrous metals (rust) is different from that which forms on parts made from other metals.

If the fastener has no washer be-

neath it or if there is a split-type lock washer, it may be held in place by extreme internal tensions in addition to a locking layer of corrosion. Cutting away the washer with a cold chisel may therefore help in the case of exceptionally stubborn bolts. If there are exposed bolt threads extending through a nut or beyond the part into which the fastener is threaded, dirt and corrosion in that

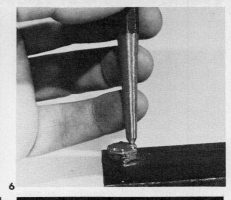

4   **5**   **6**

1. Tin hunters will yip in glee when they find a relic as complete as this 1926 Buick, but they will cry if it turns out all the fasteners are solidly rusted in place. If it is apparent that a lot of damage to otherwise good parts will occur when trying to unwind corroded screws or bolts, consider the purchase carefully before carting the derelict home.

2. The correct wrench is usually a 6-point socket, but metric tools (left) and assorted old tools that came with your (or any other) car are sometimes a big help. Square-set screw wrenches are often a boon.

3. The frozen fasteners should be treated with penetrating oil daily for about a week before you attempt to take apart old machinery. Liquid Wrench is a good brand.

4. After applying penetrating oil, tap the parts and fasteners repeatedly with a hammer to set up vibrations that help break rust and let the penetrant flow into threads.

5. If oil and repeated hammering won't do the trick, use heat. Heating and cooling of parts helps break the bond between them, due to expansion and contraction of the metal.

6. Bolts that have become rounded off can have their corners squared by striking each point of the hex with a center punch. Then use a 6-point socket wrench—carefully.

7. Bolt heads that are badly tweaked can sometimes be removed by drilling crossways and inserting a steel pin as shown here. Now the wrench has something to grip.

8. A tool like this can be ground from an old hacksaw blade. It works well for removing headless brass screws.

9. Hacksaw blade slotting tool is the most valuable on broken, small-diameter screws that cannot be drilled for the use of an extractor. Cut a slot as shown, then use a screwdriver.

10. If a broken bolt must be removed with an extractor, use a center punch to help get the hole started in the exact center and to avoid damage to the female threads.

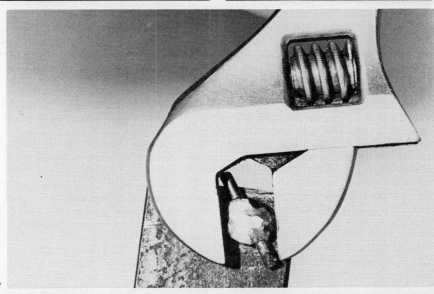

7

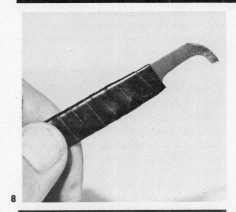

8

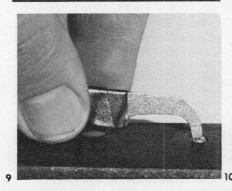

9

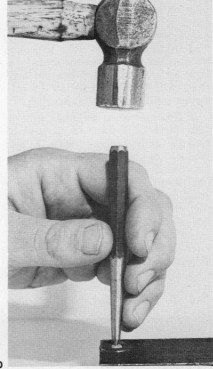

10

area may be hindering removal of the bolt more than the presence of internal corrosion. This is always a distinct possibility on bolts that pass through spring hangers or other once-lubricated assemblies. Clean off the exposed threads with a wire brush or thread chaser, apply penetrating oil, and they'll usually come right out. Try the brute force approach and you're only likely to get somewhere you don't want to go.

How you grip the fastener is highly important. Pipe wrenches, adjustable wrenches, and vise grips invariably do more damage than good, often making it impossible to ever get the fastener out intact. Use metric wrenches on cars having metric fasteners. The U.S. "equivalent" size is always a compromise. Some early car makers used nonstandard hex and square sizes. Metric tools will sometimes fit these better than U.S. sizes. Occasionally you can locate some of the original tools supplied by the car maker, and these can be lifesavers for certain special jobs. Six-point socket wrenches are superior to the 12-point variety for popping frozen fasteners free after years of neglect, and any kind of box or socket wrench is better than an ordinary open-end "spanner."

If a fastener is accidentally broken or damaged by your efforts, you must decide the best manner of extracting the threaded portion remaining in the hole. If the fastener itself is "standard hardware," you may choose to cut, break, burn, or grind it off and replace it with a new screw or bolt upon reassembly. In some cases the old bolts will have become so weakened by metal fatigue or internal crystalization that they will break off when merely struck solidly with a hammer!

If time permits, all fasteners on your piece of vintage tin should be given a daily soaking with Liquid Wrench or some other good rust-dissolving penetrant. Keep this treatment up for five days or a week, wire-brushing away any loose rust around the exposed parts of the fastener. Copper polishing cleanser, made for keeping the bottoms of kitchen pans bright, can be obtained at any supermarket. Apply this stuff with an old toothbrush and a little warm water to dissolve the corrosion that forms around brass screws threaded into brass parts.

After the fasteners have been saturated as thoroughly as possible with penetrating oil, tap them and the metal surrounding them repeatedly with a hammer. This will set up vibrations that help break up solid rust and aid the flow of the penetrant into the threads. Select a good, properly-fitting tool and apply "exploratory pressure." If the fastener does not turn, continue the penetrating oil/hammering routine a bit longer before trying again. Should it become possible to turn the fastener even slightly, add more penetrating oil and alternately loosen and tighten the fastener to help work the lubricant deep into the threads.

If hammering doesn't help, heating usually will. A propane torch is the safest bet, since it is not so likely to overheat the metal parts to a point that might cause permanent damage. Alternate heating and cooling will cause the parts and their fasteners to expand and contract, breaking the rust bond between them. Continued oiling and hammering may be used in addition to the heating/cooling cycle until the fastener can be worked free with a wrench.

If someone else has already failed at removing the fastener, or if your own efforts have gotten too brutal, the head of the bolt may become so rounded or broken that it is no longer possible to grip it in the normal way. Keep up with the oil/hammering/heating, but seek a means of getting a better grip on things. If the corners of the hex have been only slightly rounded off (by a poorly-fitting wrench or a 12-pointer with too much force applied), you can restore its corners by striking a deep "dimple" into each angle of the hex with a center punch. Use a 6-point socket after this operation.

When bolt or screw heads have become completely deformed, try drilling a hole through what remains of the head. Insert a steel pin through the drilled head so that it can be gripped with a wrench. This works especially well on soft brass bolts that tend to "crunch up" if vise grips are used.

Bolts with broken-off heads can often be removed using extractors. Once the head is gone it is actually easier to get penetrating oil down into the threads, and by drilling completely through the remaining threaded part of the bolt, penetrating oil can be gotten to the very bottom of the bolt as well. Drilling the full length of bolts that are still intact for the sake of filling the lower part of the hole with penetrating oil is an occasionally-used trick.

Several important points must be observed for successful extractor work. First, always use the drill size indicated on the extractor. It will bore the hole diameter that allows the best possible grip. Next, use an extractor that is small enough to leave at least 1/16" of metal around the hole drilled in the fastener, but large enough to provide the greatest possible grip area. Finally, make sure the hole you drill is dead center in the broken bolt. This will prevent local deformation of the threads as the extractor is driven in and will permit a more efficient use of twisting force.

Do not hammer the extractor into the drilled bolt with great force. This would only tend to expand the threads and cause them to seize even more tightly in the hole. Because of this possibility, extractors may not be the best choice for broken screws that are made from soft metals. In such cases you may find that slotting the bolt shank's end for the insertion of a screwdriver will offer a greater chance of success than is likely with an extractor. This is especially true if the diameter of the threads is too small to permit adequate room for drilling.

Make a slotting tool by grinding away all but two or three teeth

---

1. It's important to use the size drill that is called for on the shank of the extractor being used. This denotes the best hole size for maximum gripping of the tool.

2. A sharp drill bit is a must when drilling into broken bolts. A dull one tends to wander and will start its hole off center if at all.

3. Drive the extractor into the hole using just one or two light taps. If you drive it in with too much force, you'll only expand the threads and make things tighter than before.

4. A T-handled tap wrench is better for holding the extractor squarely than an awkward crescent wrench. This tool centers the force and avoids breaking the extractor.

5. There is such a thing as a nut splitting tool, but a cold chisel will work about as well. If the stubborn nut is holding a piece of sheetmetal, though, use this method only as a last resort.

6. This is the preferred way to get sheetmetal-retaining nuts or boltheads out of the way. Grind the nut away with an abrasive stone in a drill motor, lift or carefully pry the sheetmetal off stub, then drill remains of bolt and use an extractor.

from the end of an old fine-tooth hacksaw blade. Wrap some tape around it for a handle and use it as shown in the photos. Make sure the screwdriver you use accurately fits the slot you have cut into the broken screw end. Good-fitting screwdrivers are vital to removing any frozen fasteners having a slotted or special head.

Bolts that hold two sheetmetal sections together or hold sheetmetal parts onto the frame or other heavier pieces of metal require special care. Any cutting of fasteners or hammering to get a stubborn one free may deform or tear holes in the sheetmetal parts you are trying hardest to preserve. In cases like these it is usually best to grind the heads off the screws or bolts to separate the sheetmetal parts from their mountings.

Various small abrasive stones and wheels are available which are well suited to the above work. An electric hand drill and a bit of patience are all that is required to use them for cutting away old rust-locked fasteners with a minimum of damage to the surrounding metal panels.

If it proves to be impossible to remove a bolt or screw that is threaded into a casting, forging, or other heavy metal part, you'll have to drill it out and tap the hole for slightly larger threads. Choose a thread size that is about 1/16" greater in diameter than the original and has the same number of threads per inch, if possible. A 5/16"-24 thread will, therefore, be the best replacement for a 1/4"-24, since the pitch of the threads is the same (24 per inch). If any of the original threads remain after drilling out the broken bolt, they will be deepened rather than cross-cut.

Work carefully and follow the hints outlined here and you'll end up with more top-grade vintage tin in your shop than the guy who does everything with a cutting torch and a crowbar. If flawless restoration is your game, you'll be able to save most of the original nuts and bolts that are so necessary for a truly detailed piece of work. The successful freeing of frozen fasteners is far more a result of patience, know-how, and the right tools than it is of hurrying, hammering, and brute force. Spare the care and spoil the car! 🎬

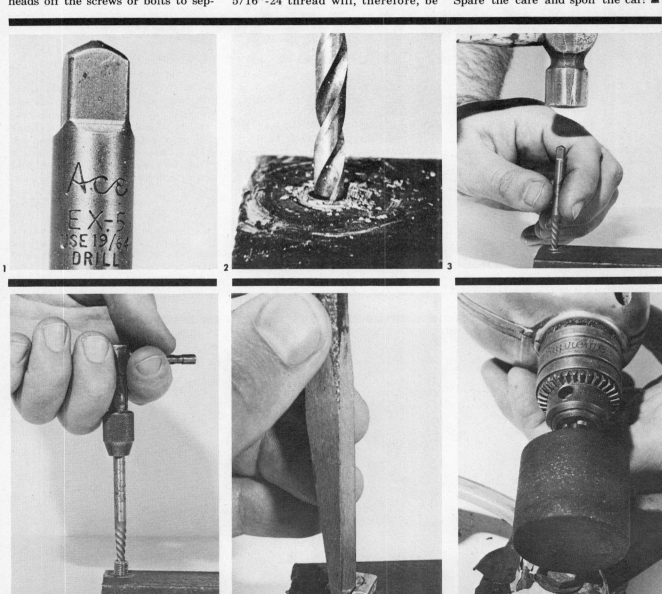

MACHINE TOOL TIPS
ANYONE WHO WORKS ON AN OLD CAR WILL EVENTUALLY USE ONE OR MORE OF THE COMMON POWER MACHINE TOOLS. HERE'S HOW TO KEEP TRACK OF YOUR FINGERS

If you've ever tried your hand at building a car, or any part of one, then you can appreciate the value of a well-equipped machine shop. The only problem is that few of us can afford one. Even if you're a newcomer to the hobby and just thinking of restoring that first car, setting up a rear end for the first time, or reworking the old buggy's tired engine, you're going to have to face up to the need for specialized tools and equipment that you probably don't have at hand.

Of course, you could go the route of having the work done for you by others, but where's the creativity or fun in any project as personal as your car if you're going to let it all out for someone else to do? And pay out hard-earned cash besides? So you trade on personal friendship with those who have the tools you need, or you enter into a "let me use it and I'll pay for the time" arrangement with a local machine shop or well-equipped garage.

We'll leave it to you and your own devices to figure out precisely how to get your hands on the specialized tools needed to do the particular job you have in mind; what we have for you are hints on how you can best do the job. As power tools vary considerably in what they'll do and how they're used (depending upon age and manufacturer), we could fill this entire book just with instructions on how to operate lathes, drill presses, mills and so on. But we have to assume that you're at least familiar with the fundamentals of measurement and tool operation . . . and with that assessment of your ability under our belt, let's take a look at some of the tools you might be using and how you can get the job done quickly and safely.

Actually, safety is a key word whenever you're working around

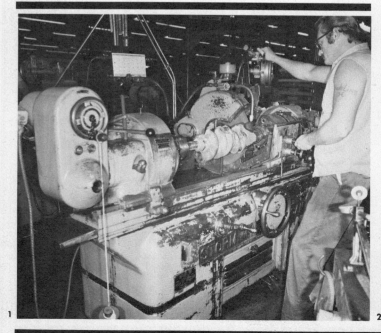
1

2

power tools of any kind. The very first time that you use a bandsaw, you'll start off with a healthy amount of respect and fear for that moving blade. It can remove one or more fingers should you slip. As long as you have this combination fear/respect, you're okay. It's after you've used the saw for a while that overconfidence creeps in and your actions tend to become automatic. Let's face it—you can't make an intricate cut with a fast-moving saw blade while carrying on a conversation with a buddy at the same time. Either the work or you are going to suffer if your mind isn't *right on* what you're doing at the time.

Nor is it worth it to save a few seconds here and there by ignoring those little things that common sense tells us we should do, like wearing safety goggles or glasses when working with a bench grinder. Remember, those sparks aren't just a pretty little shower of light kicked up for your entertainment. Most of them are tiny pieces of metal heated so hot by contact with the grinding stone that they glow momentarily as they flick into the air. One such

tiny piece of flying metal in the eyeball and it's all over—a loss hardly worth the inconvenience of wearing safety equipment.

There's no reason why you shouldn't be able to safely operate any power or machine tool, as long as (1) you understand its proper operation and (2) you maintain a respect for anything that's strong and sharp enough to cut through metal. To begin with, let's take a close look at that most common and innocent of all shop tools—the bench vise.

BENCH VISE

Here's a piece of equipment that's indispensable—you'll probably use a vise more than anything else in a shop. There's no better way to hold a connecting rod, piston, etc., so that it won't move, while leaving both hands free to work. Obviously, the vise has to be mounted *securely* to the bench or it may move, and there are many other fun ways to mash a finger or your toes without dropping 10 to 60 lbs. of metal on them.

1. If you're a machinist by trade, you probably spend your days with equipment like this crankshaft grinding lathe. We can't teach you much, but if you're a novice, we've got a few handy hints on using machine shop tools.

2. This is the usual bench vise; turn the handle and the jaws close together. Cloth prevents jaw imprint on precision parts.

3. Air vise uses foot pedal and compressed air to close the jaws. Note that this vise is also securely fastened to the bench. Keep your fingers clear of jaws when using an air vise.

4. Air vises come in different shapes and sizes, but this one is typical. Jaw A is stationary while jaw B moves forward under pressure to close. The adjusting wheel C can be set for various size openings.

5. Hold the workpiece firmly and rest it on the guide platform when using a bench grinder.

6. If you're using a wire wheel instead of an abrasive wheel, hold the work to the edge of the wheel as shown. Holding it directly in front as you would for grinding tends to cause the workpiece to flip up and away from wheel.

7. While some disc sanders are combination units with other power tools, the one shown here is a separate unit operated directly from the motor shaft. Work is held on the down side of sanding disc's rotation.

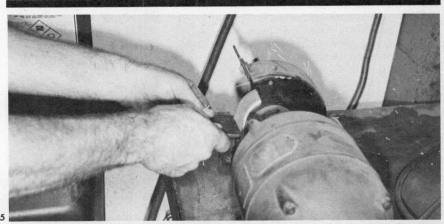

Most bench vises you'll encounter are simply a pair of metal jaws which open or close by turning a handle that rotates a steel screw. A heavy-duty vise can clamp shut with a force of up to 6000 lbs., providing that you've tightened the jaws securely. But here's where many users go wrong—they forget the one extra turn which assures that the workpiece will *not* move—leaving anything to happen when force or pressure in the form of a power grinder or drill is applied.

Besides taking the pains to make sure that what you are working on is not going to move, you should also consider what result the vise's holding force and jaw faces may have on it. If it's a soft or malleable stock, you may find a nice imprint of the jaw faces on its sides when you finish. And if the piece isn't held securely enough, the chances are excellent that you'll get both the imprint and a goodly number of scratches as the pressure you apply forces it out of the vise's jaws and onto the bench or floor. You can prevent many such problems by lining the jaw faces with a cloth to prevent imprints, scratching or marring if something slips; and the slipping can be avoided by tightening the jaws *that one extra turn.*

If you happen to wander into an up-to-date machine shop, you just might come across an air vise. This dandy but quite expensive piece of equipment operates hydraulically with compressed air, eliminating the need for "that one extra turn." And once it's locked in place, it's locked until you release the pressure. Most such vises are foot pedal-operated. Just insert the workpiece, step on the pedal and bang—the vise shuts. As long as you keep your foot on that pedal, the vise will hold whatever's between its teeth in a death grip. Just be careful that your fingers are not in the line of fire when you step on the pedal; when those jaws come together, it's a darn sight more painful than if you pinch your finger while manually tightening a regular vise.

One other precaution when using a bench vise—if the one you're working with has a swivel base that lets you position its jaws to suit your needs, be sure that the base is locked in place before setting to work. Otherwise, you may end up with a ⅜-in. hole in a finger or hand if the jaws move under pressure and that high-speed drill slips off.

GRINDERS

Bench grinders are invaluable for many kinds of jobs: You can rough-grind to shape, finish grind, buff, polish, brush or even sharpen hand tools. When new, most come equipped with flip-up polymer eye shields, but for some unexplainable reason, the shields are almost always missing after the grinder's been in the shop for a few weeks. Few mechanics seem to want to bother with them, preferring to work only with safety goggles or glasses. And if you hang around a single shop for very long, you'll notice that the use of these safety items is a rare sight. But just because others are careless is no good reason why you should risk your eyesight in the same way.

Grinders are dual-purpose tools, as there's an abrasive wheel mounted on each end of the revolving shaft. This lets you have two different grades of abrasive at hand without having to stop and change wheels. Use the coarser stone to remove lots of metal at one time and the finer one for sharpening or dressing your work. By removing one or both of the wheels, other tools such as wire or buffing wheels can be substituted.

The wire wheel is useful in removing rust, paint or deburring metal and gives soft metals a satin finish. Used with a bit of buffing compound, the buffing wheel will put a nice high-luster finish on metal surfaces. You can even fit an emery belt to the buffing wheel for smoothing metal surfaces.

When using a bench grinder, take care to hold the metal being worked on tightly and by the sides so that an accidental slip will not bring your fingers into contact with that aluminum-oxide wheel. If the piece is very small, clamp it in the jaws of vice-grip pliers. And if you use the small platform in front of the wheel to support the workpiece, you can feed or angle it with a great deal more certainty. Grinding wheels will gradually become clogged with use and must be "dressed" to restore their shape and efficiency. While there are several ways to do this, the most economical is a wheel-dressing tool that uses replaceable high-carbon steel cutters to dress, shape and remove unwanted glaze.

Some bench grinders are equipped with a disc sander, but you may also find this as a separate tool operated by its own motor. Nothing more

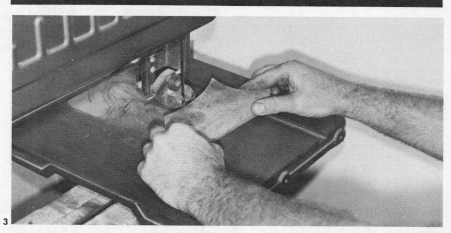

than a flat wheel which has a circular sheet of grit paper fastened to it, a disc sander is unfortunately a low-priority tool in many shops. Thus you'll often find it mounted wherever there's spare room, which usually means the end of a workbench that's too close to a wall.

When using a disc sander, always work *with* the rotating disc. This means using the "down" side as the sander travels; using the "up" side will cause the work to lift away from the disc and can result both in ruin to the surface being sanded and injury to the user. To obtain a flat edge, hold the workpiece flat as you bring it to the moving disc. Curved or circular pieces should be turned lightly as you sand. You can smooth odd angles freehand, but using the sander table will provide the greatest degree of accuracy. If the shop hasn't removed and lost the table, you'll find that it can be tilted for uniform bevel or cross-bevel cuts.

Use caution when working with the disc sander. As you're applying pressure toward the moving wheel, a slip of the fingers would mean several inches of flesh sanded painfully raw. Safety glasses are also in order to protect the eyes. And don't force

the work to the sanding wheel; while the abrasive particles act as cutting teeth, they can only remove a certain amount at one time. Forcing the issue will prematurely wear out the abrasive surface.

Belt sanders use a continuous abrasive belt that travels over a drum at each end. They are available in a variety of different shapes and sizes. While some are positioned vertically and others horizontally, most are adjustable for use in either position. Working with the horizontal is best for surface sanding, while a vertical position is preferred for end or edge sanding. The belt sander is really a rather versatile tool. You can use it when working with irregular and odd shapes, since the back of the belt is unsupported. Its idler drum can be used instead of a drum sander for working on the inside edge of a curved piece. Although belt widths vary, this doesn't interfere with the size of material that you can sand. When working with material that's wider than the belt, simply make repeated passes.

Make sure that the belt tracks over the two drums evenly before starting work. If it moves to either side, it should be adjusted before

proceeding. And don't use the table stop when sanding small pieces, because if you apply too much pressure, it's possible for the belt to pull the work from your fingers, resulting in a painful injury to the fingertips.

SAWS AND PRESSES

One of the fastest and most capable of cutting devices, the bandsaw is an essential tool in any general-purpose shop. Although used primarily for cutting curves, rough cutting of any form is commonly done on the bandsaw. Similar in operation to the belt sander, bandsaws use an endless blade that revolves over two wheels. Wheel size is important, as the smaller the wheel, the greater the number of flexes that take place during its rotation. Such flexing of the band causes a crystallization of its metal, ending up in a broken saw blade. What's important here is that you don't try to do too much with the smaller units—one with 12-in. wheels and a 2400 fpm rotation will not slice through a driveshaft easily.

Since the blade of a bandsaw is fairly narrow (⅛ to ½-in.), you can make some pretty intricate and delicate cuts, but don't attempt to turn corners that are too tight for the

1. This type of belt sander is commonly found in shops; the unsupported back of the belt allows sufficient "give" to use it for contoured edges, and removal of the idler drum shield lets you use it in place of a drum sander.

2. Belt sanders are also a useful specialty item; this one uses an endless emery belt for polishing camshaft journals.

3. Bandsaw can be used for rough cutting as well as intricate designs. Be sure to keep your fingers well to each side of the blade when holding small workpieces, and don't force-feed the saw blade.

4. The support plates used with a hydraulic press differ in size and shape depending upon their use. This is for removing bearing from shaft.

5. With outside support plate positioned on the press table, slip the two-piece plate between bearing and gear and fit in place. Then use the jack handle to lower the hydraulic ram and press the bearing off.

6. The same outside support plate is used to replace the bearing on the shaft, but the inside plate is solid this time.

7. To reinstall the bearing, rest it on the inside support plate and let the ram press on the gear face.

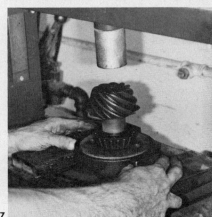

blade width. Make radial or tangential cuts instead to help the blade turn a corner and you'll save blades, as well as the time spent in changing broken ones.

When using the band saw, feed the material to be cut slowly and let the saw blade do the cutting—don't push the stock against the blade. If you force-feed it, the blade will bend or bow while cutting and the result is an uneven cut from top to bottom. Watch blade tension, as it affects the length of blade life. If you keep the tension too tight (and most of us do), you'll break blades for no apparent reason. Somewhere on most bandsaws you'll find an engraved scale or table which specifies the correct amount of tension to be used with each blade size. As you most often use the bandsaw for cutting curves, the work must be moved around the blade, but bandsaw tables do tilt for bevel cutting and can be used with various types of fences and guides. When using such, feed the material slower than usual, as it has a natural tendency to creep or move away from the fence.

Next to a vise and the various grinding/sanding tools already mentioned, you'll probably have more occasions to use a hydraulic press than any other auto shop equipment. Many bearings and gears require the use of such a tool to remove and reinstall them, and there's just no way around this need. How else could you apply 1000 lbs. or more of force? As long as you use the proper support plates for the job at hand, the press is as simple to operate as it is heavy. Just position the adjustable base table or platform at the correct height required for the job at hand and use the necessary support or press plates. Let's assume that you're going to press a bearing from its shaft. After centering the shaft and support plates beneath it, a worm screw head is turned down on the shaft. Now simply swing the press arm downward slowly, and the two parts separate like a torch passing through an ice block.

There are some cases when you can do the job without resorting to the use of a hydraulic press. For example, let's suppose that you need to remove and replace the distributor drive gear or timing gear from an old crankshaft. While a press is needed to remove the old gears, you can put the new ones on without it (if you're not in a hurry) by heating a small container of oil with the

gears in it. Let them stand for 10-15 minutes, remove from the hot oil and they'll slide onto the crankshaft and into place just as quickly and easily as the old ones came off.

The hydraulic press comes in handy in any number of ways, from installing piston wristpins to removing and replacing valve guide inserts in a cylinder head. The main thing to remember when using it is that you're applying a tremendous amount of force. Whatever you're working on should be centered under the press head so that uniform pressure will be exerted over the work surface; use no Rube Goldberg-type arrangements.

Make certain that the shaft, bearing or whatever you're applying the pressure to is firmly supported at each side on the press base; the best way to do this is to use the support plates specifically designed for the job. But if you have access to a press and no support plates, grab onto a couple pieces of ½-in. steel plate. Place one on each side of the

bearing, shaft, etc., and you're in good shape. But again, exercise caution when applying the pressure (do it slowly), and if the steel plates show any sign of weakening or slipping, back off the pressure to readjust before continuing.

LATHES

An expensive but versatile machine tool, the modern metalworking lathe in its simplest form is nothing more than a device to hold and rotate a workpiece against a singlepoint cutting tool. The tool is fed up to the metal stock and along its rotational axis to produce the desired cylindrical contour. Contouring the outside of the stock is called turning, while work done on the inside is called boring. These two operations comprise the primary functions of any lathe, but if you know what you're doing, the lathe can be used for threading, facing, reaming, drilling, polishing and even knurling.

You'll find a wide variety of lathes in use—engine, turret, speed,

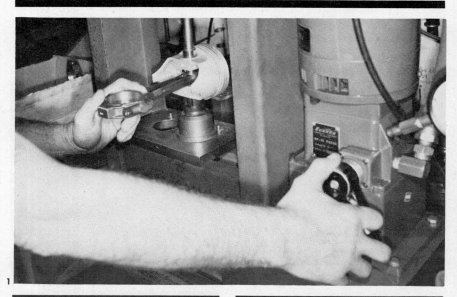

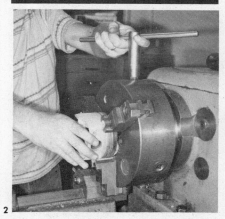

vertical, automatic—but all perform the same basic function of rotating metal stock against a fixed tool. Bench lathes differ from floor models only in size and the way in which they're mounted; a small engine lathe can be bench mounted, while larger ones must necessarily rest directly on the floor. So if you've been told that what you need is the use of a bench lathe, don't pass up the opportunity to use a floor lathe if it comes your way.

As a lathe is a basic tool to any metalworking shop, the chances are good that you'll run across a floor-mounted engine lathe. Most have spindles equipped with a universal three- or four-jaw chuck controlled by a single screw and pinion gear to automatically center the workpiece. Occasionally, however, you'll come across some odd-thinking genius who has fitted his with an independent four-jaw chuck. As all four jaws work independently of each other, all kinds of unusual and irregular shapes can be held and centered.

The larger engine lathes use a carriage to support and feed the cutting tool over the work. The cutting tool is inserted in the tool post and fastened for certain types of work, but it can also be mounted in place of the tailstock center and used for boring, drilling or reaming. Controls for positioning and feeding the tool are located on the face or apron of the carriage, while those used to select and change the speed at which the spindle rotates are found on the side of the headstock, behind the chuck. The less expensive and smaller units for bench mounting are often 3- or 4-speed combination wood/metal lathes, fitted with a sliding compound or tool rest that can be swiveled up to 180° and locked in place on the bed.

To get the most from any lathe, you must learn to use the cutting tools properly, and this takes a bit of experience, as well as a good understanding before you start of exactly what you must do to arrive at the precise shape and dimensions required. When feeding tools into contact with the work, move them slowly and with a steady hand. If you must hand-hold the tool, do so

1. The hydraulic press has a large variety of uses, including installing piston wristpins.

2. This is typical of the well-equipped automotive machine shop and uses a floor-mounted engine lathe. Fitting a piston into the universal chuck is done just as with smaller, bench-mounted units.

3. Lathes are often used with other specialized machine shop tools. This grinder/lathe combination is used in camshaft grinding.

4. Drill presses come in many sizes and shapes. This small shop unit has simplified controls and a rigid press table. Slots in the table accommodate a table vise for precise drilling.

5. There are four operations involved in using the drill press to drill and tap a hole like the one in this carburetor spacer plate.

6. As precision placement is required and the hole is on an angle, a special jig to hold the plate is clamped to the table. Start off with an undersize drill for a pilot hole.

7. After drilling the pilot hole, the flange surface is counterbored.

8. Step No. 3 involves redrilling the pilot hole to exact specifications.

9. Final step comes with threading the hole. Note the jig clamped to the angle iron on the press table; using an arrangement like this, you could drill any number of spacer plates exactly alike.

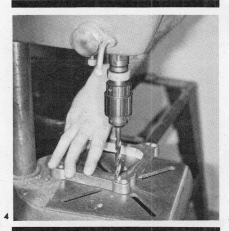

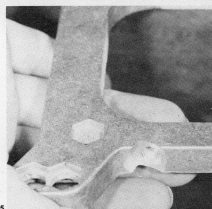

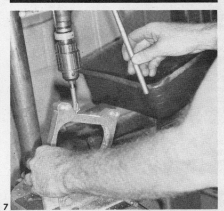

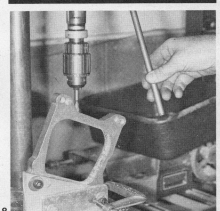

firmly and use the other hand as a guide to control the depth of cut and help move the tool to one side or the other. Use the compound or tool rest for a pivot point as well as tool support and you'll have maximum control over your work. The ideal for those with little experience is one of the larger engine lathes which allow you to fit and lock the tool in place, controlling its action with the micrometer-graduated hand dials.

When using a lathe to work metal, keep in mind that the larger the size of the piece on which you're working, the slower the speed you should use. When the work begins to chatter, it's a danger signal that either you're turning the stock too rapidly or that you're cutting too deeply. Slow down the lathe speed or apply the tool with a lighter touch until the chattering stops. Metal cutting tools designed for freehand turning are tipped with tungsten carbide, which holds a good edge for a long time, but because this edge is also somewhat brittle, use and store them with care.

DRILLS

One of the most common opera-

tions you'll need to perform is the rather simple one of drilling holes. Drilling is a step required in making virtually any metal product that you care to name, and while a great deal of work can be accomplished with a hand drill and a set of twist drills, the precision required for exact fits leads us sooner or later to the drill press.

The drill press is a method of accurately rotating a cutting tool, and moving it along its own axis at the same time, into a stationary piece of metal to create a hole the same size as the tool. Rotating the drill is a simple enough task when compared to moving it along its own axis . . . did you realize that it takes more than 1000 lbs. of axial thrust to move a ½-in. drill through mild steel? Next time you fit a drill into that powered spindle chuck, do so with just a bit more respect!

Drill speeds are important—the larger the tool, the slower the speed must be. And don't overlook feed pressure. When you feed too hard, you're forcing the cutting tool beyond the capacity for which it was designed, and the result is either a broken tool or poor work. Select a tool speed and feed pressure combination that will let the tool cut

easily, at a steady rate. Don't try drilling completely through the metal in one long press, as metal chips and shavings will make the cutting tool bind and overheat. Pull the drill up often to clear the hole of metal particles whenever it's necessary to drill deeper than the length of the drill's flutes.

When using a drill press, it's a good idea to clamp the workpiece in place to the worktable. This can be accomplished with large C-clamps, or if you want to go first class, with one of the large variety of drill press vises available. The workpiece is located in the vise, which is then bolted in place to the table. Fine adjustments in centering the hole to be drilled can then be made on the vise, which usually adjusts in at least four directions and may even swivel.

Securing the workpiece is required if you want absolute precision in drilling, and it's also a darn good idea from a safety standpoint, as drills occasionally grab and bind in the hole. If you're drilling a series of holes with a common centerline, the use of a fence along which the work can be positioned and moved makes matters much simpler. And unlike the hand drill, a drill press guaran-

1. The circular guide plate fastened to the press table here is marked off in degrees and has a center cutout to hold special workpieces for producing a large number at one time.

2. A mill operates in a manner similar to that of the drill press, but you can do a great deal more with it. The nozzle is held in a table vise for flaring—a simple operation.

3. In addition to the micrometer adjustment of the table in all directions, the table vise can also be adjusted to center the work exactly.

4. By adjusting the automatic stop control on the spindle, the depth of a cut can be preset for production work, eliminating all guesswork.

5. As the cutting tool rotates in place, the milling table is moved to cut away the inside of spacer plate. Sure beats grinding by hand, and you know that it's exact.

6. Sheetmetal squaring shears are a handy but dangerous machine. Use the side of your hand as shown to position and feed material—this is the safe way to do it.

7. Watch out that you don't tromp the treadle down on the other foot when operating shears. Keep fingers well away from cutting area; position of hand as shown here prevents it from protruding into the cutting area accidentally.

tees that the hole you drill will be perfectly perpendicular. But you still have to use care in locating exactly where it's supposed to be.

The best way to drill any hole is to start off with a drill that's undersized. Position the bit and drill a lead or pilot hole, then change over to the correct size drill and finish the job. Doing it this way makes things easier both for you and for the machine—don't forget the amount of thrust required to cut through metal! To create some holes exactly as you want them, it may be necessary to change drills several times. Whenever you're drilling a series of holes that must all be to an exact depth, preset the quill extension stop and lock in place; this will let you bring the drill down to that depth and no further.

A big brother to the drill press, the boring mill is also considered to be a basic tool in a machine shop layout, but by comparison, it's considerably more advanced and sophisticated in what it will do. In fact, it's not uncommon to find the mill taking the place of a drill press in smaller shops. Where the press will move a rotating cutting tool in a vertical motion, a mill is capable of both rotary and reciprocal compound cutting motions, and in the hands of a skilled user, can replace lathes, shapers and planers.

In its most elementary use, the milling cutter produces flat, recessed or contoured surfaces whenever the workpiece is fed at right angles to its axis, but by feeding the work along the axis of the spindle instead, it can bore and drill. And by rotating the work into the milling cutter in an exact relationship, it's possible to cut gears and sprockets or even mill threads and spirals.

Unlike the drill press table, which at best can only be tilted, the mill is equipped with a table that's fully adjustable on its saddle and can be moved from left to right, front to back, up or down and tilts in addition. Used in combination with a vise similar to those used on drill press tables or a fence, there's virtually no limit to what can be done. Variations in spindle speed are produced by the use of a V-belt with stepped pulleys on both the spindle and motor shaft, and like the drill press, the larger the piece being worked on, the slower the spindle speed must be. In fact, everything that applies to the drill press also applies to the mill.

CUTTING IT

For those who are interested in doing their own bodywork, sheetmetal squaring shears will prove quite useful when cutting up to 16-gauge stock. If you have very much cutting that needs to be done, it's a tremendous timesaver, and there comes a time in every man's life when his old reliable (but sharp) tin snips just meet their match. Spare them (and your hand) the agony and switch from snips to shears. If you can find a body shop equipped with squaring shears, well and good, but chances are that you'll have to con a regular sheetmetal shop into letting you use theirs.

Although it's an odd-looking device, the squaring shears are relatively simple to operate. As long as the hold-down bar is properly adjusted, you can cut sheetmetal almost as fast as you can feed and position it. But a word of caution here—don't take up a buddy's offer to help you work this one. It's a one-man machine. The books are filled with stories of amputated fingers when four hands go to work.

A correct setting of the knives requires that a shearing cut be made by the top blade, which is set at an angle that leaves large open spaces in which unwanted fingers can disappear. And if your friend should happen to decide that everything is ready and stomps down on the foot treadle, you'll lose most of the 10 best things that ever happened to your hands. Incidentally, before you stomp that treadle down, either move your left foot or make sure that the treadle-stop works. Otherwise, you just might crush a few toes should the treadle go all the way to the floor.

While there are numerous other machines and tools that you'll run across in a shop, we've covered those that will let you accomplish the majority of things you'll need to do. Remember, if you approach each and every one of them with the proper amount of respect and fear, you should have no problems in getting the work done safely. And if you come up with any questions while operating one, it's best to shut the machine down and find someone in the shop who can give you an answer—trying things out on your own when you're not thoroughly familiar with what the machine will do is probably as great a hazard as any you could create.

Take your time, do the job right. It's worth it in the end. 🎬

5

6

7

YOUR CAR HAS BEEN FRAMED THE HEART OF A CAR IS ALSO ITS SKELETON

If your frame or chassis is wracked or tweaked in some manner from a long-forgotten altercation, your car may motor along the highway crabwise. Hopefully for a budding restorer, the tweak will be much less drastic than this case of the extreme result of two autos attempting to occupy the same space at the same time. But prior to any restoration operations, each frame, during the initial teardown period, should be completely inspected. Never assume the frame is straight and square without a close, thorough inspection.

A chassis, by modern definition, is what's left after the body and sheetmetal have been removed from an automobile. Essentially, then, the chassis proper would thus amount to the engine, transmission, driveline, front and rear suspension, axles, steering components, wheels, tires and, by all rights, the frame or skeleton to which these components are fastened. But in this day of widespread unit construction, the chassis is the complex folds and interweavings of the lower body sheetmetal, the floorpan and some structural sheetmetal boxes that actually provide the support for the heavy powertrain and suspension. The sometimes awkward and always heavy formed steel frame rails and crossmembers used in the earlier days of automobile manufacture have essentially been disposed of in the ongoing search for lighter cars and simplicity of manufacture.

"Frameless" car design began to become fairly widespread in the domestic industry with the unqualified structural success of the Chrysler Corp. Airflow series, introduced for the 1934 model year. The Airflows failed dismally from a sales standpoint, however, due to the public's apparent reluctance to accept the innovative body design. The Airflows, available in the Chrysler and DeSoto lines until the model's phase-out after 1937, did not entirely get rid of a frame in the general sense, but the body-supporting skeleton wound throughout the body in an unconventional (for the times) cage form. This cage allowed a far lighter and less complex system of under-floor girders than was then the industry norm.

Chrysler engineers had originally hoped to go to a true unit-body type of construction at the outset of design, but the haste needed to get the radical car into production resulted in at least a semblance of a frame being retained. This eased car assembly, since it provided a basis to which the other components could be attached.

But Chrysler did not invent unit-body construction, nor was it even a development of the U.S. auto industry. Proper credit must go to Vauxhall of London, which offered a true frameless car as early as 1903. The English Lagonda for 1913 used a similar method of construction, followed by the Italian Lancia, which appeared in 1921. The Budd Co., starting in 1912 as a supplier of automobile bodies for many major makers of American cars, began toying with unit construction in 1928, resulting in a design patent involving a combination frame/body unit. The development, however, first appeared in mass production on a French car, under a licensing arrangement with Budd: the 1934 Citroen.

1

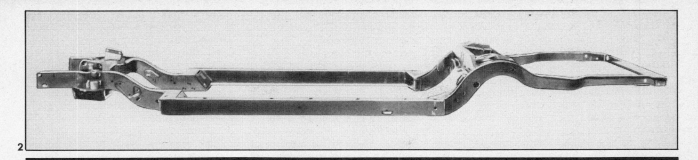

The 1931 Hupmobile was the first U.S. car to take advantage of the frameless construction, and while GM was interested early in this method of car building, it wasn't until 1937 that the giant firm adopted the system. GM, however, left it to their foreign subsidiaries, Opel and Vauxhall, to break the ice with consumers.

Unit-body construction did not spread rapidly. While there was, to be sure, a material saving in using frameless construction, the necessarily complex body structure required heavier tooling investments than a conventionally framed car. Thus it was suited only to very high production runs and meant that a basic body design must be retained for several years. This would create no end of hardship for the stylists, who, during that era, were forever developing radical and streamlined body shapes.

The lightweight construction possible with frameless design lent itself not only to cars with high manufacturing runs but at first only to small or compact cars. The 1941 Nash 600, not quite a full-sized car by U.S. standards at the time but nevertheless a bigger one than had been previously produced, cut back

1. Lift the body off a car and you have a chassis, like this Kaiser-Darrin 161. Its heart is the skeleton to which the engine, suspension components and so forth are attached.

2. Stripped of all removable parts, a frame is a single welded or riveted unit which must be carefully checked for "squareness," tweaks or cracks before the restoration work begins.

3. Some very early cars used frames of wood, a holdover from the days of the horse and buggy. This frame belongs to a 1910 Stanley Steamer.

4. Bill Chisolm of Vanowen Brake & Wheel shows one way to check for a longitudinally twisted frame before the car is dismantled for restoration. Note difference in distance between the ends of the trammel bars, one at front of car, the other at rear.

by 500 lbs. on the steel necessary for its construction by using a unitized body. The ill-fated Tucker, which bowed for 1947, went the unit route. Hudson for 1948 featured a frameless design for the body proper, but a subframe, carrying the engine, front suspension and forward sheetmetal, was added to it during final assembly.

Back in the general time period with which this book is involved, though, it is far more common to find a full conventional frame under your project car than not. So that type of construction is our primary concern.

The chassis, as stated, normally consists of the basic frame, the front suspension with axles and wheels, the transmission and driveline and the rear axle with its suspension. Naturally, this also includes the brake system (mechanical or hydraulic) and the cross-shafts and pedal assembly. The steering is a part of the chassis as well. For all practical purposes, however, we are considering the drivetrain (engine, clutch, transmission, driveshaft and rear axle) as a separate entity in this book and deal with it at length elsewhere. This leaves us with the frame, front suspension/axle assembly, rear springs, brake system and steering as our "chassis."

The paramount component of the chassis is the frame itself, to which all other assemblies are attached. Stripped to its essentials, the usual frame has two main side rails joined by two or more crossmembers. Hefty X's are also utilized on many later cars to bridge the central portion of the frame and help support the drivetrain components.

In the early years, the side rails were little more than straight lengths of U-shaped steel beams. Through use of varying-width crossmembers, though, the side rails might taper inward near the front of the car to allow clearance for the steerable front wheels. The crossmembers could be essentially straight lengths of similar-sized, U-shaped steel, but often they were arched to go either up and over the driveshaft or down and under the engine and/or transmission. Crossmembers were coupled to the side rails through welding, riveting and/or bolting, often with fishplates or gusseting to help the frame remain "square."

As cars grew heavier, longer and more complex, added cross-supports became necessary, especially when arches, termed "drops," were developed where the side rails kicked up and over the rear axle. "Double-dropped" means that the side rails arched up at both ends, for suspension clearance as well as to gain lower body lines. Ford introduced its double-dropped frame with the '32 model, the first year of the famed V-8 engine, but the frame was hardly innovative in the broad sense.

There are many things to look for on as simple a component as a bare frame. Has the vehicle been damaged and improperly repaired? Have age and stress fractured any vital components? Do any welds show signs of separating? Are any bolts loose or missing? Are the rivets tight? Are there any signs of butchery by torch or chisel? Has rust or other deterioration begun to set in? If so, how far has it progressed? These points and others must be given careful consideration before proceeding with simple frame cleaning and repainting.

Assuming you've stripped the car completely and are down to the basic skeleton, place the frame on a concrete pad or other floor that you *know* is flat and level. All the lower points of the frame may or may not touch the concrete, depending on how complex its shape is. The central portions of the side rails may lie on the floor, but the tips or frame horns (the extreme ends of the side rails) may be several inches above it. No matter—*provided* each front tip is exactly the *same* height above pad level, and that the rear tips are also at the same height. A simple steel rule can be used to measure their height. If things check out

okay here, you can be sure the frame hasn't "warped" from a long-ago accident, buckled from overloading or been twisted longitudinally.

However, even if such measurements are on the money, there is another, more important measurement step, one which will require a

1. Bill suspected that this Model A had been "crunched" in the past, due to this unusual bend at front of the valance panel. Use of trammel bars in previous photo verified it.

2. Unit construction cars, like this 1950 Hudson Commodore (with a forward stub frame to support the engine and front suspension), are very difficult to salvage if they've been badly wrecked. Note how the girders are integral with the body sheetmetal.

3. A careful check should be made of all four frame "horns," as they carry the bumper brackets and are prone to damage. Be sure your horns are true before measuring diagonally.

4. A frame is checked for "square" by cross-measurement, as shown. By comparing the distance between the same points across the other diagonal, a lot can be told about a frame's past history.

YOUR CAR HAS BEEN FRAMED

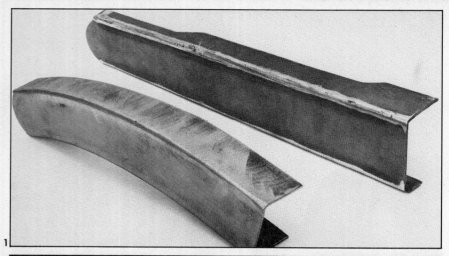

steel tape longer than the everyday 6- or 8-footer. This measurement is the "diamond" test.

An accident may have knocked a frame out of true alignment or out-of-square. To check this, take measurements from one rear corner (measure from matching holes or rivet heads) to the opposite front corner, or diagonally across the frame. Note the measurement, then stretch the tape across the other diagonal and compare the figures. Frames are not manufactured to very close tolerances, so if your frame is out-of-square by ⅛-in. or less, that's right on in Detroit parlance. If it's more than this, though, then you'd better seek the expertise of a frame shop. Judiciously applied force, via a jack or the more professional hydraulic push/pull rams, can usually bring the tweaked frame back within tolerances.

If at this point the frame is found to be square, it's worth trying to salvage, and you can proceed to the next logical step of cleaning. Don't waste too much time trying to discover kinks in the side rail flanges, loose rivets or cracked fishplates just yet, because the grease and grime that have accumulated over the years may hide more trouble spots than you can see while the frame is still dirty.

The best way to thoroughly clean a frame and prepare it for painting is a combination of two cleaning methods described in more detail on the following pages: steam cleaning and then sandblasting. If these operations are done correctly, your frame will be thoroughly cleaned, rid of its original paint and rust scale. Now it's ready for your close inspection. Are there wear splits, cracks, broken pieces, rippled flanges or any other problems?

As stated, the juncture of cross-members to side rails may have been welded, riveted, bolted or any combination of these. If any joints show signs of having "worked" and loose rivets or cracked welds are in evidence, repair them in the same way they were originally fastened. Don't, for example, weld a joint that was originally riveted. Riveting, while it provides a secure fastening, allows for a certain amount of flexing, as when the car is driven over rough roads. If a once-riveted joint is welded, it may crack as soon as the car is driven, since it's no longer free to move as originally designed.

If a rivet is obviously loose, chisel or drill out the offending part and re-rivet. If hole has become elongated or egg-shaped, drill the hole to the minimum size needed to produce a round hole and use a rivet that is a near press-fit in the opening. Few at-home restorers are equipped to do this, but your friendly frame shop is—if you tote your assembly to them.

Before hauling the steel home from the frame shop, go through the measuring procedures again. After all, the shop's personnel are not infallible, and it could save two trips and some temper flaring if the frame turns out to be still slightly tweaked. That way you'll make certain that the frame is square and true before spending any more money on your restoration. 🏛

1. At least one firm has come to the aid of frame restorers. Rock Valley Antique Auto Parts, 122 S. Pine St., Stillman Valley, Ill. 61084, fabricates frame horns for the '32 Ford. They can be butt-welded on after damaged horns are torched off.

2. Even a partial restoration should include wire-brushing the frame and the attachment brackets. Then inspect them and follow with repainting.

3. It's not the easiest way to clean a chassis, but if you don't have access to a sandblaster, clean off all rust scale after steam cleaning.

4. A Model A stripped of its many essentials looks like just so much scrap iron, but it's the basis of a show-stopping restoration.

5. After steam cleaning and sandblasting, check riveted joints for loose rivets and welded joints for cracks and fractures. Cleaning showed up this badly rusted joint.

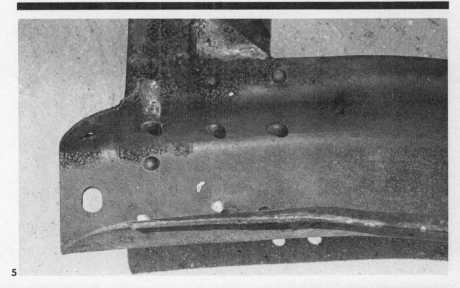

BLAST IT! AIR AND SAND ARE COMBINED TO PROVIDE AN EFFECTIVE GUNK REMOVER

An alternative to chemical stripping, sandblasting can be performed on both the frame and body of a vintage car. When handled with care, blasting can quickly and safely remove rust and corrosion from all but the most delicate parts.

Hambro's Sandblasting (9235 Glenoaks Blvd., Sun Valley, Calif. 91352) has been dealing with vintage tin for a number of years. They've developed their own techniques to protect valuable metal. Nozzle angles, grit so fine it is unavailable from commercial sources and personal experience are all part of this technique.

Personal experience is the overriding factor here, and it led Hambro's to the proper use of air pressure, correct nozzle angles and a successful search for the special abrasive needed for use on older cars. Hambro's has the experience and can be trusted, but can your local sandblaster? Can he be trusted with that one-of-a-kind fender you need cleaned? This you'll have to check out for yourself. Watch your local man at work. Does he specialize in stucco removal or can he also clean metal? If an antique auto club is headquartered nearby (you should be considering membership anyway), ask if any members have had dealings with this man. If he's given a good recommendation by these folk, you should be able to trust him and his work.

Suppose you've found your man and you're ready to proceed. Can you save money by preparing a frame or fender beforehand? Yes! The first stop is a "quarter car wash," the neighborhood do-it-yourself, coin-operated, quasi-steam cleaning center. Degreasing the frame, running gear, body parts, etc., prior to blasting will save the sandman time and you money. If the gummy, years-old collection of grease, dirt and what have you resists the frontal assault of the 25¢ car wash, visit a professional steam cleaner (covered elsewhere in this book) en route to the sandman.

Any wood panels should also be removed prior to blasting. Although Hambro's masks off any wood near target metal, it's safer to remove it. However, if the wood panels are new and need to acquire an antique appearance, slight sand brushing will

PHOTOS BY ERIC RICKMAN

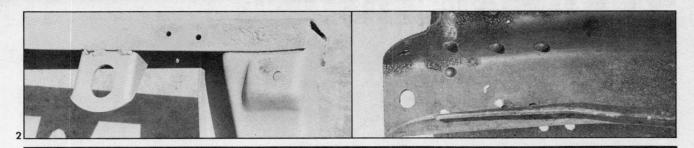

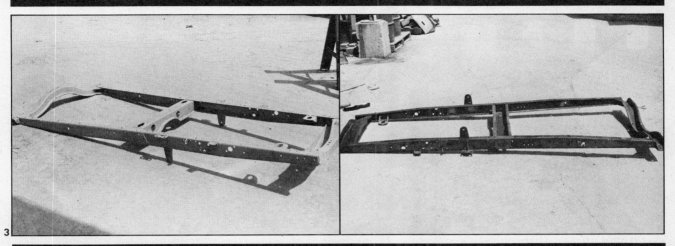

1. A sandblasting booth is not the place to be without a breathing mask. The gun is working on a frame, with a welded-spoke wheel awaiting its turn.

2. Before and after photos show how much rust and old paint is removed, leaving clean, bare metal.

3. Sandblasting is an excellent preparation for painting. After blasting, surface is lightly pitted, providing excellent adhesion for paint.

4. This is the steel backing wall behind the blasting room's workbench. In the hands of a novice, a sandblasting gun can be very destructive. These holes were worn through over a period of years, however.

soften the grain and bring out an old and weathered look. Sand brushing means just lightly brushing across the wood face with the nozzle, enough to etch but not hard or long enough to cut.

Ron Hambro has discovered that commercially sold abrasive is far too coarse to use when sandblasting valuable sheetmetal or even vintage frame rails. However, each time a grain of sand passes through the nozzle to strike something, it is reduced in size and sharpness. Eventually, after being used many times, the grain will become a mere dust mote and pass out of the blasting booth to be caught by the filters. Just prior to filtering size, the grain

has about the consistency of powder. Ron recycles this powder and uses it for cleaning sheetmetal. Coupled with very shallow nozzle angles and lowered air pressure, he has found that this sand powder works great on vintage tin without harmful side effects.

One step up the ladder from powder, the grain is still a grain of sand, but with very soft, rounded edges. Ron recycles sand in this condition for blasting vintage frames. He feels even No. 60 grit is too coarse for older frame metal. New sand and

normal air pressures can warp body metal and even some frames very quickly.

Sandblasting is also an excellent preparation for painting, but don't hold off the paint job too long! Rust visits blasted metal very quickly. Ron's company will prime bare metal with zinc chromate—but only if requested to do so.

In the hands of an expert, a sandblasting gun can restore a rusted hulk of metal to a valuable piece of vintage tin—but make certain the sandman *is* an expert.

STEAM CLEANING
THE FAST WAY TO DE-GUNKING

You've managed to transport your recently discovered vintage tin home. Now what? Do you jump right in and begin work, separating pieces and parts and placing them in their new resting places, various well-marked containers? Not really. It is much easier to work with clean, non-greasy components (they don't slip through your fingers as readily). But trying to clean each individual part separately can also be a real chore.

For quick and easy cleaning, you can't beat steam. Steam cleaning can quickly eat away in minutes patches of grungy mess that would otherwise occupy many hours of scraping, applying solvent, hosing everything off and then repeating the same drill over again.

There are a few do's and don'ts applicable to cleaning with steam. Most of these concern simple safety procedures or just common sense. First and foremost, decide if you wish to perform the task yourself or pay for a pro. Either way, implement that familiar slogan and "Let your fingers do the walking through the yellow pages."

If you've decided on using a pro, call ahead first to ascertain whether the shop can or will handle vintage tin. If it can, make reservations for a particular time—especially if you wish to watch. Some professional companies may even offer curb service—there are portable cleaners that can degrease your chassis right in your own driveway.

If you wish to save labor costs, you can rent a portable unit to use on your car and do it at your own speed and convenience. Look through the yellow pages under "Steam Cleaners, Rentals." In any large city you should find many firms advertising rental units. Large national stores such as Sears or Wards also offer units suitable for home garage use, a definite consideration if you are planning more than one restoration. Each unit should come with a complete book of instructions, but if you've ever patronized a 25¢ car wash, you'll be able to use the portable unit with no problems.

PHOTOS BY ERIC RICKMAN

A few basic safety hints, however, may or may not be included with the instruction booklet. Protect yourself; cover any skin that could come in direct contact with the hot steam to avoid burns. Eye protection is a must, even though the man in the photos has temporarily misplaced his. Anyone using a high-pressure steam nozzle should definitely wear goggles or glasses. Wear old clothes, because hot grease will splatter whatever you wear with hundreds of spots that leave the appearance of dried mildew.

As for protecting the car, avoid spraying near good paint. The caustic cleanser used in conjunction with the steam will etch and streak whatever paint it contacts. So be careful. Care should also be taken with wiring. Late-model insulation is plastic, which is very different from insulation used during pre-12-volt days. Steam has a negligible effect on plastic, but early insulation is almost completely destroyed by steam cleaning. So if your wiring is pre-plastic OEM, be prepared to replace any wiring located in the steam-cleaned area.

Most freshly cleaned surfaces have to be painted almost immediately after cleaning, because the grease and dirt that have been protecting the surface for years are no longer there. Also, all U-joints, bearings and lube points will have been cleaned out and are now running dry, so lubrication must be applied again—immediately, before damage can occur.

Now that the clean components can no longer slip through your fingers, it's time to remove and mark them. Store the smaller parts and fasteners in containers that clearly identify them and take plenty of photos every step of the way. 🦂

3

4

1. A hoist (either air or hydraulic) really helps the operator to clean otherwise hidden areas. If the paint job is a good one, stay away from it!

2. An empty engine compartment is very easy to clean, compared to some more modern engine compartments that appear to have been stuffed full with a shoehorn. Operator should be wearing long-sleeved shirt and goggles.

3. The engine and transmission from this T-bird really aren't very dirty, but a clean assembly is still easier and better to work with.

4. It's easier to clean, the engine and trans assembly outside the car.

ON STRAIGHTENING A BEAM AXLE NOT AN AT-HOME PROJECT, THIS JOB CALLS FOR ACTION BY A PRO

BY BOB KOVACIK

The beam axles used under most older cars, particularly in the Ford line, were well engineered and manufactured from steel alloys that were almost unbelievably strong. Seldom during a car's normal lifetime did these hunks of metal sag or bend, but an unfortunate front-end accident was something else again. Sometimes the offending axle, if not too badly tweaked, was brought back to original shape, but because the units were inexpensive and widely available during their era, most front-end shops simply slipped in a replacement axle in place of the bad one. The customer went away secure in the knowledge that the beam that separated his front wheels would never again give trouble—unless another front-ender came his way.

Your restoration may or may not have its original beam axle; who knows the past history of a derelict car? It may or may not have been in an axle-cruncher early in its life; if it was, was the axle replaced or merely straightened? Or has the axle suffered a worse fate, such as acting as a support for a tow-truck hook or a mounting point for a cable when the car was fished out of a swamp? Whatever the state of your car, it's essential that the front suspension be given a thorough going-over and the bushings, bearings, etc., replaced whether they appear to need it or not.

Of more importance is the beam axle itself; only a pro's check with the tools of his specialized trade will tell you if the darned thing is bent, bowed or otherwise tweaked.

Because of the super-stout metals used in the manufacture of axles, it is not expected that many at-home restorers will have the equipment at hand to right the wrongs that may exist. Thus this is another chore for the specialist—who will probably insist, mind you, that the axle be brought to him with the rest of the car attached to it.

Bill Chisolm at Vanowen Brake & Wheel took us through the procedure on a rather tired-looking Model A. The fault in this (basket) case was found to be a rearward bend on the right side of the axle. Bill mentioned that when straightening a bend like this, the load applied (by hydraulic jack) must be distributed across nearly the entire width of the axle. If not, a kink will result and the later caster and camber adjust-

PHOTOS BY ERIC RICKMAN

ments will be woefully short of specs. Bill put a round billet of steel against the front of the axle, then mounted his ram with its two clamps astride the axle's bent point. Hydraulic pressure did the rest, while Bill carefully monitored the amount of pull to make sure he didn't go too far.

Since beam-axle Fords had no provision for precise adjustment of either caster or camber, the axle itself must be "adjusted" by bending it in a vertical plane for camber, and by similarly tweaking the wishbone arms, also vertically, to "adjust" the caster. Toe-in, the third critical factor in a car's front suspension, is, thankfully, adjustable through the clevises on the tie rod.

Since caster, camber and toe-in can only be checked properly with the car on a front-end rack *and* embodying most of its running weight to simulate its road stance, forget about taking just a front axle to the fix-it man. If your car is in such sad condition that it must be totally dismantled and the pieces repaired or replaced bit by bit, be sure to take the car to the front-end shop *before* it's disassembled. If the car is incomplete—minus its engine, for example—add ballast weight, via sacks of cement or whatever, to bring its total weight back to where it belongs.

By doing the axle work in this way, it doesn't really matter where or how the various frame and/or axle straightening devices are mounted or levered for pushing or pulling. Woe to the restorer who waits until his car is nearly completed before fixing the axle; those high-powered hydraulic rams and jacks can make a real mess of fresh paint. 🛠

2

3

1. Only specialized equipment like this hydraulic ram can be used to straighten a beam axle; the tough alloys used in their manufacture can be moved around in no other way.

2. On Fords, the axle itself must be bent slightly for setting the camber. Similarly, caster is set by bowing the wishbone legs as required, a job requiring a setup like this one.

3. Toe-in on Fords is adjustable via the tie-rod clevis. The first step is to scribe a line around the circumference of each front tire.

4. A trammel is set to gauge the distance between the tire scribe marks at front, and then it's carefully checked on the back side of the tires. Model A's require ⅛-in. of toe-in.

4

KINGPIN REPLACEMENT
A SMALL BUT IMPORTANT STEP ON THE ROAD TO RESTORATION

BY ERIC RICKMAN

Normal kingpin replacement is not a particularly difficult job, but it does require patience and some knowledge. The real challenge comes with a car that's been sitting awhile and has its components pretty well rusted together.

When kingpins are frozen in the spindles, you may need a specialist to do part or all of the replacement.

The installation you see here was especially hard, and was done by Bill Chisholm at Vanowen Brake & Wheel in North Hollywood, Calif.

The first step, of course, is to get to the kingpin itself. This means removing everything attached to the end of the axle. Generally it's not necessary to disassemble the brakes if your car is equipped with front brakes. You can just unbolt the backing plate from the spindle and remove the entire backing plate, brake and hydraulic cylinder assembly (or mechanical accuators). It's not necessary to disconnect the hydraulic brake hose, if your car has this newer braking system.

Don't let the backing plate hang on the brake hose, though. It should be fastened securely under the fender while you're working on the spindle.

Most kingpins have a locking bolt or pin of some kind that secures the kingpin to the spool on the end of the axle or knuckle support. Once this locking bolt is removed, the kingpin comes out easily . . . unless you're dealing with something like our derelict Model A pictured here.

To remove this heavily encrusted unit, Bill Chisholm used a torch to cut off the ball end of the kingpin. This allowed him to get a drift onto the pin itself, in order to drive it out. When a drift is used, it's important that it be of the proper diameter to prevent the soft metal kingpin from mushrooming and creating an even more difficult problem.

In this particular case, hammer and manpower weren't enough. It became necessary to use a torch and

PHOTOS BY ERIC RICKMAN

cut through the crack between the spindle bosses and axle end. This helped free the kingpin and bushing and burn out the old thrust bearing. Even then, a special pressing clamp was needed to push out the final piece. The kingpin was finally removed in four separate sections.

At this point, Bill had to dress off the top and bottom surfaces of the axle ends with a grinder to remove the melted metal bits that accumulated. Never ream the axle ends to fit the new kingpin. If the boss is narrowed slightly, don't worry—the new kingpin kit comes with shims to take up the space.

The next step is to press or drive out the old bushings. Use solvent and compressed air to clean and blow out the grease passages. When the new bushings are pressed into place in their spindle bosses, be sure to align the grease-fitting holes. In the Model A, Zerk fittings are a drive fit. Don't thread the holes and install Alemite fittings, because they will destroy the original integrity of the car. That means you'll get docked points at a concours for a non-stock modification.

New bushings are undersize and must be honed or reamed to fit the new kingpin. A controversy exists over these two methods of opening up the bushings. Some say the honing tool gives a perfect fit because it doesn't remove too much metal, while a master mechanic will tell you he can do the job just as well with an adjustable reamer. One caution: Beware of nonadjustable reamers made for Ford kingpins—many aren't the proper size.

In this installation, Bill used a

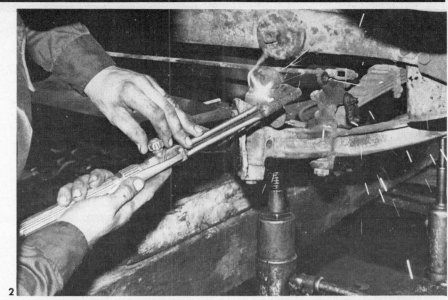

1. Almost half a century of rust has frozen this Model A kingpin solid, which means the job ahead will be tough. But it's not an uncommon one.

2. This kingpin has probably never been replaced before, so it becomes necessary to cut off the top with a torch in hopes of driving out the pin.

3. A proper-size drift is essential when driving the pin out. Otherwise the relatively soft metal of the kingpin will mushroom. Sometimes even this is not enough to free the pin.

4. This stubborn pin required torching between the spindle bosses and axle end, plus the use of a special pressing clamp, before it could be extracted.

5. Never ream the axle ends to fit the new kingpin. However, it is necessary to dress off the top and bottom to remove burned metal and burrs.

reamer. It's necessary to measure the new kingpin first. Then expand the reamer a little at a time as you drive the kingpin through the spindle bosses until it is a snug push-fit through the bushings. During this procedure, the reamer pilot must be used carefully to keep the reamer in line, because the two bosses must be reamed on a common axis or the kingpin will bind when pressed in place.

Don't use a hammer or other tool to drive down on top of the kingpin ball. It should fit without force. The ball top may distort if you use the hammer tactic.

Properly fitted kingpins will result in a spindle that flops from side to side with the slightest touch, yet when you lift up and down on the extreme end of the spindle, you feel no play whatsoever.

Grease the thrust bearing and bushings, then place the spindle on the end of the axle with the thrust bearing in place. You may have a certain amount of up-and-down play, which means the spindle is sliding along the kingpin. Here's where the shim washers come into use. These are placed between the spindle and the spool in order to take up the play.

Before finishing kingpin installation, take a look at the steering arm. A very common wear point is on the end of the steering arm where it connects with the drag link. If the wear is excessive, you have two alternatives: (1) replace the steering arm, or (2) find a compe-

1

2

tent repairman. Chisholm has a fellow who actually replaces the ball forged into the steering arm by drilling it out and welding in a new one.

To wrap up your kingpin job, all you need to do is insert the kingpin lock (a tapered pin with a threaded tip and flat side) from the front. Whack it lightly a few times. Then install the keeper nut on the threaded end of the lock pin.

Wheel alignment is necessary to assure proper caster/camber whenever kingpins are replaced.

1. Old bushings must be pressed or driven out of the spindle and new bushings driven or pressed back in. Be sure grease fitting holes align.

2. Grease thrust bearing and bushing. Put the spindle in place with thrust bearing. Then check the shim thickness to take out any vertical play.

3. Don't drive the ball on top of the new kingpin. It should fit easily and lock into axle with this pin, which seats with a few light hammer taps.

4. Don't forget the felt dust seat and washer at bottom of axle. Also check wear on end of steering arm where it connects with the drag link.

5. The final step is front end alignment. Since it's inexpensive but requires professional equipment, let the pros do it. Nearly all older cars can be done on modern machinery.

ADJUSTING MECHANICAL BRAKES A HARD JOB MADE EASY

Nearly anyone with a smidgen of mechanical aptitude and a little experience with modern-day hydraulic brakes can overhaul and adjust a set of mechanical brakes. The shoes must be checked for warpage and replaced if they're bad enough. The lining, once riveted in place, must be arced to the inside drum diameter after the drums have been cleaned up on a drum lathe. All the mechanical components must be checked against severe wear and replaced, if necessary, by less-worn used parts, NOS or repro items. This is all pretty straightforward. It's the final adjustment that will drive you bananas if it's not done in the correct manner.

Everyone knows that brake pressure must be applied evenly to each wheel in order for the car to whoa to a stop. This is no problem on a properly working hydraulic system, since pressure applied to one end of a column of incompressible brake fluid exerts an equal pressure at the other end, and thence equally to each individual wheel cylinder. On mechanical brakes, though, the individual wheel pressure is applied via a complex linkage system. If any one of the links is loose, too tight, worn or whatever, the braking effort will be unequally applied to the wheels, and the car may skitter all over the road before you can bring it to a full stop.

Ford, the last holdout on mechanical brakes, finally made the conversion to hydraulics for the 1939 model year. Ford easily produced more brakes of this type than the rest of the industry combined. Because of this, there are undoubtedly more mechanically braked Fords undergoing restoration than any other make. We'll take a look, then, at rejuvenating the stoppers on a Model A, courtesy of Sparks Automotive, 1965 Gower St., Los Angeles, Calif.

With all the NOS, repro and good used brake pieces available for not only the A but all Fords, suffice it to say that all the individual brake parts at each wheel should be checked for warpage, wear, breaks and so forth and discarded if not suitable. Shoe lining is available at

1

PHOTOS BY ERIC RICKMAN

1. Newly relined Model A brake shoes should be "arced" to inside diameter of brake drums—after latter have been turned to rid them of scores, high spots.

2. Since your car (to say nothing of your life) depends upon your brakes, use new or quality repro parts when doing an overhaul. Make sure springs have required tension and that all parts are lightly lubed.

3. So far, the mechanical braking system is very close to that of the later hydraulic brake but without the actuating cylinder, pistons and hoses. The real trick with these Ford brakes is in the final adjustment.

4. Here's the Model A brake ready to receive its drum. At top of shoes is housing which encloses the adjuster; at bottom is the actuator.

5. The brake actuator is a wedge (arrow) that is forced downward by a rod passing through the kingpin, motion being imparted by an enclosed cam on the end of the brake shaft. Here the shoes are withdrawn.

6. Pedal pressure transmits force through linkage to rotate cam on end of brake shaft, forcing operating shaft and its wedge downward. This expands the shoes against inside of the drum. Here wedge has expanded the shoes.

7. Brake shoe rollers must be free to rotate or the wedge will wear flat spots and cause uneven brake adjustment.

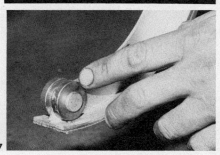

any firm dealing with old car parts. Most will simply exchange your shoes for reconditioned ones fitted with new, riveted lining. A brake shop will inspect your drums to make sure they're not worn too far oversize or scored too deeply to be "cleaned up," then turn them for you. They'll also arc your shoes to the drums' new inside diameter, something best left to the pro who has the proper equipment.

Inspect all the bits and pieces before reassembling each brake, and discard those that are badly worn. Use new or repro parts wherever possible, for despite the fact that brakes are unseen, they're the only thing that's going to keep your beautifully restored car from coming acropper against a tree or in a roadside ditch.

Brake synchronization follows assembly of the fourth brake, and this is where the novice who has never tackled a mechanical system will probably go mad. It's largely a matter of adjust and try, adjust and try, adjust and try, in order to get all four wheels to respond equally to pedal pressure. But there is an easy way to go about it.

Disconnect all the mechanical links between the pedal and each individual brake. Put the car up on jack stands so that all four wheels hang in the air. Starting with whichever wheel is the handiest, rotate the wheel with one hand and tighten the adjuster with the other hand until the wheel is locked up. Now, back off on the adjuster in small increments until the wheel can be turned again, but with a little drag. Repeat the process at the oth-

er three wheels, doing your best via "educated feel" to get the same amount of drag.

Inspect all the brake rod linkage, especially the adjustable clevises. Over the years, a clevis pin may have egg-shaped its clevis hole, making precise adjustment impossible. New clevises and pins are available from many suppliers in repro, but there are also oversize clevis pins that allow you to ream out the clevis hole so that it's round again.

Look carefully for any welds on the brake rods. In the old days, people often shortened the rods by cutting a short section out and welding the pieces back together when they "ran out" of adjustment at a wheel. Obviously, such rods must be deep-sixed and new ones substituted.

After inspection, reassemble all the rod linkage except the clevises and the brakes' actuating arms. Run one clevis at a time in or out, whichever is required, on its thread-

ed rod until the clevis pin hole aligns exactly with the actuating arm hole. The clevis pin should slide easily through the holes. Repeat the process at each wheel, remembering to use a new cotter pin on each clevis pin.

With the car back down on all fours again, take it out for a trial run and try a couple of hard stops from about 20 mph. Be ready for at least a little swerving the first time or two, because no matter how carefully you set up the brakes and adjusted the "drag" at each wheel, some unevenness will occur. Determine which wheel(s) are grabbing, remove the cotter and clevis pins, turn the clevis a half turn "out," reinstall the clevis pin and another new cotter pin and try it again.

There'll still be a lot of cut-and-try before you can near-panic stop in a dead straight line, but the chore is much easier if you have preadjusted each individual wheel first and achieved a near-equal drag all the way around. 🎬

4

1. After making certain all parts move freely and the wheel bearings are properly lubed, slide drum on.

2. Even Ford manuals of the time do not specify degree of tightness of the spindle nut, saying merely to tighten it good and snug, then back off a notch or two. Sparks Automotive, however, has learned that nut should be tightened to 15 ft.-lbs., then backed off two nut castellations.

3. Always—and that means *always* —insert new, proper size cotter pin; never reuse one after removal.

4. Here's the mechanical actuating mechanism of the Model A, with the wrench on the adjuster. With wheel on car, rotate by hand and tighten adjuster until wheel locks, then back it off until wheel can be turned with a slight drag. Repeat at each wheel in turn.

5. With brake shaft arm (A) firmly against its stop and pedal linkage similarly set, adjust clevis (B) until its hole and hole in shaft arm are exactly aligned. Pin should slide through without binding. Though location of parts on rear brakes vary from the fronts, assembly and adjustment are similar.

6. Lock nut is tightened against the clevis, the clevis dropped over the front brake shaft arm, the clevis pin inserted and a new cotter pin installed. Now it's time for the road testing.

7. If one or more wheels grab during trial stopping, their clevises should be backed off a half-turn and the stopping procedure tried again. Use new cotter pins every time.

5

6

7

OVERHAULING EARLY HYDRAULIC BRAKES

THERE HAS BEEN LITTLE IMPROVEMENT IN 42 YEARS, SO A REBUILD IS EASY

Fundamentally, hydraulic brakes have changed little since their introduction to the mass American car market in the '34 model year and filtering down to all major makes by 1936—with the exception of Ford Motor Co. which resisted the change until 1939. To be sure, brake shoe sizes, drum diameters, lining materials and other bits and pieces have undergone many changes over the years, but it remains that the basic hydraulic system used today is essentially the same as the system which replaced the older, purely mechanical brakes.

It isn't really necessary to thoroughly understand the principles of hydraulics in order to overhaul a set of brakes, but perhaps a bit of background would be wise so that the first-time tackler of such a project will have more of a regard for the components with which he will be dealing.

Hydraulics are quite simple and easy to understand, and are based on the simple principle that fluids cannot be compressed like gases. It is therefore possible to move a column of liquid (hydraulic brake fluid) from the actuator or master cylinder, through a pipeline system, to the slave or wheel cylinders, whose movement causes the friction material (brake lining) to come in contact with the wheel-driven drum and force it to slow or stop.

The master cylinder is filled with fluid and has a piston at what might be termed bottom dead center, with the connecting rod linked to the brake pedal itself. Hydraulic lines connect this cylinder with the slave units at the wheels. These are best described as a cylinder with a piston at each end. As the pedal is pressed, the master cylinder piston pushes the fluid through the lines to each wheel cylinder, causing the

wheel cylinder pistons to push outward, forcing the brake shoes against the drum. Since this pressure is equal to all wheel cylinders, effective braking pressure cannot be applied to any one wheel until all the shoes on the wheels are in contact with their respective drums, providing a self-equalizing effect.

From the foregoing it is easy to understand why hydraulic brake systems should be virtually surgically clean and why air cannot be allowed to get into the system. For this reason, all work on master and wheel cylinders should be done with as much precision and cleanliness as possible, and if the novice at the game is afraid he has neither the tools nor the expertise to proceed on his own, then he'd best seek the competence of a reputable brake specialist.

We noted earlier that Ford had resisted the conversion to hydraulic

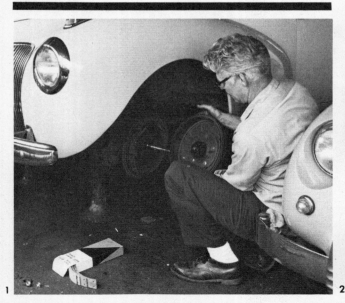

PHOTOS BY ERIC RICKMAN

braking until well after the other major makers had changed over—1939 being the model year that Ford finally relented and introduced his version of the system across his model lineup (Lincoln-Zephyr, Mercury and Ford). But the senior Mr. Ford had valid reasons for not making the switch until that time, and then only because his dealers forced the situation due to growing buyer resistance against the "archaic" mechanical system he had so long employed.

One reason that Ford held out against hydraulic braking was his personal satisfaction with his mechanical arrangement—and that the simple, occasional adjustment could be carried out by either the owner or a blacksmith-level mechanic. He was also dead set against the increased manufacturing cost that hydraulic brakes would introduce to his cars—what with the necessary plumbing and myriad fittings, etc.—since his great success in the automotive world was largely due to the low prices for which his cars were sold.

There was however, despite widespread belief today that just the opposite was true, experimental hydraulic brake work going on behind closed doors at Dearborn early in the Thirties. This can be accredited to Mr. Ford's reasoning that although "everybody" else did things very much alike, there *had* to be a better yet easier and cheaper way to accomplish the same purpose. This lead to experimentation with systems even as exotic as Rolls Royces which utilized all-steel components—no "slip shod" fabric or rubber seals to make up for inaccurate machine work. But this proved to be "out" as far as Ford was concerned with his high-production rates and in the end, he settled for the tried-and-true system based on the Bendix patents and which the other manufacturers were also largely employing.

Though an individual hydraulic brake system on one make of car may differ slightly in mechanical link-up between the wheel cylinders and the shoes, drum diameters and widths, and so forth, all are basically alike and the system pictured here, while on a 1941 Lincoln Continental, is pretty typical of all early hydraulic brakes in every regard except dimensions and tolerances. The latter, incidentally, are easy to come by in factory shop manuals which are available for virtually any car through reprints offered by several publishers or from original editions which can be found at swap meets. Follow along, then, as we go through a routine brake overhaul on

the '41 L-C at Vanowen Brake & Wheel, 11576 Vanowen Blvd., No. Hollywood, Calif. 91605.

Bill Chisolm at Vanowen, who admits to having worked on almost every make of car produced in this country, at one time or another, made some interesting points during our conversation. When digging into a newly acquired and restorable car, whether a basketcase or one already (but perhaps poorly) rebuilt, make *sure* that the hydraulic brake components are *of the original type*. Cars of the Thirties or Forties may have had, by now, dozens of owners. As the car began to age and deteriorate, less care was probably lavished on it and no insistence was made that parts needing replacement be genuine. The last owner—before you—probably did everything he could to jury rig the car just enough to get it from his backyard to the junkyard or pasture, so you're just as apt to find Chevrolet brake shoes on a Buick as a Ford master cylinder on a Lincoln-Zephyr. Factory shop manuals usually depict such important pieces as brake parts with line drawings or photos, as well as singling out the proper part numbers which are embossed or stamped onto the pieces, so you shouldn't have too much trouble deciding whether all of your parts are "real" or not. If, however, you're not certain your parts are all factory-type originals, the chances are good that any reputable brake shop can help you discover the truth.

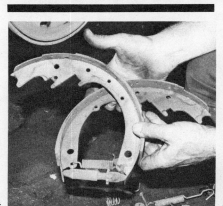

1. Vanowen's Bill Chisolm starts the brake job on a '41 Lincoln Continental the same way he would on a later car: He removes the wheel, then the drum.

2. The shoe's return spring comes off next. Note how similar components are to a modern car despite their 35 years.

3. Shoe retainer is removed from the hold-down "nails." Check the latter where they go through the backing plate, as this is a wear point. Replace them if necessary.

4. Shoes are spread at the top to allow removal from the wheel cylinder pushrods. Look carefully at clevis end of pushrods; replace if worn.

5. The shoes' upper ends are crossed to ease removal of the star wheel adjuster at the base. Finally, spring can be removed.

6. Several situations could have caused old shoe lining to wear like this. Drum could be bell-mouthed for one of several reasons, or shoes could be bent. In this case it was the latter problem, and the shoes will have to be straightened or replaced.

The first order of business is to dismantle all of the brake pieces at any given wheel, and if you've done a brake job on a modern car, the steps are the same for the old one.

Check all the parts carefully for cracks or warps, severe wear, corrosion, and so forth. Since hydraulic brakes date from only 1934, NOS or repro parts are relatively easy to come by, or some salvage yards may have used components that go back quite far. Also easy to obtain are rebuild kits for wheel and master cylinders, for many modern cars use pistons, cups and seals of the same dimensions as older ones. It is important, though, to use pieces of the exact required dimensions.

The brake drum itself is subject to the most wear, and to scoring if the car was driven with the shoe lining material worn completely away or at least far enough that the rivets came into contact with the drum. Few home shops are equipped with a special drum lathe, so the drums should be taken to a specialist for turning (if needed). First, though, the inside diameter of the drum should be checked with a drum micrometer and compared against factory specs. Vanowen says

that .090-in. oversize is the maximum a drum should be turned, but that .075-in. maximum is better (and safer). If the drum doesn't "clean up" at this figure, the drum should be discarded and a new or not-so-well-used one obtained.

If the drums come out to be within tolerance, check next for cracked, worn or thread-galled wheel studs. Clean the threads with a wire brush and inspect them carefully. New studs should be pressed in if necessary, another job the brake shop can easily do. The car pictured was equipped with incorrect wheels, which egg-shaped the wheel stud holes, wore out the base of the stud threads from the improper fit, and since the wheels rode directly against the brake drum, the drums were distorted slightly.

The brake shoes should be arced in a special machine (again, your friendly brake expert has one) to conform to the new inside diameter of the turned drums. It's also wise to order oversize lining to help make up for new, larger inner drum radius.

The wheel cylinders should be checked carefully for wear, corrosion or pits in the cylinder bore. If the

bores clean up within tolerances, fine. If not, sometimes the bore can be enlarged sufficiently to allow the use of a sleeve, which is then bored to exact original tolerance. Don't, whatever you do, simply bore the cylinder out and then use oversize pistons and seals. The brakes were engineered to have precise cylinder bores, and each must be the same as the others, and they must be in the proper bore relationship to the master cylinder. Reworked wheel cylinders often need expanders behind the rubber cups to insure a good seal. They come in some rebuild kits, but often they'll have to be obtained separately.

On the front wheels, carefully inspect the wheel bearings for wear, flat spots, galling, cracks, or other problems. Wheel bearings all conform to certain standards and it is possible to obtain a brand new set of bearings for virtually any car. Clean the used bearings in solvent and blow dry for inspection, but don't let the cage rotate via air pressure. Wash the bearings in very hot water, too, to ensure clean surfaces.

Brake lining, particularly Bendix, is available for every old car. Lucky

for you, the Brake Lining Mfgr's. Assn., publishes a book entitled *"Friction Material Standards Institute,"* (F.M.S.I.) which has brake specs for all domestic cars since development of the hydraulic brake. This will help you and your brake man get the original type of lining that your car was designed to have.

Reassembly of the wheel cylinders should be done using Hydraulic Assembly Fluid (better than brake fluid). It's a moisture inhibitor and deters rust. No telling how long it will be after you do the brakes that the car will actually be driven, and you don't want your job ruined by simply sitting still for a long period.

Clean all threaded parts with a wire brush, inspect the threads, then put things back together with a good anti-seize compound on lug nuts and studs, star wheel adjuster, etc. One good brand is GM's Anti-Seize, available at parts counters.

Pack the wheel bearings following the shop manual for your car, drop them back where they belong, then install. Not everyone has a torque wrench, so a time-proven rule of thumb is to tighten the spindle nut until some small resistance is felt when rotating the brake drum, then

back it off to the first cotter pin hole to line up.

Go over the master cylinder thoroughly, again looking for pits, wear or corrosion inside the bore. Rebuild kits are available for virtually any cylinder, or if yours is too bad, new or replacement ones are easy to come by at swap meets or salvage yards. Even if the flexible brake lines from frame to backing plate appear to be sound, it's a good idea to replace all of them. You never know how soon an apparently good line may blow out on you, and on older cars with a single master cylinder fluid reservoir, it's goodbye restoration.

As stated at the outset, doing a brake job on an older car is just the same as it is today. The same precautions are necessary, the same order of assembly and reassembly, the same techniques and the brake shop's tools—nothing's really new. Any brake shop can do a total or partial rebuild on any U.S. car with hydraulic brakes (though it may be left to you to scrounge new or at least salvageable drums and shoes if needed), so this is one area where the restorer will have very few problems. 🏁

1. All the "innards" from one '41 L-C front brake shoe system, together with new, readily available lining.

2. First step in drum-checking is to mike the I.D., compare size against original specifications and discard if it won't "clean up" to a maximum of .090-in. oversize, with .075-in. maximum a more desirable margin.

3. If the drum will "save," check the studs next; they can be replaced individually. In this case, wrong wheels had led owner to space the wheel out with washers.

4. Spacer washer had seriously galled the lower thread portion of this stud. This one stud is pointed to simplify wheel mounting. If a stud is too bad, it can be pressed out and a new one pressed back in. Studs are to standard dimensions and are easily available.

5. Incorrect wheel rode on outer drum edge; could have caused drum distortion and brake overheating. Luckily, this drum was salvageable.

6. Here's the culprit: a wrong wheel. Whatever it was for, it is ruined now, since the too-big stud hole has become egg-shaped through use.

7. Wheel cylinder overhaul is discussed in text. Last step before reassembly is to clean, check, then repack the wheel bearings—or use new ones. Like brake linings, wheel bearings have been manufactured to rigid standards for years; hence there are no oddball ones to contend with.

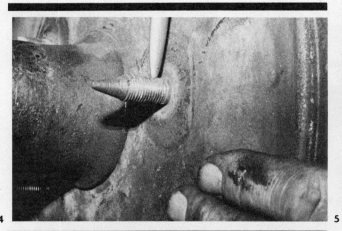

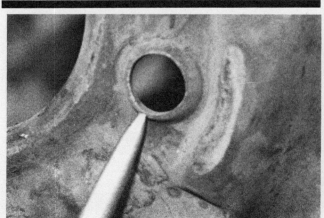

USING BODY TOOLS
USING THE RIGHT TOOLS IN THE PROPER MANNER IS THE BASIS OF A PERFECT FINISH

What makes really fine quality bodywork so expensive? The two main factors, particularly where old cars are concerned, are time and skill. Restoration of a 40-year-old car is nothing like everyday bodywork, such as fixing a crunched Pinto front end, for several reasons. First of all, when a Pinto is crunched, you can buy new fenders right at your local Ford dealer, but unfortunately, they're not making nice new fenders and such for your basketcase '39 convertible. So the restorer faced with damaged sheetmetal must refinish to shining perfection panels that a regular bodyman wouldn't think of working on. And the quality of restoration work must be higher than regular

bodywork. While the repaired collision job goes right back out into the traffic and parking lot wars, the restored old car has to withstand the detailed scrutiny of other finicky restorers at antique car gatherings and shows.

No question about it, old car bodywork is expensive when done professionally and done right. What this chapter will attempt to do is show you the proper tools required and their uses, so that you can practice the techniques we describe. Even if you don't wind up capable of doing *all* your own work, at least we will have provided you with the knowledge of how the work *should* be done, and you may save considerably if you can do the preliminary

work yourself, leaving the finish work up to a professional.

TOOLS AND HOW TO USE THEM

Hand tools used to straighten sheetmetal accomplish the job in one or more of the following ways: by striking a direct blow on the metal surface, as resistance to a direct blow struck on the opposite side of the metal, and as a lever prying against the surface. For the enthusiast, this means bumping hammers, dolly blocks, bumping spoons, body spoons, pry tools and caulking tools. Unfortunately, none of these tools is automatic. Each requires some semblance of dexterity, and the body man must practice before

learning to strike a blind dolly or slap a spoon just right.

HAMMERS

Hammers come in a variety of styles, sizes and combinations. There are many small manufacturers of body tools, but most auto parts stores carry a reasonable supply, as do the larger mail order houses. (Sears Roebuck, Montgomery Ward, etc.). This is especially true of hammers.

The large, flat face of a body hammer spreads the hammer blow force over a fairly large area of the metal surface. This is essential when working with sheetmetal, and is one of the reasons a metal man will visibly wince when he sees metal being struck with a ball-peen hammer. It is difficult for the beginner to accurately strike a hidden dolly (one that is being held behind the panel), so the large, flat-body hammer face reduces the chance of a miss. The best hammers have a dead flat spot in the center of the head, blending into a slight curved edge to prevent making sharp edges.

For the home enthusiast, the number of body hammers necessary may be as few as two, this is usually determined by what is on the opposite end of the head from the flat surface just described. The combination hammer is the most common, and may include a slightly smaller, more rounded head, or a picking end. The rounded head is great for working out raised sections of metal without a backup dolly, and the picking head is used to raise stubborn low spots.

1. Whether you're an old craftsman or a beginning restorer, good results are never achieved without the right tools. That, plus lots of practice!

2. As an amateur restorer, you won't need every tool we have pictured here, but all of them serve a purpose for the pro who must work on many types of cars. From the top we have some hook-type pry bars, rubber mallets and steel body hammers, several shapes of dollies, and (lower right) spoons.

3. Even if you only have one or two hammers, you'll eventually need several dollies of different shapes. Look in any pro's toolbox and you're likely to find several homemade ones, too, built for some specific past job.

4. The body hammer, dolly and file should be considered the "basic trio" of bodywork. Never use any body filler until you've exhausted their talents. The pointed ends are picking hammers.

Under no circumstances should a carpenter's or claw hammer be used for metal working. Its head is rounded to help prevent bending a nail if it is struck off-square. Using it on sheetmetal will only tend to give you stretched round areas.

DOLLIES

Dolly blocks come in every possible shape and size, but the most common are the general-purpose, low-crown general-purpose, heel, and toe. The general-purpose dolly is often nicknamed the railroad dolly because it is shaped something like a piece of railroad track, with a variety of curves. The low crown, general-purpose dolly has a flatter main working face, better suited to working flatter panels. When working in narrow confines, the special designs of the heel and toe dollies come into play because they are thinner. These dollies have sharp edges for working flanges.

A dolly can be used as a handleless hammer. Watch a good body man at work and note how he will strike a low dent from the back with a dolly during the hammer and dolly phase. This raises a low spot so the hammer work will be effective

as the dent is being raised. A dolly is not an anvil. That is, it is not intended as a place to smash the sheetmetal. Instead, it serves to raise metal with its working face, whether struck directly by the hammer or from a nearby blow. The correct dolly will weigh about three times as much as the hammer, and when used by a good body man, the dolly/hammer combination is hard to beat for near perfect surface finishing.

SPOONS

If the restorer contemplates any kind of extended body repair or modification, a selection of spoons is desirable. A spoon is a bar of steel, forged flatter and thinner on one or both ends. It may be bent in a number of shapes, with the forged end serving as a working face to use against the metal. A spoon can serve as a means of spreading the force of a hammer blow over a large area, as a dolly block where access to the inner face of the panel is limited, and as a prying or driving tool.

When working on badly damaged panels, the pry or pick tool is an invaluable ally. When inner panels restrict access to a panel area such

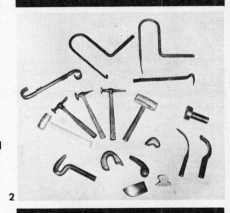

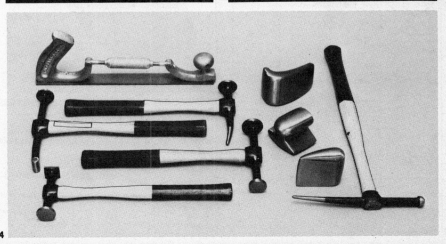

It is really just a form of dolly for getting into very tight places or for prying, and should not be used as a dolly substitute if the latter can be used. The body spoon can be left in the toolbox until the hammer and dolly are mastered.

PRY BAR

Another tool the beginner should understand, but does not necessarily

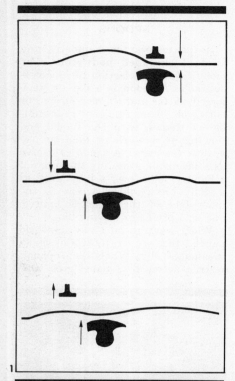

need at first is the pry bar. A pry tool is used when the damaged area cannot be reached from the inside, such as the lower portion of a door panel. A prying tool is usually considered a kind of last resort, because the surface will always be roughened. When using a pry bar, avoid too much force; it is better to work up the area with a series of low-force pries than with a single pry that may raise a bump. The problem with the bump distortion is that it may grind down too thin (or even clear through). Go slow with pry tools!

FINISHING

After the hand tools have been used to straighten a damaged section, the metal must be finished preparatory to painting. In bodywork, metal finishing means restoration of final surface smoothness after straightening has been carried as far as practical. This means that areas which are still too low (or too high) can be picked up or lowered—whichever is necessary.

The file and disc sander are the two prime tools of metal finishing. The beginner should become thoroughly familiar with the file first, since it does not work as fast as the sander, and consequently will not make as great a mistake.

FILES

Body files are usually fitted with flat, 14-in. blades, with the wooden

file holder preferable. Metal file holders are available, some with adjustable blade surface. The beginner who contemplates extended bodywork should also equip himself with files of various shapes that will conform to the sometimes odd curves he will be working.

When a file is used correctly, the many cutting blades down its length remove minor surface irregularities. When a file is drawn over a freshly straightened surface, the blades will cut on the high or level spots and leave the low spots untouched. So, the file becomes a sort of tattle-tale straightedge.

The file should always be moved in the general direction of the flattest crown of the panel in order to show up the greatest imperfection in the panel. At the same time, the file must be shifted to one side slightly during the stroke to get maximum area coverage. During the filing stroke, the area covered will not be as long as the file, usually, and several inches wide. At the same time, the blade is curved very slightly so that the stroke starts with the front of the blade in metal contact and ends with the rear. But restorers can take note that a perfectly flat file can be used to ensure maximum smoothness of a panel. The flat file will cut slower, but the finished job is better.

After the file has been passed over a straightened area, any excessively high spots will show up as sharp

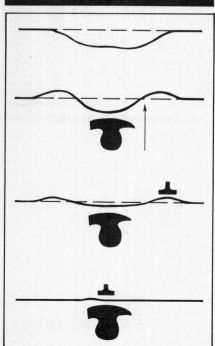

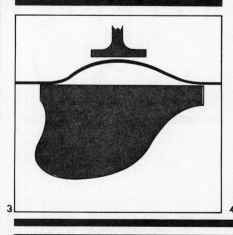

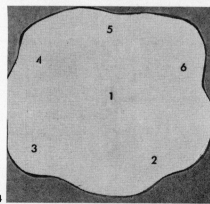

cuts from the file and should be worked more. Usually, however, the appearance will be of low spots spread throughout the filed area. These spots can be lifted with any blunt-ended tool, but the best is the pick hammer. Here is where the home body man can do an excellent job—or get into serious trouble and ruin a panel.

Coming under the heading of a file, but actually a tool that uses coarse sandpaper as a cutting medium, is a relatively new piece of equipment called an air file. It works off of air pressure and will run up to 3500 strokes per minute,

with each stroke ½-in. long and moving straight back and forth. Different sandpaper platens are available; one with both shoulders "hard," another with one "soft" for use in tight, concave areas. This is a great time and labor saver in the hands of a pro, but works too fast for a beginner to use without mistakes.

PICK HAMMERS

It is very difficult to "hit where you look" when learning to pick up low spots. Since the pick hammer is being driven toward the user and is out of sight behind the panel, the normal reaction is to hit below the desired spot and often off to the left side. Learning to use a pick hammer is a matter of practice, but the way to begin is to bring the hammer into view at first, then move it up to about where the low spot should be. A good guide to keep the hammer working in the same spot is to rest

the arm on an available piece of metal, which will keep the hammer from wandering during use.

Start with a gentle tap to the metal and see where the blow lands. It may be difficult to locate this spot at first, so lay the flattened hand against the metal as a guide. The small bump can usually be felt and the pick adjusted to then hit the low spots. Low spots will feel like high spots on the inside of the panel, so the pick head can be rubbed against the metal to locate the spot if the touch is sensitive. As with the pry bar, go easy and slow with the pick hammer, as too much metal can be hammered up.

Use a blunt pick unless the area to be lifted is very small, then a sharp pick may be desired. In any case, it is possible to create a pick dolly which will limit metal displacement. These dollies are not normally sold in stores but we have seen several being used by bodymen.

1. Most dents will take a combination of hammer-on and hammer-off dolly work. The preliminary work here (top) is done on-dolly at the edges of the dent. Then the dolly is used *off* to slap up the center while the hammer brings down the outer high spots.

2. Here's another combination of techniques on a stretched area. The dolly is used first to slap up the low spots, then the hammer works on the high spots progressively until it is working on-dolly. This type of damage would also require the use of the torch to shrink the stretch spots.

3. Shrinking with heat (using torch) is an essential of bodywork. Shrinking this high spot (exaggerated here) means heating the area, backing with a dolly and striking the high spots directly with the on-dolly hammer.

4. This is the sequence for a heated high spot to be struck with a hammer, using light blows. Work around the edges more than the middle.

5. Pry bars and picks can be very useful when raising low spots behind blind panels, but the sharper the point on the pry bar, the easier you have to go with it. Because of the leverage offered by the long handle, a sharp picking pry bar can poke the tip right through sheetmetal if you don't take it easy. Until you know it's working right where you want it, just pry till you see the high point it leaves on your outer panel.

6. A vixen file with an adjustable turnbuckle like this one can be set for various low-crown contours. Here the file is being used in its most common mode, to find high and low spots.

7. A file board, which accepts long thin strips of sandpaper, can be very useful in smoothing low-crown areas. It's versatile because the grit of the paper can be varied for smoother or coarser cutting action.

8. When using lead as a filler, a fine-toothed body file is used to cut down the filler metal to the height of the rest of the panel, then using primer and block-sanding to fill the minor imperfections. Don't use a file like this without a handle.

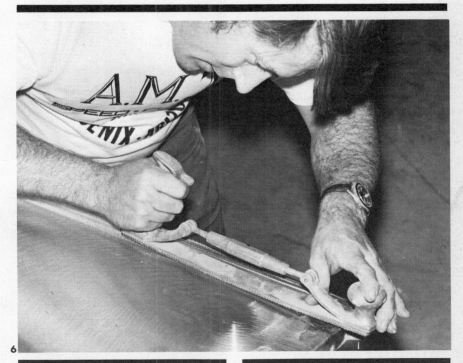

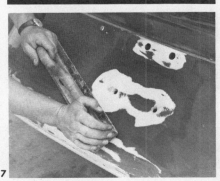

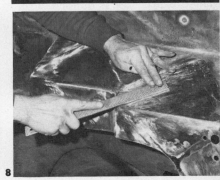

After the area has been picked up lightly, use the file again. Repeat the pick and file operation until the damaged surface is smooth.

DISC SANDER

This is one of the most versatile of power tools, and fills the need for a lightweight, heavy-duty grinder on the toughest of jobs. Good used sanders can often be purchased at very low prices from a body shop with newer equipment. Often, broken sanders require only minor repairs, and can be bought at bargain prices.

The sanding discs are fiber discs coated on one side with an abrasive grit, usually an aluminum oxide. The grit size is identified by number. Disc size refers to the disc diameter, with 7 and 9⅛ ins. the common sizes, smaller discs being made by cutting down the larger units.

Grit size is designated by a number, such as #34 or #36, etc., and refers to the size of screen which the grit will pass through. These discs are available in open- or closed-coat types, with the open-coat discs commonly used as paint removers. The closed-coat discs have a heavier layer of abrasive for heavy-duty use in metal grinding. The open- and closed-coat discs are available in glue bonding only, as the resin-bonded discs come in a single style.

Grit size determines how the disc will be used, with the coarse #16 selected for paint removal and coarse cutting. A #24 disc is most commonly used as an all-around grit since it will cut paint and finish off the metal smoothly. However, a #36 grit is better for finishing.

A professional body man will use the disc sander as a file substitute, but the beginner should not. At any rate, the sander is intended as both a substitute and as a method of finishing off the rough file marks. Learning to use a disc sander on sheetmetal is a skill not easily picked up, but seldom forgotten.

When using the sander rather than a file, the disc is run across the surface at such an angle that the grit swirl marks will bridge across the low spots. This allows the low spots to stand out as with the file, and is accomplished by moving the sander back and forth across the panel following the flat direction of the panel as with the file. The sander is held so that the disc approaches the metal at an angle, and pressure applied to cause the disc pad to flex slightly. This will pro-

duce the best cutting action but the sander motor will not be loaded so much it will slow down. During the side-to-side strokes, the sander is tilted first to one side and then to the other. That is, when going toward the right, the left side of the disc is working; when moving back to the left, the sander is twisted slightly and the right side of the disc is working. Moving the sander this way will cause a criss-cross pattern which will show the low spots better.

If there has been considerable metal work involved in an area, it is advisable to go over the area with a file after the sander has been used. This is a final check for low spots and is particularly suited to the beginner.

After the area is smooth, a #50 or #60 grit disc can be installed on the sander and the metal buffed. While the sander follows the flattest plane of the panel, usually length-

wise with the car, the buffing is done across the greatest crown, usually up and down. The sander is not tilted on the edge quite so much, so that a much larger part of the pad contacts the metal surface during a stroke. The final buffing cuts down the deeper scratches of coarse discs or a file and is a preliminary to the painting operations.

When using the sander around a reverse-crown area, it is advisable to cut the disc into a "star" shape. The round disc edge will have a tendency to dig into the reverse crown, while the floppier corners of a star-shaped disc will follow the crown contour. A disc may have any number of points, depending upon how severe the reverse crown is, but as a guide, the more severe the crown, the more points on the disc.

Never use the disc sander without some kind of eye protection. Although the flow of particles may be away from the face, they can and do glance off other surfaces and can cause serious eye damage. Also be careful how the sander is handled, as the disc will cut a nasty wound in a leg or arm. Be especially careful when resting the sander on the leg during work, as the disc can wind-up loose clothing (such as coveralls) rapidly.

SHRINKING

As far as the body man is concerned, shrinking really means the

use of heat from an oxygen-acetylene torch to soften metal for a specified upset. A propane tank without oxygen will not give enough heat. When an area is being shrunk, a spot—or group of spots—is heated and worked with a dolly and hammer, then cooled. While shrinking looks easy, it is a precision job and requires more "feel" than ordinary bodywork.

Damage at any part of a car body may require shrinking to some degree, but it is usually more prevalent in the low-crown sections, such as door and quarter panels, top and hood.

Stretched metal will have an in-

1. For straightening low-crown areas quickly, especially where fillers have been used, an air-operated file can be very helpful, but disastrous in the wrong hands. Like other files, it is always used in the direction of the lowest crown of the panel.

2. The body grinder can be indispensable to the body man, for truing an edge to be hammer welded, grinding down welds, or just removing paint and rust. Abrasive discs are available for fast or slow cutting.

3. You can "scallop" a grinding disc like this to make it conform easier to crevices and difficult contours.

4. When the contour is too tight to grind even with a scalloped disc, you can use sanding cones or mushrooms like this 50-grit Bear unit.

as a door skin, the pry or pick can be inserted and used to push metal around slightly.

ROUGHING THE METAL

The initial step of any body repair after disassembly is roughing the metal into shape. This first step will be followed by bumping (hammer and dolly work) and finishing (filing and grinding). Aligning is also part of the repair and is usually included with roughing.

Repair of sheetmetal is something like building a house in that each step builds upon those taken previously, with a mistake made at first likely to be magnified several times at the finish. With automotive bodies, roughing means bringing the particular piece of sheetmetal back into general contour, including supporting members and reinforcements. When a panel is being roughed into shape, it may have force applied by using a hammer and dolly, by pushing with a jack, or pulling with a jack. Sometimes a combination of these methods will be required, or all three may be involved.

The vital importance of initial roughing cannot be over emphasized, since the newcomer to bodywork will have less tendency to make mistakes if the roughing is reasonably successful. The cardinal rule is to always pull if possible, and never push or hammer major damage unless absolutely necessary.

Once the rough shape has been attained and the panel at least looks like part of an automobile, the second and third phases of repair start. This begins with the hammer and dolly, two hand tools that can easily be misused if the workman is not careful. While the dolly can be used as a hammer, it is primarily used in conjunction with a hammer in both the hammer-on and hammer-off methods.

HAMMER-ON TECHNIQUE

When the neophyte begins to learn metal work, the hammer-on method seems the most difficult. This entails placing the dolly behind the panel and striking it through the metal. It is very difficult at first, but can be mastered with brief experience. It is advisable to practice hammer and dolly coordination on a discarded piece of metal before attempting an actual repair.

At first the force of the hammer blow on the dolly is not nearly so important as hitting the dolly at all.

It is important to learn a technique wherein the hammer hits with just the right amount of force, time after time. Further, the hammer is allowed to "bounce back." That is, the dolly should remain in constant contact with the metal, with the hammer rebounding from the blow. Improper use of the hammer and dolly can be expected at first, with the hammer striking the metal, causing the dolly to bounce away and restrike the backside of the metal. The dolly will bounce away slightly when the hammer is used properly, or snapped with a definite wrist action, but it will not be a pronounced "limp-wrist" bounce.

The hammer-on technique is especially effective for raising a low point in metal, as the hammer first tends to flatten the metal being struck. This is followed by the reaction of the dolly as it slightly rebounds from the hammer blow. If the hand holding the dolly increases its pressure, then the tendency of the dolly to raise the low spot also increases.

It is advisable to use the hammer-on technique sparingly until the

body man knows just about how much the metal can be expected to "stretch" during the operation. It is not entirely correct to say the metal stretches during hammer-on work, but this is the common body shop term. At any rate, too much use of the hammer-on technique will cause the beginner to end up with too much metal in the right places.

HAMMER-OFF TECHNIQUE

In the hammer-off technique, the dolly is placed adjacent to the hammer blow, but not directly under it. Learning the hammer-off style is easy after learning the hammer-on. The spot struck by the hammer drives the metal down, since it is not being supported by the dolly. Movement of the metal transfers the hammer-blow force to the dolly, making it rebound the same as with the hammer-on technique. The effect is to drive the low spot up (from dolly force) and the high spot down (from hammer force) with a single hammer blow.

When using the hammer-off technique, the hammer blow should always be on the high metal adjacent

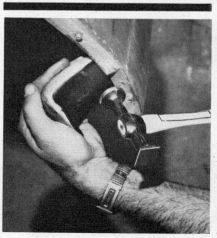

to the low spot, never anywhere else! Learning to "see" with the hand palm is part of metal work experience, and feeling to locate the low and high parts of the damage becomes a natural reaction. The dolly should be of the high-crown type, or the portion used should have minimum contact with the metal, and hammer blows should be just enough. Too much hammer effort will cause extra damage. Normally the dolly would be about ¼-in. away from the hammer blow, depending upon the metal "springiness."

The bumping spoons are used differently than dollies in that they are really methods of spreading out the force of the hammer blow. They are used to straighten long, smooth buckles. There is a paradox in the type of spoon to be used with a particular panel, in that a high crown or combination panel needs a very low crown or flat spoon, and a low-crown panel needs a high-crown spoon. This is so because the high-crowned panels are stiff and need lots of force spread over quite an area for straightening purposes. The low-crown buckle has springy metal on either side, so the force should be concentrated directly on the buckle.

When using a spoon, place the center directly over the area to be worked, then strike with a ball peen or similar hammer. Never use the body hammer. Grip the spoon only lightly to allow the spoon face to conform to the panel. If the spoon is gripped too tightly the hammer-blow force will be transferred to an edge, causing damaging marks at that point. Move the spoon over the entire buckled area, striking it with the hammer as it is placed in a new spot, starting as far from the main damage as there is sign of distortion. A common mistake is trying to use the bumping spoon on too sharp a buckle. If this is the case, the area must be roughed into near shape and finished off with the spoon.

Unlike the bumping spoon, the body spoon is used like a dolly, held

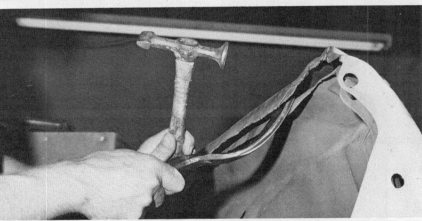

5

6

7

1. Rubber mallets are sometimes used in bodywork, along with steel hammers, to bend an edge without denting it.

2. Unless you have a shop full of big sheetmetal tools such as an English roller or a plemishing hammer, some of the curves and crowns you need to form in a sheet of metal can be done with homemade hammers and/or dollies made from lengths of scrap wood.

3. No one can teach you exactly in words and pictures how to get the "feel" of using a hammer and dolly, but your first few jobs will show you how helpful these tools can be.

4. Sometimes a dolly may be used by itself before the hammer is brought into play. In the case of this crease the dolly will be used from the backside, to "slap out" the crease before finishing up with the hammer.

5. In some instances, you may want to spread the blow of your hammer over a wider area than the head can provide. This is where a spoon will prove its value in restoring contours.

6. Spoons are especially useful too, being more or less flat and thinner than a dolly, in areas that can't be reached with a regular dolly, such as in straightening these flanges.

7. Doors, especially on open cars, will always be a restorer's biggest headaches. Using a spoon as a dolly behind a blind panel may save using filler to get this phaeton door as wave free as a restoration should be.

crease in surface area, either in length, width or both. In collision damage, the stretched area may be confined to a rather small section, and may show as either a depression or bulge in the panel. If a large section of the panel is stretched, it is usually advisable to replace the entire panel if a replacement can be found.

A panel can have a false stretch which is easily confused with a true stretch because the false stretch will tend to "oil can" or have a raised hump. A false stretch will always be smooth and unworked and next to an area that has been upset; the raises are being caused by the gathering effect of the upset. A false stretch is usually found around the reinforced edge of doors, hoods and deck lids where there has been a rolled buckle and the upset has not been relieved completely. Beating out a stiff buckle which should be straightened under tension is a typical cause of false stretch.

When an area of sheetmetal undergoes the shrinking operation, the high crown, or bulge, must be upset to bring the bulge back down to its original contour. If a bulge is struck cold, the hammer force is transmitted out through the metal toward the edges and little or no effect is usually noted. However, as the bulge is heated the metal at the hot spot will tend to upset readily. When the heat is first applied, the bulge will grow noticeably, but will return to the bulge shape as the metal cools. If the metal is upset while the spot is still hot, the metal will shrink to

a state smaller than the bulge. Of course, the hot spot will tend to begin cooling as soon as the torch is removed, so hammer and dolly application must be immediate. The hammer does not drive the bulge completely away, leaving a perfectly level surface while the metal is still hot. If this were to happen, the metal would be over-shrunk as it cooled.

The rate at which the metal cools will have an effect on the total shrink; therefore it is possible to use a sponge or wet rag as part of the shrinking procedure. If the heated spot is cooled faster than normal, more of the upset can be retained. That is, the shrinking can be more

1

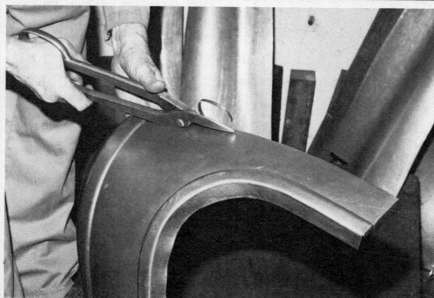

2

effective if the metal is quenched immediately after working with hammer and dolly. The rapid cooling stops the yield of the heated area to contraction/tension, but must be done while the metal is still quite hot (the water will steam on metal contact). It will take a little experience to learn when and when not to use quenching. If the metal appears to be approaching the original contour during the hammer and dolly work, chances are that little or no quenching will be necessary. If the area receives too much quenching, buckles will often appear in the surrounding panel and must be worked out with the hammer.

When an area is overshrunk, this will have a puckering effect on the surrounding metal. If an area has been overshrunk, some hammer-on dolly technique will often stretch the spot just enough to relieve the stress. Space the hammer blows well over the area and do not apply heavy pressure to the dolly from the back side. As the hammer strikes the metal, it will tend to spread it just enough to compensate for the overshrinking.

When shrinking a gouge, the dolly must supply the force to upset the metal from the backside. A small gouge can be bumped out from the back and then shrunk as a raised bulge, but this is limited to very small damages. The more common gouge will require use of the hammer and dolly as follows: The gouge is heated to above 1400° F., or good and red, which will deepen the gouge. The dolly is used as a hammer from the backside, knocking the gouge outward at the deepest point and driving the metal adjacent to the gouge higher than the original contour. The dolly is then held hard against the low point and the hammer used in a hammer-off technique to drive down the surrounding high metal. When the gouge is very close to the original contour, the hammer should then be used directly against the dolly to relieve some of the stress that might cause overshrinking.

A small gouge is usually removed with one or two heatings; a long gouge may require a number of heatings down its length as the hammer and dolly work progresses. Usually, quenching is not needed for a gouge shrink.

Learning to get the proper heat application will be the hardest part of shrinking for the novice, as heat requirements will differ with each type of shrink. The problem is getting just the right amount of heat in just the right size and spot. If a large bulge is involved, the heat should be spread out, but not necessarily red hot. Sheetmetal will begin to soften where the first color begins to form, so the large bulge can be shrunk very well (the upset will be considerable) when the metal just begins to turn blue. On large areas the shrinking spots may be spaced out over a wide pattern, but the temperature should be kept relatively low.

In a severely stretched area, such as a gouge, the temperature must be higher, usually to the bright red range, and must be concentrated in

small areas. Several of these bright red heatings may be necessary in a typical gouge. Incidentally, much of the crease in a minor gouge can be removed without heat, but requires the hammer-off dolly technique, with the hammer striking very close to a high-crowned dolly. Keep heavy pressure on the dolly and tap both sides of the crease lightly for an inch or so. Then tap the crease directly over the dolly for an equal space, and again revert to the hammer-off technique. Slapping the crease in this way will remove most of the damage rapidly.

Shrinking is not difficult to master, but it definitely requires pa-

tience and practice. After a few gouges have been attempted with success, the beginner will learn to remove much of the gouge with one heat application and rapid use of hammer and dolly.

INSPECTING THE DAMAGE

There is much that can be learned about a damaged panel during the initial inspection, and the following hints will apply to all types of collision damage. First, locate the point, or points, of initial impact. Then decide if there are two or more points of impact. If so, are they equal or is there a significant major impact point with others secondary? How are the secondary areas of impact related to each other, and will repair of any area be related to the others? Should any specific area be repaired first? When looking at a collision damage, categorize the type of damage involved (buckles, displaced metal, etc.) and then decide how each will be best repaired.

Obviously, proceeding with a restoration plan without some kind of organization will be chaotic, something a neophyte soon learns. For this reason, the best way to go after the inspection is to decide where to start, and whether the repair should be roughed out by driving, pushing or pulling. Thought must be given as to what the panel or area will look like after the initial roughing, and which panel should be repaired next. After some kind of organized plan is formulated, the problems of doing the job are quickly dispatched.

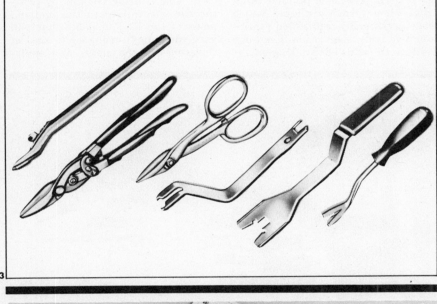

1. Your common electric drill will find many uses in restoration work. Here it's used with a countersink bit to clean scale out of a welded hole before leading work is started.

2. Whenever you're making new panels to replace rotted-out sections in an antique car, you'll be using snips to trim them. A heavy-duty pair of snips like these are good for straight cuts, and there are special "aviation" snips for both left and right-hand curves.

3. Doing bodywork will eventually require you to have some other, more specialized tools also. At left is a rough panel chisel, snips, two types of door handle removers, and a pry bar for removing upholstery tacks.

4. One of your first investments in body tools for restoration will have to be a set of torches, since there's only so much bodywork that can be done cold. You can take a course at your local trade school or a night course to get some practice in first.

BODY FILLERS EVEN THE CHERRIEST OF PARTS MAY NEED SOME FILLER FOR "100 POINT" RESULTS

Sooner or later in your restoration work, you will encounter a sheetmetal panel that is going to require a thin coating of a filler material after the basic hammer and dolly work has been completed. There should be no stigma attached to using such materials, as long as they are used judiciously; even the professionals must use lead and/or plastic fillers to get perfect results without beating and grinding the metal paper-thin. The negative connotations of body fillers arise because they can so easily be used excessively, to cover up for improper metalwork. It is very easy for a beginner to form the unsatisfactory habit of filling a low spot when very little effort would be required to straighten the damage. In many cases, it would be much faster to repair the metal, and save the added cost of the filler. Excessive use of filler breeds poor work traits and, usually, poor workmanship. This has become especially pronounced with the introduction of quality plastic fillers which can be applied by the very unskilled, normally with poor results.

The employment of plastic or lead is an essential part of body repair, but their use should be limited. When fillers are used, they must be applied with care. Experience comes with use, and as more experience is gained, the less fillers will be used.

Lead solder has been utilized in basic automobile construction for decades, and will undoubtedly continue for many years to come. Plastic fillers are relatively new, and while they do some jobs quite well, they are not to be considered a total replacement for lead. In this respect, the neophyte restorer would do well to concentrate on learning the use of lead first, then go about picking up the few remaining secrets of plastic.

Practically all automobile bodies use lead to some degree during the initial construction, usually at the visible points of panel mating. This would be where the top panel mates with the quarter panels, where the deck-lid skirt panels mate with the quarter panels, on the cowl panels, etc. However, the amount of lead used here is very small, and it's sometimes necessary for the restorer to melt this lead when replacing the panel.

Lead is not an unusual substance, but it does have some peculiar properties when correctly alloyed which make it especially well suited for automotive body application. Lead can be heated and easily shaped, it

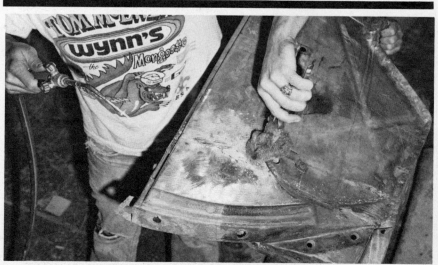

bonds perfectly and permanently to sheetmetal, it is easy to finish very smooth, and it will accept paint like sheetmetal.

Lead will bond to metals because it will tin the surface with its own properties, although tinning is often accomplished with a secondary compound, but the lead itself can be used. This is made possible by heating the sheetmetal to the melting point of the lead (a point that will vary with alloy), using some kind of flux to clean the metal, and apply-

PHOTOS BY JAY STORER

ing a thin coat of lead. If the metal is the right temperature and has been cleaned well, the lead will flow across the metal surface like water.

Lead that is alloyed for body and fender repair has its own peculiar melting characteristics, in that it does not melt from a solid to a liquid immediately. Most body leads start to soften at about 360° F and become softer as the temperature is raised. The point at which a particular lead compound will melt is determined by the percentage of tin in the mixture. Furthermore, the body lead alloy will melt below the melting point of pure lead, 620° F, and it may be below the melting point of tin at 455° F. The higher the amount of tin in a compound, the lower the melting point, and this must be understood when lead is being purchased.

LEAD ALLOYS

For all-around shop use, especially where considerable work is involved, the 70-30 alloy is best (70% lead and 30% tin). This alloy melts just under 500° F, which gives a wide latitude or plasticity for working in pro-

longed areas. Lead is available in a wide range of percentages, but anything other than 70-30 or 80-20 is not easy to use. A good example of this is the solder (lead is really a solder) used for other types of repair work, such as radiators. This particular compound is normally of the 50-50 variety, and the temperature range between where it becomes soft and where it melts is very narrow.

The necessity for lead is usually restricted to filling up low spots if good repair practices have been followed, and even then the area to be filled should be minor. However, this is not necessarily the case when a "patch" panel has been hammer-welded in place where a rusted-out area was cut out, or anyplace where lead is used to cover a welded seam or as a filler to make a difficult reverse crown. No matter where the lead is used, the steps for application are similar.

There are certain basic steps involved in using body fillers, whether they be lead or plastic. In the case of lead, the area must be cleaned, tinned, filled, shaped and finished. With plastic, tinning is not involved.

In the case of the beginner, nearly every one of these steps can lead to unsatisfactory results if these correct procedures are not followed. Remember, if the surface is not cleaned right, the lead may not stick. If the surface isn't tinned right, the lead won't stay in place. It is not easy to apply at first (especially on vertical panels), and shaping can be overdone. The entire job can be botched by careless finishing. Even so, leading is not difficult to

1. A graphic comparison of the lead vs. plastic filler techniques is this layout of the tools required for each. At left are the various tools needed for application of lead: torch, 70-30 lead sticks, tinning compound, steel wool, lead paddles and beeswax. The spreader at right is all that's used for applying plastic, or "cool-lead."

2. We used two identical areas on a '36 Ford cowl for our comparison. The lower corners had been rusted out, a common problem, and pieces from a good cowl were cut and hammer-welded in place. Now the welded seams needed to be filled. Body man Carl Green begins by warming the metal and wiping with the steel wool, which had also been warmed and dipped in the lead/flux.

3. After the area is tinned, the flux residue must be removed, or the lead still won't stick. Once again Carl lightly heats the area and wipes it quickly and lightly with a rag. You can't wipe too hard or you'll remove the tinning lead, too. Arrows indicate shiny areas that have been wiped clean.

4. Now the area is heated again, just enough to allow the lead stick to melt in crumbles, and stick to panel.

5. When enough lead has been applied to cover the area, the real work in leading begins. The body man has to heat the lead *just* to the workable point and spread it around evenly with his paddles. Keeping the lead workable requires frequent application of the torch in quick passes.

6. To keep the wooden paddles from sticking to the hot lead, they must be frequently dipped in beeswax. A quick blast from the torch melts the beeswax, and the paddle is dipped in.

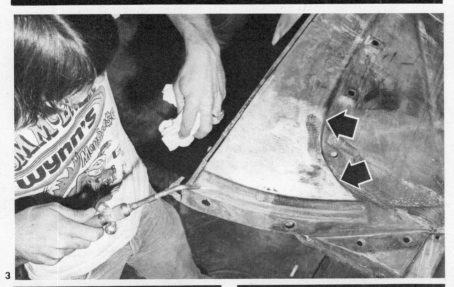

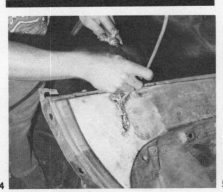

master if the beginner is patient and willing to practice.

Paint, welding scale and rust are the foreign agents that are normally on any surface to be leaded. It is necessary to clean a larger area than will be covered with lead, since the filler must blend perfectly into the surrounding metal. An open-coat disc on the power sander will remove the initial paint, while a cup-shaped wire brush on the same sander will make short work of any weld scale or rust in the cavities. If this type of wire brush is not available, a smaller brush in an electric drill, or even a hand brush, can be used. The small abrasions left in the metal from the disc sander make an ideal surface for the adherence of the lead.

Acids have been used as cleaning agents, but they are more trouble than they're worth. Muriatic acid can remove weld scale and rust; paint stripper will take off paint, but these chemicals do seep down in hidden cracks and will come out and haunt you later after the finish has been applied.

After the surface has been cleaned of all foreign materials—that is, the surface is all bright and shiny (this is difficult if a welded seam is to be leaded, but it's essential)—the entire area must be thoroughly tinned. Lead will have difficulty sticking to the metal unless it has been properly tinned.

TINNING FLUX

Some kind of tinning flux is necessary, as the flux is a chemical cleaner of the steel. Since this is usually a two-step operation in bodywork, the flux will leave a burned residue after tinning and must be wiped away before lead is added. Tinning flux comes in a variety of types, but the kind normally associated with other forms of soldering is not acceptable in bodywork. Auto supply stores carry a wide range of tinning agents, including the pure-liquid type and the popular compounds, composed of flux and powdered lead. The compound has the advantage of applying the tinning lead at the same time cleaner is being applied.

When tinning with the compounds, some method must be devised to get the compound onto the heated surface. This can be nothing more than a wadded rag, but the best is a piece of tightly wound steel wool gripped in pliers. The steel wool is pushed around in the tinning powder then applied directly to the heated panel.

When a liquid flux is used, the area to be tinned is first lightly heated then the flux brushed on. *Remember: heat applied during leading must be very closely controlled since it can distort panels, particularly those of the low-crown variety.* After the area is brushed with tinning liquid, heat the metal with brief passes of the torch until it is hot enough to melt the lead pressed against the surface. When pressing the lead bar, just a small mound will melt; then as the metal becomes too cold, the bar crumbles. A slight twisting motion of the bar will help get the correct amount. Repeat this brief heat and solder treatment to about one-third the area to be covered with lead.

At all times, the heat is applied in very brief brushing strokes, then removed. This controls the heat of the panel and the lead at a fairly constant level, somewhere between initial lead softening and actual melting. Of course, during tinning, the lead is actually melted.

To spread the lead over the surface and thereby gain the full tinning advantage, heat an area around a lead mound or two. As the lead changes appearance from the solid, grainy look to a shiny look (careful here because the change is rapid), wipe it across the panel with a wadded clean rag. Make all the wipes in the same direction, and make sure the entire area is tinned. There will be a series of overlapping wipe strokes, and when slightly cooled the tinned area will appear dull in contrast with the freshly sanded steel. While the lead is being wiped over the surface to get a good tin, the flux residue is being wiped away. It's obvious that tinning is an alternate heat-and-wipe situation. Compounds are best wiped with a rag after application, also.

Be careful when using heat and the rag on a tinned area. If too much pressure is applied to the rag, the tinning film can be completely wiped away. If too much heat is used over a tinned surface, the film can burn away. If a surface will not take a complete tinning, that is, if there are some small spots of bare metal that continue to show, it means the metal is not completely clean. Don't leave small, uncleaned and untinned spots and hope to bridge over with lead, such as craters in a welded seam. Get the metal as clean as you possibly can!

CONTROLLED HEAT

Up to this point, it is possible the lead procedure could have been accomplished with a welding torch, or a blow torch, or even a cutting torch. Practically any kind of heating flame could have been used, provided the heat was used sparingly. But from now on, the heat must be controlled more carefully, so properly adjusting the torch is of utmost importance.

Unlike other phases of welding, leading only requires a soft flame, a flame that is spread over a wide

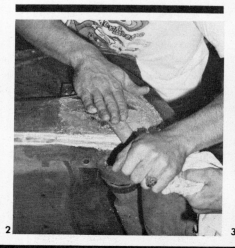

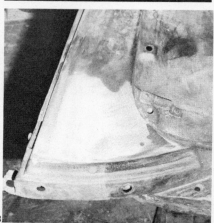

area. Generally, a medium-size tip is selected, one that might be used for welding slightly heavier steel gauge than sheetmetal. The acetylene is turned on as with welding and the torch is lit. Next the oxygen valve is opened slightly. The idea is to get a long, fuzzy flame, which is usually made up of a long, irregular blue cone with touches of yellow at the extreme tip. Even if the flame is toward the yellow side, it will still work properly.

When applying this flame to the metal, keep the tip well back and use just the end of the flame. Let it "lick" at the work. This will get the temperature up near where you want it and keep it there without undue heat concentration in a single, small area. Use the flame on the lead similar to the way it is used with brazing; flick the flame tip onto the metal, pass it across the lead, then flick it away. Now repeat this process until the desired results are achieved.

It is important to learn good torch control before the application of lead can even be considered, since merely keeping the unfinished lead on the panel will seem almost impossible at first. The secret is in

1. A variety of paddle shapes may be necessary for various contours, and you may have to make one or two from wood yourself for difficult areas.

2. A body file is used to take off ridges and show up the low spots.

3. If the leading process warped any of your panel, now is the time to hammer it and refile. Power sanders can save a lot of time, such as here, but only an experienced body man has the "touch" to use one without damage.

4. Final block sanding is done with a rubber sanding block and #80 paper.

5. With several coats of primer on the cowl, no one would ever guess it was ever patched together. A *good* lead job will never crack or peel off.

keeping the lead at that particular temperature between first softening and melting.

The beginner is advised to work on horizontal, flat panels at first, until some experience has been gained in learning to recognize when lead is beginning to soften and how to control the torch flame. The beginner trying to lead a vertical panel, such as a door, will find most of the material on the ground. At the same time, using a relatively flat practice panel, such as a hood, will encourage good heating habits. Remember again, too much heat and the panel will distort.

APPLYING LEAD

Lead can be applied in one of two basic methods: from the bar or from a mush pot. The former is the most common for smaller areas, the latter is better for large areas or for beginners who have trouble keeping the bar at the right application temperature. The mush pot is nothing more than a melting container in which lead bar(s) have been melted. The torch is kept directed toward the pot when not being played over the metal surface to keep the lead plastic, but not at the runny, melted state. The lead is then scooped out of the pot on a leading paddle and applied to the metal surface, like stucco on a building wall. The metal surface must be kept at the right temperature, too, but since the large mass of lead is well heated, it can be spread with the paddle (a kind of wooden trowel) over a relatively large area. A mush pot can be anything, even an old hubcap. However, such a large amount of lead would mean either poor metalwork, or a very large welded seam. In these cases, it is best to hammer weld the seam, but if this isn't possible, the leading practice must be accepted. Even so, the lead is applied over a relatively narrow band.

More common is the application of the lead directly from the solid-

bar state. If the panel is horizontal, this isn't too difficult since the melted lead will run onto the metal and puddle. Anywhere else, however, the puddle will continue to run onto the ground. When applying lead in this manner, heat the panel until the right temperature is reached, then the flame is played over the tip of the lead bar, usually about 1 in. of the tip. As the bar tip softens it is pressed onto the panel and the bar will break off right where it is too cold to stick. This can be accentuated by twisting the bar slightly as it is being pressed onto the panel. This procedure is repeated over the panel until enough lead has been applied. It is better to get too much than too little but more lead can be added as needed. Until experience is gained, keep pressure on the lead stick and make it crumple onto the panel.

The appearance of the lead is the key of successful working. When the solid bar begins to get shiny on one of the exposed edges, the temperature is about right for the plastic state. If the torch flame is kept on the lead, the shiny appearance will spread throughout the bar, which usually means the temperature is too high. When this happens, the lead will suddenly become liquid and run off the panel. Keeping pressure on the bar as it is heated will cause the bar to fold into the metal when it is hot enough, yet well before it becomes liquid. As a rule, apply the rough-lead buildup in the center of the working area.

Lead paddles are rather peculiar things in that any specific paddle probably will not feel exactly "right" when new, but even the beginner may find that an older, used paddle feels perfect the first time. Generally, new paddles seem large, sometimes unwieldy. There are good arguments for all sizes of paddles, but one about 4-ins. long, excluding the curved handle, is good for beginners. Paddles are made of quality

hardwood, with a variety of face shapes ranging from flat to very high crowns. At least one flat and one half-round design should be in every toolbox.

The hardwood paddle can be burned by the flame, as most well-used paddles invariably are This is bound to happen with so much alternation between flame and paddle on the lead surface, but burning will be reduced to a minimum as more experience with flame control is gained. Also, lead will tend to stick to the plain paddle. To counteract this tendency, the paddle face must be treated with a thin film of oil or beeswax. An ideal paddle lubricator can be made by cutting the side from a polish tin, then folding in an oil soaked rag. Very lightly heat the paddle face and rub it on the rag, repeating as found necessary during the paddle process. Some body men feel beeswax has a better lubricating quality than oil. The minute the lead seems to drag or stick to the paddle, it should be lubricated as soon as possible.

PADDLING LEAD

Getting the lead onto the panel initially will seem extremely simple compared to paddling the lead out, simply because there is a certain amount of manual dexterity required in coordinating the flame and paddle. Still, paddling lead is not unlike plastering a wall. Imagine yourself standing at a wall. The plaster trowel is usually held in the right hand, and the mortar board in the left. As a glob of plaster is stuck to the wall, it is immediately troweled out, otherwise the glob would fall. This alternating between left and right hands becomes a smooth movement with practice.

The same goes for paddling lead. The paddle is held in the prime working hand (left or right, as the case may be) and the torch in the opposite hand. The beginner will have a tendency to overheat the area at first, which may cause the lead alloy to separate into lumps of lead and tin. If this happens, more lead must be applied. The direct reaction to this overheat is an underheat, where the beginner then tries to work lead that is too cold to be spread.

Getting the lead and the surrounding metal up to the right temperature is done by holding the flame well away from the panel, with the tip of the soft flame just licking the surface. Move the flame

over the area to be worked, which includes the metal and the lead, never stopping in any one spot. The idea is to heat everything uniformly, but it does not mean heating an area bigger than can be worked with a few paddle strokes.

Watch the sharp edges of the lead during this heating; mash down on the lead buildup often, as a test. The minute one little edge of lead starts to brighten, the entire area of lead being heated is close to the plastic working state. Move the torch rapidly from this point on, flicking back to the lead only momentarily to keep the heat up.

The beginner will keep the lead in place by mashing down on it at first, which will show how soft and workable it really is. The torch plays across the lead and the paddle is used to push the lead around where it is needed. Rather than scrape the lead across the panel, it should be pulled. That is, do not lower the leading edge of the paddle and scrape, but raise the leading edge and pull the softened lead along. If the lead starts to get too hot, it will get brighter, so skip a couple of passes with the torch. If the lead is getting too cold, it will be harder to spread, or won't spread at all. Paddling lead across a metal surface is like buttering bread. If the butter is too warm, it flows too thin; if it is too cold, it doesn't spread at all.

Be careful not to keep heat on a lead area too long, as heat will cause the lead's grain structure to become coarse. Heating an area several times and repaddling it may cause this structure change, which leaves pit holes in the finished job.

At the same time, do not get the surrounding metal too hot, as this will raise the temperature in the lead and cause it to run off. Too

high a temperature will also encourage metal distortion. If some distortion is apparent the leaded area can be quenched with water after the paddling is finished but before the lead has become too cold. Throw water on the leaded surface with a rag or sponge, then as soon as the lead is cooled, rub the sponge or rag over the surface. Don't attempt this water quenching while the lead is still very hot (after paddling is the correct time, with no additional heat applied) as it will ruin the leading job. If the lead is too cold, the distortion will not be pulled out.

The beginner will find that not having enough lead to work will be his major trouble once the paddling technique is mastered. It is difficult to go back and add lead, since the temperature must be brought up carefully. The new lead must be applied and worked without overheating the already paddled lead film, and the two areas of lead must be heated enough to flow together at the mating point. If there is too much lead for a particular spot, it

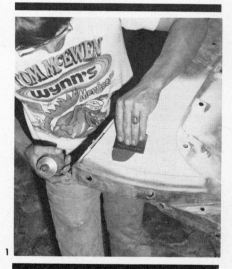

can be removed with the paddle while it is still in its plastic state. Ideally, the lead surface should be reasonably smooth and only slightly higher than the surrounding metal.

FILING FILLERS

Both lead and plastic fillers file and grind away faster than the surrounding metal, so care must be taken not to cut the filler too much, nor to make gouges and scratches in the filler's surface. The beginner is cautioned to use the file for final finish work on either lead or plastic, as it will cut slower than a disc sander, and the long surface of the file will level the filler with the area of the surrounding metal.

The file will cut deep gouges if allowed to run uncontrolled over the lead. If the file is not held firmly, it may skip up on one edge, which will make a very bad cut, a cut that may not file out. It is possible to learn a lighter filing touch for filler by pulling the file rather than pushing it.

Another common mistake begin-

1. Small dabs of glazing putty will take care of the minor pinholes or scratches in the leaded areas.

2. Now for our "bondo" example. As with leading, the surface must be perfectly clean for even the plastic fillers to adhere well. This cowl was dipped at a metal-stripping plant, and Carl gives it extra "tooth" with light passes of the body grinder.

3. A glass plate or clean piece of sheetmetal makes a good mixing board for plastic filler. Don't use paper or cardboard. These are about the proportions for filler and hardener.

4. The hardener is usually a dark color so you can tell when it is thoroughly mixed with the white bondo. Knead it quickly for about 30 seconds with a *clean* spatula or squeegee.

ners fall heir to is cutting away too much of the filler, whether lead or plastic. There is almost always a crown to the surface being filed. If the file or sander is run across the filler only, until the edges are feathered, chances are the filler will be flatter than the crown. The correct procedure is to start on the edges and work to the middle, running the file lengthwise to the crown. This keeps the file cutting the minimum amount of filler to reach the level of the surrounding metal, gradually forming the correct crown in the filled area. The filler in the middle of the repaired depression is the last to be filed.

When the area is finished with the file, all the edges should blend smoothly into the metal. If there is a tiny, low spot at the edge that does not smooth out, it may be picked up slightly (with the pointed end of a lightweight body hammer) or filled with putty later. A large, unfilled area indicates the lead was not run into the surrounding metal far enough, or the metal has distorted. Additional lead is the usual remedy if the panel cannot be picked up with the hammer.

After the initial filing, the area should be block sanded with #80 grit production paper. This paper is coarse enough to cut the file marks from the filler without loading up. It is only intended to finish off the filler and not to shape it, although such paper can be hand-held to finish off difficult areas, like reverse crowns. The disc sander should be used on a filler only by a professional. Of course, the beginner is not going to know the disadvantages of improper sander use unless he tries it, but the trial should be only on a practice panel. Generally, the sander cuts so rapidly that the beginner finds the filled area cut too low and flat. There is a certain health hazard associated with using a disc sander on lead also, in that the sander causes a fine lead dust that can be absorbed into the skin and/or breathed into the lungs. This can cause lead poisoning if kept up over a long period of time.

In summary, lead is an invaluable aid to the body man, but it must be used properly. Never use lead where the spot can better be repaired or shaped; only use lead if it is an economical and fast method of repair.

PLASTIC FILLERS

Plastic and fiberglass repair procedures are often mistaken for one

and the same thing, but they are not. The so-called plastic filler is basically a substitute for lead, while the fiberglass repair is primarily for fiberglass surfaces, but may be used on sheetmetal. In this respect, the latter is almost always used only as a repair of a rust-rotted area that could only be repaired by panel replacement or patching.

A tremendous amount of energy has been expended during the past two decades in plastic filler research, in an effort to create a true no-heat filler that will work as well as lead. While a perfect plastic filler has yet to be found, the product of today is vastly improved over that of a few short years ago. Today, plastic can be relied upon to give a good, hard finish that will not shrink or crack with age, yet will adhere to the metal even under the most extreme temperature conditions.

There are many companies making plastic fillers, since the composition lends itself to small, local production as well as major company manufacture. Prices for such fillers range from very low to quite high, and about the only guideline for the beginner is to use the filler that the majority of local body men use. A plastic filler usually takes about 30 minutes to harden, which means that where time is an important cost factor, the use of lead may be faster. It takes less skill to apply a plastic filler, but the dust created from grinding some plastics can injure the lungs. By and large, the plastic filler has a definite place in auto body repair techniques.

Because the metal cannot be worked after a plastic filler has been used, it is imperative that all high spots be driven down before the application of plastics. The area to be filled must be cleaned of rust, paint and welding scale, as with lead. Grind the metal with a #24 open-coat disc to give a rough metal surface for good plastic "bite," then wipe away any oil or waxes that might prevent a good bond. Clean an area larger than that to be repaired with the surrounding paint featheredged before the repair is started. This will allow the filler be spread onto the surrounding metal to ensure the necessary buildup. Do not spread the filler over any paint, as it will probably peel later on. To cut down on the labor involved, do not fill more than is absolutely necessary.

Plastic fillers of this nature include a resin base and a catalyst.

Unmixed, the two agents remain pliable over a long period of time, but once the catalyst is added to the resin, it will harden in a matter of minutes. It is possible to control the hardening time somewhat by the amount of catalyst (hardener) added, but the best course is to follow mixing instructions on the containers.

The most common type of plastic filler kit includes a specific amount of resin (usually contained in quart cans) and a small tube of liquid hardener. Normally, no more than two small drops of hardener are required for a golf-ball size hunk of resin. Any type of plastic filler must be thoroughly mixed. Since the mixture should be kept free of any contaminants, a piece of safety glass is the best mixing "board" available. It is easy to clean and store. Cardboard will work in a pinch.

Never mix more plastic than immediately needed, even if the fill will require several coats. The filler on the panel and that on the mixing board will harden at the same rate, so the unused portion is useless once it has been mixed.

Plastics can be applied with a wide putty knife, a rubber squeegee, or practically any kind of flexible straightedge. The rubber squeegee is perhaps the easiest to use, since it will tend to follow body contours and leave a smoother finish than the others.

As soon as the plastic is completely mixed, it should be applied to the work area. Apply the mixture onto the area with a downward-sideways motion to force out any air bubbles. These bubbles must not be left in the work, as they will shrink or burst later after the paint is applied. At the same time, this pressure will cause the plastic to gain maximum bond with the roughened metal.

If the area to be filled is more than ¼-in. deep, successive filling is necessary, with each coat allowed to dry before the next is applied. Such a deep fill might be a gouge, in which case the deepest part of the fill would receive the plastic first. No plastic would be feathered to the edges, instead this would be kept for the last coat.

If too much hardener is used, or if the material stands too long before it is applied, it will tend to roll up and pull loose from the metal. Don't bother going further; mix a new batch and start again.

Finishing plastic can be either very easy or extremely difficult, de-

pending upon how long it is allowed to set before the finishing process is started. It is not uncommon to see a gouge obviously filled by the car's owner with plastic. Usually the owner has applied the filler rather roughly and apparently waited until the plastic has become very hard before attempting to file or sand it smooth. By then, it required a very sharp file, a disc sander, and lots of elbow grease. He had none of these.

A regular body file is not used to work plastic. The type of file used is referred to as a cheese grater, the kind of file often found in woodworking. Blades for these files are available in a variety of sizes, as with normal lead files, for unusual contours. Special holders are also available, although the blade can be used without a holder.

Plastic fillers set up hard because of chemical interaction, thus they do not "dry" in the normal sense of the word. However, they are affected by high temperatures, so they will harden faster on a very hot day. To speed this hardening, lamps used for paint drying can be directed on the mixture. At any rate, it is best to begin working the material while it is still "soft." This can be determined by touching the surface lightly with the grater. When it is just right to work, the plastic will peel through the grater openings in long strings.

Work the area with the grater and a very light touch, shaping carefully

until the filler is almost down to the desired height. Let the plastic harden for a while longer, then finish it off with a long, flat block and #180 grit sandpaper. Coarser paper will tend to leave scratches. The long sandpaper "file" will smooth the filled spot into the surrounding area just as the lead file does. Air files, pneumatic tools having a long, narrow platen taking coarse sandpaper up to about 4-ins.x16 ins., should be kept out of the hands of the novice. They cut too fast, at up to 3500 strokes per minute, and will eliminate a carefully formed crown of filler in short order. Used judiciously, though, and with experience, they have made the use of plastic fillers populars due to the speed (thus, time-saving) at which they operate. Finally, finish the area for painting with a regular rubber sanding block and #220 grit sandpaper or garnet paper.

If the plastic is allowed to become too hard, it must be worked out just as lead with a regular metal file and/or a disc sander. The beginner will find the file as necessary here as with lead since the filler can be cut down too low. If the sander is used, a respirator or some kind of nose protection should be used to protect the lungs against the plastic dust.

Plastic fillers should not be used as a substitute for poor body repair no matter how easy they are to apply. Using too much plastic filler is just asking for trouble. Plastic

should never be used where the body is liable to flex or where strength is required, just as lead should never be used to bridge a gap that should have been welded. Nor is plastic acceptable as an edge. If an area must be filled out to an exposed edge or lip, lead should be used at the edge, then the plastic

1. A wide, thin coat of filler is best, even though most of this will be filed and sanded off anyway. Never use fillers to make up for poor work.

2. After the plastic has set up but not hardened completely, use a "cheese grater" file to level out the filler.

3. A disc grinder can be used if you know what you're doing, but a slip-up will cut into the bondo even faster than it would through lead filler.

4. Final sanding, as always, is done by hand, working from about 80 grit to 180 grit for finishing. Be sure to thoroughly feather the edges.

5. Several coats of primer, a few dabs of spot putty on any pinholes and the job is done. Wet-sand and prime this panel and it's ready for final paint. In the case of this '36 Ford phaeton, the owner specified lead be used, so this plastic was removed after our photo session, but properly applied, plastic fillers are every bit as suitable for antique car work as lead, and in some ways better.

added. The lead won't be as strong as sheetmetal, but it won't chip like plastic.

In areas where there are extreme temperature fluctuations during short periods of time, plastic fillers have been known to give problems. If this is the case, local body men will have found which plastics should be utilized.

Apply a primer/surfacer that is recommended for use over plastic, as some paint compounds have a bad effect on fillers. The auto parts store specializing in paints will know what compounds will work. Should problems occur after the paint is applied, it will be only because of poor filler application (surface not clean, etc.) or because the paint is reacting to the filler.

OLD FILLER

There are yet a few final words to say about the use of fillers, both lead and plastic. If you have not yet begun to restore a car but are still in the looking stages, examine a potential restoration with care. If the car has been previously restored, or if it suffered body damage an unknown number of years ago, it may show up in the form of imperfectly adhered filler.

Perhaps some long-forgotten body man used the wrong lead alloy mixture, or perhaps the surface he was leading wasn't entirely cleaned. Or maybe the car fell into a "quick-and-dirty" body man's hands just about the time the plastic fillers were first put on the market and the chemical technology wasn't what it is now. Whatever the case, a poor filling job may show up as a broken line of paint indicating the lifting of the filler from the base sheetmetal underneath the paint finish. It will take close examination, perhaps, to determine whether an unknown type of filler is actually beginning to curl up at the edges, or whether the break line in the paint is caused merely by an old finish that is beginning to severly weather. But the point is, be aware that an earlier "fixer-upper" may have unknowingly created more of a problem than you're willing to cope with. It just may take too much time and/or too much money to restore a car that has been improperly fixed long years ago—or, the present owner of the derelict that you're itching to buy may lower his price if you can convince him that the condition of the car is not as sound as he says it is.

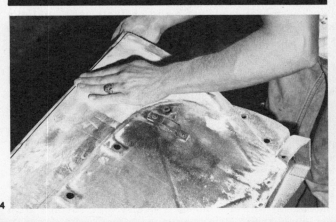

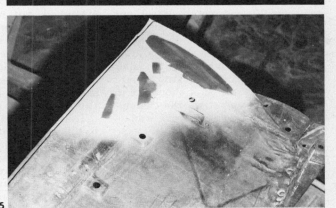

HAMMER WELDING
THIS USEFUL RESTORATION SKILL TAKES PATIENCE AND PRACTICE

Late-night TV watchers have probably seen blacksmiths in old Western movies heat two pieces of iron in a forge, then join them by pounding them on an anvil. This is not hammer welding by today's bodyworking standards. Hammer welding as it's done in the bodyworking trade is ordinary gas welding followed by some tricky hammer and dolly work on the welded joint to provide as smooth and distortion free a seam as possible.

Among the several facets of bodywork and painting that require a certain finesse and "feel," hammer welding is perhaps the most prominent. It isn't difficult, but because several basic tenets of metalworking are involved, very few metal men practice the art. While it may be easier for a quick repair to use a filler, the workman who strives for quality will take a moment longer and do the best job possible.

Restorers particularly find hammer welding advantageous, usually in situations calling for maximum strength and minimum filler. The finished job is far superior to the use of lead or plastic. It also allows the metal man to gain better control over the panel, to shape and mold it the way he wants it with stress in the right place.

Hammer welding is normally involved in only three bodywork situations: repair of a tear, replacement of a panel and modification of a panel. In all three, the emphasis is upon quality and metal control, not economy. A commercial body shop cannot expect to include hammer welding on a large scale, simply because every minute spent in labor reduces its profit margin. Where quality is stressed, as it should be in a restoration operation, the customer demands premium work and is willing to bear the extra cost.

Consider a metal tear in a quarter panel. It is easy to rough the panel into shape and then weld the tear quickly. The bead is then ground off and beaten down so filler will cover the depression. Most modern body

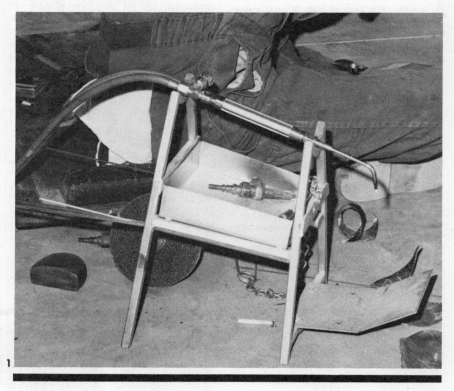

shops rely solely on plastics for this repair job. Obviously, there is some unusual stress buildup around the welded area, which may cause problems elsewhere in the panel.

It is also possible to rough the panel back into shape until the torn metal edges can be aligned carefully, then hammer weld the rip closed. With such a situation, the area adjacent to the tear will probably be stretched, but when the metal is welded and hammered, a natural shrinking force is introduced that tends to pull the stretch out. After the initial hammer welding, the area may be treated as a gouge—keep on shrinking and working the panel until it assumes its original shape.

It is in panel replacement and modification that hammer welding takes on such importance. Unless the panel is shaped properly (with seams hammer welded), there will be a need for an excessive amount of filler material. In some radical cases, the entire panel will end up with a

filler coat to varying degrees. Anyone can sling lead and plastic, but it takes a craftsman to work metal. That's what counts.

This is not to say that every seam should be hammer welded; far from it. When a panel can be replaced and the joint made by spot welding, riveting or even ordinary fusion welding—and the joint will not show—fine. But if the seam is in the open and affects the panel's strength, hammer welding must be considered.

Take the situation where the bottom edge of an exterior panel has rusted away. Only about 2 ins. of the metal is really cancerous, but the replacement strip will be from 3 to 4-ins. wide. This strip will usually have very little (or no) crown and will generally include a folded lip of 90% or more. Whether the panel is on a door, cowl or quarter area, it does not matter. The metal man will be working directly in the middle of a nearly flat surface with heat. That means a high distortion possibility, which requires torch control.

AN IMPERATIVE

It is absolutely imperative that all hammer welding include the smallest possible weld bead. To accomplish this, the panels to be mated must fit as closely as they can. The replacement panel should be shaped and trimmed first, then held over the area to be replaced and well marked. It is wise to cut away the bad metal with as little distortion as possible, so this rules out the "hot wrench" immediately. A manual or air-operated chisel can be used, but there is a rather rough edge left which must be worked. Better yet, use a saber saw or nibbler.

After the initial rough cut, try the replacement panel on for size. It will generally be off just a whisker, because there is usually too much metal remaining on the parent panel. This thin strip may be trimmed off with a good pair of aviation tin

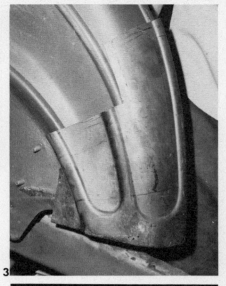

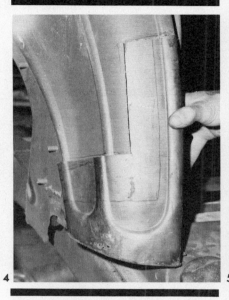

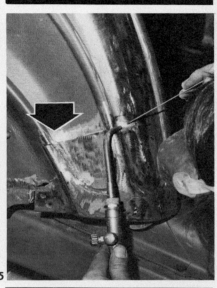

1. Hammer welding is a time-consuming technique not often seen in regular body shops. One of the prime tools needed is a (homemade) torch rest like this one, which has a shield to keep the lighted torch from scorching the floor, a tray for tips, and tubes to hold various welding rods. This one's in use at Carl Green Enterprises in Van Nuys, Calif.

2. Here's a typical butt-joint of two pieces of sheetmetal which has been hammer welded. A few passes of the grinder and this undistorted seam is almost ready for primer and a few dabs of glaze. Normal overlap seam would have been quicker, but would have required lots of filler.

3. Here's a common auto restoration problem. The rear corners of this '32 Ford roadster were rotted out and no good roadster panels could be found. On some bad advice as to the interchangeability, a coupe rear was purchased. It took careful cutting and hammer welding to make the parts fit.

4. With part of the rotted section trimmed off and the coupe piece held in place, the fit looks okay except for the outside two beads.

5. A thin strip was trimmed from the left-corner piece so that the center bead would line up on the body, and this was hammerwelded in place. Fit of the fenderwell bead (arrow) was accomplished by using again the wedge end of the finishing hammer. Corner finally takes shape.

6. After grinding down the seams, a little primer and putty brings this part of our roadster project that much closer to completion. No one will ever know (except you) what went into these stock-looking corners.

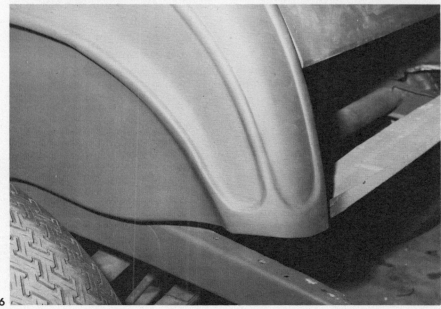

snips, although such snips have a tendency to roll the tiny edge rather than make a clean cut, while the body grinder will make the ultimate fitting easier. The two panel edges should fit flush along the full length, with no more than 1/16-in. gap at any part. If the edges touch, all the better. A gap requires too much filler rod, resulting in a larger bead, and as the bead size gets larger, the hammer weld becomes increasingly poorer.

Clamp the pieces together and tack weld the edges. Use very little or no filler rod and make the tack tiny. Speed is important here, as well as a very small flame. Often too large a tip will be used, resulting in too much heat immediately adjacent to the edge. This causes the metal to crawl excessively and makes a perfect fusion weld almost impossible. A correct hammer weld cannot be made if the edges lap.

Make sure the edges are level during and after the tack weld. If not, heat the tack in a restricted area and use the hammer and dolly to level the edges. This means a few light taps, not heavy blows, as the metal is hot.

After the panels are tacked about an inch apart all along the seam, start at one end with the hammer-welding process. Be prepared to travel rapidly, not so much with the torch as with the hammer and dolly. The railroad dolly is well suited to hammer welding, since it has a number of convenient crowns and is easy to hold. The hammer face should be nearly flat.

Hammer welding calls for an alternate use of torch and hammer/dolly, so some sort of torch stand is required. This will allow the torch to be hung out of the way and remain lit, yet close at hand. A bucket of water will be useful if an extensive weld is involved, as the dolly will become hot after awhile and can be cooled by dipping it into the water. It is also wise to wear a glove on the dolly hand, to protect against a burn from either the dolly or slag falling from the welded surface's underside. Remember, every tool must be close at hand to ensure speed.

There are two ways to make a hammer weld. The simplest method is to weld the entire seam at once, then follow with spot heat and the hammer/dolly. A better way is to weld a short 2-in. section, then use the hammer, then weld again. This way the area is still hot from welding and does not need reheating, al-

lowing better control of the metal.

Lay the torch tip flatter to the plane of travel than with normal fusion welding, thus reducing the heat to the metal. The filler rod can also be held at an opposite low angle to shield the edges. Although the two metal pieces touch, they will tend to grow toward each other even more when the heat is applied, allowing the edges to melt and flow together without the necessity of the filler rod. Such flowing may be difficult at first, but can be accomplished easily as experience is gained. An occasional hole will develop which must be filled by a drop from the rod, but the idea is to make the weld rapidly and with as little heat and rod as possible. At the same time, the edges should be kept level.

Immediately upon setting the torch aside, place the dolly against the underside and hold it firmly to the weld. Slap the bead rapidly with the dinging hammer—working back and forth from one end of the seam

to the other. This will cause the bead to flatten out and have a shrinking effect on the panel, which has tried to grow with the heat. If one panel has not stayed level, that area must be reheated and hammered until it is level across the bead. The objective here is to flatten the mating joint so as to minimize follow-up work.

Continue across the entire joint in this way, alternating between torch and hammer/dolly. It is possible to feel the area with a palm, but remember that the metal stays hot. Wipe the hand quickly across the surface to detect stretched spots and to determine how the panel contour is being affected.

STRETCH MARKS

After the seam has been hammer welded, check for a stretched area. Wherever one is found, shrink the panel as necessary. The welded seam should look almost flush with the

surrounding panel, or even be in a very slight valley. If the bead has been too big, it will have been flattened on top and bottom by the hammer and dolly, but will still stick up from the surface slightly.

Grind the weld with a disc sander, using a flexible disc pad which will allow the disc to follow the contour rather than cut into it. This grinding should cut down the bead ridges and will show up the low spots along the bead that must be picked up. Use a picking hammer from the bottom and a picking dolly on top (an ordinary dolly will substitute) and raise only those low craters that remain. At this stage, hammer welding is very similar to crease repair and requires a good deal of patience, particularly from the beginner.

Resort to the file and grinder often during this picking operation, as no filler will be used since the two panels have become one. As the small craters are raised—and the high spots taken down with normal hammer/dolly technique—keep running the hand across the entire pan-el. Look across the panel from several different angles, trying to find a break in the contour. For the most part, the problems will be confined to the immediate seam area.

After as many of the craters and tiny low spots have been removed as practical, wash the surface thoroughly with a good metal prep, using a wire brush to clean out the minute depressions that remain. Finish off the surface with the smoother grinder discs, followed by a "jitterbug" oscillating air sander. Prime the bare metal and allow the primer to set completely before going over the seam with a thin coat of glazing compound. This glaze will get down into the small pockmarks that remain, resulting in a perfectly smooth job.

There is no substitute for hammer welding on a panel that's being re-paired or patched, if both sides of the panel will be visible. Though this is not common in ordinary bodyworking, it's becoming more prevalent on restored cars slated for display, where onlookers or show judges may inspect the underside of a fender as closely as the top side.

For a number of years now, it has been common for the more experienced automotive enthusiasts to extol the virtues of hammer welding. There are a number of restorers famous for this type of work, and their products show the quality. This kind of technique requires practice, no doubt about it, but the results are immediately apparent. Fortunately, the student need make only a few short hammer welds to get the idea. From there on it's a matter of using his new-found secret technique.

1. Another typical problem that is best solved with hammer welding is replacing a lower, rusted-out area on an early car's cowl or quarter. Here the rusted section is cut off and the trim line ground straight. Flush fit of the panels to be welded is critical.

2. Anytime a butt weld is being made it can distort nearby low-crown panels. The torch should have a very small flame; the tip may be laid flatter to direct flame at area just welded.

3. Hammer each tack immediately, as this will tend to shrink the area and eliminate any distortion caused by the heat. It also keeps the edges flush. Don't worry about distortion in larger panel at this time.

4. Pick hammer is used to raise the low spots, but dolly is kept on top to keep from raising spots too high. This is where experience with the hammer will begin to pay off.

5. After the new section is hammer welded, the surrounding panel may be worked as necessary since "growth" through heat of welding may cause distortion. In this case, original part of weld needed several shrinks (arrow) to remove "oil-canning."

6. Although it usually isn't to be found in the average body man's kit of tools, the shrinking dolly is a handy item. It is grooved to "grip" metal and is used in conjuction with an aluminum hammer.

7. This is the panel as it appears in nearly finished condition. Some tiny low areas remain to be picked up and filed, then panel will be primed. Remaining imperfections are glazed.

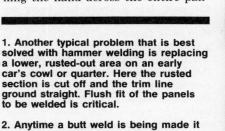
5

6

7

SAVE THOSE PANELS
SKILLED AND UNSKILLED TECHNIQUES FOR SAVING "UNSALVAGEABLE" BODY PANELS

Old-timers to the hobby of restoring old cars have a favorite saying about the quality of body and fender work. "If it's flawless, paint it black." Indeed, black is the most unforgiving color that can be sprayed on a surface. The slightest imperfection, something the eye could never discern otherwise, will stand out like a sore thumb when painted a shiny black. And black, as you surely know, is the most common color encountered in old cars.

A person doesn't have to be an accomplished body and fender man to give his vehicle a thorough detailing. He does have to pay strict attention to the small things.

Nothing detracts from a beautiful restoration job as much as poor panel preparation. This doesn't mean the paint, because a good paint job over a wavy panel indicates either a lack of talent or a lack of interest in preparation. Since patience is 90% of talent, the answer is lack of interest.

In preparing the metal and fiberglass panels of a vehicle, it is easy to overlook the tiny dings and waves that will show so blatantly later on. It is very easy to throw a prime coat on the car and follow immediately with color, impatience being what it is.

OLDER CAR PROBLEMS

Take the early cars, for instance. When a 1947 Ford tudor sedan is being restored to original condition, even down to the dark maroon paint job, there are plenty of things to consider—not the least of which is replacement of a few bent chrome strips and replating of all the other chrome. Obviously, the car would not be as perfect if this chrome were overlooked. But what about the waves in the hood? These older cars were prone to develop hood waves, an imperfection that shows up almost immediately.

Such a problem usually does not stem from damage, it's just old age and quite difficult to cure. Yet a weekend spent on making the panel perfect is invaluable. More of a problem is the damaged area that

has been straightened poorly. This is not uncommon on older cars, and will usually include a fender or door panel. If possible, replace the panel. If not, straighten what is there.

On pre-1935 cars, the experts look for imperfections in a number of significant places. First of all, has there been a repair of rusted areas? This would be the base of the cowl and quarter panels, bottom of the doors, and around the panel beneath the deck lid. If there has been no repair, the rusted surface is obvious. But more important, has there been a poor repair?

The point here is to keep everything the way it is supposed to be, not half way. When the real enthusiasts begin picking a particular early car apart, they look for bad metal in the deck lid (flat spots that run across the lid, very common), high and low spots in the metal panels directly above and below the deck lid, short vertical waves in the quarter panels above the rear fenders (also quite common), flat spots in the hood, and irregular fender edges.

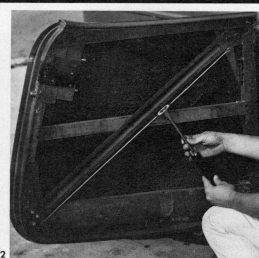

SPECIAL PANEL PROBLEMS

Fixing up an early car deck lid can be a study in maximum frustration. This is a relatively low-crowned panel, but it normally has a curve in both directions. When it gets flat spots, they usually appear almost as bands, about 4-ins. wide, from one side to the other. How they get there is anybody's guess—by people leaning on the lid, things piled on it, etc. Whatever the cause, it should be cured. In some cases where a rumble seat is installed, the body stops have been damaged, allowing the lid to contact the lower body panel. But in this instance, the spot will be a definite crease and not a wide band.

The quick and dirty way to repair a "banded" deck lid is with large amounts of plastic filler, but this isn't the best way. The metal should be worked. Raising all the low bands can be accomplished by either picking and prying, or by cutting the inner panel away and working with a dolly and hammer. The latter is preferable. When the inner panel is cut out, use tin snips or a panel cutter. Do not use the torch, as it tends to cause distortion unless handled by a professional in the business.

With the inner panel removed (same goes for doors) work up all the low spots. Since the metal will tend to work harden during this process, the panel will hold shape better after working. Always check the progress with an adjustable body file. Since the flattened spots will have displaced the panel elsewhere, the edges of the bands will tend to be high. After the panel is perfect, the inner panel is spot brazed back in place (do not localize heat which will cause external panel distortion).

The body panels directly above the deck lid on older cars are not as large as the deck lid, but often cause as much trouble. The upper panel normally requires work to smooth out low spots. Again, these spots can be filled with plastic, but since the panel is easy to reach it is better worked out in the traditional manner. The lower panel is not so easy. This particular piece of sheetmetal is usually hemmed over a rather substantial brace. In the case of

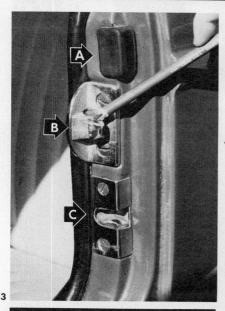

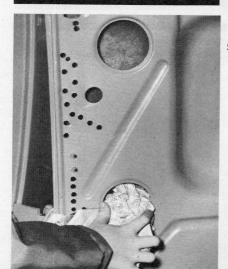

1. Good alignment and fit of all body panels is particularly important on a restoration. Things like the gaps around doors and other panels will be subjected to close scrutiny. If yours has been a ground-up, body-off-frame restoration, don't *finish* any panel until the body and other parts are securely bolted back down on the frame.

2. Doors, their shape, alignment and fit, are always a problem on old cars—especially open cars. Wood-framed doors usually develop a sag which can be reduced by installing a tension strap with a turnbuckle, as here.

3. Three sources of early car door alignment are right here; A, the rubber door bumper, B, the striker, and C, the dovetail assembly. Worn striker tips can be built up with arc welding, rubbers replaced, and both striker and dovetail can be shimmed or moved slightly to affect a change in door fit and alignment.

4. Door alignment can be frustrating and time-consuming, but the answers aren't complex. Sometimes a simple bend against an object in the jamb can realign a tight hinge area.

5. If there's no other way to do a good job straigtening a door skin, cut out the inner structure so the outer panel can be worked with the hammer and dolly. When the work is done, weld the inner panel back in.

6. Rather than cutting up the inner panel, this door was fixed by drilling holes for a prybar to fit through in working on the outside skin. Never use newspaper stuffed into a door as sound deadener, though. Not only is it a fire hazard but the paper will hold moisture in the door, promoting later rust-out problems. Better to use boat-type pour-and-set foam.

7. Older hinge pins tend to wear and must be replaced as a rule. New stock pins can sometimes be located at new car dealerships that can be trimmed to fit early cars. Also you can check the antique parts houses.

some specific old cars, such as the Model A, specialty parts houses stock new replacement panels. Otherwise, it's a matter of repair.

Here is one place it pays to use the plastic rather than fight the inner reinforcement. There is seldom room to get a dolly, or even pick of some kind, inside this bracing. The alternative is to weld up any cracks (they usually start at the upper and lower edges where this panel is riveted via a flange to the quarter panels), grind and lead if necessary, and straighten the flanged lip along the deck lid opening. To get a perfectly smooth contour often requires the use of plastic, usually more as a thick putty than anything else. When working such a large area, which has a very low crown in both directions, it is an advantage to rely primarily on large sanding files.

One area of preparation that is often overlooked about the deck lid is the flange lip itself. This should be cleaned very thoroughly with a rotary wire brush, both inside and beneath. Clean out all the old paint, rubber and cement, etc., then weld up the minute cracks that are sure to be present. Do not prime the lip heavily; instead rely on a thin coat of primer/surfacer and a thin coat of color to reduce its tendency to chip.

Quarter panels are the dead giveaway as to quality of bodywork on older cars. While rust is possible at the bottom edge, vertical waves are common in the area around the fender opening. These imperfections may have been caused by a rear-end collision at some time, but many undamaged bodies also have them.

If the problem was caused by a collision (look on the inside of the trunk to find marks left by hammer or dolly), chances are the panel is stretched ever so slightly and will need a bit of shrinking. When no previous damage has been involved, the low/high spots can be worked out with hammer, dolly and spoon. The beginner will find it difficult to get an absolutely perfect panel in this instance, since feel is the only way to locate the definite ripples. For this reason a thin coat of plastic filler may again be used as almost a putty. It is most effective.

FENDER BUGABOOS

Irregular fender lines are the worst enemy of the restorer, since they are so prevalent, and so difficult to repair. The problem is accentuated by a case of poor repairs. Older fenders display a marked tendency toward splitting, due to vibrations and lack of support.

About the only way to diagnose fender edge waves is by a critical eye looking down the fender line. This will disclose high and low areas along the edge, and will usually

show if one end is out of alignment with the other. But it is not always a good proof, especially when the paint is dull. A sure-fire check is with either a plumb level or plumb bob. Position either of these vertical plumb devices at stations down the

1. Irregularities in fender edges are sometimes difficult to see. Draw a straight reference line on the shop floor and run a straightedge along the fender bead while holding a piece of chalk. Line shows waves.

2. Door fit and body rigidity were both improved on this roadster with addition of a crossbrace behind seat. Not seen here is turnbuckle (arrow) which provides for adjustment of the tension. Tension brought one door in and the other out. Both now fit.

3. So you think your panels are straight enough for black lacquer? This door looked fine until a guide coat of light primer was lightly scuffed with sandpaper to show many, many highs and lows that needed work.

4. Old car bodies are actually quite flimsy when off the chassis. When you have everything bolted back on the finished chassis for the last time, then you can use shims under some of the bolts to align cowl, doors, etc.

5. The lower portions of cowls and rear quarters are convenient places for water, snow, etc. to have built up over the years, along with the rustout they develop. The only good solution is to cut it out and weld in a new panel. Reproduction "patch" panels are available for most Fords, and others can be made at your local sheetmetal shop quite reasonably.

6. Welding will warp sheetmetal, unless you hammer weld using a dolly behind the panel. This patch panel was hammer welded for most of its length, but lower-heat brazing was used at the ends, because there's no way to dolly the backside there.

fender edge and make a chalk mark on the pavement below. Connect these marks with a line to determine how straight the fender edge really is. This plumb check will show up major ripples or waves, but it will not show small dings. Only the block sander will give them away. Also, wetting down a dull fender can help you discover minor problems, that otherwise would not be apparent until the fender was painted.

Fender edge repair on older cars is best done with a hammer and dolly, at least until all the workable metal is straight. Because some fenders used wire in the rolled bead, it will be practically impossible to get each tiny dent out so follow with a filler.

HINGES AND DOORS

When it comes to the doors, older cars have a corner on the "bad news" market. Big, heavy cars may experience some trouble in keeping door alignment (usually sag results after several years), but most older cars were built with thin, lightweight doors. This means there will be trouble with alignment to some extent, but the mechanical door

4

parts are likely to wear rapidly. A beautifully-restored open car can have its image ruined by ill-working doors.

Alignment of a coupe or sedan door is not nearly as difficult as on its roadster counterpart, since the closed cars generally have three hinges to the roadster's two. Dual hinges became almost standard after 1936, but they were made stronger at the same time. Whether two or three hinges are involved, alignment will be handled in the same manner.

Many times a sloppy fitting door is due entirely to worn hinge pins. This may not be apparent when the door is opened and moved up and down as a check, since the wear is very little and limited to a small area of both hinge and pin. As a guide, if the pins haven't been changed (few have) on a car made before 1948, new pins will be needed.

Drive the old pin out and inspect for wear. Also check the hinge pin holes, as they may have elongated ever so slightly. If the holes are larger, it may be necessary to drill the hinge to a slight oversize. Pins are available from a number of sources, including Antique Auto Parts, in Rosemead, Calif., the local hardware store, and the local Volkswagen dealer. It is best to lubricate the pin with a dry graphite before installing it.

If the doors still sag after the hinge adjustments, there may be some other trouble. This is true of roadsters that have another body adjustment at the front body-to-frame bolts. By shimming between body and frame at the bolt nearest the door, it is possible to raise or lower the door in relation to the rear post.

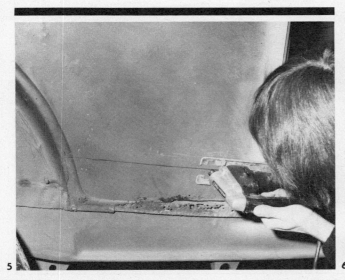

5

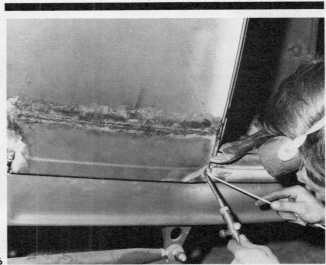

6

Wooden framework doors have problems all their own when it comes to vertical alignment. After the hinges are checked and repaired, loosen the framework screws slightly. Swing the door closed, but do not latch it, and place a small jack under the door rear. By raising the jack in small adjustments, the door can be aligned perfectly with the opening. The screws must be retightened. If they do not hold, additional screws should be added. It also helps to pour a quality-wood glue in the joints.

On larger wood-framed doors there will often be a diagonal support brace running from the top of the hinged side to the opposite bottom edge. Make sure this brace is rigid, and replace it if necessary. A piece of thin steel strap 1-in. wide may be added for more bracing if desired.

In many cases, the bottom of the door will stick out (see chapter on alignment). This presents a very special problem with wood-framed doors. Using normal screen-door tighteners available from any hardware store, attach one end to the door top near a hinge and the other at the opposite bottom, just like the brace. With the framework screws loosened, tighten this adjustable rod to the desired shape, then retighten the screws and add glue.

Quite often the door may fit perfectly, but a worn latch assembly keeps the final fit sloppy. In the majority of old cars, the latching system is a simple sliding-bolt arrangement wherein a bar with a beveled end slides back and forth in the metal housing. This housing is composed of two sides, in a sort of sandwich, held together by screws or bent metal tabs. When these tabs are carefully bent straight, the housing will separate. Every part of the latch should be washed and wire brushed, since rust is the usual cause of poorly operating doors.

The sliding bar tip may be worn and must be welded, then ground or filed to stock configuration. If a good arc welder is available, this tip may be hard-faced to reduce repeat wear. Thoroughly lubricate the sliding bar sides and corresponding moving parts in the housing, then reassemble the complete unit.

The door post striker may also be worn and can be built up with weld as was the sliding bar. Since new parts are seldom available for older cars, this rebuilding procedure is often the only way to make doors fit and operate well.

Bringing a post-1948 car into outstanding shape is not as hard as with older cars, at least not from a sheetmetal standpoint. The larger body panels are easier to work with and alignment conditions are easier to control. Still, the newer cars present some special problems of their own.

After about five years, the rubber around doors and deck lids begins to deteriorate. The small rubber bumpers used to keep the hood in tension will crumble. Finding original replacements will be very difficult, since most manufacturers do not stock such parts for a long time. It is often possible to locate these items in well-established new car agencies, and occasionally usable rubber can be found on wrecked cars. When nothing else works, adapt rubber parts from newer automobiles. Most agencies stock a formed door rubber, and while this may not be exactly like the original, it will work. When attaching this type rubber, use the yellow 3M cement. It works far better than the black.

SEALING

One final area the body man will need to investigate is how well the body is sealed. Dust can enter a car through the tiniest of openings, as can water. Seal around all leaking windows with special sealing compound, dousing the area with a hose as a preliminary check. Be advised that nothing will show up a water leak like a good rain storm, so the vehicle should be checked during a rain and the leaking area marked for repair when dry.

Dust can enter the passenger and luggage compartments from any opening, but the culprit is almost always improperly sealed doors and deck lid. To check for seal, close a sheet of typing paper in the door or deck lid. Do this completely around the sealing surface, and if the paper will pull out when the door is closed, that point is not sealing. This may be a problem of alignment, or the sealer may have failed.

The super-sanitary car is that one which has received attention to detail. Not just the addition of new gimmicks, but the restoration of all stock items to like-new operation. It means, simply, that the car has been inspected from head to toe before being given that final nod of complete approval.

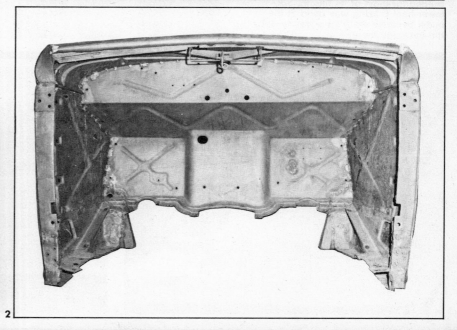

3

4

5

6

1. Before removing the bolts for any body panels such as a hood or trunk, where there are slotted holes for alignment, scribe a reference line where the parts mate to give you a starting point for later realignment.

2. Unless your project car is 100% original, you may have to undo some hot-rod butchery perpetrated long ago. This is particularly true of Fords, and many you may find will have cut-up firewalls from engine swaps. You have two choices, do a lot of time-consuming metalwork to restore the existing piece, or cut it out and weld or braze in a stock firewall from another car, as on this '36.

3. Speaking of hot-rod butchery, Ford fenders were also targets for the customizers, who "bobbed" them short such as at right. We're going to graft on the rear portion of an otherwise unrestorable '36 fender.

4. Transfer of shape of fender piece needed would be difficult with curved edges, so it was further cut in a series of straight lines for easier measurement. Snips follow tape line. Shape of needed piece was transferred to junked fender, but overlap of about 1 in. was allowed.

5. Body man Carl Green tacked the new piece on, after it had been scribed and trimmed with snips and a grinder, about an inch apart to prevent warp, then entire seam was hammer welded.

6. A light grinding to show up the remaining high and low spots, and the fender is almost new. No fillers were needed, just priming and block sanding to fill grinding marks.

SOMETHING FROM NOTHING

Sometimes it's possible to unite several assorted pieces into a single usable part. Using a door as an example again, one may have a structurally sound inner framework but with the outer panel badly rusted or shot full of holes. Another door scrounged from a wrecking yard or off a hulk rotting behind a barn may have a bent or badly deteriorated inner structure but a salvagable outer skin. The solution is to unite the best parts of each, and in restoration work this is often done.

Here are a couple of examples of what we're talking about. The first problem was with the left front fender of a '36 Ford, almost as sound as the proverbial dollar except that the trailing edge had been trimmed away by some forgotten hot rodder who wanted to sport about town minus his running boards after the fashion of the day. The rear edge of the fender had been what they called "bobbed." When this fender was bolted on the car undergoing restoration, there was a roughly pie-shaped gap up to 8-ins. wide between it and the running board. Still, the majority of the fender was in very good shape, and it was the best of several junkyard choices.

A second left front fender was obtained whose entire front p o r t i o n had been the sad looser in a battle with something very solid. Someone had evidently tried to salvage this one by bashing the damaged surface into something not too close to original shape, grinding the metal to tissue paper thickness, then laying on heavy slabs of plastic filler. To a restorer, the front half of this fender was literally useless, but the trailing edge was rust-free and straight. This particular project, then, shows joining the better parts of the two identical fenders. The trick, and there really is one, lies in accurately joining the pieces so the alignment of bolt holes and final contours is identical to the original, yet with as little metalworking as possible.

FENDER SURGERY

To follow this sequence of events we dropped by the shop of Carl Green of Van Nuys, Calif. Carl is an experienced bodyworking technician who was about to perform the surgery illustrated. As the photos reveal, only ordinary body tools and equipment were used. One accompanying photo shows the bobbed fender which was to be repaired. Notice how the cut rear edge is rounded where the original "butcher" wanted some semblance of grace on his shade tree reshaping project. It would have been time-consuming and wasted effort to transfer the outline of this irregular cut to the other fender, for there were no straight lines for accurate measurement and reference. So, the job was begun by cutting away even more of the fender.

Before work was attempted, however, the bobbed fender was solidly bolted to the car. This was not only to keep from having to chase the fender all over the shop floor when attacking it with hammer and dolly, but to hold it rigidly in position during welding so that the tendency of the metal to shift around or warp when heated would be reduced.

Masking tape was placed on the installed fender to define straight-line cuts to be made. Snips, aviation snips if you prefer, were used to follow the tape's outline as shown. This eliminated the original curved edges of the earlier trimming job.

By careful measurement from various reference points on the original fender (the bolt holes along the flanged inner edge) more tape was placed on the spare fender. About an inch of excess metal was allowed for precisely matched trimming of the edges to be butted.

The slightly too-long fender segment was cut off with an electric saber saw, a useful body shop tool that does not bend or chew up the edges of cuts in body steel. The severed piece included one of the mounting holes on its inner flange, so it was bolted on the car right where it belonged. Precise measurements were next taken to assure perfect alignment, then the piece was clamped solidly with vise grips.

A sharp-pointed awl was used to scribe a fine line on the fender segment, using the cut edge of the other fender as a template. Next the piece was removed from the car and the line followed with the snips, then dressed off with the body grinder. Now the pieces could be accurately butted together without overlap. The segment was rebolted to the car, the mating running board edge was checked for alignment then, finally, welding began.

HAMMER WELDING

The fact that body sheetmetal expands at approximately 6 millionths of an inch per degree of heat, doesn't sound like much. But when you realize a welding flame is about 1800° to 2000° F, some distortion is going to occur. Even the most carefully aligned edges of butted panels

will spread from each other at one end when welding begins at the other. To prevent this, or to at least greatly reduce this tendency, a series of short tack welds are made at widely spaced intervals.

Carl began his welding procedure with one tack weld at each end of the cut separating the fender pieces. A third tack in the middle pretty firmly joined them and would prevent movement and misalignment through heat distortion. Then, by adding additional tack welds at alternate ends of the seam, the pieces became joined, yet without a concentration of heat at any one point.

When there were enough individual tack welds so the spaces between them were about 1-in. long, Carl welded up all the gaps, hammer- and dollying each one as he went.

See the chapter on hammer welding for details on this restoration technique.

Once the accessible areas of the fender seam had been entirely welded, and the two pieces had become one single fender, the fender was once more removed from the car. The difficult and inaccessible seam areas, such as the inner flange and the outer stiffening bead, could now be finished off with torch and rod.

Light surface grinding with a small, air-driven body grinder cleaned up the welded seam of scale and burned paint, and also showed up small low and high spots that needed a little more dinging. These were places where heat distortion had moved the metal either above or below the desired level. Shrinking the spots by heating them cherry red then quickly hammer and dollying them, as when hammer welding,

shrank the metal and brought it to proper contour.

Beyond this it would be a matter of dressing the area and preparing for paint, so we'll let the matter go for now and move to the second problem on the '36 Ford.

BACK TO THE BACK

One rear fender now on the subject car had been severely bobbed, evidently by a long-ago hot rodder that preferred cruising minus running boards. Again, the area that adjoined the running board had been completely eliminated, but this particular fender is a scarce item and neither a substitute nor a second fender, damaged in another area

1. This bobbed rear fender was also a mess, with a very bad fender bead, and no place to mount running board.

2. EMT tubing, or electrical conduit in ½-in. size was a perfect substitute for the rolled fender edge. Carl brought it forward and later curved it to form the corner of the fender and a strong rim for attaching new metal.

3. A cardboard pattern was taken from the other fender, and various small patches of sheetmetal were massaged with torch and hammer until you couldn't tell the fender from an original. A 3/16-in. plate was added at the lower edge to stiffen the running board attachment point, as the fender was stiffened originally.

4. Here you can see the corner taking shape. Skillful hammer and dolly work by Carl Green saved an otherwise unusable fender. Patience in this work is a paramount virtue, of course.

5. Finished fender took only a skim coating of filler to bring it to the primer stage. Now only we know!

but from which the proper chunks could be salvaged, could be found. This would be purely a case of make-do, and a perfect example of what to do to repair body panel when another original piece can't be located.

As before, the first step was to temporarily but securely bolt the butchered fender to the car, then align and secure the running board. The huge gap between the two showed the area that would have to be entirely hand-formed.

THE CONDUIT TRICK

The outer edges of most older fenders have a rounded-under lip that strengthens the fender and prevents the start of vibration cracks. The radius of these rolled beads is approximately ½-in. in diameter. To change the beaded edge normally means hammering the rolled edge flat, making the repair or modification, then re-rolling the edge back under again with hammer and dolly. This is difficult, time consuming, and usually ends up with warped fender surfaces.

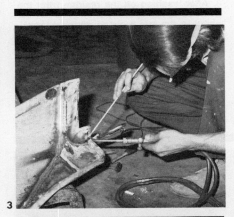
3

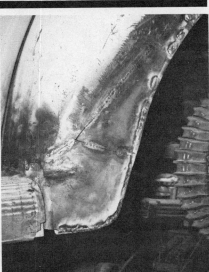
4

But there's a better way. Carl obtained a length of ½-in. diameter electrical conduit, a thin wall, low-grade steel tube with a zinc coating to prevent corrosion. It can be welded or brazed without trouble since the coating quickly burns away. The EMT, as it's called, is pliable enough in ½-in. diameter, to be formed to almost any desired contour, and it can be curved to a 1 ft. or even smaller radius if you're careful and go slowly. Carl curved the conduit by the simple expedient of bending it around a tire, then worked it more between his hands until it assumed a smooth arch matching the curve of the original fender opening.

Next, the conduit was clamped in proper alignment inside the fender where it was tack brazed at 6-in. intervals. At this point the front part of the conduit curved out into thin air, as the photos show. The conduit, if you haven't been paying attention, will form the new bead edge of the fender; it prevents the need to roll the metal under with hammer and dolly, and it provides greater strength in the bargain.

Brazing is best in a situation like this where a raw edge of metal must attach to the conduit. Welding, with its hotter flame, would distort the fender panel since its stiffening edge had been cut away, and the arched conduit itself might tend to wrinkle or collapse if too much heat were applied in one spot. By tack brazing at widely spaced intervals, though, the heat was controlled, and shortly the conduit had been solidly brazed where it joined the fender, or about half-way around the radius of the wheel opening.

5

Carl now had a rough outline of the area that would have to be bridged with new sheetmetal; one that coincided with the bobbed-off front edge where the running board must meet it.

The lower front edge of the original fender had been manufactured as a double-thickness, to provide strength where the running board bolted. Remember, all this had already been trimmed off.

A hockey-stick-shaped piece of 3/16-in. steel plate was cut using a cardboard template made from the rear running board flange. This produced a true lower edge contour of the missing fender portion, and it was tack brazed to the inner fender flange.

Various small shapes and sizes of 20-gauge sheetmetal were cut like a steel jigsaw puzzle to fill in the missing areas of the fenders. Carl preferred working with the relatively small pieces rather than a few large ones. Each was tack welded after being trimmed to fit between the cut edge of the fender and the conduit. He eyeballed the general contours as he went, using ingenuity, common sense, and several photos of 1936 Fords that clearly showed how the rear fenders originally looked. When the pieces were all tacked in place, each seam was hammer welded as discussed previously. However, where new metal was mated to the lip-forming conduit, it was brazed instead to keep welding's higher heat from buckling the thin-wall tubing.

The whole operation was brought to the roughly metal-finished stage in approximately three hours, as compared to the front fender on the same car that had required about one hour. Again, the body grinder cleaned the rear fender of weld and braze scale and burned paint, and disclosed some high and low spots that were then shrunk to proper contour with the torch, hammer, and dolly. Finally, the virtually hand-crafted rear fender was removed from the car so that the inaccessible inner flange could be properly welded. All that remained now was to permanently reinstall the fender, and prepare it for painting. It had been a tough job, one that certainly could have been eased had a complete fender been available. But it was a good lesson in making-do and proves that no matter how formidable a bodyworking job might be, forethought, patience and experience can make a complex operation really quite simple. 🐞

METAL STRIPPING

THE DIRTIEST 4-LETTER WORD IN RESTORATION IS: RUST! HERE'S HOW TO ELIMINATE IT

Next to the bane of all car enthusiasts, the "crusher," the number-one enemy of any restorer is *oxygen*. While we must have it to breathe of course, our beloved old cars decidedly don't need it. When combined with the vintage steel in their bodies, frames and chromed parts, oxygen creates what must be the nastiest four-letter word spoken in old car circles: RUST!

Whether you're restoring a Duesenberg on a $50,000 budget or a '40 Ford for a tenth of that, rust is a villain that plays no favorites. Even plastic-bodied Corvettes can suffer frame damage when exposed to the elements of air and moisture long enough. So furtive is rust in its attack on our precious sheetmetal that it can hide in areas where it can't be seen, such as in seams, behind blind panels, etc. Only after the fender has been pounded, painted, rubbed out and fondled does the villain reappear, in the form of bubbles under that new lacquer job.

Traditionally, sandblasting has been used to remove not only rust from metal, but also the many layers of just plain paint, bondo and dirt that have accumulated on a piece of sheetmetal 30 or 40 years old.

While sandblasting can be used for this purpose, unless it is done properly it can also damage fragile, contoured sheetmetal components such as quarter panels and doors. You can't just find a sandblaster in the phone book who makes a living blasting stucco and hand him a gennie fender to strip the paint off. Additionally, sandblasting will not remove anything from areas that are inaccessible to the nozzle of the gun. Many times, seams and folds in sheetmetal that can't be sandblasted are the prime rust pockets in an old car body. Often, sandblasting will leave rust in the metal that is below the surface, which will continue to

eat the metal even after the paint is applied. Sandblasting will not remove vinyl or rubber coatings, nor will it have any effect on undercoating. There are few things more difficult to remove than 40-year-old undercoating.

Sandblasting will also work-harden the surface of sheetmetal (like a shot-peening process), which makes it awfully tough for your metal man to straighten out wrinkled panels. There are other reasons that illustrate why sandblasting is not the way to strip sheetmetal, but these are bad enough. Sandblasting has been the way to go for many years only because there wasn't anything better...until now.

CHEMICAL STRIPPING

If you're just trying to remove paint and dirt from your metal parts, you can use many available

1. Redi-Strip's Bob Deringer oversees a customer's '40 Ford coupe as it is lowered into the huge tank of heated paint stripper. Even this tall a car will be completely stripped, but for a small portion of the top, which will be later hand-stripped.

2. This T body has been in the tank less than five minutes, and already the 50 years of paint and dirt are dissolving. Cars can be stripped as a complete unit, you need only remove aluminum and pot-metal parts, which are processed separately at Redi-Strip.

3. After washing off the residue from the paint-striping operation, this '40 is now about to dip into the rust removal tank. This sunken tank takes off rust with an electrolytic action that uses no metal-robbing acids.

4. Another power rinse after the rust removal, and parts are then washed down with a hot spray of phosphate, which prepares the surface for paint.

paint removers to do the job. Just be sure you do it outside (because of the toxic stripper fumes), and wear rubber gloves and eye protection. Paint strippers are not meant to be Ivory-gentle to your skin. If, after 'the paint is removed, you discover any evidence of rust, then you'll have to take a different approach to the problem. There are chemical rust removing solutions available, from the "Naval Jelly" in your local hardware store, to the chemicals advertised in some of the antique car publications. These are fine for small parts like taillight brackets, but what about the main body? When you're only restoring one car, it's foolish to buy hundreds of gallons of the stuff to dip your body parts in. Refinishing a car isn't like refinishing an old chair or table; you can't tip the car over to apply stripper on the other side. And how would you get your paintbrush full of stripper inside the water passages of your engine block to remove the scale and rust not removed by normal "hot-tank" degreasing at the machine shop?

Luckily for car enthusiasts, there is a better way, and more and more restorers are taking advantage of it. What we're talking about is complete chemical stripping and total rust removal by a commercial stripping company. There are an increasing number of such plants springing up across the country, offering paint removal for the antique furniture restorer, and paint and rust removal for the car collector. Let's take a look inside one of these plants to see how metal miracles are made.

REDI-STRIP, INC.

The Redi-Strip Co. has been doing industrial stripping of all types since

2

3

4

1953. As a matter of fact, the greatest percentage of their volume today is large-quantity industrial stripping. Their customers include aircraft and aerospace firms, computer companies, and amusement complexes like Disneyland. (Imagine having to strip the paint off 2000 trash cans every year or so by doing them one at a time). They have stripped parts for the Lunar Rover, they've done furniture and cabinets (yes, they can strip wood, also), burnt car bodies, wooden and metal-spoke wheels and guns, among millions of others. A common order for derusting might include 10,000 small brackets that have been allowed to rust before they could be used. A trip through the Redi-Strip tank can save a company thousands of dollars.

ELECTROLYTIC DERUSTING

The 11,000 sq-ft. Redi-Strip plant in El Monte, Calif. has seven large tanks for stripping, the largest a 4600-gal. paint remover. Others include an electrolytic deruster, three other paint tanks, a phosphate tank, and a chromate tank.

The process used for stripping paint involves the use of caustic (for iron and steel) and non-caustic (for aluminum) chemicals, and is well-known industrially. However, the derusting process was developed by Bob and Paul Deringer, owners of Redi-Strip, and is a closely guarded secret.

A typical paint and rust stripping job of a steel car body (a 1927 Model T Turtledeck Roadster is shown) would involve the following steps:

1. Caustic Paint Tank: The caustic paint stripper tank, in which the chemicals are heated by burners under the tank, will strip most any body of all paint and undercoating in a matter of minutes.

2. Rinse-Wash: A fresh water rinse to check for complete paint removal. Perhaps another dip in the caustic tank will be necessary.

3. Derust: The body is submerged in an electro-chemical solution and the rust is separated from the metal using an electrolytic theory of molecular separation. When it comes out of this tank, all rust has been eliminated, leaving only healthy metal.

4. The body can now be rinsed off by high-pressure washers. The controls on the washers are then changed, and now a phosphate coating is applied by the hot, high-pressure washers. This not only etches the metal slightly (like Metal-Prep) to give your paint a toothed surface for adhesion, but keeps the part from rusting until you can get out the spraygun and lay several good coats of primer on.

ALUMINUM

All parts should be as free of oil and grease as possible when sent to Redi-Strip. This will save time and keep costs down. Assemblies which include dissimilar metals—for example, steel studs in an aluminum head—should be broken down as far as possible to eliminate having to fit special electrodes prior to stripping.

Aluminum can be stripped of corrosion (water jackets), and acid-dipped if specially requested. Aluminum must be handled separately from steel parts so don't leave any aluminum castings bolted to a steel body. They may melt in the tank. Ordinarily, the crew at Redi-Strip is very conscientious when handling customer parts, but it might be possible to miss one.

The derusting process won't affect organic material like wood, rubber or hemp. The stripping will dry out the wood, thoroughly cleaning it, and perhaps raising the grain. In many cases the wood can be used without any problems, although laminated woods such as plywood may separate if the solutions dissolve the glues in the wood. Excessively dry wood can be used again

1. Parts are sprayed thoroughly top and bottom to ensure that rust doesn't start again on the now-cleaned metal.

2. Smaller parts are dipped into the tanks in these baskets. Here some of the '40 Ford parts are waiting for the tank, in company with two antique cast-iron bed frames!

3. This before and after comparison of the '40 Ford engine compartment vividly shows why this is the best starting point for a restoration. It's a lot easier to work on a *clean* car.

4. Most stripping processes leave a black, oxidized effect on aluminum parts, but Redi-Strip has cleaned these rare, early Healey panels to bright, like-new appearance.

5. Stripping is really the only way to completely clean out the water passages in engine blocks, like the flathead Ford and 283 Chevy hovering here over the bubbling tank of hot rust remover and electrical plates.

6. The lot outside of a Redi-Strip facility usually contains a variety of parts awaiting stripping, rusty steel shelving, corroded lawn chairs, and a melange of antique car parts.

for patterns. It is amazing to see the dirt and grime literally pour from rubber tires when they are submerged in the tank. The tanks are drained and cleaned once a month and the residues that accumulate on the bottom are disposed of in an approved industrial fashion; they are definitely not flushed into the sewer system.

The Redi-Strip derusting process is patented and is their exclusive property. However, the company is currently involved in an expansion program, franchising the process to operators around the country. In fact, they now have a total of six locations. What's interesting is that, even though the "Mother" plant in Los Angeles does 90% industrial work and 10% antique car parts, the newer franchised locations are dealing mainly in automotive work. Bob Deringer says that at least two of his franchise holders are car nuts themselves who learned of the company through the third edition of our *Complete Ford Book!*

Bob Deringer and engineer Eric Price are always anxious to help you with any problems or questions you might have regarding a stripping project so feel free to call them before shipping your project their way. They do a lot of classic-car work, stripping parts that are nearly irreplaceable, so you can trust them with anything.

Redi-Strip derusting is really the only way to completely remove rust from the water jackets of a cast iron engine, so the company is now doing quite a few engine blocks for restorers and rodders. It's *the* guaranteed method of achieving like-new cooling for your older engine block.

Rodders and restorers in the Los Angeles area have been taking advantage of the fabulous Redi-Strip derusting service for years, as have builders from all over the country who ship parts to them. The time and money saved more than compensates for the shipping charges, especially when you consider the cost of improperly handled parts lost or damaged by other methods of stripping.

About the only thing that the Redi-Strip people can't remove from your sheetmetal is the dents. But you can be sure, aside from that, when they are through with it, it will be as good as new in all other respects.

RESTORING STRUCTURAL WOOD QUALITY WOOD PARTS DON'T GROW ON TREES; HERE ARE A FEW TIPS ON HOW TO BUILD 'EM

BY JAY STORER

If you're new to the auto restoration field, you may not realize how extensive a part wood can play in restoring an old vehicle. Wood was the traditional construction material in the pre-gasoline-engine period for coaches and carriages, and its use in bodybuilding continued for three decades or more into the automobile's development. Woodworkers have told us they have seen cars as late as 1954 (Mercedes) with wood still used in the doors, and undoubtedly there are custom-crafted cars being built even today in Europe in whose construction wood still plays a role.

If you've ever worked with wood, you may find it a frustrating material, but for custom bodybuilding it has many desirable properties. Until sheetmetal stamping development brought all-steel construction to all major manufacturers, wood represented the major structural strength

of many of the vehicles we're most interested in.

Since the carriage-building days, the percentage of wood used in auto body construction has continuously declined. Some of the earliest cars, like the buggies that preceded them, were almost entirely wood except for the engine, the screws and the tires. Some early cars even used wood in suspension parts: One horseless carriage we've seen had a wooden front axle. Also, many of these low-torque conveyances got by with wooden frame rails. As engine power escalated, the chassis and suspensions were made of steel, but coachwork was still largely wood, since it was easy to shape and hand labor was still cheap.

A little later, manufacturers discovered they could build better-looking cars more quickly by using stamped-steel fenders and covering the wooden body shells with sheet-

metal panels, which accepted a nice paint job a lot better than their "lumbering" ancestors.

This type of construction became more or less the standard for most cars for the next 20 years or so, with Fords being the outstanding exception. Mr. Ford pioneered the use of more and more steel in his Model T's, until wood was basically being used only to facilitate the attachment of hardware and upholstery. While other cars were being built out of wood and covered with sheetmetal, Fords were built out of steel and lined with wood.

This may sound like a merely semantic difference, but you General Motors enthusiasts will bear witness that this can make all the difference in auto restoration. For example, let's take two cars, a 1928 Ford sedan and a 1928 Chevrolet sedan. Let them sit outside in the elements for, say, 40 years. If all the wood rots

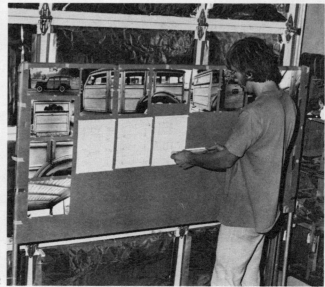

PHOTOS BY JAY STORER AND ERIC RICKMAN

away on the Ford, you still have a recognizable automobile, while on the Chevrolet, the rotting of the wood means that the doors, rear body and perhaps even the cowl have lost all connection to the car and have fallen off, to further accelerate their decay on the ground. This is an extreme comparison, but it illustrates what a difference these two construction methods can make when it comes time to restore one of our favorite vintage cars.

DON'T JUMP THE GUN

If the particular car of your dreams, when it finally finds its way into your garage, dates from the Twenties or Thirties, chances are there is at least some structural wood in it that may need replacement. (We're not dealing with woodie station wagons, Sportsmans or Town & Countrys here; external "beauty" wood is discussed elsewhere in this book.) The absolutely first thing for you to do is to resist the tremendous temptation to do something. As with anything else mechanical, and particularly when you're talking about restoring things, your first move should be toward detailed study and investigation rather than immediate and wanton disassembly. Failure to do so has caused many a machine to appear in the Sunday classifieds de-

scribed as "1927 _ _ _ _ _ sedan, complete but disassembled; needs work, must sell."

Borrow a quality camera, roll the car outside on a sunny day and take a roll or two of black and white pictures before you disassemble anything. You'll be miles ahead later on when you try to piece the jigsaw puzzle back together again. If you can, get a camera that is capable of

fairly close work, to allow you to shoot as close as 2 ft. away for details of complicated structural joints. Shoot closeups of all the metal brackets as they look when installed. The photos will be an invaluable aid, as many of the metal support braces and brackets may look similar but fit only one way.

It would also help to make a complete schematic of the wood pieces

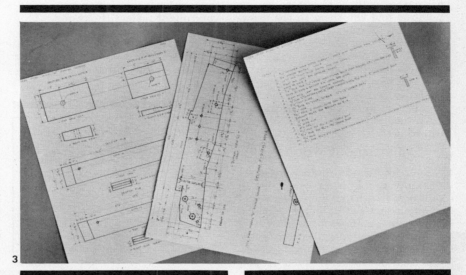

3

4

5

1. Hopefully your first venture into antique auto woodworking will be less of a challenge than this 1926 Buick, but with patience and determination even it can be a concours winner.

2. Before taking out that first screw, make a photographic record of all the wood pieces in your car, especially joints and unusual parts. The photos, plus photos of restored examples of the same year and model, will come in extremely handy for later reference.

3. Woodworker Bradley Brown makes detailed "blueprints" of original wood parts before he duplicates them. These '32 Ford woodie parts sheets include detailed notes on holes, etc.

4. An otherwise sound wood part with a crack in it can be repaired with today's "superglues," but most restorers replace any damaged structural wood.

5. In some cases, a repaired crack should be further strengthened with the addition of a wooden dowel.

6. Even if new and old pieces are mated in the finished woodwork (as on this '30 Cadillac, where only one section needed replacing), your primary consideration should be the strength and authenticity of your woodwork. Alas, none of your hard work will show after the car's upholstered.

6

in your car. In other other words, make a drawing showing the location of all the parts. Add to this drawing notes on the measurements of all these pieces, lengths and sizes of screws and their locations, and the diagonal measurements (from corner to corner) wherever there is a "box" formed by four or more pieces of wood, such as in door frames. Then you can mark the ends of each piece with code letters and/or numbers and key them to the drawings and photographs. With this "blueprint" mounted on the wall of your garage for reference, you can begin to disassemble the wood from the car. Even with these graphic guides to go by, it may still be safer to work on only one side of the car at a time, so the other, stock side can be used for reference.

A BIT ABOUT WOODS

Your first venture into woodworking can be confusing when you're confronted with the incredible variety of nature's building materials. There are hundreds of wood types, all with varying qualities that make them suitable for some uses and impractical for others. Even if you study wood all your life, there are varieties which, stripped of their foliage and bark, you still can't positively identify in their board form. So how does the restorer know what to shop for? Luckily, there are only a few types of wood suitable for structural use in antique automobiles.

Most wood originally installed in cars for structural purposes was oak, although ash was used on some Fords and maple and birch on most woodie station wagons. Oak may not be the best material for the job, but it is the one most widely used in restoration, and it is certainly adequate in terms of strength and dura-

bility. There are many cheaper woods than oak, of course, but structural wood is no place to cheapen your restoration project.

A hardwood like oak is needed because of the stresses and strains an automobile body is put through in normal driving, because it is resistant to decay and because it will hold screws and upholstery nails firmly. If you really wanted to do the finest possible job on your wood, you might select boxwood. This wood is about three times as expensive as oak, but extremely durable. A framework of boxwood in your car would probably outlast the sheetmetal.

The oak you shop for should be seasoned red or white Eastern oak. Naturally seasoned wood is really the best, because it dries out the wood's natural juices the slowest and makes wood its hardest. However, naturally seasoned wood will be impossible to find at your local hardwood supply, since oak takes 2 to 5 years to season naturally. Most wood that you'll encounter at a lumberyard has been artificially seasoned by kiln-drying. Make sure that it *is* kiln dried, though; the only thing worse than artificially seasoned wood is *green* wood, and some lumberyards sell it.

If there is a choice available, choose the red oak over the white. While the white oak is slightly more resistant to decay, the red oak is less apt to split when screws are driven into it and is less prone to shrinkage and swelling. When you're pawing through the selection of boards in the oak section of your local lumberyard or hardwood supply, look for pieces with the straightest grain. If there are several price grades, get the best grade offered.

Not that it will make much difference in your shopping, but we can tell you that the wood should have been felled in midwinter, too. At this time the vegetation is at rest and the sap is down, so less seasoning is required.

We all know that wood "grows on trees," but what we may not realize is that when round logs are cut up into flat boards, there are any number of ways to cut the logs, with each method making for a different grain pattern in the boards. The chief sawyer of a lumbermill has a heavy task. As a huge log of oak or other expensive wood heads toward the blade, he must quickly determine exactly how this log is to be cut, a decision that could mean thousands of dollars lost if he is wrong.

Stay away from the curved end grain (see illustration) and look for the pieces with the straightest grain, because these have the least tenden-

4

1. It takes an experienced eye to really select the best wood, but you can get in the ballpark by examining the end grain. Boards like one at top are not as suitable as the example below, because some of the grain lines run from the top to the side, which may induce splitting. Look for oak with the straightest grain patterns.

2. Trace the shape of your old part onto the new oak, leaving a safe margin around the edges. Cut the part to shape with a bandsaw or table saw, but bring it to its final shape and size only by sanding.

3. A car like this, with its sheetmetal-over-wooden-framework body, is a restoration project not to be undertaken lightly. Note the kickup at the rear of the "frame" and the curve of the deck support. These pieces can only be duplicated by laminating pieces together. Hanging the doors, decklid and golf bag door were no easy tasks either. This is for pros.

4. Here California Metal Shaping is building virtually a brand-new body, both wood and sheetmetal, for this rare phaeton. Don't finish any of your wood parts until you've checked them for fit with the metal skin.

5. Some of the wood you'll replace will be a tough fit inside the steel, such as this front header. Remember that you're building backward from the factory, where all the metal was added only *after* the wood structure.

6. The canvas top on closed cars is one of the first parts to deteriorate on a wood-based car. Arrows indicate the all-important upper stringers which hold the doorposts in alignment. Bradley Brown is adding the slotted side pieces which will hold the main structural top bows in place.

5

6

cy to warp. If any of the pieces you're duplicating will be exposed when the car is done, you'll be glad to know that these boards also have the prettiest grain patterns after varnishing.

DUPLICATING WOODEN PARTS

Even when dealing with good-quality oak, your biggest problem will be possible warpage of the wood after you've cut it to size, since the wood you're buying is artificially seasoned. Your best approach to this problem is to do the woodwork in your car *last*. Naturally, if there is a lot of structural wood to replace in your car, you can't restore everything (like paint and upholstery) before the wood is done, but wait as long as possible. Before you do any other work on the car, buy all the oak you think you'll need (if in doubt, buy extra) and store it in a dry place. Stack the pieces alternately (criss-cross) so that air can move around and between them. This is natural seasoning, and the longer you do it, the less prone to warpage the wood will be. Then start your restoration on the chassis and driveline. A year or two later, when that's all done, you can take down your oak and start cutting out the new pieces for the body.

On most cars you won't need to replace every single piece of wood, but even those original pieces that appear in good shape should be removed for repairs, cleaning and sealing. Use your own judgment when you inspect wooden parts. If the part is basically sound, even though it may have a crack or two, it can be repaired, but a thorough restoration would require that it be replaced.

Some compound-curved pieces may be very difficult for you to du-

plicate, so the original piece can be repaired if salvageable. Cracks are repaired by opening them with a screwdriver, squirting in wood glue, removing the screwdriver and clamping overnight. A part or joint of two parts that needs further strengthening can be drilled and a wooden dowel inserted. If you do any doweling, be sure to clamp and glue the piece beforehand. Use fluted dowels, too, because they hold a quantity of glue as they are driven in.

There are several routes that you can go in restoring your structural wood. You can do it yourself, buy a ready-made wood "kit" or take your oak stock and your old parts to a local woodworker for duplication. Shop wisely for a kit if you take that approach (check our directory

of suppliers), since the kits we've seen vary widely in quality. Some kits even employ softwoods, which will not hold your screws or upholstery nails firmly.

If you like the idea of doing the wood yourself, then don't make any plans for the winter; the woodwork will keep you busy enough. You'll need to borrow, buy or rent three basic shop tools: A table saw and bandsaw are necessary for cutting out the straight and curved sections, and a combination belt/disc sander is a must for final shaping and smoothing.

The basic procedure is to trace the pattern of the old piece directly onto the new oak, giving yourself a good margin around the edges. Cut the straight sides with the table saw

and the curved sides with the band-saw. After trial-fitting the piece in the car, sand the wood to remove all saw marks and arrive at the final size and shape.

The wooden pieces in just one car are so varied that it is impossible to describe duplication procedures for all of them here. You will encounter joints and shapes that are difficult to duplicate. Some of these you can make on the table saw, and some will have to be cut with a router. Even the very complicated finger joints sometimes used on early cars can be duplicated on a table saw if you have an indexing head. Make one cut at a time, then index over a precise amount and make your next cut. Above all, go slowly and carefully. Hand sand the fingers if you have to, but get a tight fit with no gaps. This precision fit is important to the strength of the joint.

Hand sanding, though, can be as dangerous as machine sanding, even with a sanding block. If you don't think so, practice for awhile on a scrap piece of wood. Take a piece with rounded edges and try to sand them all square and sharp by hand. Chances are you will tend to round off the edges when hand sanding. If you're aware of this tendency, you can work to avoid it.

Inletting door posts for hinges and latches is done with a router by most pros, but a slip with this tool and you'll be starting over with a new piece of wood. A hinge gets its support from a very tight fit into the wood, and your woodie/steelie needs all the support you can give it. The easiest way to do it *right* is to mortise the hinge areas by hand, with a hammer and a very sharp wood chisel. We didn't say it would be quick.

To get properly started on a tight fit, don't make the mistake of tracing the hinge's outline with a pencil, because cutting along that line will make the mortised area slightly oversize. Use a knife blade to trace the outline more closely. Doing the inletting by hand is slow and takes practice (on scrap wood), but it can produce a job to be proud of.

Something to remember about wood is that it warps toward the *bark* side (outside of the tree). Therefore, never construct a joint in such a way that the natural tendency of the two pieces of wood is to ruin the joint. You can tell which is the bark side and which is the heart side by examining the end grain. Another construction tip that early bodybuilders went by was to build door pillars with the heart side to the outside of the body and stationary pillars with the heart side to the inside.

INSTALLING YOUR NEW WOOD

When every piece has been trial-fitted in place on the car, it's time to drill countersunk holes for all your screws. The drilling has to be precise, so you need a full set of drill bits, plus a countersink bit. Follow our chart to find the recommended clearance and pilot hole sizes for various screws. You're dealing with very hard wood, so if the holes aren't drilled big enough, the screwheads will give up before the oak when you try to force them in.

Where you're mounting two pieces of wood together in a corner, clamp both parts of the joint together and drill them as a unit. If you drill them separately, there's always some misalignment.

Fit together, drill and screw all your pieces and assemble them *in the car* at least once before final installation. It's not enough to trial-fit all the parts to the car body individually. They have to fit each other *and* conform to your original blueprint for diagonal and other measurements.

Since you'll be dealing (at least in the case of a closed-car body) with quite a number of fasteners, you can buy them in volume for a good

1. The structural bows are notched at the ends to fit into slots on the side pieces. Assembly is tricky here, because the side pieces must spread enough for you to insert the bows.

2. The thin wood battens that give the top upholstery its support are nailed to the structural bows but must be drilled and screwed at the ends, where they might split if nailed. Beeswax is used to lubricate screws.

3. Some of the shapes you'll come across will have to be duplicated with a router, so you may elect to take those to a professional woodshop if you don't have router experience.

4. Rebuilding a wooden car is just like a jigsaw puzzle. You may have to clamp many unfinished parts in place and go on to the next parts before checking for final fit.

5. Woodworker Frank Fowler deepens a notch here to fit the upper part of this phaeton's rear door jamb. A part is never nailed back in place until it has been thoroughly sealed.

4

5

price. Get high-quality, plated screws. There's absolutely no sense in reusing any of the original screws. After you've measured them and marked your "blueprint" to pinpoint their location, throw the old screws away. When shopping for screws, look for clean, sharp threads and well-cut screwdriver slots. In case nails are also used in your car's body, and undoubtedly they are, don't buy standard supermarket nails. Use nonferrous *marine* nails of the same sizes as those originally used on your car.

To fasten the lengthwise top battens to the bows (in cars which don't have an all-steel roof), you should probably use brass screws instead of steel, due to the danger of rust in this area. Always mount a thinner piece to a thicker one rather than the other way around. Also, a screw should be twice as long as the piece you are mounting is thick.

A very important step before installing any of your wood for the last time is to apply two coats of *marine* wood sealer to all sides of your parts. All your cast iron and sheetmetal angle brackets and braces should be sandblasted or stripped perfectly clean and painted with Rustoleum or epoxy paint. Of course, if you have any plywood flooring in your early vehicle, it should be replaced only with *marine* plywood. These parts should receive extra coats of sealer as well, especially around all the porous edges. After the parts are nailed and screwed into place inside your car's body, you may want to dab another light coat of sealer over the fasteners and on any spots where you may have nicked the wood with your tools.

For the sake of your car and your sanity, don't use any *glue* if you can help it, certainly not on any parts that were not glued originally. There are two reasons for this, and they're both good ones. First, glue makes your wooden parts virtually impossible to replace in the future without cutting the parts out or breaking them. Second—and more important—glue will make the body too stiff. Most of your hard work will be for naught, as you drive down the street to the accompaniment of creaks, groans and even the sound of your new wood cracking and splintering. All-steel bodies may be designed stiff, but a sheetmetal-over-wood body such as yours is designed to flex a little as the car travels over uneven roads, and all

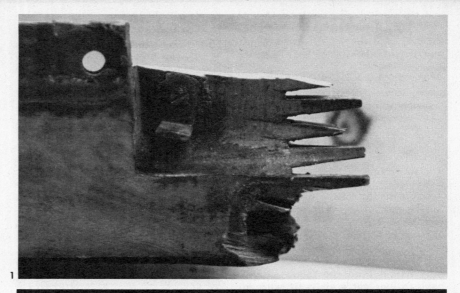

1

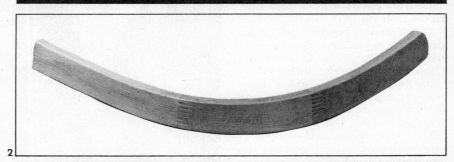

2

3

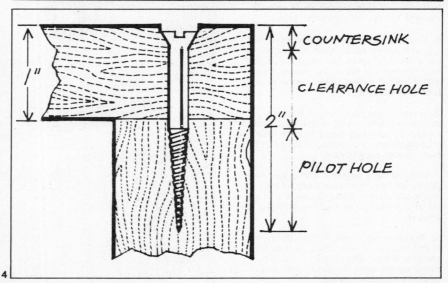

COUNTERSINK

CLEARANCE HOLE

PILOT HOLE

1"

2"

4

the joints take part in this flexing. If you glue everything together at each joint, there's no chance for the wood to "work" and it will crack or split.

Even if you have restored other cars before and are fully competent in mechanical work, bodywork and the other skills called for in a complete restoration, this may be your first "adventure" in woodworking. You have to learn a new approach, because wood has many desirable working properties, but you can't treat it as you would metal. If you cut a piece of wood too short, for instance, you can't weld on another piece, grind down the weld and paint over it so no one will ever know. Wood can be very unforgiving of mistakes, so the best advice is to measure and trial-fit constantly. And go slowly. We'll quote here the motto of a famous wood shop teacher, which bears hanging on your shop wall: "Measure three times . . . cut once."

WOOD SCREW SIZE	CLEARANCE HOLE	PILOT HOLE	
		SOFT WOOD	HARDWOOD
#4	1/8''	1/16''	5/64''
5	9/64	5/64	3/32
6	9/64	5/64	3/32
7	5/32	3/32	7/64
8	11/64	3/32	7/64
9	3/16	7/64	1/8
10	3/16	7/64	1/8
12	7/32	1/8	5/32

5

6

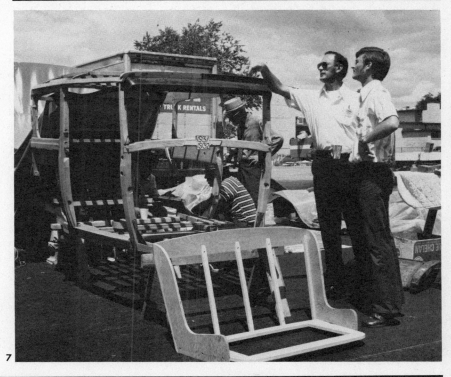

7

1. Even a complicated finger joint can be duplicated at home with your table saw and a dose of patience.

2. Finger joints were used on many antique cars, where they provided a strong joint for curved shapes made from several different pieces.

3. There are places in your wood where parts are attached with bolts rather than screws. For them you'll use threaded inserts. The two at left here are originals which were screwed or nailed to the wood, while the one at right is a modern piece which you drive into the wood with a hammer.

4. Ideally, a wood screw should be twice as long as the piece it is used to mount. Notice here that the screw *shank* is long enough to extend a bit into the second piece, giving the joint a dowelling effect for strength.

5. The proper size clearance and pilot holes are extremely important to get screw tension without splitting the wood. In the hardwoods you'll be using, it's even more important.

6. Plywood flooring should only be replaced with marine-quality plywood. This should be thoroughly sealed, especially around the porous edges and wherever you drill for screws.

7. Many wood kits are becoming available now, including these for Chevrolets, seen at the national meet of the Vintage Chevrolet Club. You should get a written guarantee of satisfaction before you buy through the mails, though. We've heard of kits that don't fit and use poor wood. Check our list of suppliers for kits.

PAINT: FROM THE BEGINNING HOW PAINTING DEVELOPED, FROM CHARIOTS TO SOYBEANS

BY RICHARD T. PARKER

Tombs in China, Mesopotamia and Egypt disclosed that dyes, inks and paints had originated far back in the mists of history. Chariots of the Egyptian Empire era (call it 1200 B.C.) were already expertly painted and gold-leafed. Pigments were local, blood was a popular binder, and brushes were made from animal or human hair bound to reeds or twigs. The world has never lost its interest in painting...nor its interest in chariots. Seemingly paint and pigment technology progressed little in the next 2500 years, which brings us to the renaissance (say the 1400's), when painters spent much of their time experimenting with sticky tree saps, searching for suitable metal oxides for pigments, scraping soot from hearths, and climbing mountains in quest of colored rock outcroppings soft enough to grind into pigments. Eventually their efforts were rewarded, and the information was disseminated, despite their living in an era of illiteracy in which little technical information was transmitted other than from father to son. Considering that many pigments are color unstable (like the beautiful blue-green copper oxides) and chemically incompatible with other pigments, one must respect the accumulated knowledge of those renaissance painters who were able to grind and mix their pigments with oils and solvents such that now, 500 years later, their surviving paintings still retain brilliant colors! Little wonder that 10 and 20 year apprenticeships were required to learn the complex arts of the master painters.

Again, let us jump several centuries to the 1700's, when specialized carriage painters were developing their skills on royal coaches. By then, ochre; umber; indigo; cochineal; red oxides from lead, iron, cadmium and mercury; yellow and green oxides from chromium; gray and white oxides from lead; and carbon black (saved by chimney sweeps) were available, as were turpentine, linseed oil and bristle brushes. Some of these were the valuable cargoes of sailing ships visiting major world ports.

BRUSHES

Quill pens, sponges, and rollers were easy inventions. Surely someone in antiquity discovered that blowing through a quill dipped in paint would spray paint a surface. For at least the last century, the best brushes have been made from Manchurian boar bristles. Rather significantly, during WW-II when their supply was interrupted, painters became desperate: they decried the rayon fiber substitutes. (American hogs and cattle have hair too short to make good bristle brushes.) Egyptian camel's hair is still the favorite for varnish and striping brushes. Painters have always been real individualists in the selection of their brushes. For painting automobiles, painters liked to buy the most expensive brushes—especially when their employers paid for them. Some painters, presumably inferring loudly how hard they worked, claimed that they would wear out a brush in a day; others were satisfied to use a brush gently for a year. Because new brushes shed some bristles, and because camel's hair brushes shed minute whiskers (known on TV as "split ends"), new brushes were "worked in" by a "boy" who sat down with a bucket of dirty varnish, and, for hours, painted varnish back and forth across a board grooved like a butter paddle. Hopefully, this removed all of the loose debris. When not in use, varnish brushes and striping brushes were dipped in slow-drying raw linseed oil and stored flat on a pane of glass. Early striping brushes consisted of a little bundle of camel's hairs about 2½ inches long, pulled through a quill. A drop of glue down the quill secured the hairs. Sword stripers (larger bundles of camel's hairs trimmed to a point and tied to a short handle with a fishing line)

appeared in the Twenties, and are still used. Painters could easily spend half an hour in the morning and another half hour at the end of the day performing rituals for their brushes.

RUBBING COMPOUNDS

Only vaguely can one conjecture when scouring powders, rubbing compounds and sandpaper first came into use. The surfaces of Egyptian chariots were smooth, indicating that some form of polishing compound had been used. In Egypt, volcanic ash (pumice) was readily available. Straining it through cloth to obtain various degrees of courseness would have been easy; sifting it onto sticky papyrus would have made "sandpaper." Well into this century the numerous coats of paint on carriages and automobiles were rubbed smooth with blocks of wood, water and suitable grinds of pumice. The finest grind was called "Fuller's Earth." By the Twenties, rubber blocks had displaced the wood blocks. Otherwise, hand rubbing compounds and techniques have changed little in 3000 years!

THE MEN

Artisans and craftsmen have always been members of caste systems, reinforced by guilds and unions. Among the men who applied paint and varnish to carriages and automobiles, unskilled laborers performed the wiping and cleaning operations; mechanics were called to diassemble and reassemble components for the painters' convenience; artisans performed the sandpapering and rubbing operations; skilled craftsmen mixed and applied the paint; varnishers (who were to paint shops what prima donnas were to opera) applied the varnish; and artists striped the bodies. Rather interestingly, at the Ford factory when they were building 900 Model A's a day, one striper, chewing a water-logged cigar (the only man in the factory permitted to smoke on the job), striped every car body as it came from the assembly

Early finishing techniques were laborious and time-consuming, slowing the capabilities of production lines. The simple economic truth behind the famous Henry Ford statement, "You can have a Model T in any color you want, as long as it's black," was that Mr. Ford found it the fastest-drying paint color then available!

line. One wonders what happened when he was home ill for a day. Master painters also dealt in "snake oil" additives, secret pigment mixtures, and they developed intense loyalties to certain expensive brands of paint (possibly aided by under-the-table benefits from the paint salesman). Although all businesses decree im-

mediate dismissal for drinking alcoholic beverages on the job, painters have been tacitly exempted from that rule. Customarily, painters keep a bottle of whiskey in their paint locker "to cut the paint out of their throats." Considering the many things which could go wrong during an automobile body's long stay in the paint and varnish shop, being a lucky painter was often better than being a skilled painter. Sometimes paints, for inexplicable reasons, refused to dry; roof leaks dripped muddy water on fresh varnish; sunshine coming through the windows caused fresh varnish to blister; dust storms wrought their havoc; there were flying insects, runs, smears, fin-

ger prints (curious passersby have an uncontrollable urge to put a finger in the center of a panel to check if the paint is dry), scrapes . . . . Hell knoweth no fury like that of the master painter after a mechanic scratched a cowl while installing a windshield frame. Little wonder painters were superstitious.

THE BASIC INGREDIENTS FOR OIL-BASE PAINT

Ground gray lead oxide is chemically stable and is the cheapest pigment. Note how well it lasts on battleships! The oxides of lead, titanium, cadmium, iron, mercury, and chromium provide most of the colors. Mixing with white lead or white titanium oxide lightens the colors; mixing with carbon black darkens the colors. The iridescent shell of the Brasilian cochineal bug, when ground, makes the magenta and burgundy pigments (and, incidentally, red and violet ink). Being an organic compound, cochineal powder oxidizes and discolors in the sun and rain. Being quite translucent, it must be painted over a red iron oxide primer or a black undercoating. Linseed oil, pressed from linen seed, is the popular binder for paint, although, in the Orient, tung oil, soy oil, and sap from the broad leafed tree, Rhus vernicifera, are used as binders. Unlike motor oil, these oils oxidize and dry, leaving a shiny surface. Raw linseed oil dries very slowly and is used principally for protecting metal, as in bridge paint. Boiled linseed oil, mixed with pigment, becomes carriage and automobile paint. Pine tree sap, when distilled, produces volatile turpentine and a sticky residue called rosin. (Chemists distinguish the synthetic product by spelling it "resin.") Rosin mixed with linseed oil makes varnish. Pigment mixed with rosin and linseed oil makes enamel, or color-varnish. Turpentine is the thinning and drying agent. Fortunately the petro-chemical industry developed synthetic thinner, resins and pigments just as the paint industry was confronting the awkward fact that there were not enough pine trees in the world to satisfy future demands. Painters liked to paint automobiles black: there were less complaints from customers. A little yellow pigment added to black made Brewster Green. The predominance of white lead oxide in light-colored paints caused these paints to "chalk." Light colors and bright colors tended to fade badly. Light blue was the most fugitive of all: so, if you wished to give the impression of magnificent opulence, you had your McFarlane Roadster painted in Robin's Egg Blue—and then kept it out of the sun! A gray-purple pigment, for reasons not clear, was called "Lake." Perhaps to a mentality still remembering the mauve decade (1890-1900), it was "the most elegant of all colors," and was most appropriate for Pierce Arrow limousines.

Mixtures of these many variables were the secret art of the master painters and varnishers: after all, handling the bristle brush and the camel's hair varnish brush were arts akin to violin playing!

During the one to three months

the automobile body was in the paint shop, it received 6 to 12 coats of paint and varnish, and, after the last coat of varnish was applied, the body remained in the paint shop two weeks to a month for the varnish to harden sufficiently for the body to be handled by the trimmers and assemblers. By necessity, paint shops were enormous. After arriving in the paint shop on a dolly, the new body was sandpapered smooth; it was then brush painted with a gray primer, a mixture of lead oxide, boiled linseed oil and turpentine. After drying several days, the primer was dry-sandpapered or "blocked out" using a block of wood, water and pumice. The primer sequence was repeated several times until the painter was satisfied with the surface. Then the more expensive color pigments were mixed with boiled linseed oil and turpentine, applied, dried, rubbed. Rosin was added to subsequent coats and called color varnish: it did not sandpaper well. The last coat of clear varnish was applied in a hosed-down, dust-free area with northern light. Where the environment was too dusty, the varnish was applied in a closed booth, often without windows. The varnisher would stand or squat on the wet floor holding a drop-cord light in one hand and his varnish brush in the other hand. Once started, the varnishing would continue till complete, regardless of the hour. Varnish was not "brushed in," as this was said to "beat the life out of the varnish." Instead, it was daubed on and immediately finished with a minimum of up-strokes. Runs were pulled down. After each brush full of varnish was applied, the brush was wiped over the edge of the "dirty varnish can" to remove the remaining varnish plus any dust picked up from the surface or corners. When dust particles settled on the fresh varnish, they were called "lice," and were laboriously picked up with a small brush with a little sticky varnish on the tip. The best varnish was imported from England. The finished varnish had a beautiful shine, showed no brush marks, and was not rubbed down. New car owners were advised not to use body polish for at least a month lest it imbed in the surface, and they were advised, likewise, not to park in hot sunshine lest it melt the rosin or blister the varnish. One of the standard rainy day chores was drying the car with a chamois skin immediately after the rain, or immediately after

garaging. The more prudent person did not take his car out in the rain.

A varnish job was expected to last about 3 years before it checked and discolored. Aluminum hoods and close fitting hoods were mortal enemies to the paint on them. In Europe, polished aluminum hoods with no paint on them were popular, but in the U.S. unpainted aluminum hoods developed a coating of aluminum hydroxide, and pitted. Americans didn't want to bother with the daily oily rag treatment. Varnish finishes had other mortal enemies: sunshine bleached the cowls; bird spots etched the surface; rain drops left permanent discolorations; and sap dripping from trees left sticky spots in the varnish. Even scratches and minor collision damage required tediously refinishing large areas, and never, never did the repainted area match the rest of the car—unless the car was black! A 1925 Nash advertisement stated: "28 days are required to apply 10 coats of paint to a Nash." Depending upon weather and temperature, painting an automobile required anywhere from three days at the Ford factory to three months for elegant multi-color paint jobs on fine cars. Obviously, Henry Ford was smart in offering "any color you want so long as it's black." Ford weakened in 1926: the sedans were painted in burgundy and the coupes were in green. (The following year, Model T sedans and coupes were spray painted in Duco.) By 1915, spray equipment was available for painting trucks, for applying gray primer, for applying cheap varnish, and for applying black baked enamel on radiators, hoods, fenders, lamps and aprons. Gas heated drying booths were already being used, although they had a bad habit of exploding.

BAKED ENAMEL

About '15, a chemically very stable synthetic resin was developed, which would dry only at elevated temperatures. The drying was a combination of oxidation and polymerization. Mixed with carbon black, this was known as black baked enamel. It retained its shine, did not check nor bleach, and was immediately accepted. On cheap automobiles, even when the body was a different color, the hood was finished in black baked enamel. Naturally, bodies with wood in them could not be baked. However, in 1912, the Budd Company had developed and shown all-steel bodies. When the Dodge was introduced in 1916, it

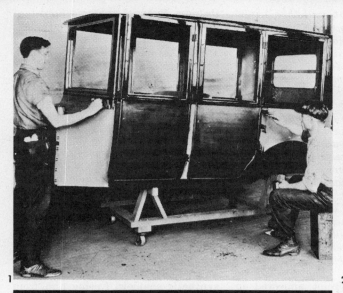

1. Early paint jobs, consisting of lampblack and varnish, were applied by hand, dried between the many coats and then rubbed out with pumice and water. It could take as long as 4 weeks to complete a paint job. Photo courtesy of Du Pont.

2. The 1924 Oakland introduced Duco nitrocellulose lacquer, a production breakthrough. Not only was it more durable and faster drying, but could be applied by spraygun rather than by hand. Photo courtesy of Du Pont.

was furnished with a Budd all-steel body finished in black baked enamel. The ovens were so large as to be a source of great amazement in the industry. Then, in '26 and '27 the all-steel Ford Roadster and Touring Car bodies were finished in black baked enamel. In '23 some other colors, including red-orange, were available in baked enamel, but they chipped easily. But wait. Something better was on the horizon!

REPAINTING AN ENTIRE CAR

This was considered to be quite out of the province of the do-it-yourselfer. True, one-coat enamels were available, and some eager souls even painted their cars black with stove enamel. For reasons not always clear, they seemed always to be proud of their work. A good repaint job necessitated de-commissioning the car for one to three months. Fenders, hood, lights, aprons, runningboards, wheels door handles and accessories were removed and spread out on saw horses around the car. Tacks and trim strips were removed from the cloth tops and the upholstery, and the top and uphol-

stery were either removed or tied back out of the way. The chassis was steam-cleaned, which removed some of the body paint, too. Sodium hydroxide paint remover was a mixed blessing: it seemed to destroy everything except the old paint. Sometimes the old paint was burned off with a plumber's gasoline blow torch held in one hand while a wire brush was held in the other hand. Prudently, someone stood by with a fire extinguisher. Painters did not like to use a blow torch around a gasoline tank because the results were rather frighteningly unpredictable. Masking tape had not yet appeared, altho glue-backed butcher's tape was tried. It was difficult to soak off. Repainting automatically included re-nickeling headlight rims, door handles and small parts. Some of the bumpers were "Old Hickory." When spring steel bumpers came into use, they were re-nickeled, too. Seeing your car in its new color and its new glory could be a shock. The color was never what you had visualized, nor was the bill, and the striper had taken certain artist's liberties which distressed you. Tires were generally messed horribly. Because the fenders were installed with new welt, and all of the accessories were installed with lock washers, all of the old rattles and squeaks were gone. When you arrived home, you parked in front of the house. All of the neighbors gathered for a social and to inquire if the color came out as you had expected. The "experts," bless their devilish souls, looked for wiggles in the striping, counted the varnish runs, and looked under the fenders to see how conscientiously the painter had treated the chassis.

With qualifications, this was a great day.

DUCO

"Varnish was good enough for my grandfather and it's good enough for me." Such was the attitude of established automobile painters until about '27. Rapidly they were losing a battle in a technological revolution which commenced in the early Twenties when the gun-powder manufacturer, E. I. duPont de Nemours, developed a new petro-chemical (nitro celulose) finish called Duco. Yes, it was explosive, and had to be applied in well-ventilated areas. The first sales promotion suggested that it could be applied with a brush, but gave better results when applied with a spray gun. They did not use the name, lacquer, although some licensees, making similar products, suggested that it resembled the beautiful hand-rubbed lacquer finish on Japanese and Chinese wooden items, a finish distilled from Rhus vernicifera, a broad leafed tree. The seemingly French name, lacquer, is derived from lac of Burma, which is the gummy excreta from the insect, Coccus Lacca. The gum, when dissolved in alcohol, is known as shellac, or, elsewhere in the world, goma lacca. Thus, lacquer was a name erroniously applied even to the Japanese and Chinese finishes.

Like countless preceeding new paint products, Duco came with extravagant claims. In 1923 some local re-paint shops advertised that they would "Duco" your car by spraying this new "eternal" paint right over the old paint on your car. Predictably, the results were disappointing. General Motors' '24 Oakland, the first automobile to be factory-painted in "satin finish Duco," offered only one color: "True Blue." (The fenders, aprons and headlamps were still black baked enamel.) Here are Oakland's claims:

"Through all these years, buyers have admired beautiful and new cars. Yet while they admired, they knew that, at best, the delicate finishes of these cars would be dimmed and aged after a few short months of ordinary usage. But no enduring body finish was available that would withstand the constant daily use to which automobiles are increasingly subjected.

Happily, those days are gone forever! Oakland has revolutionized motor car body finishes by the development and application of a radically different substance—Duco. It is a beautiful, durable, weatherproof coating, impervious alike to sun and wind, rain and snow, salt air from the sea and alkaline conditions of the deserts.

Oakland's Special Satin Finish retains its newness indefinitely. Wiping with a dry cloth will restore its original lustre without scratching, even though the car be covered with dust, rain spots, mud, oil or tar. And it is a fact that the more frequently the finish is rubbed, the more beautiful it becomes.

Oakland's Special Satin Finish is more than capable of meeting the severest demands of all-season motoring. Even sulphuric acid, or the chemicals of fire extinguishers, have

been sprayed on it, and then wiped off, leaving no marring trace. Certainly, therefore, no road or weather conditions met anywhere in the country or city driving, winter or summer, can harm this remarkable finish.

While durability is its prime virtue, everyone who has seen this new finish enthuses over its beauty and individuality. Its satiny sheen is distinctive and different. It breathes refinement and richness.

How fitting that the True Blue Oakland—the car with the new 6 cylinder engine, 4 wheel brakes, permanent top, automatic spark advance, centralized controls, and so many other exclusive features—should be the first car to offer this remarkable finish."

The 1925 Chevrolet appeared in Satin Finish Duco in several colors, and in a late 1925 Duco advertisement, duPont listed the following cars which would have Duco finish on their 1926 models: Franklin, Oakland, Kissel, Buick, Nash, Cleveland, Chandler, Moon, Diana, Cadillac, Chevrolet, Marmon, Oldsmobile, Maxwell, Meteor, Hertz, Gardiner, Rolls-Royce, Chrysler, Paige, Jewett, Hupmobile, Flint, Premier and Rollin "There is only ONE Duco—duPont Duco." Duco was "Satin Finish" because it was sprayed on and not polished. However, the 1926 cars were polished, whch nullified one of the manufacturing advantages claimed for Duco. Critics pointed out that Duco tended to chip around the moldings, joints and hood. In 1927,

Peerless, Pierce Arrow and Ford (enclosed bodies) appeared in Duco, and in 1928 the entire line of Fords had Duco. This grieved Henry Ford's soul, because GM owned 39p of the duPont stock!

The more recent history of paints and painting is dealt with elsewhere in this book, and though developments in application and chemistry were at first slow in coming, painting today is still undergoing changes at a rapidly increasing pace. Ford began early to experiment with soybean-based products, including paint, as a way for the rural American to partake of the heightening economy produced by the automotive industry. The culmination of this was his pyroxylin paints used in the late '20's and '30's. By 1938 Ford had moved to synthetic enamels, freeing him from the duPont stigma. Twenty years later Chevrolet, Oldsmobile and Pontiac adopted Acrylic Enamel. And the search continues for the "perfect paint," one which is somehow applied instantaneously, cannot by harmed by weathering or age, which needs no maintenance whatsoever, yet provides impervious coverage for the delicate metallic surface beneath it. 🐾

The paints available in your store today represent years of continuing research by manufacturers to find new formulas for paints that last longer and are easier to apply. In paint-exposure centers like this Du Pont facility in Hialeah, Fla., thousands of painted panels are tested under harsh conditions. Photo courtesy of Du Pont.

PAINTING PREPARATION AND APPLICATION
THE MORE TIME INVESTED IN THE START, THE BETTER THE FINISH

BY JAY STORER

If you've read the previous chapter, you know how the development of sprayable paints contributed to the high-speed assembly of automobiles. Paints have come a long way even since then, and today there are almost as many choices of paint types and related chemicals as there are vehicles to put them on. The chemical research done by the major paint manufacturers continually brings us improved products.

Early cars were sprayed with pyroxylin or nitrocellulose lacquers (the same thing). Cotton fibers, too short for spinning into cloth, were treated with acids to make them into pyroxylin, a fibrous mass which was then dissolved in alcohol and other lacquer solvents. Adding powdered pigment made this into colored paint. Today our lacquers are called "acrylics," because acrylic resins have been added to them to make them harder and longer-lasting. The plain nitrocellulose lacquers are seldom seen today, and even then only in primer systems, not for topcoat applications.

In Detroit's continual search for quicker and better methods for finishing cars on the assembly line, the use of lacquer as original equipment gradually gave way to the harder enamels, which could be oven-baked on the line for a super-hard finish. More importantly, they needed no rubbing out to achieve gloss. The enamels used on these cars had an alkyd base of phthalic anhydride. Just as acrylic developments have increased the durability of lacquers, acrylic resins are now part of the enamels we use today.

ENAMEL VS. LACQUER

These are the two basic families

The equipment to perform quality paint work will be one of your best restoration investments, but it can be rented in most locales also. You'll need at least a 1½-hp unit.

of paints you'll be choosing from when it comes time to repaint your restoration project, and they represent quite different routes to the same objective: a beautiful finish. Lacquers are very fast-drying, as opposed to enamels, and herein lie their differences.

Lacquers dry by evaporation of the solvents and are thinned out considerably before spraying. Because they are thin in spraying form, it takes a number of coats to build up a good finish. When you're done, the body must be color-sanded with fine sandpaper, then rubbed out with abrasive compounds to achieve a high gloss.

The durable enamels are thicker, take fewer coats to do the job and use less solvent ("reducer" in the case of enamels) than lacquer. Enamel dries by a chemical reaction within the paint, a long process but one that results in superior gloss and a hard finish that requires no rubbing out or sanding.

The drawback of enamel is that since it takes so long to dry, there is a much greater chance of dust getting into the sticky surface before it is dry. Unless you have a dust-free spraybooth (preferably with infrared lights to speed up the drying process and produce a "baked enamel" finish), the chances are good that some "glitches" will show up in the paint job.

In other-than-spraybooth conditions, lacquer is ideal, because its quick drying time allows less dust to get into the paint. Even if some dust does adhere, you eliminate it when the paint job is color-sanded and rubbed out. Also, lacquer is eminently more repairable than enamel. Because it is generally thinner than enamel, a chip or scratch in lacquer can be sanded out to a featheredge much more easily. If you do make a run or a goof in spraying lacquer, you can sand and respray it as soon as it is dry, which may be as quickly as an hour.

With enamel, on the other hand, it may take a week or even several months for the chemical reaction to produce a finish hard enough to sand and respray. As far as glitches in the drying paint go, it is possible to color-sand and rub out enamel also, but it must be done carefully and only after the enamel is thoroughly hardened. Unless the finish was baked on or a hardener was used, this may take about two months.

The debate between the two paint families has raged for years, with proponents of each claiming theirs is

the only route to a flawless deep finish on a restoration. We've seen "perfect" results with both methods, so our conclusion is that either system can yield the desired results, but only when conscientious attention has been paid to the preparation and application.

EPOXIES AND POLYURETHANES

The search for ever-more-durable finishes for such heavy-duty applications as aircraft, trucks and buses has given us a new family of "plastic" paints. These are derivatives of acrylic enamels, but feature the added ingredient of a "hot" reacting catalyst. The catalyst works just as it does with fiberglass products and those household epoxy superglues. It "kicks" the paint into a super-hard, super-glossy finish.

Once they're hardened, chemicals such as brake fluid, oil and gasoline, which would ruin an ordinary paint job, have no effect on these paints. They are also highly resistant to road chips (hence their use on the 18-wheelers and buses) and the occasional dropped wrench or spark plug.

Epoxies and polyurethanes are not the same. The epoxies are generally used as primers and fillers, due to their excellent adhesion and ability to fill surface imperfections. They are also used on engines, driveline parts and chassis, but they don't have the resistance to fading of the later-developed polyurethanes.

The polyurethanes do have their drawbacks, though. Once they're dry, there's almost no way to get them *off*, if you should want to for any reason. Also, they're several

times as expensive as standard paints. They come in a limited range of colors, too, although we are told the paint selection is growing all the time. You must also be extremely careful when spraying polyurethane paints. A good respirator/mask with replaceable filters is a must, because these paints contain chemicals that can attack your lungs, with unhealthy results.

The pure polyurethanes are quite expensive. In restoration work, they are usually used only on the drivetrain and chassis, where their chip resistance is especially appreciated. One that has found favor with many restorers we've talked to is Du Pont's Imron. It's mixed in a ratio of three parts of Imron to one part of the special catalytic hardener. You can buy three quarts of paint and one quart of hardener (at about $40 total) and have enough to do your chassis parts. The Imron is meant to be used unthinned, although Du Pont does make a special reducer if you need it. You must also use a special primer beforehand (#825-S zinc-chromate epoxy primer). The primer dries in about 2 hours and the Imron in about 6 to 10 hours (2 to 4 hours if a special accelerator is added). We don't recommend that you sandblast any *body* panels, but this is the route for chassis parts, as it provides a perfect "tooth" for the epoxy primer and Imron.

Considerably less expensive than the pure epoxies or polyurethanes are the two-part enamels. Most of the major paint companies make them. Basically they are standard acrylic enamels to which you can

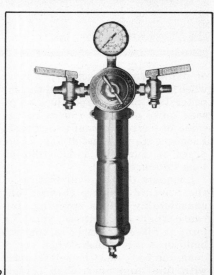

add a hardening agent that imparts most of the good qualities of the pure polyurethanes without the expense.

An example would be Ditzler's Delstar/Delthane system. Delstar is a synthetic enamel, available in just about any "book" color, and you do use a reducer with it. Enough material to do most types of cars would require a gallon of Delstar, two quarts of reducer and a pint of Delthane hardener. The beauty of the Delstar is that it dries like lacquer, almost as quickly as you can walk around the car with your spraygun! It can be force-dried in as little as 20 minutes. However, it takes 4 to 6 hours to get hard enough to retape and spray over (for doing a body panel in a second color). Such two-part enamels (Du Pont has one also, called Centari) are perfect for the restored car that is going to be driven instead of hoarded away in a garage most of its life.

Whatever type of paint you do select, stick with one brand and use it for your whole system; intermixing paints, primers, thinners and agents from different brands usually results in disaster. When you pick a system, do yourself a large favor before you open the first can . . . read the directions.

PREPARATION

Talk to any professional painter and he'll probably admit that the righteous paint job everyone works toward is 90% preparation and only 10% paint application. Even the pros are tempted now and again to rush through the preliminary steps to "get some color on," usually to the detriment of the final results. As marvelous a protective system as a paint job is, it can't hide improper bodywork or sloppy preparation. We've seen otherwise beautifully restored cars that couldn't stand a very close inspection of the paint and bodywork because the refinisher skipped some of the block sanding, forgot to feather out a paint break or allowed carelessly corrected rust areas to reappear right through his glossy new paint.

Let's start our preparation by assuming that you have the car basically together; that is, the body is back on the frame and all your bodywork is done. You probably have the fenders and other removable body parts scattered around the garage. All of these smaller parts are best painted off the car. Since you're probably installing new door hinge pins as part of your restoration, you can paint the doors off the car as well, since this makes painting the jambs a lot easier.

Remember, you can't go from your post-metalwork primer right on to your topcoat, not if you want everything smooth and ripple-free. First spray a *very* light mist of silver (or other color that contrasts with your primer) on all your panels. This is your guide coat. A light block sanding or scuffing will reveal any remaining high and low spots that need to be taken care of. Without the guide coat step, there might

1. This Binks #69 is typical of a good quality gun. Here it's fitted with a quick-locking 1-qt. paint cup, so there's no fumbling with threads when attaching a filled cup.

2. When you're painting a restoration, it's essential that all water, oil and dust be removed from the air before it gets into the paint. Use of an air transformer (or filter) such as this DeVilbiss P-HB is a must. This unit incorporates a regulator and features a replaceable element.

3. An optional purchase for the part-time restorer but a must for the pro is a touch-up gun. This DeVilbiss EGA model is ideal for doing spot repairs, door jambs and painting small parts.

4. For production work, a gun with a separate paint cup makes the job easier on the painter's arm. Also, there's no chance of dropping paint out of the siphon hole onto the car, and the cup holds more paint. The cup is often attached to your belt.

5. After all your bodywork has been completed, the real work begins. This panel is full of grinder marks that must be reduced with finer sanding. The paint skirting the area must be featheredged by hand and remaining scratches filled by repeated priming and block sanding before painting.

6. Bodyworked panels that are down to bare metal must be treated with metal conditioner, which etches the surface so that paint and primer will adhere.

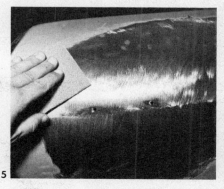

be some dimples that otherwise wouldn't be noticed until the color coats went on.

Wetting down the panels is also a good way to show up problem areas, because the reflective quality gives an indication of panel straightness.

When you're absolutely sure that no more bodywork is necessary, tape off the glass and other areas you don't want painted. Then wipe down the panels with a wax- and grease-removing solvent like Pre-Kleano or Prep-Sol. Any areas that have been sanded to bare metal should be treated with a metal conditioner to etch the surface and sanded with No. 180 paper so that the primer will adhere. Now you can spray on several heavy coats of primer, which hopefully you strained beforehand.

When the primer is thoroughly dry, you can begin the laborious process of block sanding. Using a hard rubber sanding block and No. 320 wet-and-dry paper, wet-sand all your body panels. Use plenty of water to keep the paper from clogging up. If you don't have a hose handy, use a large car-washing sponge. Keep it full of water and above the area you're sanding. A slight pressure on the full sponge should keep a steady sheet of water flowing over the area you're sanding.

At this time, you may discover some tiny pinholes or mistakes in the primer or underlying bodywork. Fill these with glazing putty (actually just very thick primer), applied very thin with a small rubber squeegee. When these spots are dry, wet-sand and feather these into the rest of the primer. Let the car sit for several days, as both the glazing putty and the primer itself may

shrink, exposing new areas that need sanding or filling.

Spray on a few more coats of primer next and let it harden. This should be carefully wet-sanded with No. 400 paper, wiped down with a cleaning solvent again and any dust cleaned off with a *new* tack rag. Many painters use a tack rag only between color coats and not on sanded primer, but a little extra protection never hurts.

Now you're about ready for the nerve-wracking stage of applying the actual color coats. All the hours you've put into your restoration will finally bear fruit after just a few more passes with the spraygun.

SPRAY EQUIPMENT

It's perhaps proper to mention here a few points about the equipment you'll be using, as this is no place for shortcuts. You need *good* equipment. If you can't afford to buy it, you'll have to rent it. First you need a quality spraygun. Binks or DeVilbiss are two brands we can

think of offhand. For the fast-drying paints you'll be using, the spraygun should be of the external-mix type with suction feed. The paint and air are mixed just as they leave the gun, controlled by the air cap and fluid tip, which are available in various sizes for different paint flow rates. A suction-feed gun has a bleed hole in the top of the cup which allows atmospheric pressure to enter above the paint. This way the suction created at the gun nozzle draws the paint up through the gun head. Later, in the spray technique section, we'll explain the significance of this little air hole.

We've already discussed paints and primers, so the only item you need besides the paint and spraygun is air. It may be free all around us, but compressing enough of it to work your spraygun (and smoothly) is what runs into money. A good spraygun can cost from $75 to $150, but an air compressor big enough for automotive spraying can cost you two or three times that, espe-

1

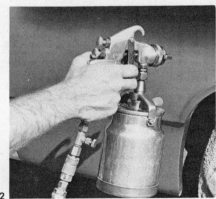

2

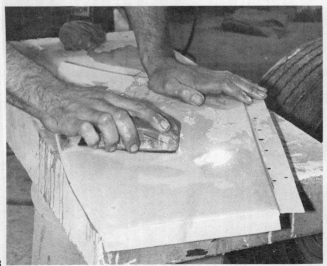

3

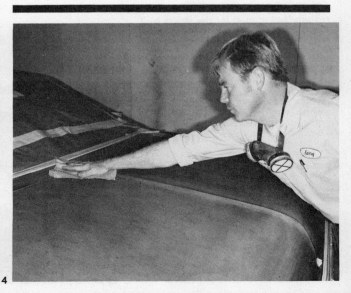

4

cially counting the hose and regulator as well.

Compressors are rated according to their output of air, which is expressed in cfm (cubic feet of air per minute). This expresses the amount of work that can be accomplished in a given time. The pressure (or force) necessary to move the air is measured in psi (pounds per square inch). The air delivery (cfm) is one consideration which determines the type of paint and the amount of atomized paint which can be

---

1. Another treatment, this one for bare *and* painted surfaces, is a wax and grease remover. Use it and your tack rag before any spray painting.

2. If you desire the best possible paint job, take as much time and trouble in your primering as you do for final paint. This includes using the tack rag and solvent, adjusting your spray pattern, straining the primer and using a quality thinner.

3. Final wet-sanding of your primer coats is the last step before you apply a topcoat. Get the surfaces as smooth as possible, and if you break through the primer somewhere, you must apply more primer and resand.

4. After all your sanding is done, make one more pass with two rags, the first with wax-and-grease remover and the second a clean tack rag. If the car is assembled at this point, be sure to clean all the crevices at panel edges and door jambs, too.

5. Whatever you're painting, be it primer or topcoat, every time you mix paint or fill your spraygun cup the material should be strained.

6. If you're using one of the new epoxy or polyurethane paints, the hardener should be added just before the material is to be sprayed.

---

sprayed per minute. Thicker or heavy-bodied paints require high air pressure to atomize. Most paints you'll be using require lower pressures.

The two most popular types of compressors are the diaphragm type and the piston type. Either may be operated by gasoline or electric motors. Most portable units are electric-powered diaphragm jobs developing 30-40 psi. They are suitable for most small jobs, but can't keep up the air supply during sustained spraying. The spray equipment dealer where you purchase your gun can tell you the cfm capabilities of the particular gun and sprayhead combination you select. Then, using the charts in this story, you can determine what size compressor you'll need to buy or rent. It'll probably be a piston type in the 1½- to 3-hp range.

Remember that the longer your air hose is, the more of a pressure drop will be incurred at the gun. Don't count on getting away with a short hose, either. The compressor heats up the air it takes in and compresses, so you need at least 25 ft. of hose (either standard flexible rubber hose or metal pipe mounted stationary to the shop wall) to cool the air off again before it reaches the paint gun.

Unfortunately, this heating and subsequent cooling can induce condensation of moisture in the lines, and you don't want that to reach the gun either. You'll need an additional piece of equipment to do the job right: an air transformer or extractor. This filters the water out of the air. It also removes any oil that gets past the rings in a piston-type

compressor. Ideally, the 25 ft. of metal pipe should run from the compressor to the extractor, and your flexible hose should connect to the other side of the extractor. Obviously, with a portable unit, particularly a rented one, you can't have 25 ft. of permanently mounted pipe hooked up, so just run 25 ft. of regular hose to the extractor and then more hose to the gun.

A final piece of equipment, more important than the compressor, the gun or even the paint job, is an air respirator with a replaceable filter element. No paint job is worth the ruin of your health, and automotive spray paints are definitely unhealthy for your lungs. Don't settle at the last minute for one of those paper "surgical masks" they give away at the paint store. You need the best protection possible. With the newer epoxies, polyurethanes and two-part enamels, such breathing protection is imperative.

PAINT APPLICATION

Assuming that you've prepared the car as previously described, you're now ready to make all that work seem worthwhile by applying some color and bringing that 40-year-old sheetmetal back to life.

Something we didn't mention before and perhaps should now is masking. It may seem to some of you that masking is so easy that it needs no explanation, but it can be the difference between a professional-looking paint job and an amateurish one. A perfect masking job doesn't take practice and skill so much as it does time. Taking an extra hour or so now will pay dividends in the finished job. In a resto-

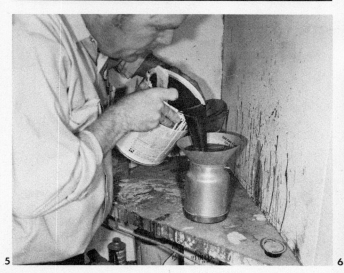

5

6

ration job, you have the opportunity to do the best possible paint work, because the car is dismantled. Overspray is less of a problem, and items that normally would need to be masked off, such as lights, chrome trim, etc., are not even in the same room as the parts being painted.

For the rest, masking tape is great, but there are some things it can't do, such as follow a tight curve. Use ½-in. or ⅜-in. tape for curves and then overlap with your normal ¾-in. tape. The skinnier tape won't wrinkle or lift as readily in the corners as the wide kind. Even so, press down hard on all your taped edges shortly before you begin spraying, especially if your masking was done several hours before you were ready to paint. And don't ever leave masking tape out in the sun or on for more than 36 hours—it hardens, cracks and gives up its sticking power, leaving a difficult-to-remove gummy residue on the car.

Now mix your paint and thinner. Strain the paint before it is mixed with the thinner and once again after it is mixed and you're pouring it into the spraygun cup. If you're us-

ing a paint with a hardener, don't mix any more than you can use right away. If you have access to a professional paint booth, put on your mask and paint away. Most of us don't have a booth at home, but perhaps there's a friendly body shop near you that will rent their booth for a few hours. It may be a hassle to get the car there, but it'll be worth it to have a dust-free atmosphere to paint in.

If you're stuck with the garage or driveway at home, as we have been on occasion, don't despair. Many fine jobs have been done at home by amateurs who took pains to do things right. Dust will be your biggest problem. Sweep out thoroughly, wash down the floors and take out boxes of parts, etc., that may have a layer of dust or overspray on them.

You've probably heard backyard paint experts advise you to wet the garage floor before painting to keep the dust down. This can be disastrous advice, particularly with lacquer paints in hot weather. The water on the warm concrete can create localized humidity that can cause your paint to "blush" or mottle. In

addition to the humidity problem, you have to watch for the air hose. If dragged across a wet floor, the hose can create havoc if it touches a freshly painted part. The floor can be *damp,* but never wet.

Another way to reduce dust problems is to attach a ground strap or length of chain to the car frame and run it to a ground connection. This keeps the car from becoming a storehouse of static electricity during sanding and wiping.

Going by the recommendations of the paint salesman and the directions on the paint can, adjust your regulator for the desired air pressure. Open the fluid adjustment knob on your spraygun about 2½ turns out from fully closed and make a spray pattern test on a sheet of cardboard or other object. The fluid and fan (paint and air) adjustment knobs should be turned only a little at a time while getting your spray pattern just right. What's desired is a pattern that allows you to work about 8 to 10 ins. away from the surface, giving you uniform coverage without a lot of dry overspray around the edges.

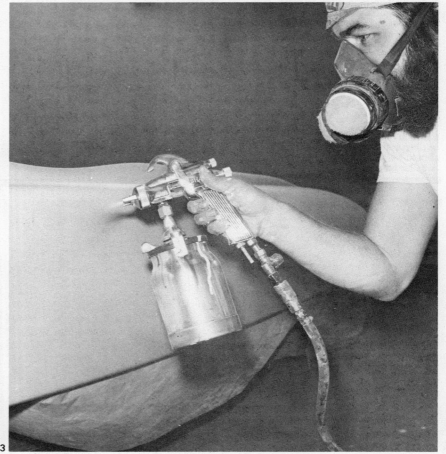

When your pattern is right, put the gun down and dust off the car one last time with a tack cloth before painting. Since you will not be painting as fast as a professional can, it will take you longer to get all the way around a car. Thus there may be blending problems if the area where you started is partly dry when you come back around to it. One way to get around this is to start at the hood, then do both front fenders, then go down one side of the car. When you get to the rear, go back to the other front fender and run down that side of the car so your two passes meet at the rear around the decklid.

While you are painting, there are several things to watch out for. First of all, don't drag the air hose across the doors, hood or decklid when you're reaching to paint the roof. Also, remember that little air hole in the top of the paint cup? Be sure it doesn't get clogged with paint or it will ruin your spray pattern. At the same time, be careful when tilting a full gun of paint or it will drip out of the hole and onto a fender. Keep the air hole at the rear of the gun and wrap a rag around the top of the cup (still allowing air to get in the hole) to catch any paint drips.

When the paint is sufficiently dry (follow directions on the can for how long between coats, how long before retape, etc.), remove the masking tape and paper and survey your artwork. There's a temptation to remove the masking right after painting, but don't succumb. Premature masking removal can leave ragged paint edges or let sanding dust hidden in your masking paper fall out onto still-tacky paint.

With some types of paint and if there was any dust in the paint job, you may have to color-sand the paint with No. 600 paper, used wet. Then buff out the finish for gloss with rubbing compound and finally apply wax. With enamels, you will have to wait two or three months before color-sanding any glitches, unless you've used a hardening agent. And don't wax a new enamel job, either, unless it has had hardener added.

If you've followed us all the way through and are still afraid to paint your own car, at least we've shown some of the work involved and the attention to small details that it takes for a clean job. Now you know why the pros get as much money as they do for this work.

If you've done your own paint job, then sit back, take a well-deserved beer break and admire what you've done. Not every restorer is capable of doing every bit of work on his car, and most of us farm out one job or another. But the paint job is one of the most important aspects, since it is seen first, and knowing that you did yours yourself is something to be truly proud of when you show your car. 🛠

1. On siphon guns, use a wire to keep the air hole clear, keep the hole at the rear when you attach the cup and use a rag to catch any drips.

2. The spraygun pattern differs according to the various materials and air pressures used, so always adjust the gun before painting the actual car. Top knob is the fan adjustment, lower one is for fluid adjustment.

3. No paints, and that includes primers and even pure thinner sprayed for gun cleaning, should be sprayed unless the painter is wearing a good mask. Throw the dirty, replaceable filters away after each paint job.

4. Proper, even coverage is essential for a professional job, particularly with lacquers or other paints that will be color-sanded and rubbed out. ..

5. Lacquer paints are easy to use, but they do require rubbing out, a job that can easily ruin the paint if you cut through with the buffer. Work by hand, first buff with fine polish, then with cornstarch/water paste.

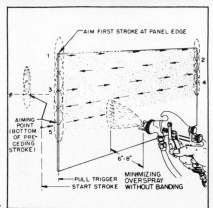

WHEELS ANY SHAPE IS O.K. AS LONG AS IT'S ROUND

BY JIM BRIGHTLY

If you have wire wheels on your Ford, they're welded. All Ford wire wheels were of the welded variety and were not adjustable. This made them much cheaper to manufacture, but much more difficult to repair. Spoke replacement is just about out of the question. Each bent spoke must be individually straightened, because replacement would be very impractical, if not impossible. Spoke stock of the proper size and length is very hard to find, and the process of swaging or welding the spokes is extremely time-consuming and quite expensive.

If your rims are slightly bent or out of alignment, you may be able to straighten them. But if they've had many spokes broken and the rims are egg-shaped, forget it. Slightly bent rims have a kind of memory built into the metal; when heated, they will usually return to the original shape. Oval rims, however, have stretched metal that can never be trued again. They should be junked.

Straightening begins in the cleaning tank. All rust, caked-on dirt and flaky paint are washed away in Valley Wire Wheel Service's ultrasonic tank. The tank solution consists of phosphoric acid, a wetting agent and a detergent. An ultrasonic unit facilitates cleaning, as it can do the equivalent of a 24-hour soak in a normal hot tank in only about half an hour. Ed Werndorf of Valley Wire Wheel Service, 14725 Bessemer St., Van Nuys, Calif. 91411, bought his ultrasonic unit at a government salvage sale. It had been used in the aerospace industry for cleaning ceramic nose cones. Ed's unit has two 1000-watt, 60-cycle units, providing a total of 2000 watts of ultrasonic action. The unit has paid for itself by labor costs (time) saved in cleaning the wheels. Ultrasonic energy cuts loose dirt from the tiniest crevices, and the wheel comes out of the tank squeaky clean.

For cleaning at home, when a hot tank is unavailable, the local 25¢, do-it-yourself car wash works great for dirty wheels, while sandblasting will clean up the more grungy rims.

To begin the straightening process, Ed places the bent rim in his hydraulic press, which roughly corrects both lateral and radial runout. He corrects to within 1/16-in. to 3/32-in. initially. Later, using more closely controlled methods, he will work the rim to a tolerance of .030-in., both laterally and radially.

Upon completion of the preliminary rim truing by the hydraulic press, Ed goes to work on the bent and broken spokes. He'll repair the broken spokes by brazing them with a torch. Welding is too hot and may warp the rim. While the torch is on, he heats any bent spokes and pries them back straight. In some cases he may be forced to use a drift punch from the rear to bend spokes forward; in other cases a hammer or pry bar will suffice. When all the spokes are straightened or brazed, Ed must go back and grind down the brazing beads so they'll go unnoticed after painting.

With the spokes out of the way, Ed returns to the rim to straighten it to within his own personal specification of .030-in. Using the torch, he heats minute sections of the rim, working his way inch by inch around the rim. Using specially shaped tools, Ed rebends tweaked sections. A hammer and dolly are then used to achieve proper rim bead radius and edge shape after dents are bent out. Even the hubs used to rotate the rims while work is being performed are becoming scarce; consequently, finding a shop set up for this type of work is very difficult.

Another factor is liability. While it is very expensive (because of the tediousness, time and knowledge required) to have a rim straightened, there still isn't enough money involved to pay for liability insurance. And if an old wheel that has recently been repaired fails, guess who is responsible.

Balancing wire wheels can be a problem. Wire wheels are much less rigid than solid steel wheels, which allows them to flex at high speed. High-speed flexing can really play havoc with a wheel that has been bubble balanced, and it could even ruin a newly completed straightening job.

Wire wheels should always be balanced on the car. First, two wheels are spun and stroboscopically balanced on the front spindles, removed and mounted on the rear. Then the remaining two wheels are balanced on the front and remain there. A spun balance of this nature includes wheel bearings, linkage play, brake drums, etc. Owners of older cars that aren't driven much over 40 mph needn't worry too much about balancing—it could even be done on a bubble machine. Balancing is not very critical under 40 mph. Types of weights are optional. You may prefer the glue-on magnesium wheel type, and these can be used on any

PHOTOS BY ERIC RICKMAN

wheel. But in some cases, an abundance of weight may be needed. If so, this will require using the more normal crimp-on style.

Welded wire wheel straightening is a slow, time-consuming, tedious and expensive operation. So many rims were manufactured that it might still be cheaper to buy a used wheel than to repair your bent one.

ADJUSTABLE-SPOKE WIRE WHEELS

Restoration of an adjustable spoked wheel is decidedly easier, cheaper and quicker than rebuilding a welded wheel. Threaded spokes are simple to replace because they are still being produced today. Many of the more popular and late-model brands were interchangeable: Kelsey Hayes, Cadillac, Buick and T-Bird all used standard spokes.

Originally there were many, many different thread patterns. It seems every individual wheel brand had its own pattern. Buchanan's Frame Shop, 629 E. Garvey Ave., Monterey Park, Calif., has an inventory of spokes on hand that can match nearly any threaded spoke made in the U.S. All of Buchanan's spokes, however, no matter what the application, have the same thread pattern.

Buchanan can perform all or any portion of wheel restoration, but if you wish to do the work yourself and have a sense of accomplishment from a job well done, you should prepare by taking pictures of the spoke lacing pattern from many different angles. The lacing patterns can be very intricate, and these pho-

1. The wheel will have to go into the ultrasonic hot tank before being inspected closely for any cracks in the rim or hub. The dents indicated by arrows will also be dressed.

2. To correct runout, the wheel is mounted on the hub and straightened hydraulically. At this stage a pointer is sufficient for checking the rim.

3. The preliminary rim dressing is done with a pinch tool and torch.

4. Ed uses a hammer and dolly just before the final dressing of rim. The dial indicator is for checking the rim bead radius and edge shape.

5. Bent spokes are heated during straightening. Ed also uses the torch to braze any broken spokes.

6. After grinding, sand and paint.

tos will lessen the chance of a mistake during reassembly. You should also try to draw a diagram for later reference.

Even though there were only two basic lacing patterns and an expert can relace a wheel in about 2½ hours, we are not all experts and need all the help we can get. Dave Moore, Buchanan's resident expert, can assemble a wheel in less than 3 hours and does it 90% from memory.

To remove the old spokes, you'll either have to cut them out or (if you're lucky!) unbolt them. Preparing the nipples for removal should begin 24 hours before attacking them with a wrench. Liberally soak the nipples with penetrating oil or soak the entire rim in kerosene.

You should also mike the size of the nipples and order the corresponding size of wrench from Buchanan's. Due to the many different sizes of nipples, Buchanan's was forced to develop these special decimal-size wrenches in order to keep from rounding off the nipples' edges.

If the nipples are still too stiff after soaking, apply some heat with a small propane torch. Heating the nipples forces the oil further into the threads. More heat while applying wrench pressure also helps dislodge rusty nipples. Don't be discouraged if you break a few. Very seldom can you save old spokes—they're usually too badly rusted in.

You should have any wheel straightening finished prior to plating; after all, you wouldn't want to ruin a neat chrome job with scratches from a hydraulic press. Spokes just aren't strong enough to use as a means of straightening the rim. About all they can handle is hub-to-rim alignment. If your hub is okay and the outer rim is pretty well banged up, Buchanan's can also remove the proper-sized rim from a solid steel wheel, drill and dimple it and lace it to your hub.

When you take your spokes in for chroming, remind the plater about protecting the threads of the nipples and spokes. Most platers know this, but it never hurts to be certain. All freshly chromed spokes—and some platers may *not* be aware of this—should be baked as soon as possible after plating (within 24 hours) at 350° for at least 4 hours. This cooks the hydrogen out of the metal.

Hydrogen embrittlement has been the bugaboo of chrome-plated wheels; the welds were hydrogen impregnated and they fractured. If hydrogen gets into the metal during the plating process, it can also cause fractures as the hydrogen tries to works its way out of the metal. Fatigue testing shows a ratio of 4:1 in strength between a baked plated spoke vs. an untreated chrome-plated spoke. The higher the quality of steel used, the greater the problem. Rims are made of cold-rolled carbon steel and present no embrittlement problem. However, spokes are of a high-quality steel and will absorb hydrogen in plating.

Now sort out the spokes according to length. The wheel in the accompanying photos has only two sizes, so it's easy to sort. Some old Cadillacs have four different spoke lengths, and they only vary by about ⅛-in., so you can get into trouble if you mix them.

Next comes indexing, and this is important. Some wheels will only go together one way. There are wheels with three spokes in the bottom and two in the top. With some wheels it is critical as to which hole you start lacing from—a specific hole in the hub must be aligned with a specific hole in the rim or the pattern won't work out correctly. The wheel in the photos is a standard type, with an even number of spokes, so it can be started anywhere.

Begin lacing by dropping the short spokes through the hub holes. Block the hub up to proper height level inside the rim. Observe closely in both rim and hub which way the dimples face, because this indicates the direction in which to aim the spokes. On the wheel we're working with, there are two rows of dimples for each spoke length, making a total of four rows in pairs of two.

Remember that your wheels may differ from one another, so refer to the photos you took before disassembly for correct indexing. Or you can always keep at least one wheel fully assembled for easy reference.

After you've inserted the short spokes through their corresponding holes in the rim, start the nipples and thread them on a few turns. Then you can turn the wheel over and begin indexing the long spokes. Again, the upper row of spokes in the hub goes to the upper row of holes in the rim, and the lower row

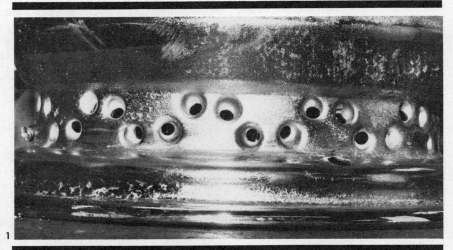

crosses over and goes to the lower holes. Lace all the long spokes and start the nipples. Use a few drops of oil on each nipple and leave everything loose until all spokes are located.

Screw all the nipples down until only a couple of threads are left showing on each spoke. Now you're ready to start fine tuning and tightening the spokes. To do this, mount the wheel on one of the car's spindles. It'll be much easier to rotate while tightening.

To eyeball alignment accuracy, a dial indicator is not necessary; a rigidly mounted pointer will suffice. Alignment tolerance depends on the condition of the rim; the better the condition, the closer the tolerance. Read on the bead side of the rim for concentricity and at the inner edge of the bead side for runout. The two outside edges of a rim never seem to match after much road abuse, so you can only average the runout as closely as possible between the two. It is more important to have the bead seats run true for proper tire support than it is to have the outer

flange of the rim running true. Truing the wheel is a slow process of loosening and tightening opposite sides to draw the rim into alignment and concentricity.

Theoretically, now that you've aligned the wheel and all the nipples are snug, you can take ⅛ of a turn on each spoke as you work your way around the rim and the wheel should stay true. All spokes must be snugged down very tight, but evenly. The tighter you can get the spokes, the longer the wheel will stay true. Get each nipple as tight as you can, right up to just short of damage.

Finally, check the outer end of each nipple closely to be sure none of the spoke is poking through. If any metal is showing, it must be ground off flush to prevent puncturing the inner tube later on. After a final inspection, wrap the spoke area of the rim with duct tape or a rubber wheel liner.

Now that you know how it's done, you can decide whether to restore your own wheels and save money or let Buchanan's or a similar shop do it and save time.

WOODEN WHEEL RESTORATION

The wooden automobile wheel has two mortal enemies. The first, of course, is outright breakage, the result of an unfortunate accident. The wheel may have hit an unseen chuckhole or bashed against a curb. This situation may or may not have occurred to the wheel you're considering restoring. But really inevitable is the second enemy, over which neither the car's former owner nor you have the slightest control: time. That's right, age alone can negate the restorability and usefulness of the wooden wheel, even if the car on which it's mounted belonged to the well-known little old lady from Pasadena who drove it only once to the Rose Parade. It's not a matter of whether the car was babied over the years, always garaged, kept serviced and clean; it's a matter of how *old* the wheel is.

Unfortunately, there is no hard and fast rule-of-thumb which can be applied to the wooden wheel. You cannot simply say that if it's over 40 years old, discard it, and if it's younger than that, it will positively last another half-dozen years. Entering into wheel deterioration are humidity, harshly cold winters contrasting with very hot summers and so forth. There are so many other factors that enter into wood's longevity that it's impossible to examine a wheel and make the decision to keep it or have a replacement built. But since the steel wheel took over the wheelwright's trade in the late Twenties, a "late model" wooden wheel is 50 years of age at

1. Closely inspect the direction in which the dimples face before attempting reassembly. This wheel has two rows of paired spoke holes.

2. After the spokes have been plated and baked, they must be sorted out according to size. This wheel has only two different spoke lengths.

3. After the indexing pattern has been carefully checked (some lacing patterns must start and end with specific holes), begin lacing by dropping the appropriate spokes through holes in the rear of the hub.

4. Start the nipples and thread them on a few turns before turning the wheel over and inserting the long spokes.

5. When all spokes are in place, fingertighten the nipples and mount the wheel on the car's spindle.

6. A drop of oil on each nipple will ease the chore of tightening them during the alignment process.

best. And 50 years is too long a time for even the best-made wooden wheel to stay healthy. So the situation is that *any* wooden wheel should be replaced—if the car is to be driven hard.

The damage that time does to the wooden wheel is shrinkage. No matter how "dry" the wood was after any of the several drying processes preferred by wheelwrights, it did in truth still contain some moisture. As time progressed, the little-remaining moisture dried out, causing the wood to shrink and the joints to loosen. A temporary cure of a loose wooden wheel is an overnight soaking in a swimming pool or nearby creek, in which case the wood will absorb moisture again, swell up slightly and become tight again. But this newly induced moisture will dry up in just a few weeks and the wheel will become loose again.

Another cure might be to soak the wheel in hot linseed oil. This process will make the wheel usable for up to 2 or 3 years, but eventually it will dry out again and be useless for anything more than pure display.

Even such sage advice may sometimes fall on deaf ears, so rather than go through a how-to on wheel construction, let us repeat a sad tale that recently occurred.

The split, obviously badly distressed wheels pictured here came from an electric car of circa 1910. Because the car would not be driven any further than across a concours' grassy sward once or twice a year, and because the wheels had never been accidentally damaged and appeared to be in really pristine shape, the owner decided to restore them. But while the wood itself was in very good condition, the old finish had deteriorated to the point where it had to be removed and a new finish applied.

Now, there are many ways to

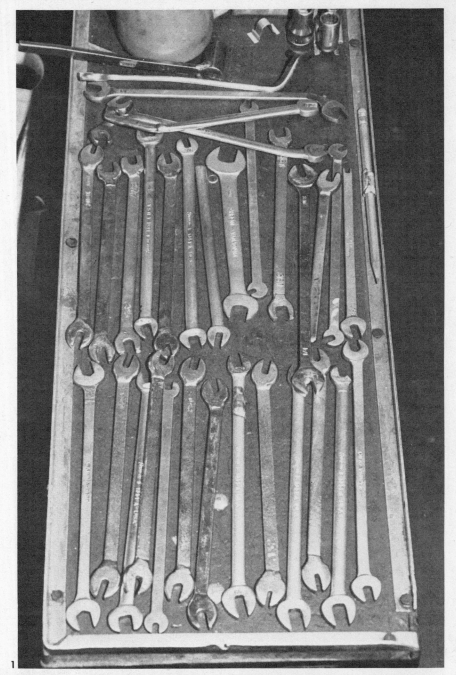

1

2

3

strip finish from wood, but the owner in question opted to take them to a professional stripper, who had all the necessary tanks and equipment. The wheels needed dunking for only about 10 minutes in a strong caustic solution, but unfortunately, after immersion they were forgotten for several hours, with the results pictured here.

Professionals at the wooden wheel restoration trade have told us a few interesting things about the nearly lost art of wooden wheel construction, but to a man they suggest that while an original piece can be made to look as good as new, such a wheel should be used strictly on a display-only car. Even short trips on today's vastly improved roads should be avoided.

Quality wooden wheels were made from kiln-dried ash or hickory. As stated, such wood is subject to shrinkage, loosening of the spokes at their juncture with the felloe and also loosening of the iron band that circles the wheel's rim. Sometimes the iron band can be removed and a very small slice cut out of the band. After rewelding and replacement, the wheel may regain some of its tightness. Other times, the minute gaps that have opened up where the spokes fit into the felloe sockets can be carefully shimmed with thin pieces of metal.

Another method that has been used with varying success is soaking the wheel in a 50/50 mixture of hot linseed oil and turpentine. However, this process can "kill" whatever life the original wood has left in it.

It is also possible to disassemble the wheel, drill holes in the butt ends of the spokes, pour in the linseed oil/turpentine mix and reassemble the pieces. This latter method may be the best, as the wheel may stay tight for up to a half-dozen years. However, if the wheel's bearings have gone bad and grease has gotten onto the wood, the pores in the grain have closed and the linseed oil cannot penetrate. If this is the case, or if dry rot has attacked the wood, a new wheel is the only way out of the dilemma. ♟

4

5

1. Many of these wrenches were cast and milled to decimal sizes by Buchanan's Frame Shop. By closely matching nipple size with the proper wrench, Buchanan's no longer rounds off the corners of the nipples.

2. With all nipples snug and the wheel mounted on spindle, final alignment can now be accomplished with a rigid pointer and lots of care. Finish wheel job by tightening all nipples as much as possible short of damage.

3. These wooden wheels were chemically stripped of old wood finish. But too-long immersion in the solution caused them to split and crack.

4. A closer look at the splits in the spokes and the general deterioration of the felloe (wood rim).

5. Wheelwrights are few and far between, but this is an example of what a brand-new wheel should look like. Metal parts have been repaired and refinished, and all the new wood has been meticulously shaped to match that of the original wheel. This kind of work is expensive: You can pay as much as $1500 for a set of four.

PLAY IT COOL DON'T NEGLECT YOUR RADIATOR OR COOLING SYSTEM

BY FRANK ODDO

Regardless of design, the automotive cooling system has but one purpose—to maintain the engine at an efficient operating temperature under all driving conditions and car speeds. Admittedly, the man whose car does not include a radiator may be more fortunate, but over the years the vast majority of American automobile manufacturers have elected to install a liquid cooling system. Typically, such a system employs a belt-driven pump to circulate a coolant through "jackets" around the cylinders and valve seats and out to a radiator. Atmospheric heat transfer occurs in the radiator, and the coolant is returned to the engine and recirculated.

"Efficient operating temperature," though, is restricted to a narrow band, with 200° F. as a midpoint. If the engine overheats, lubrication breaks down; if too little heat is developed, thermal efficiency (that relationship between power output and the potential energy in the fuel) drops off significantly.

In order to maintain that precarious balance, the cooling system must carry away about 35% of the heat generated by combustion. Even in low-compression, low-rpm powerplants, combustion temperatures reach as high as 4500° F. Although much of this heat is passed out through the exhaust system, cylinder temperatures beyond 600° F. will break down the lubricating properties of the most modern oils. It is of paramount importance, therefore, that the automotive restorer pay close attention to the restoration of cooling system *efficiency* as well as external appearance. So put the polish away for a few minutes and consider the inner workings of that imposing honeycomb of copper and brass forward of the engine.

The radiator is a device that permits a large volume of air to pass around a large volume of coolant in order to effect a transfer of heat from the coolant to the atmosphere. It has two separate components: Air passes through one (the fins) and coolant through the other (the

tubes). Although only two core styles are in standard use today (tube and corrugated fin, and tube and plate fin), over the years auto manufacturers have experimented with several configurations in attempts to increase efficiency. That some of these configurations are particularly attractive is only a secondary benefit.

One of the earliest designs (and most elaborate) is the tube and helical fin. In this, a thin copper fin is coiled around each vertical water passage tube. As in all designs, the fin is to improve heat transfer, but here it literally circulates air around the tube. Replacement cores such as this have not been commercially available for many years.

Another design, also long since gone to its reward, is the air tube cellular core. Here, horizontal tubes were stacked one atop the other in an attempt to better capture and channel the air through water passages looped in and around the air tubes. Its limited use and very complicated construction assured a lack of favor with manufacturers long before labor costs were what they are today.

One of the most handsome radiator designs is the ribbon cellular core. In this configuration a large number of narrow water passages are formed by pairs of thin copper ribbons soldered together. Higher-priced cars of the late Twenties incorporated the most elaborate variations on this design, but surprisingly enough, a modern counterpart is sometimes available through radiator shops specializing in custom work.

Practically speaking, however, the restorer of a special interest car is going to find himself limited to the aforementioned tube and corrugated fin, and tube and plate fin core design. These are the most economical to manufacture and meet reasonable expectations in terms of cooling efficiency. Most larger radiator shops stock a fairly wide variety of sizes and thicknesses, and for a moderate increase in cost, they can special order a core of unusual dimensions from a core manufacturer.

But a radiator is more than just a collection of fins and tubes. It includes water chambers or tanks, traditionally at the top and bottom of the core. The top tank receives the hot water from the block, while the lower tank passes the cooled water back into the engine. Early water tanks were almost always made of heavy gauge brass, and it is not too surprising to find a 40-year-old tank in usable (or at least repairable) condition. And that is fortunate, because each brand of prewar automobile frequently has a unique tank shape, conforming to the design of the grille shell or front end sheetmetal.

Common fatigue points are at the soldered joints where the core and side supports meet and where the filler neck is soldered to the tank. Pinholes and minor fractures can be easily repaired, and if need be, all joints can be cleaned and completely resoldered. However, if the tanks have become so embrittled (through excessive expansion and contraction) as to need replacement, relatively simple designs can be reproduced by hand in the radiator shop. Compound curves, though, will require the services of a sheetmetal craftsman, and the car owner is going to have to seek out such skills in body shops that cater to the antique and classic trade.

Postwar radiator tanks show a similarity that makes life somewhat easier for the restorer . . . as long as he is willing to compromise a bit in his desire for authenticity of design. Most radiator shops stock tanks for late-model cars that are close enough to satisfy all but the most discriminating purist. And just as with cores, the practical man should find himself thinking in terms of operating efficiency rather than concours points.

Which brings up yet another potential compromise. Should the restorer of a special interest automobile build in a wider margin of cooling safety than the original radiator provided? This is a point worthy of consideration, particularly when the car is powered by a valve-in-block, long exhaust port engine.

True, if the engine is in perfect condition, i.e. not a bit of scale in the water jackets, etc., chances are the original radiator capacity is adequate. But alas, not all engines can boast such an enviable state of internal affairs. Years of corrosion will have eaten away metal, hot tanking *will not* remove all rust and scale, and other undetected flaws will

1. Even as nicely restored a car as this 1940 Hupmobile Skylark can have its cooling system problems.

2. Carbon monoxide leaks from a defective head gasket or cracked block are serious and should be corrected immediately. Corrosive acids are formed when the gas enters the cooling system. To detect their presence, a syringe-type instrument called a Blok Check is inserted into the filler neck and pumped several times. Blue test liquid turns yellow within 60 secs. if there is a combustion leak, no matter how slight.

3. Clogged radiators are best cleaned by strong chemicals to remove all rust and scale. Afterwards, leak test is accomplished by pumping in air, submerging radiator and watching for bubbles.

4. Pressure flushing a radiator is best left up to a shop. Although not a complicated procedure, it does require proper equipment.

5. One of the most common passenger car radiator designs in current use; the tube and corrugated fin. Air passing around the tubes carries away the heat. Cores are manufactured with 7 to 20 fins per linear inch; the higher the count, the heavier the duty.

6. Another common radiator core currently available; the tube and plate fin. Tubes are typically 7/16-in. by 3/32-in.

7. Well-stocked radiator repair shops can come up with almost any size core you want—if you're not adamant about fin and tube design.

8. A mint example of a classic radiator design; the very expensive ribbon-cellular on a '25 Jordan. The core is 3-ins. thick. Similar cores can still be special ordered, but be prepared to pay plenty.

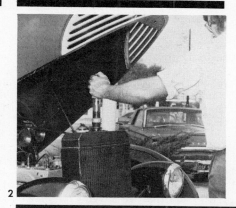

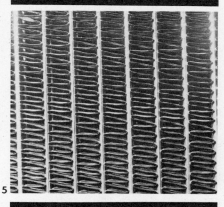

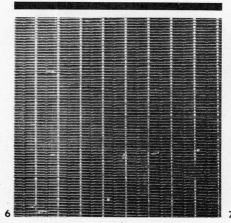

haunt the owner of a "freshly rebuilt" engine. In short, a greater-capacity radiator just might make the difference between overheating and cool running.

Ideally, a radiator would be one row of tubes thick... and 10 ft. by 10 ft. square. Ideally, but not practically. So radiators are built with smaller frontal dimensions by placing the rows of water passage tubes one behind the other, usually to a maximum of four. (Beyond that depth, there is a diminishing return, eventually to the point of cooling *loss,* inasmuch as the hindmost tubes just aren't receiving the flow of cool air.) But a four-tube radiator is a good bet over a three-tube original. Consider it if you are planning to order a new core.

Along these same lines, the conversion of a non-pressure cooling system to one that is pressurized is an excellent way to improve cooling efficiency. Atmospheric pressure is about 15 psi at sea level, and that's the level where water boils at 212° F. But with each added pound of pressure, the boiling point increases 3¼° F. That means that the coolant can be circulated at higher temperatures without boiling in a pressure boost system, and when it enters the radiator, heat is more quickly transferred to the air. In addition, coolant evaporation is reduced, because the boiling point is higher.

It is relatively easy to convert a *good* non-pressurized radiator. All that is required is to solder on a filler neck with the appropriate pressure cap. Pressure caps are designed to provide up to an additional 12 psi, which increases the boiling point of water to 250° F.

Another inconspicuous cooling system component that a prudent restorer will want to make sure is fully operative is the thermostat. The thermostat closes off the water passages between the head(s) and the top of the radiator in order to allow a cold engine to quickly reach operating temperature. They are as nearly foolproof as an automotive part can be, but they do occasionally go sour.

The thermostat consists of a bellows and a valve. The latter is closed when the bellows is cold, but as engine temperature rises, the bellows expands and opens the valve so coolant can circulate between the engine and the radiator. Thermostats are calibrated to open within specific temperature ranges; i.e. a 160° F. unit starts to open between 157° and 163° F. and is fully open at about 183° F. Most older cars operate best with 160° or 180° F. units.

The final compromise component we'd like to consider is the "coolant" itself. Now, coolant is not just a fancy word for water. Conventionally it is 50% water and 50% ethyl glycol antifreeze/antiboil concentrate. Pure water runs significantly cooler without the addition of any concentrate. Unfortunately, it also oxidizes the devil out of everything it comes in contact with. The restorer who wants to experiment without paying that high cost might try running soft water and a pint of water-soluble oil during the warmer months. Of course, antifreeze is still necessary during the winter for those of you who live in colder climates.

Before we go any further, we hasten to add that we haven't forgotten the water pump and the fan in our survey of cooling system components. Rather we have saved them for last because the restorer has little or no choice in their selection, even though the water pump is the primary mechanical component in the system.

For all practical purposes, all water pumps are the same. They consist of a housing, an inlet, an outlet and an impeller. Granted, they all look different, and impellers come in various designs. But the water pump is not a compromise component. If you are restoring a 1932 Plymouth, you will use what is essentially a 1932 Plymouth water pump. The same holds true for the fan.

Troubleshooting the cooling system is a task that can be started at home, but will probably require the services of a radiator shop to finish off. The first consideration is a complete inspection of all system components. Look through the radiator inlet for corrosion, scale or plugged-up tubes. If the coolant is muddy or rusty, flush and replace it. Check the condition of the fins. If they feel soft, then chances are you will soon be in the market for a new core. Check around soldered joints for telltale corrosion (green residue).

Remove the bottom hose and insert a garden hose in the top tank. Turn on the faucet and note how fast the water runs through the radiator and out. If it drains slowly or fills up, you can be certain that the passages are badly clogged. You may want to try one of the cooling system flushes found in the local parts house, but they offer temporary relief at best. Sooner or later you can bank on a trip to the radiator shop for an inexpensive boil-out. (But don't be surprised to find leaks you didn't know existed. Chemical clean-

ing removes scale that had plugged up holes.)

Although it is difficult to determine the condition of a water pump, some idea of its efficiency can be measured by squeezing the upper hose while the engine is warm and running. You should be able to detect an increase in pressure as the engine speed is increased.

Also, look back into the radiator inlet. Watch for small bubbles traveling across the top of the coolant. They are a dead giveaway that the water pump is sucking air and needs to be replaced or rebuilt.

With the engine shut off, grasp the fan and try to pull it up and down. The bearing that supports the water pump impeller shaft should not give at all. (On engines where the fan is driven by means other than direct connection to the pump, merely grasp whatever pulley is attached to the pump.)

Naturally you should inspect the hoses, radiator cap and fan belt. Periodic replacement is a matter of course.

As we draw this chapter to a close, we might point out that sometimes engine overheating is not entirely due to malfunctions in the cooling system itself. Insufficient oil, engine overload, improper ignition timing, high-altitude operation or simply very hot weather can contribute. By the way, don't be misled by normal after-boil or heat buildup.

This occurs when the engine is shut down following sustained operation. The engine still contains heat, and because the circulation system is no longer functioning, coolant in the water jackets may boil.

The automotive cooling system is not at all mysterious. Indeed, its basic design hasn't changed in years. But its components are subject to wear and tear, and it doesn't take much to drastically reduce its efficiency. If you are experiencing cooling problems, the troubleshooting procedures recommended above should help pinpoint their origins. Otherwise, equipment found only in repair shops will be required. Fortunately, repair and replacement are often much less expensive than the potential engine damage that is foretold by a rising temperature gauge. 🐞

1. This 1921 Dodge is equipped with a round tube and plate fin radiator. The tubes are ¼-in. diameter and are spaced about 1-in. apart for superior (it was hoped) cooling.

2. This '35 Ford radiator may look passable from the front (11), but reversing it (12) reveals years of torture. It should be recored, but the tanks and side panels can be saved.

3. A variation on the ribbon-cellular theme was used on the '32 Plymouth.

4. Radiator corners and edges are critical, and those exposed to ocean salt air will soften and eventually crumble. Check for leaks at all soldered joints.

5. Although this is a fairly late model water pump, the design of the impeller has remained essentially the same for many years.

6. An important little aid to improved cooling, even on an older radiator. This is the pressure cap.

7. Equally as important is the thermostat. Did you ever know anyone who removed his thermostat, and the car ran hotter? Why is this? Coolant doesn't stay in the radiator sufficiently long to cool.

8. Check the appearance of your coolant from time to time. Flush and replace as necessary. And don't use the same pressure cap for more than one year.

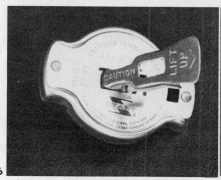

BASIC ENGINE REFURBISHING
NO MATTER HOW BAD IT IS, IT CAN USUALLY BE RESTORED

PHOTOS BY ERIC RICKMAN

Everything you have read so far has told you how to restore your treasured find to its original mint, stock condition. Unless you plan on parking it in your garage permanently, or hauling to shows on a trailer, you will want to complete your restoration by putting the little jewel in running condition. Needless to say, this isn't going to be something you will be able to completely do yourself, as there is usually a good deal of machine shop work involved in a project of this scope.

One often reads or hears about the one-in-a-million find of a classic car with low mileage, but it will have to be assumed that your restorable find will be pretty well worn out when you make your purchase.

The biggest problem in embarking on a project of this type is finding an engine rebuilding shop that will take the time and care to do this type of work properly, it takes another dedicated classic aficionado to even consider this type of job. Fortunately we were able to locate a few of this vanishing breed that are still around and willing to tackle any job.

Unless your engine has suffered a major disaster, such as a broken crank or rod that has destroyed the block, almost any engine can be rebuilt. Wear is not the major problem! Internal rust and cracks are the principal obstacles to be overcome in engine rebuilding.

You may save some money on this job: after reading our section on Freeing Frozen Fasteners you will be able to tackle the dismantling of the engine—one of the more time-consuming aspects of this job.

The engine will have to be removed from the vehicle, and cleaned

1. An elephant graveyard, typical of long-established engine builders' stock of cores. This yard belongs to Motor Mart in Anaheim, Calif. Typically the goodies are buried in back.

2. Here are a few little jewels we dug out: Model A's, some flathead V-8's, even a T or two. This stuff is still around; you just have to know where to look.

3. A crude block repair, but it did save the block. With a little finesse this could be cleaned up and made to look more presentable. Often there is no alternative if the block is good.

4. Leaking head gasket allowed water into combustion chambers and badly eroded top of block around valve ports and water passages.

5. Partially repaired area is filled by cast iron welding; entire surface will have to be filled and a new deck cut made. Valve ports will be cut out and new seat inserts installed.

6. A magnet and silver-colored iron powder locate a bad head crack. This is typical. Cracks usually occur between valve ports.

7. The Salsbury method of crack repairing utilizes various sizes of tapered and threaded cast iron plugs. Cold installation process does not warp the head or block.

8. After drilling a series of holes along the crack, the holes are tapped, prior to driving in the tapered plugs. Holes are drilled very close together.

9. Locktite or K&W Block Sealer can be used on plug threads. The proper touch is needed here; too tight and the plug will open the crack further.

10. Plug heads are cut off with a hacksaw blade. Note proximity of plugs. If casting wall is too thin for plug to hold properly, welding is the only alternative, used as a last resort.

11. Plug heads are ground off flush and additional plugs installed in between the first set, allowing the plugs to overlap. A plug must be located at the end of the crack to prevent crack from advancing.

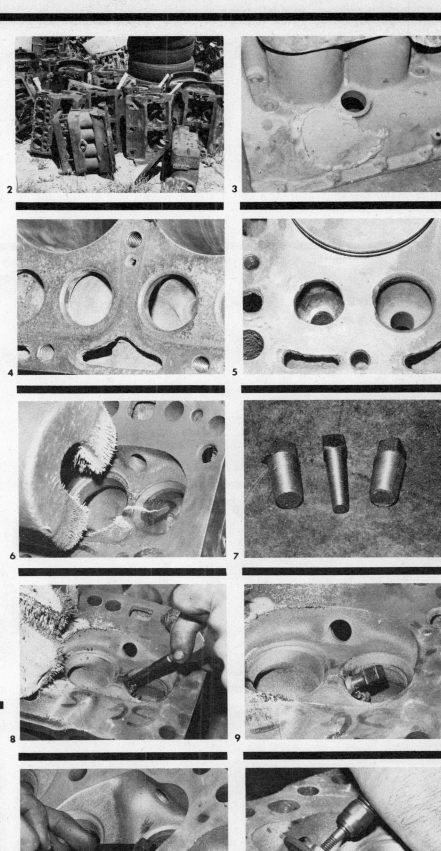

thoroughly before you begin taking it apart. As advised in Freeing Frozen Fasteners, be as careful as possible, try not to chew up the original nuts and bolts any more than necessary. You will want the restored engine to be as near stock as possible, and this means using all the original fasteners. Have plenty of boxes handy and organize all the parts into separate boxes, you will have enough trouble finding parts as it is without losing any you already have. Clean and inspect everything thoroughly. The machine shop will give everything another cleaning, but there is no such thing as having parts too clean.

A word of caution is in order here, if you are not familiar with engines, check with the shop that is going to do the machine work for you, they may prefer that you not attempt to dismantle the engine. You will more than likely do more harm than good if you don't know what you are doing.

It is interesting to note that there are so many remanufactured, and new old parts available for the most popular classics that it is almost possible to build a complete car using the currently manufactured repro parts and pieces. This is particularly true in the case of the early Fords. Unfortunately, the repro parts manufacturers haven't gotten around to engine blocks and cranks yet. They do make pistons, bearings, and valves, however. And cam grinders can build up and regrind your old cam to spec.

Detroit is required to stock parts for their various cars for a period of 10 years from the model year, after that it is scrounge around the dealer's shelves in hope of finding the part you need buried somewhere in the back under layers of dust. We're personally experiencing this problem in trying to refurbish a '64 El Camino, the parts man's usual retort is, "Sorry they don't make that anymore." We would have much more success with an older classic restoration.

We have been able to locate several of the older long-established engine builders who are rebuilding the more current engines on a semi-production line basis, but will take the

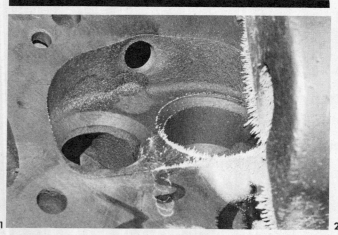

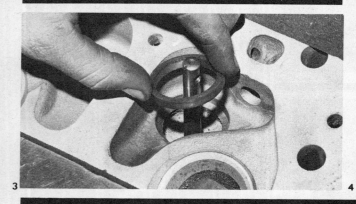

time and care needed to rebuild one of the older classic engines as a special project. We say, "older, long-established engine builders," for a reason. Most of them were in business when these engines were in current use, and as seems to be the case with these people, they never throw anything away. This holds true not only of engine builders, but the clutch and transmission rebuilders as well. We have seen whole sections of warehouses literally stacked to the ceiling with mountains of old parts.

We have also seen acres of old engines dating back into the Twenties, with a few even earlier Model T's lying about for good measure. The stuff is turning into solid gold as time goes by. We wonder if they planned it that way, or just lucked out? Hang onto things long enough and they come back into style.

External rust from lying out in the weather is no great problem, since the rebuilder will usually blast the block with glass beads or some other mild abrasive after a soaking and high pressure bath in an alkali-filled hot tank. Internal rust is another problem that occurs when the old engine is left standing with water in the block. The head gaskets deteriorate, and water works its way between the head and block sur-

1. Magnetic powder reveals a row of overlapping plugs extending into the combustion chamber and on down into the valve port.

2. Valve port is cut out after crack repair for installation of a new valve seat. This system is also used to replace badly worn valve seats.

3. New insert is dropped into place, then driven into the head. Insert is slightly larger than opening to provide an interference fit so seat can't work loose. Seats are available in various degrees of hardness, from cast iron to stellite steel.

4. New seat is ground into insert using same pilot shaft that cutter was centered on to ensure concentricity. Stellite inserts are used with lead-free gasoline and dry gaseous fuels.

5. Head or block surface is finished in a grinder or a mill to ensure a smooth, flat mating surface. Cutting beyond specifications will raise the compression ratio of the engine.

6. Clever jig used at California Engine Co. in Van Nuys, Calif. shop has multiple arms to close off water passages. Air pressure and a soapy solution are used to find leaks.

7. If cylinders are worn out, rusted or cracked, cast iron sleeves can be installed to bring bore back to stock size. Sleeve is miked to determine necessary bore size.

8. Boring bar is used to cut an oversize opening to take sleeve. Cylinder is bored .002-in. undersize for interference fit (read tight).

9. Where possible, a shoulder is left at bottom of the bore to prevent sleeve from dropping into engine if it works loose—an unlikely event. If sleeve must extend into crankcase, a stepped sleeve is used and a step cut made at the top of the block. Either way, head locks sleeve in block.

10. Aluminum paint is sprayed into bore to seal surface. If there is a large crack, Irontite ceramic sealer is used. Head/block can be flushed with sealer in water jacket as a final precaution against leaks.

11. Sleeve is driven home with a trusty sledge hammer. Remember, it's an interference fit. Dale Drake, owner of California Engine Co., did this job for us. Dale is a collector himself.

12. Sleeve protrudes above block, boring tool is changed and bar is used to cut top off sleeve flush with deck. Entire block can be sleeved back to stock or just one cylinder can be repaired this way.

faces, leaving both surfaces badly pitted and erroded. This calls for building the area up again with cast iron welding—an art unto itself. The proper preheating and cooling of the pieces to avoid warping and cracking is another science. After the surfaces are filled, the head and block are machined with a light surfacing cut to restore the original smooth and flat deck surface.

Badly rusted and worn cylinders are no problem in most engines as it is a simple matter to bore the block out to accept insert cast iron sleeves that will bring the bore back to stock size. A stock bore will give you a much wider selection of pistons because you can use any oversize available if stock pistons can't be found. The sleeved block can be bored oversize to fit the piston, or the piston can be turned down to stock size. Valve ports are machined out to accept new insert valve seats if worn beyond saving. The old guides are pressed out of the heads and new guides installed in their

1. Complete small foundry at Egge Machine Co. in Santa Fe Springs, Calif. If owner Nels Egge doesn't have it in stock, he will cast a set of pistons for you in short order.

2. Pistons are cast as oversize slugs, to be machined to customer size on order. Nels has dome head slugs in any compression range in stock too.

3. After rough machining to size and cutting ring grooves, piston is cam ground and given final finish on this special grinding machine.

4. Just one of many shelves of semi-finished pistons. Auburn, Hupmobile, Rolls Royce, Caddie, Erskine and Mercedes are there, with lots of old Ford and Chevy sizes too. Over 20,000 pistons sold last year.

5. One of the warehouse-full of shelves of new, old parts, piston rings, bearings, ignition parts. You name it and Nels will have it.

6. A fascinating aisle topped by hundreds and hundreds of head gaskets, all neatly tagged. Just send in your old gasket and it can be matched.

7. Stainless steel valve blanks are made in many sizes. Blanks are later cut down to customer specifications. Using your old valve for a pattern, Nels can make up a set to fit almost any engine you can come up with.

place, and you have a good-as-new head.

Cracked blocks and heads are one of the major problems faced by the rebuilder. If the crack is accessible and not too bad, it can often be welded, or plugged with a small tapered and threaded cast iron plug (known as the Salisbury method of repair). Plugging, being a cold process is preferred because welding or brazing are prone to distort the block or head. The condition of the block will be the deciding factor in whether you will be able to salvage it or not.

A badly worn or undersize crankshaft can be brought back to stock specs by welding or metal spraying the journals and mains then grinding the areas back to stock size. Flame spraying is preferred because it involves less heat and crank straightening after the job is done. Here again, going back to stock specs has the advantage of increas-

7

8

9

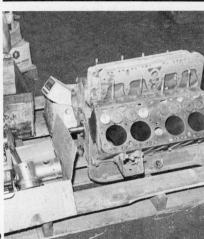
10

8. Older valves were of softer metals. Stainless steel valves require this electric-discharge drilling machine to make oval and round keeper holes in the valve stems. Egge Machine is equipped to reproduce almost any old part needed to rebuild an engine.

9. This is just part of the incoming stock that hasn't been inventoried yet. Nels has stuff even he doesn't know he has in stock. Try him.

10. Customer will assemble this '48 Caddie flathead. Nels bored block, did valves, furnished pistons, rings and bearings. Job cost about $300. Completely assembled engine with a reground crank and cam will go for $800 to a grand, depending on the amount of special work needed to salvage engine, fix cracks, etc.

11. This complete wiring harness is for a '58 Mercedes. It is completely tagged and color coded for drop-in rewiring. Egge will make harnesses for almost any old car. Note special braided loom covering on harness.

12. How's this for being specialized? Nels has both 32- and 64-spindle loom braiding machines for covering wire harnesses. Spools of thread are set up to match proper color of harness to be duplicated wherever possible.

13. Badly scored or worn crank can be built up by welding, then ground to size. Welding is used where a good deal of metal must be added. It distorts crank and requires careful realigning between centers afterward.

14. If crank isn't too badly worn, it can be ground to the next undersize. If too far gone, surface is ground smooth to prepare for metal spraying to build bearing up to stock specs. Up to .030-in. can be added this way.

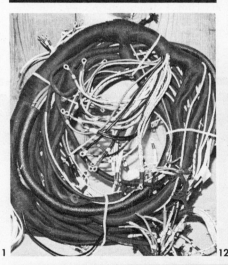
11

12

13

14

ing the availability of bearings, as you can now use any undersize bearing by having it resized to stock.

We have found companies that specialize in casting babbitt bearings for the older engines, this includes the cast-in-block and rod bearings, as well as the old thick removable shell bearings. Specify your crank size and they will cast and size the bearings to fit.

When we come to electrics, it's hard to believe, but there are complete wire looms available, color-coded and tagged just ready to drop in for a complete rewiring job. We found these looms and literally millions of other fascinating items at the Egge Machine Company (8403 Allport Ave., in Santa Fe Springs, Calif.). Owner Nels Egge has so much stuff that even he doesn't know just what he does have in stock. We did see plenty of the old-type lacquered ignition wire.

Nels even has the weaving looms to cover the wire harnesses in the proper colors to match the stock looms.

Egge Machine Company specializes in casting aluminum pistons, any make and almost any size, just send him your old piston and he will make you a set in any size and compression ratio you desire. He even has most of the piston rings to go with your pistons, and a fascinating stock of old gaskets. Egge also has a

large stock of valve blanks and can duplicate almost any of the old valves if you just send a sample.

Starters, generators, and voltage regulators are still being built, or rebuilt. There is also a huge supply of old cores available and basic rebuilding is a matter of replacing bushings, brushes, and switch contacts, then truing up the commutator bars. If the windings are completely burned out and no replacement core is avaliable, the coils can be rewound, this calls for a specialist, but it can and is being done.

We were able to round up all these services right here in the Southern California area. Having read many other publications in the classic car field we know that there are hundreds of shops throughout the United States that specialize in old, original; as well as repro parts for almost any of the more popular old cars. Any competent automotive machine shop can fix cracks, and sleeve blocks as well as get cranks refinished.

We suggest you go to some automotive swap meets and talk to the people, find the publications and read up before you dive into your project. It will take time and tenacity, not to mention money, but the end result will be worth it, and often worth a lot more than you put in if you picked the right car and did the job right. ✥

1. A coat of AntiBond material is brushed on the areas where metal isn't desired. All this bearing work was done at Nelkco Bearing & Machine Co. in Santa Fe Springs, Calif.

2. A base bonding coat of nickel aluminide is flame-sprayed on the bearing area first to provide a bond for the stainless steel that will be used to build up the bearing surface. Crank is rotating as molten material is sprayed on the bearing surface. This method uses lower heat than welding.

3. Restored cranks. Model A is on the right; the bent hairpin on the left is a Model T crank. Nelkco can grind down A mains slightly and fit an A crank in a T block—an old hot rodding trick from way back.

4. Model T block with mains cast in the block. Saddles can be bored out for larger bearings to take the A crank. Caps are babbitted separately.

5. Main caps and rods are dipped in the hot babbitt pot to remove old babbitt. Then surface is ground to provide fresh bonding surface for the new babbitt.

6. After grinding and wire brushing, bearing surface is tinned carefully to bond babbitt to body metal. Nelkco uses only high-speed nickel babbitt. No nickel is in it; it's 88% tin, 2% antimony, with copper, lead and zinc making up the other 10%.

7. Bearing core mold must be just the right temperature. Here core is heated by a gas torch. Metal will shrink from mold if chilled.

8. Tinned bearing cap is held in place while molten babbitt is poured into space between bearing cap and bearing mold core. Job takes seconds.

9. Mating faces are cleaned, then bearing caps are installed. This boring bar is used to line bore the saddles and caps to perfect alignment. Machine will also bore saddles and caps oversize for larger bearings to fit Model A crank in the T block.

10. Model A and T blocks ready for delivery with reground cranks and new main bearings. Nelkco averages 12 T's and 24 A's per month, with a few Chevy 4's thrown in too.

11. These long-legged rods are from a Buick straight-8. Rods are squared, then glass bead cleaned before being rebabbitted. Caps and rods are faced, bolted together, then bored to size to fit refinished crankshaft.

12. These unique rods are from an early Rolls-Royce 6-cyl. engine. Note wristpin oiling system. Nelkco gets all types of jobs, from air compressors to windmill bearings.

13. Later cars began to use heavy insert-type bearings. These rebabbitted bearing shells can be machined to fit any reground crankshaft size.

14. This machine flycuts rebabbitted bearing shells to size. New undersize shells can be cut out to stock.

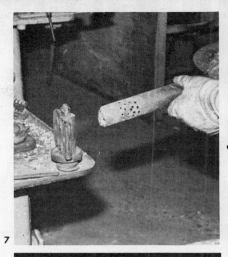

9

7

10

8

11

12

13

14

FLATHEAD V-8 ENGINE REBUILD THE OLD RELIABLE CAN BE MADE MORE RELIABLE THANKS TO MODERN ENGINE TECHNOLOGY

Webster's Seventh Collegiate Dictionary: *Flathead* /n, 1: a member of any of several Indian peoples of North America that formerly practiced head-flattening. 2: a member of a Salishan people of western Montana. 3: any of various fishes with more or less flat heads. 4: the goll-derndest engine ever put in an automobile.

The flathead Ford story continues: The universal engine that won't die is today the object of a great deal of interest from restorers and historians, since the tremendous rise in popularity of the Ford V-8 cars as restoration subjects. The ubiquitous flathead is many things to many people, a cheap, simple, reliable powerplant that was once the workhorse of millions of cars used for daily transportation.

Henry Ford dreamed of a cheap V-8 for his Ford automobiles back in the early Twenties. Many designs were considered: two 4-cyl. Model T blocks on a special crankcase, a pair of Model A blocks in the same arrangement, and even an X-8 (four banks of paired cylinders). But it wasn't until the summer of 1930 that the technology and metallurgy was available to design a V-8 to head off the strong sales of the unbeatable Chevy and Plymouth sixes.

The flathead V-8's most significant feature at the time was that the crankcase and cylinder banks were to be cast in one piece, an am-

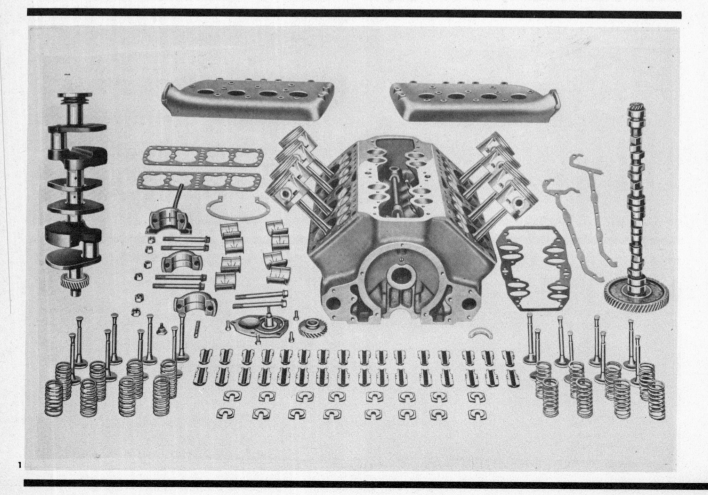

bitious undertaking for an engine that was to sell for only $70 more than the 4-cyl. Model B. This was Henry's goal and the greatest headache for the engineers. He supervised a team of his sharpest troubleshooters to make the dream a reality. The fundamental technological problems were finally worked out, and four months after the first drawings were cut, the final production casting for 1932 was struck. The flathead was born.

22 YEARS

Although the Ford flathead had basically the same design concept from its audacious debut, March 9, 1932, until it was finally set aside for the ohv Y-block in 1954, there are many differences in the engine through the years. We will concern ourselves here with the role of the flathead Ford V-8 engine in the world of genuine Ford restoration projects (as opposed to hop-up or procedures for racing) and explain how to rebuild a flathead V-8 for a restored early (pre-'48) Ford.

Our mentor and prime source of specifications for this article is Bill Wood of La Canada, Calif., whose background includes many hours as

a young man in the Denver, Colo. shop of Bill Kenz and Roy Leslie. Bill Wood is an engineer and he is often asked to lecture to the Early Ford V-8 Club on the subject of building a reliable flathead for street use. He builds many engines for club members. One of his many flathead-powered cars is a '40 Merc Coupe. He hammers out many miles a week driving to work, and seven trips to Canada have helped roll up a hefty 175,000 miles on the current engine with but one valve job for repairs. 175,000 miles on a set of rings . . . not too bad.

THE DILEMMA

Those of you who are rebuilding a flathead for a pre-'39 Ford have a choice to make: whether or not to use the exact year engine that goes with the car. Now, we realize that to suggest to a purist that he put anything in a '33 Phaeton but a '33 engine may be blasphemy, but there are quite a few restored pre-'39 Fords running around with 24-stud engines in them. And there are good reasons for doing this. It will cost you points at shows but many restorers are less interested in points

than they are in the extra horsepower and durability of the 24-stud, post-'39 motors. Or, they simply can't find the proper 21-stud babbitt pounder.

There were, in fact, numerous changes made to the engine between the original configuration in '32, and 1939 when the 24-stud 91 and 99A engines came out. After that, the flathead changed little but power was increased. The horsepower of the '46-'48 engine is nearly double that of the original model, and parts are much easier to find.

So, it's up to you. One word of caution, though. If you opt for the later 59A engine with its 100-110 hp for use in your 21-stud, mechanical-braked '35 coupe, the transmission and brakes may not be satisfactory. Keep it in mind. It's one more complication in your restoration plans.

Although there are differences in the engine, the rebuilding procedures are fundamentally the same. Our purpose here (among others) is to list some sources of supply for hard-to-find parts (those that wear out) and to enumerate some important building tips that will insure success with the engine when it is finished. There is nothing worse than listening to a lot of dialogue from uninformed friends about how unreliable the flathead engine is, and then proving them right when yours fails because it wasn't built properly.

BRASS TACKS

We are going to suggest that *if you have a choice,* if you are not bound by pure restoration considerations ('32-'39), or if you are restoring a '39 or later Ford, use the 59A engine (see listing, '46-'48 Ford/Merc). If possible, start with a complete engine. It's better than collecting one piecemeal, unless you don't mind carrying a micrometer around with you when hunting parts.

The 59A was used in the '46-'48 Fords and Mercs (identical); has 239 cu. ins., and was rated at 100 hp.

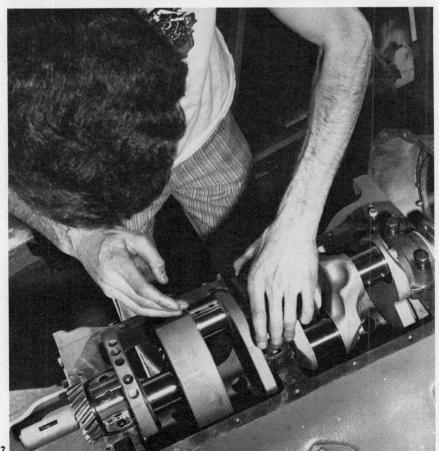

1. Here is a look at all the component parts of a 21-stud flathead engine. When this engine was announced by Ford, it was a revolutionary development for the public.

2. Crankshaft should be dropped into main bearing saddles with extreme care. Bearing clearances should be checked with Plastigage before assembly begins. One must note that this crank has had the full treatment. It was magnafluxed, ground, polished, heat-treated, and glass beaded, all for strength.

The letters 59A (or L or Z) are embossed on top of the bellhousing. If you use the 59A with its 10-in. clutch and flywheel with a pre-'39 Ford bellhousing and transmission, remember that the early clutch housing which was designed to take a 9-in. clutch will not accommodate the 59A 10-in. clutch. Also, the 59A motor mounts are integral with the water pumps, unlike the pre-'39's, so motor mount adapters must be fabricated when putting the late motor in a 21-stud chassis. These can be incorporated without welding or making any changes to the chassis. If you are using an engine of a year different than the chassis, it is the *chassis* that will determine which fan arrangement you use, and *you must use a fan!*

DISASSEMBLE THE "IRON MOUNTAIN"

Before you start work on your rebuilding project, you might explain to your wife that she need not fear: you do know what you're doing—armed with reams of reference material—and she can be assured that the filthy mountain of iron on the garage floor will indeed one day haul the family to a Dearborn meet. As added insurance, you might invest in one of the manuals for older cars like *Chilton's Auto Repair Manual 1940-1953,* or a *Motor Manual* for pre and postwar cars.

When you get your engine home (or out of your car) set aside a clean area of your workbench to prepare for the project. Disassemble the engine carefully, saving all the bolts and parts. You may want to keep the bolts in containers marked for easy reference. If the bolts are rusted or stripped you can use the size and number for reference to buy new ones. Clean all parts with solvent and set them aside. Don't throw anything away even if you think you are going to replace it later. Drain the oil before you drop the pan. Gather all cast iron (and steel) parts—heads, block, crank, rods, pan, etc.—and have them hot-tanked to remove grease, sludge, and oil. Don't hot-tank aluminum. It will dissolve!

This probably is no news to most of you but flathead engines are tough to keep cool. Every part of the cooling system must be in top shape, right? Okay, right off the bat you can get a real head start on the cooling problem by removing all the rust from the water jackets of your block. Think about that one for a minute . . . you can't do it with a

screwdriver. Send the block to the Redi-Strip Company. See the story on metal stripping for the address of a shop near you. They will remove all the rust from the block (or any other rusted parts you have) by using an electrolytic process. The water jackets will be like new.

Once the block is clean you can check for cracks. Inspect the main webs for obvious flaws. For real insurance, have the block magnafluxed ($15). Check the cylinder decks: you will probably notice cracks from stud holes to water jacket passages. Don't worry about these. But if there are cracks from a *cylinder* to a valve seat, water jacket, or stud hole, you're out of luck. Get another block.

Mike the bores and note their sizes. Run a tap into *all* holes in the block to clean the threads. Run a small rod into all the oil galleries in the crank. (On late cranks you will have to remove the "freeze" plugs.)

While disassembling, you should have been sure to mark the rod caps and main caps to make sure you don't switch them when putting the engine together. The front and center main caps look like they might interchange but they don't. Here's how to identify them: The two bolt holes in the center cap are equally spaced between the sides of the cap, but the holes in the front cap are offset slightly. When installing, align the bearing tang slots on the block. The rear cap does not interchange.

Remember this! If you buy your engine one part at a time make sure your block has *main bearing caps.* If you don't get the caps that go with the block, you will have to have the block align-bored ($40—$50) in order to use the caps from a different block. That's an expensive mistake for nothing.

When disassembling the valve gear do not mix the valves or valve guides. Make a holder to keep all

parts in the same relation to one another; e.g. No. 1 cylinder intake and exhaust valves with No. 1 guides and lifters. (The springs you can interchange. They will all be matched for pressure). Send out the block, crank, rods, pistons, and heads to your rebuilder or machine shop.

If you have a 1936 or earlier engine, the main bearings are the poured babbitt type. Bearing babbitt is an alloy that is melted in a small forge and poured into iron fixtures in the main webs and main bearing caps. The "irons" are inserted into the block and caps to make a "mold," and when the alloy cools, they are removed.

The rebuilder will make and grind your crank to whatever undersize is necessary to clean it up, and then align-bore the bearings to provide

1. A torque wrench must be used for assembly. A *Motor's Manual* will supply specifications and instructions.

2. Reciprocating assembly should be balanced for maximum power and smoothness. All pistons and rods are brought to equal weight, then crank is drilled for proper weight.

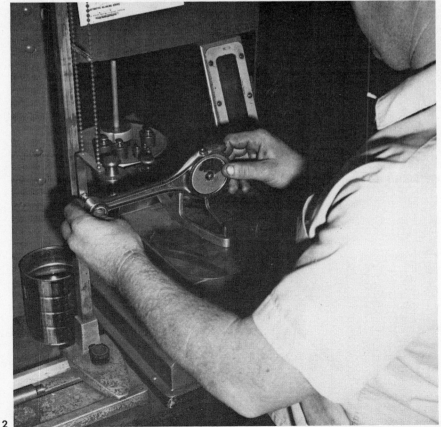
2

the proper clearance with the crank. In this way, it is easier to provide bearings for the babbitt motors because they can be cut to whatever clearance is desired. The later cranks require a regular insert type bearing and your choice will depend on what's available off the supplier's shelves. Also, late bearings are only available in selected undersizes: .001-, .002-, .003-, .010-, .020-, .030-in. whereas, the babbitt can be cut for any undersize.

On the 59A block (and other 24-studders), bearings can be had from Federal-Mogul and some other bearing suppliers. Your machine shop should be able to get them for you. You might have the decks of the block checked. Each deck should be the *exact* distance from the main bearing bores. This is something that wasn't done 20 years ago during rebuilding. It will make a big difference in the way the engine performs. The block is clamped in a saddle and each deck is cut with a huge cutting wheel to true the decks and equalize their distance from the crank.

Before you bore the block you should have the pistons you are going to use, in hand. You can bore to

fit pistons, but it may be difficult to find pistons to fit a *particular* bore. Pistons for stock rebuilds should be available at various obsolete parts houses, and some auto parts houses. Mike the bore, then locate pistons that are enough oversize to allow a clean-up bore. Usually .060-in. should clean the cylinders.

After boring it is essential that each cylinder be honed properly. This is a *must* for proper ring seating and long life. Use a 220 grit stone, lubed with 10W or 20W oil only, nothing else. The cross-hatch pattern should be between 30° and 45° from the horizontal. This is regulated by the speed at which the hone is moved up and down in the cylinder.

After honing, wipe the cylinder with an oil saturated rag to *float* the grit to the top of the grooves, *then* use solvent or lacquer thinner. Don't use solvent or thinner to remove honing grit because it won't lift the particles out of the grooves.

The valves and valve seats should be ground during the machine work stage (rather than after the block has been cleaned for assembly). So we'll jump ahead a bit and talk about valves.

Bill Woods recommends that you use Ford script exhaust valves if at all possible (pre-1949). These valves will have the letters "T-Ford-F" on them. The "T" and the "F" will be upright block letters ('32-'36) or slanted ('37 on). If you have script valves and they are damaged, salvage them if at all possible. You may have to root around swap meets, parts houses, or wrecking yards for script valves. Bill suggests that FoMoCo ('49-'53) valves are not as good as script valves. If your valve stems are worn, hard chroming may add .002- to .003-in.

Flathead valve guides are tungsten chrome steel. You must use genuine Ford valve guides, and they are hard to find. Replacement (non-Ford) guides are of poor quality, often with the valve stem hole not concentric with the O.D. of the guide. The valve won't seat if the hole is off. The exhaust guides are more often worn than the intakes. You can install the intake guides in the exhaust side, and then replace the eight intake guides.

Valve seats should be ground to widths of .060-in. for intakes and .090-in. for exhausts. A 30° angle on the intake valves will provide a small boost in performance but exhaust seats should *always* be ground to 45°. The valves should be hand-lapped to ensure a good seal.

Now that all the machine work is done, clean the block *thoroughly* with Tide or another strong detergent soap. (If your wife will go for it, toss the block in the washing machine.) Dry the block with an air hose and spray the whole thing with WD-40 or wipe it with a good film of oil to prevent rusting. Replace all oil gallery plugs. Remember the one directly behind the cam gear. Now back to the reciprocating assembly.

Piston rings are most important for long engine life and robust performance. Perfect Circle has a good ring set for flatheads. It consists of a chrome 200 compression top ring, a cast-iron 200 second ring, and a chrome 98 oil set (two rails with ex-pander). This type of ring set is relatively new and wasn't available when the flathead was still being produced. It will give a better seal and longer life than stock rings.

Ring gap should be .010- to .012-in. Be sure that when fully compressed into the piston grooves the rings do not butt together before they are flush with the piston side. Bill suggests one idea that will help ring life greatly: machine the top ring groove in the piston for a rail (spacer) that fits above the top ring. These rails are available from Perfect Circle and other suppliers and Bill credits them for his uncanny ring life.

Use heavy-duty piston pins if possible. Pins are available from your engine rebuilder. When installing the pins make sure the snap rings are firmly seated in their grooves. The pin clearance should be .0004-in., which is pretty tight. At room temperature, grip the piston firmly, holding the rod straight out. It should fall slowly of its own weight.

Federal Mogul has many rod bearing numbers for flatheads. Full floating rod bearings were used from 1932 through 1948 on V-8 engines. The floating-type rod bearing is not anchored to the rod big-end. It has bearing material (nickel/silver, copper alloy, cad/silver, etc.) on both sides of the shell, and spins on both the crankpin and the inside the rod. It is probably the best rod bearing design there is, good for many thousands of miles of service.

Floating rod bearings were replaced in the post-'49 flatheads with the more commonly used pinned-insert type. Floating bearings must be installed so that the part-lines do not hang up on the part-lines of the rod. This is done by spreading or squeezing the shells until they fit the rods and crankpins perfectly.

Your rods should be reusable with no problem (unless they're obviously

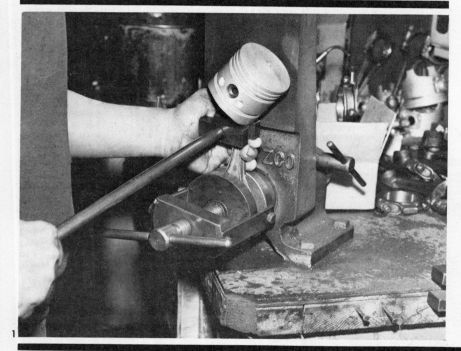

1

1. Rods are aligned on a fixture that will show if they are slightly bent. This is corrected with a large bar and clamp to bend rod.

2. Use this torquing sequence for cylinder heads. Lube threads of studs or capscrews before tightening.

3. After the block has been cleaned, don't forget to replace the gallery plugs before assembly begins. The main lifter gallery plus is behind the camshaft gear, as indicated.

4. Fresh 21-studer in this '34 will provide 100,000 miles of service if built and assembled carefully.

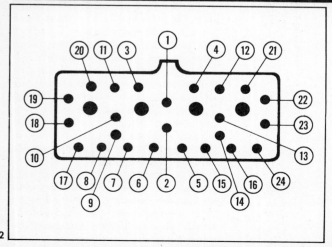

2

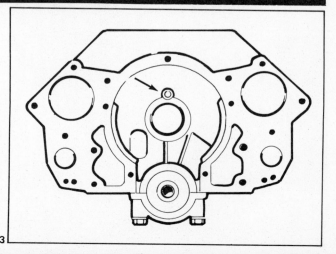

3

deformed). They should be aligned and checked for wear on both ends. If the big-end I.D. is worn it can be resized by removing material at the part-line and reboring. The little-end bushings should be replaced and sized for proper pin clearance.

The entire reciprocating assembly should be balanced by a competent engine builder. This will make a big difference in smoothness and will increase power and engine life.

Bill Wood recommends the use of the late-8BA ('49-'53) oil pump. It is shorter than the 59A pump but uses helical instead of straightcut spur gears, and pumps a lot more oil. Use the 8BA inlet screen and pickup tube. Engine rebuilders can supply new gears or a complete rebuilt oil pump for you. If you can locate one of the old Mellings oil pumps it's a great unit for increased pressure and volume to the bearings.

It is likely that you can reuse your stock camshaft. Mike the lobes and compare them with one another. Usually, when a cam lobe loses its hardness it wears fast and it will be visibly smaller than the others. You shouldn't reject a cam for lobe-size differentials of less than .004-in. If your cam is worn it can probably be reground by any cam grinder.

Check the bearing journals for wear because this will reduce oil pressure. There should be no need to change timing gears unless yours are obviously damaged. Use pre-'48 cam

followers (lifters). The lobe surface is much larger than the late units. Check the length of the followers for excessive wear. If their lobe surfaces are etched or slightly dished, you may be able to make them perfectly flat by polishing them with a strip of aluminum oxide sandpaper pressed against a thick piece of glass. However, don't go through the hardening, which is only a few thousandths of an inch thick.

Valve-to-cylinder head clearance should be at least .040-in. The head gasket will be .060-in. thick. If you remove the gasket and install the head and there is no interference, then you know you have at least .060-in. clearance.

When assembling any engine, flathead or otherwise, you must keep every part perfectly clean. Your work area must be clean and organized and you must have parts and tools handy. Always use assembly lube generously. Some fellows like STP, others use engine oil, white lead, a mixture of these, or their own special brew. Whatever, use a good assembly lube to prevent starting the engine dry.

Don't use the genuine Ford head gaskets. Use a Fel-Pro or Victor copper/asbestos sandwich type *with* gasket sealer. Follow torque sequence in the manual and retorque the heads at least three times in the first few hundred miles. The threads of the studs or bolts should be lubed

with silicone grease because it won't flow out between retorquings. Torque wrench readings depend on the lubricated threads. Oil will run out and change your readings. With cast-iron heads, capscrews should be torqued to 50-lbs. hot; studs 70 lbs. With aluminum heads, capscrews should be 40-lbs. cold, and studs 55 lbs. Prevent scrapings of metal from the studs or holes in the heads from getting between the heads and block. Tap the studs with a hammer, bending them until the heads drop onto the block to avoid scraping. Soak the main bearing seals in engine oil for a week. Bill heartily recommends the use of a Frantz oil filter, in fact he wouldn't be without one. He is also a firm believer in the Perry water filter which keeps the cooling system unbelievably clean.

The stock distributor (through '48) is probably the best unit you can use for your engine. It is a dual-point design with centrifugal advance and is far superior to the '49 to '53 type. The point plate was designed by Mallory, has 36° of dwell, and parts are available from obsolete parts houses. Of course, plug wiring should be new.

If you can secure a genuine radiator it will have more fins than some replacement cores. You must have a top-notch cooling system. Check the tubes, tanks, hoses, and make sure air has full access to the radiator. Don't restrict the passage of air with plaques or license plates. If at all possible, build a fan shroud, possibly removable for concourse events. Run a fan; use 160° thermostats. Bill suggests that you do not use coolant (anti-freeze) but stick with water. Some fellows do have good luck with coolant but others have had trouble with electrolysis of aluminum. The Perry water filter is said to eliminate electrolysis. If you do use plain water, use some sort of rust inhibitor with it.

We simply don't have space to show every construction detail of assembly of the engine. If you can find an early motor manual for your year engine you should have no trouble. Or, you may want to have your engine assembled by a pro. At least you'll be armed with a basic knowledge of what's involved and you may be able to help him find parts.

If care is taken, there's no reason why your flathead is one bit less reliable than the engine in your new car. It's just a matter of top-quality workmanship.

RENEWING GENERATORS AND STARTERS BRUSHING UP ON SOME ELECTRICAL ACCESSORIES

BY ERIC RICKMAN

Before you can get your beautifully rebuilt engine running, you're usually going to be faced with the problem of restoring the electrical system.

As mentioned elsewhere in this section on engines, there are complete wire looms available that are color coded and tagged for drop-in installation and hookup. Maybe "drop-in" is a bit too casual. From experience I have found that replacing wire looms requires a great deal of physical dexterity, flexibility and stamina when it comes to crawling around behind the dashboard. The point is that already-made-up wiring is available to take care of that problem.

Next we come to the generator, starter, voltage regulator and distributor. Any good machine shop should be able to rebuild a distributor, as the major problem will be wear of the shaft and bushings. A new shaft can be made from drill rod stock, or the old shaft can be metal-sprayed back to size, as discussed in crankshaft restoration. Bushings can be made from bronze stock, or they can be cut down to fit from some oversize existing bushing, pressed in the housing and reamed to fit the restored shaft.

Broken caps and rotors are the most difficult things to replace, since you have to find the exact piece. The molded plastic parts can't be repaired. We have no ready answer to this problem, other than attending lots of swap meets or contacting ignition rebuilding companies, the older the better. These companies are usually found listed as carburetor and ignition rebuilders. Not a bad idea, as you may need some help in the carburetor department also. Points and condensers are in plentiful supply.

Getting back to generators, starters and regulators—you should have a minimum amount of trouble either finding replacements or getting your unit rebuilt if it isn't a real oddball.

We are fortunate here in Hollywood. With the motion picture industry's constant need for older cars, a small industry specializing in the restoration and maintenance of older cars for studio rental has grown up. They handle not just classics, but all the old cars. As a result we have several automotive electrical shops that make a practice of rebuilding and stocking parts for older cars.

My first acquaintance with Ivan Cregger's Hollywood Generator Exchange occured in 1950, when I first came to work for Petersen Publishing Co. My poor old '37 Chevrolet's generator gave up the ghost after the trip down from Oakland. At that time a '37 generator was no problem. Ivan still has '37 Chevy generators in stock, so it's still no problem.

Ivan represents one of the more personalized service businesses that take an interest in older cars. It is a point of pride with Ivan to be able to supply almost any of the older electrical components. He is an admirer of classic cars and gains a great deal of satisfaction from helping to keep alive a portion of the American heritage.

Basically, rebuilding starters and generators involves replacing the bearings and brushes and cleaning up the commutator bars to service the mechanical aspect. Electrically, the wire coils are checked for continuity and condition of the insulation and internal wiring.

All old exchange cores are valuable. Even if they are completely burned out, they can be rewired and new coils wound where necessary. Don't hesitate to bring your unit in even if it appears to be a total loss. Solenoids can also be rewound and replaced, along with the internal switch contacts. Often just rotating a switch contact 180° will offer a new contact surface. There are lots of tricks to this trade. The biggest problem the rebuilder encounters is the removal of bearings and gears that have become frozen to the armature shaft.

Armatures are prone to sling out the solder and wire connections when overloaded and overheated. The wires can be reconnected and soldered back in place to salvage the unit. Worn commutator bars are trued by machining a new surface in

1. While researching this story at Ivan Cregger's Hollywood Generator Exchange, this '50 Buick drove in; owner needed a generator. No problem—Ivan had one on the shelf. There was also a '41 T&C-type De Soto station wagon in for a starter.

2. When you service the Hollywood movie studios, you have to have one of everything in stock. Here Ivan is checking a '23 Oakland generator. There is no money in storing this stuff for all these years. It's a matter of pride, and Ivan just loves classics.

3. A typical corner of the shop has rows of shelves full of starter and generator armatures, reconditioned and ready to go into a rebuilt unit.

4. A few generator shells, complete with field coils, ready for a new lease on life. There are Chevrolet and Chrysler units going back to '29, all on the shelf and ready to go.

5. These are some quite rare power top, window and seat motors from the early Forties. These motors can be rebuilt when necessary. Finding anyone willing and qualified to take on the job is the hard part.

6. This particular shelf has nothing more current than 1942. Old cores are invaluable. Even if the coils are completely burned out, they can be rewound and restored to service.

7. Look closely—you may see something you need. These are starter switches, some brand new, for Model A's, '28 Dodges, you name it. Parts can be cannibalized to fix your particular switch.

8. This is a rare '26/'27 Buick gear-driven generator with a distributor drive at rear of case. Disassembly is the first step in restoration and often difficult, since old bearings and gears are prone to freeze on the shaft.

a lathe. If this cleaning-up operation has been done too often, the armatures are sent to a salvage shop, where new commutators can often be installed. The older units were manufactured by combining components, not as one-piece items as they are with today's more sophisticated engineering techniques.

When bearings go bad, often the armature will rub against the field poles. Fortunately, the damage is self-limiting, because the unit will become excessively noisy or quit completely, thus drawing your attention to the problem before irreparable damage can be done.

Voltage regulators are another necessary adjunct to the car's electrical system that more often than not have to be replaced. There is a plentiful supply of regulators, but a problem arises for the purist in that most of the available stocks are aftermarket replacement brands. Ivan has some rebuilt original stock units on hand, or your stock regulator can often be rebuilt to retain the car's stock integrity.

Typically, the large commercial rebuilder won't waste his valuable storage space in order to keep this slow-moving stock on hand. You are going to have to look for a smaller shop where the owner is a fellow car buff. One clue in your search will be a few of the oldies but goodies parked in his service area. Happy hunting!

1

2

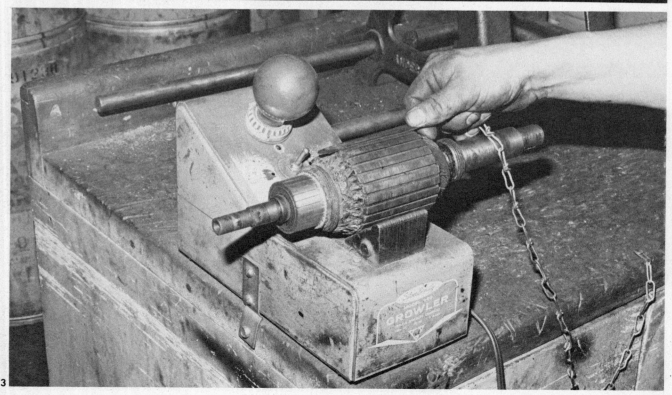

3

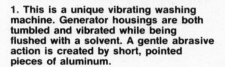

1. This is a unique vibrating washing machine. Generator housings are both tumbled and vibrated while being flushed with a solvent. A gentle abrasive action is created by short, pointed pieces of aluminum.

2. Cleaning action is so gentle that the wire coils and leads aren't damaged, yet paint, dirt, grease and corrosion are completely removed without having to further disassemble the case.

3. Armatures are checked for an open circuit on this magnetic growler. If there is an open winding, the tester emits a loud growling sound and the test light comes on.

4. Here is a stock of starters and generators going back to the Twenties. Ivan has at least one 'T' starter on the shelf at all times. There is also a stock of old voltage regulators.

5. This rear cover of a '26/'27 Buick generator will need new brushes and bearings after being cleaned up. Ivan has a complete stock of these old parts to rebuild almost anything.

6. Resoldering the armature coil leads to the commutator bars is accomplished by dipping the entire commutator end of the armature in a pot of molten solder—*very carefully!*

7. Soldered unit ready for finishing. When generator is overloaded, it overheats, melting solder. Rotation speed slings winding leads out of commutator bars; leads must be reconnected.

8. A light finishing cut is taken to renew the commutator bars' surface. This can only be done so many times before unit must be scrapped. Mica spacers between bars must be undercut and bar surface polished.

9. Ford lovers will recognize this early flathead V-8 generator.

GEARING UP
TRANSMISSIONS AND REAR ENDS NEED THE RESTORER'S TENDER, LOVING CARE

BY ERIC RICKMAN

It makes one wonder, did these people plan it this way, or is it the nature of people in this type of business to squirrel things away like pack rats? Bless 'em, where would we be today if all this stuff had been thrown out after it was worn and discarded after a few years of use? Today's restorer and collector is completely in debt to the old-timers and their saving ways, for without them, restoration would be an impossibility. In fact, there would be nothing to restore in the first place.

We chose one of the oldest companies in the business when it came time for this portion of the story. Lucas Transmission has been in business in downtown Los Angeles since 1936 (that's over 40 years), and typically they haven't thrown anything away in all those years. Besides shops and storage yards in Los Angeles, they have a 2½-acre storage lot in North El Monte piled with transmissions and differentials. The L.A. yard has parts going back to about '29, while the El Monte yard has stuff reaching back into the early Twenties, with a few even earlier Model T gearboxes thrown in for good measure.

Just to give you an idea what this stuff is worth today, we strolled through the L.A. yard with Tom Johnson, the president of Lucas Transmission, while he pointed out some of the oldies but goodies. He has early Plymouth and Dodge 3-speed transmissions, along with La Salle and Caddie boxes, '49 and '50 Mercury and Ford units, and '49 Ford overdrive and standard transmissions too. The stuff looks like junk, covered with grease, dirt, and rust. Bring your checkbook; the core charge alone on these oldies is $150 apiece, worn out yet! That's not too bad an investment for just lying

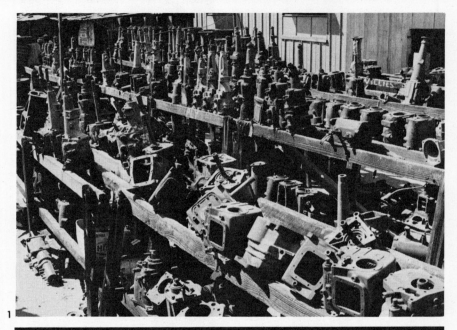

around in the weather for the past 30 or 40 years—*solid gold* Junk!

Tom has one of the very first automatic transmissions that was ever built, the forerunner of the famous Olds Hydra-Matic.

This unit was built in '38 for both Buick and Olds and utilized a clutch for the shift into 1st, and then shifted automatically through the rest of the gears. Need one? Tom can build it for you.

Tom says they have a huge stock of new old parts for almost every transmission ever built. He is presently filling an order for 200 '54 Powerflite transmissions for NATO—no problem. In addition to the usual run of Ford, Merc, and Chevy stuff, orders are beginning to come in for early Chrysler components. He has '33-'46 and '50 Fluid drive units for Chryslers and De Sotos.

Suppose you have sent in your transmission to be rebuilt. Tom's first step is to go out in the yard and dig out the proper core. After dissasembly, everything is soaked in a hot tank, then steam cleaned and abrasive cleaned in a Wheelabrader where necessary. Both transmission and differential cases are inspected very closely for wear and cracks. The thrust pads in a transmission case are the only portion subject to wear. These surfaces are machined smooth and a slightly thicker thrust washer is used in reassembly to make up for the wear and machining. Differential housings aren't subject to wear, but the bearing carrier saddles must be inspected closely to be sure they haven't become deformed.

All new bearings are used in rebuilding both transmissions and differentials; no undersize or oversize parts are used to compensate for wear. If you break down anywhere, a stock part can be used as a replacement. Heavier thrust washers are available as a stock part.

The components are checked closely, and inspected for excess wear. If reusable, the gears are touched up with a hand grinder to remove any burrs or nicks. Lucas has a huge stock of new old parts, along with their tremendous stock of cores. In a good many cases the gears can be reused, and it is foolish to lay out the money for new gears when you really don't need them.

Face it—you are never going to subject your rebuilt transmission or differential to the type of abuse it lived through in its first life. From now on it's easy does it, with lots of good old TLC. Differential wear is

1. Junk, right? Wrong! At about $150 per core, this stuff is like gold. Here are '49-'50 Ford, Merc boxes with and without overdrive—very rare.

2. This should warm the hearts of you Packard collectors. Lucas also has Packard Ultramatics from '51. Like money in the bank, this stuff just sits out in the weather and grows more valuable as the years go by.

3. After disassembled, the parts are hot tanked in alkali, then steam cleaned before close inspection. There is very little wear in a trans case.

4. Cluster gear thrust bosses at front and rear of case are only wear points. Bosses are refaced and a thicker washer is used to make up difference.

5. Gears and shafts are thoroughly cleaned and wire brushed before inspection. This will reveal any flaws, as well as polish surfaces.

6. All parts are carefully inspected for nicks, chipped and broken teeth in addition to excess wear. All new bearings are used in the assembly. Most of this stuff is still good.

7. Salvageable gears are carefully deburred by hand with a high-speed grinder to remove rough edges and restore each tooth's beveled edge.

8. One of the many aisles of new old stock in the Lucas warehouse. There are parts here for almost anything that has ever been built, in addition to new bearings for all rebuilds.

9. These parts for a '34-'35 Chevy Master DeLuxe Sedan gearbox are typical of some of Lucas' new old stock. Combine with new bearings and a salvaged case and you have a good-as-new transmission again.

compensated for on assembly when the gear contact pattern is set. The ring gear is shimmed from side to side while the pinion is shimmed in and out of the case to establish the correct gear tooth contact pattern—this takes care of the wear. Add a new set of spider gear shafts and new bearings and you're all set.

There is no shortage of bearings, because there are only a total of about 11 different sizes of bearings that were ever used in all American transmissions ever built. The part number may vary, but the basic sizes are the same. It just takes a little looking, because Lucas stocks every bearing ever made.

Comebacks are a problem in any business of this type, but Tom says they get very few, and when they do it is usually because the customer reused his old transmission cover without renewing the shift forks and detents, or the shift rails were worn out. If you send in your transmission, send in the entire unit so the job can be done properly. And when you assemble the car, use new motor mounts and shift linkage grommets where necessary. Also check the vacuum lines. You are a restorer—why am I telling you all this? Tom says most failures are caused

by the customer failing to take care of the related parts when he installs a rebuilt transmission. As we pointed out in the drivelines chapter, the driveline must be in good shape and in balance. The yoke

must not be worn. Lucas ships out a completely restored transmission, but it is only as good as the installation and related parts and pieces, just as a chain is only as strong as its weakest link.

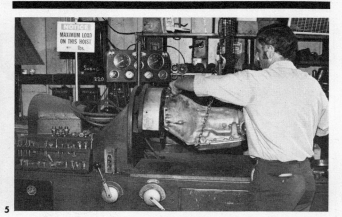

6

7

8

1. A few of the hundreds of bins of old, old stock, all perfectly good salvaged gears ready to go back into service in your restored classic.

2. Here is a collection of GM and Mopar automatics. Stand 'em on end with a coffee can over the shaft to keep the rain out and, if filled with oil, they can sit here forever.

3. This place is a gold mine of goodies. How about these '39-'40 Chrysler Fluid Drive and torque converter units? This stuff is hard to find. Freelancing scroungers comb the wrecking yards for parts.

4. This is the forerunner of the now famous Olds Hydra-Matic; it was originally used in the '38 Olds and Buicks. A clutch was used for the shift into low, and shifting became automatic through the rest of the gears. Need one? Lucas has a few.

5. Automatic transmissions are tested for oil pressure, shift points, stall speed, leaks, etc., on this special machine. All rebuilds are guaranteed.

6. A good portion of the Lucas yard is devoted to differentials also. These are third member, or pumpkin type, center sections favored by Ford and Mopar. GM uses the Salisbury differential that is integral with the axle housing; it's mean to work on.

7. All differentials are completely disassembled, then sent to the hot tank and steam cleaned before they are carefully inspected.

8. Salvageable gears are stored by make, model, year and ratio in these wall bins. Gear sets seldom wear much if lubed and not abused by drag racing. Each rebuild is carefully shimmed for proper gear engagement, which compensates for wear.

9. Old bearings are removed and new bearings are always used when a rear/end unit is rebuilt. Bearing carriers are checked to be sure they are perfectly round. Unless a unit has been run completely dry, bearing wear is the only critical factor.

10. Driveshaft yoke, crush sleeve and new rear bearing cone are pressed on the pinion shaft. Yoke securing nut is then torqued to a specified figure for proper bearing preloading.

9

10

CLUTCH PLAY

THE NEED FOR SPECIAL EQUIPMENT USUALLY MEANS FINDING PROFESSIONAL HELP FOR THIS RESTORATION

One of the more critical components in any old car is the clutch; the device that connects (or disconnects) the engine to the transmission, and thence to the rear end and, finally, the wheels. Without it, the engine would stop every time the car was stopped. Over the years clutches have had a wide variety of configurations, but most have relied on friction to transmit the engine horsepower to the rest of the driveline. Because of the nature of the beast, clutches are probably more prone to wear than any other part of a car, excepting perhaps the brakes, and like brakes, the friction material gradually wears away until it must be replaced.

Because of the great complexity of clutch types, sizes, and so on, it is impossible within the confines of these pages to present a rebuilding how-to on even the more popular style of clutches. Moreover, clutch rebuilding, even simple refacing or replacement of the lining material itself, requires special tools and equipment that the at-home restorer is not apt to have. Thus, we dropped by one of the larger and older clutch rebuilding firms in the west and came back with a how-it's-done essay in order to show the why's of a rebuild. Luckily, this is one area where the restorer can more easily rely on a specialist than try to do a fixer-upper himself. In fact, until re-

cently, the owner of an old whatever 6 could take his troublesome-clutch components to almost any modern-day clutch rebuilder, wait an appropriate amount of time, then go back and pick up his remanufactured unit. But with the spreading interest in auto restoration, there are firms that actually stock already-rebuilt units just waiting for the intrepid restorer to walk in and exchange his old unit for the fresh one—practically without regard to the age, make, and model of car. One of these is the A-1 Clutch Co., in Los Angeles.

One of the best things about an old, established company like A-1 is that they never throw anything away. Even years ago before restora-

PHOTOS BY ERIC RICKMAN

tion became the hobby/investment pasttime that it is today, A-1 hung onto every old clutch and component that came their way. As a result, they have parts for cars that we've never heard of, and for the cars that are today in high demand, they've got enough pieces to keep them running for ever and always.

A-1 owner Sidney Triggs gave us the grand tour, and pointed out that his remanufactured clutches are actually better than the original factory assemblies. New clutches are built from fresh "green" castings that haven't had time to cure and until they have aged sufficiently, are prone to warp with heat and pres-

sure. A-1 rebuilds are well cured by heat and age, and after being derusted and the pressure plates ground to a new finish, will hold their shape and settings indefinitly. In addition, Sid uses all new springs that are a product of our more modern metallurgy. Hence, they hold the proper pressure much longer. A

2

3

4

5

1. The "we never throw anything away" syndrome leads to some awfully big piles of old clutches over a period of time. These are old truck clutches that span a number of years.

2. Just a few bins of clutch discs. A-1 has literally hundreds of thousands of discs and clutches. It takes a real expert to sort this mess.

3. After the old facing material is unriveted from the discs, they are ready for cleaning. This is just a small sample of the rows upon rows of bins full of old clutch discs.

4. Rust is removed by a Wheelabrader, a machine that utilizes an abrasive blasting process. Disc looks like new and is ready for new springs, hub and new friction material facings.

5. Pressure plates are refaced in a surface grinding machine after being cleaned in the Wheelabrader. Operator uses a wood block to offset grinding wheel pressure on magnetic chuck.

good deal more TLC is used in A-1's remanufacture of small runs of clutches than was ever used in the factory assembly line runs of thousands of clutches at a time.

Typically, an old clutch assembly is taken apart, the springs discarded, and the cover, pressure plate, fingers etc., are degreased then cleaned in an abrasive blasting machine called a Wheelabrader. All the parts come out shiny new—the small parts are tumbled in an abrasive for cleaning. Where possible, fingers are rebushed, or new parts are used. Clutch discs go through the same process after having the old friction material removed from the faces. When refaced with new, more modern friction materials they will outlast the original disc by a considerable margin. Pressure plates are refinished by a special grinding process that delivers a super smooth finish.

The biggest trick in remanufacturing the older clutches is in having all the proper specifications. Sid has all the old manuals and can set up almost any clutch to original factory specs—this includes proper spring pressure, finger travel, finger height, and release point.

Having the proper jigs for assembling these old timers is another necessity. Sid has 'em all. He assembles on one machine, then sets up the clutch on another machine to ensure both cleanliness and accuracy (a tiny metal chip will throw the settings off by several thousandths of an inch).

Proper tension and finger height are critical because if the fingers are too low, the clutch won't release properly; too high, and the fingers will contact the throwout bearing after a small amount of disc wear, losing the necessary freeplay and causing throwout bearing failure.

All A-1 clutches are dynamically balanced regardless of year. Back about '35, engines began to develop a lot more revs and balance became a factor to be reckoned with—an out of balance clutch will really rattle your teeth and is hard to diagnose. Sid won't take that chance with a clutch of any year.

If you want an A-1 rebuild you are going to have to specify A-1 when you take your clutch to your local parts store or dealer (Sid does a wholesale business only). You might write Sid at 6910 Aragon Circle, Buena Park, Calif. 90620 and find out if he can do your clutch, and who your nearest parts house is that handle A-1 clutches. ♘

4

5

1. Before and after refinishing. New face is extremely smooth, and the old, seasoned casting will remain flat, giving an even longer service life than a new clutch assembly.

2. New actuating fingers, clevises and pins are installed on the newly refinished pressure plates before final assembly is begun.

3. Assembly must be done on special jigs to hold the cover down against spring pressure. An exact spring pressure is specified for each model clutch. This jig cycles the clutch several times after assembly to be sure it works smoothly and properly.

4. After several actuating cycles the finger heighth is checked and set to specification. This is critical: too high and the throwout bearing wears excessively; too low and the clutch won't release properly.

5. Along about '35, engines began to turn up more rpm, and clutch balance became a critical factor. This machine spins the clutch assembly and has a stroboscopic light to spot the out-of-balance point. Weight can be drilled out or added by driving small iron plugs into cover holes. A-1 balances all their clutch assemblies.

6. This is one of the rare items in the A-1 stock: a '23 Jewett clutch. There can't be too many of these old machines around, but if you need a clutch you know where one is.

7. This is a cork-faced Essex Terraplane clutch disc, another item that isn't too much in demand today. These discs ran in an enclosed oil bath and lasted forever if you kept the oil level up. Low oil produced fried cork.

THE COMPLETE CLUTCH SERVICE

6

7

DRIVESHAFT REBUILDING
A PRO IS BETTER EQUIPPED FOR THIS WORK, BUT IF YOU WANT TO KNOW HOW HE DOES IT, READ ON

There is little doubt that the driveshaft is the most neglected item on an automobile. Few people even realize that a driveshaft must be serviced let alone bother to have it done. The usual pattern is to drive the car until the U-joint bearings go bad and the shaft either falls out, or the vibration and klunking get so bad it can't be tolerated.

This may come as a surprise, but the factory-sealed needle roller bearings in the universal joints should be serviced at about 20,000 to 30,000 miles. This means disassemble and inspect the bearings, wash them out and repack with fresh grease then reassemble the U-joint. Some of the older cars had grease fittings on the universal-joint bearings, if you are lucky and the previous owners had kept the car lubed properly you may still have a good driveshaft assembly. To check, get under the car and grasp the driveline and twist it back and forth while watching the universal joints, there should be no play whatever, a badly worn set of bearings will have a lot of slop, and give off a loud klunk when going from forward to reverse.

The driveshaft is expected to operate under the most adverse conditions imaginable, it is exposed to all the dirt, mud, water, salt and whatever else is on the road, and at the same time turns at engine speed while delivering full power to the rear axle. There are usually just eight little needle roller bearings to do this job, with no provision for lubrication. Unless you are going for Concours points, use the later units with lube fittings when replacing the U-joint bearings, it will save a lot of hassle.

Unless there has been a complete bearing failure and the driveshaft has fallen out of the car, reconditioning is merely a matter of replacing the universal-joint bearings. You

PHOTOS BY ERIC RICKMAN

3

1. Typical of the "We never throw anything away" pack rat syndrome of the old-timers is this storage yard at Cannon Engineering in North Hollywood, Calif. Imagine the problem if the old-timers had thrown everything away! Restorers are completely dependent on this old stock.

2. The "goodie bin"—if there ever was one, it's here. Steel tube is easy to replace; it's these forged steel yokes that are hard to come by. Only the bearings wear. The yoke as the bearing carrier is usually okay.

3. Ted Cannon shows how to straighten an early torque tube. These tubes were vulnerable: Being rigidly bolted to the differential, they got tweaked when a rear wheel was hit.

4. A shaped block must be used when straightening a tube to avoid kinking. That dial indicator has seen better days, but it still works. Since a torque tube doesn't rotate, it isn't as critical as an open driveshaft, which has to be within .005-in. of true to run smoothly.

5. After the torque tube is fairly straight, it must be set up in a lathe for final truing. The ball joint is centered in the chuck first. The U-joint operating in an enclosed ball very seldom failed. The other end was coupled to the differential shaft.

6. With the torque tube running true in the lathe, a squaring cut must be taken across the differential housing mating flange to ensure a square, tight fit when bolted up.

4

5

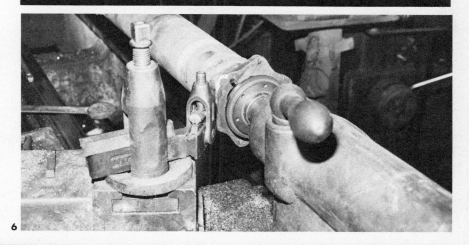

6

can do it yourself if you are familiar with the procedure, or you can have any shop do the job for you—it's not too expensive. We advise having a driveline shop do the work, since they can check the shaft for straightness and balance at the same time.

We would show you how, except for the fact that there are so many different types it would take this whole book to depict all the various methods of removal and installation.

If there has been a complete failure and the driveshaft yoke has been damaged, the old yoke will have to be cut off by cutting the weld and a replacement welded to your old shaft. Short of total failure, there is no wear on a yoke, so an old yoke is as good as a new one (it merely serves to carry the bearings, which you are replacing anyway). This is why it pays to do business with a well-established shop,

they have the pack-rat syndrome of never throwing anything away, and will always have a replacement yoke stashed away somewhere.

If the drive tube itself is badly bent or tweaked, it is no problem to cut a new length of steel tube and weld the old yokes in place, and "in time," (meaning in proper alignment with each other—a crucial factor). If the shaft is only bent slightly, it can usually be brought back to true.

If the shaft has a small dent, a hole is drilled in the shaft opposite the dent and the dent dinged out with a punch inserted through the hole. Weld up the hole afterward, check for straightness, balance and you're on your way.

Ford and Chevrolet switched from torque tube to the open driveline for the '49 model year. Torque tube housings can be straightened in a press the same way as an open driveline. However the flange joining

the tube to the differential housing must have a squaring cut taken in a lathe to insure proper alignment. The inner driveshaft may also have to be straightened.

A shaped block should be used at the pressure point when straightening a tubular shape to prevent kinking the tube.

A good driveshaft is considered straight if it is within .005-in. of true. If it gets out of line by .030-in. you will feel the vibration in the seat of the pants, and t&e rearview mirror will be giving you double images. A perfectly straight driveshaft will vibrate if the bearings are worn. If the car has been operating with a worn driveshaft for any length of time, the front slip yoke in the transmission will have ruined the transmission tailshaft housing bearing and oil seal. This is an item to check if you discover a bad front U-joint.

1

2

3

4

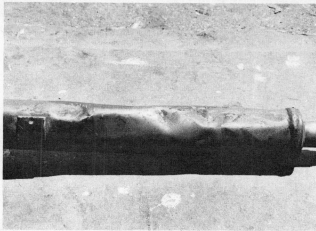

5

6

1. Unlike the torque tube U-joint, the open driveline U-joint is exposed to everything the elements have to offer. The tiny needle bearings are dependent on the sealing ability of a small rubber or cork ring, which can deteriorate quickly in the harsh environment of dirt, mud and water.

2. Lack of maintenance makes the bearing crosses begin to look like this. Cross on left has provision for lube; someone got lazy. When they get this bad, it's only a matter of miles until you will be walking.

3. The catastrophic failure on the right allowed the driveshaft to drop out on the road and be destroyed. It is quite apparent that the trunnion tore out of the bearing cup after the needles wore out. New unit is on left.

4. The yoke in #3 is a bolt-in unit. Usually the yoke has to be put in a lathe and the weld machined off to remove it from the tube. This too was a lubeable joint, but somebody goofed. Such neglect gets expensive.

5. This new cross and bearing have a provision for lubrication. That little rubber ring seal is all that stands between you and disaster. An occasional shot of grease pushes the dirt back out before it gets into bearing. Seal does harden with age.

6. If your project car has been ill-used over the years, the driveshaft will often look like this, due to high centering over rough roads. Small dents can be dinged out by drilling a hole opposite the dent, punching it out, then welding up the hole. A condition as bad as this calls for a new drive tube.

7. Here is something to watch for—if the front slip yoke is badly worn, it will develop a lot of side play and vibration which will destroy the transmission tailshaft housing bearing and grease seal (arrow).

8. The final step is to have the restored driveshaft balanced. Remember, it turns at crankshaft speed. This is a Bear Dual Plane balancing machine. New bearings, balancing and a few shots of grease from time to time and you will go a long way.

7

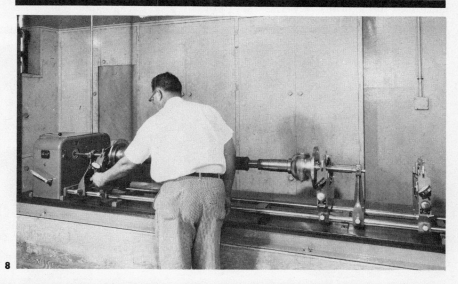

8

MODEL T SURVIVAL TRICKS
DON'T DO IT IF THE SHOW JUDGE IS LOOKING, BUT HERE ARE SOME TIPS TO KEEP THAT T GOING

Despite the fact this book is largely a catchall of how-to restoration tidbits, and thus is rightly dedicated to the purist restorer who is seeking to make his project vehicle a faithful as-built rejuvenation, we couldn't help but pass along a few tricks for the Model T. Tricks, that is, that have evolved or been developed long after the last of Henry Ford's miracle cars rolled from the assembly line in May of 1927.

While the *really* purist restorer, as well as the typical car show judge, will cringe at the suggestions depicted here, there are Model T buffs who are after improved reliability of their cars. Not the buffs who relish the trailered trek to the Model T Nationals—wherever they are held—but the guys who restore their cars so they can be driven reliably on tours, caravans or merely extended weekend jaunts. We're referring, of course, to the T's inherently mediocre oiling system, its tendency to overheat, proclivity to destroy valves and the eternal transmission band problem. Here are a few choice "fixes" by Fred Upshaw, a Model T enthusiast for 55 of his 75 years. ♣

1

2

3

4

PHOTOS BY PETER READ MILLER

5

6

1. Fred Upshaw in a typical situation; at the "helm" of an engine stand with his favorite, Ford's Model T engine.

2. No, this isn't a suspension "fix"; it's a rather rare Model T, especially in the Western states where Upshaw holds sway. A limited number of '13 T's were manufactured with 60-in. wheel tread (normal was 54 ins.) to better conform to wide-rutted "roads" in the deep South.

3. "Ford Faithful Oiling System" reads the special transmission cover plate, a popular T accessory. The T suffered in its engine oiling system, and this was one addition offered in the T's heyday to help solve it.

4. Mr. Ford reasoned that thermosiphon of cooling water (where hot water rises as cooler water sinks) would handle the T's circulation system. Accessories such as this "Camel" water pump became available when the theory didn't work in practice.

5. Here's what we meant by a trick. Oil dippers from pre-1955 Chevrolet 6-cyl. engines are brazed to drilled rod caps to help the T scoop up the oil it deserves—and needs.

6. The Model T relied on magneto for generating electricity. Magnets are spaced around flywheel, should be remagnetized to assure proper spark generation.

7. Chevrolet parts again. This time it's the valves from a 327-cu.-in. Chevrolet V-8, which fit most T engines.

8. Only work necessary to install the Chevy valves is a reaming of the valve guides. Springs and cups are T.

9. Tired of rebanding the T trans? Try slipping in a set of bands from a GM Hydra-Matic transmission.

10. If you're unhappy with the performance of the T's ignition system, you might consider adapting a distributor from a '28 4-cyl. Chevy.

11. The redoubtable Model T is still a favorite in Argentina, where, because of new car prices and extreme duty charges, old cars must be kept chugging. Here's a new Argentinian accessory, a water pump.

7

8

9

10

11

SAVE THAT TANK
NO MATTER HOW BADLY PITTED OR CORRODED, YOUR ORIGINAL GAS TANK CAN BE MADE LEAKPROOF

BY JIM BRIGHTLY

After many hours of hard work preparing your car for a concours, losing points because of a reproduction fuel tank can be very discouraging. A few extra hours of effort and some Tank Seal can save those points. It might make the difference between winning a ribbon and nothing.

A polyvinyl chloride compound was originally developed to seal aircraft fuel tanks and has been commercially available for add-on RV gas tanks for many years. However, the normal commercial grade compound is too thin for use in restoring older tanks; it easily seals on bright, new metal, but not scaly, rusty gas tanks from the Twenties or Thirties.

Tank Seal is also a polyvinyl chloride (PVC) in a solvent carrier, but thanks to its thickness (it has the consistency of pancake syrup), it will cover rust patches and fairly large cracks and weld or solder leaks. Bill Holiday, the chemist who developed this particular compound, recommends about three applications to thoroughly seal a badly corroded tank. He said, "Thinner sealers would require many, many more applications to even approach the ability of this new compound to seal older tanks."

Before applying, the surface must be properly prepared. Any dirt, rust or scales must be removed through a vigorous washing and blown dry with air pressure. Next, dissolve any oily deposits or grease with either lacquer thinner or acetone. (Gas tanks may also be cleaned in a hot tank in a radiator shop.) Remember to do all work in an area with very good ventilation, as the fumes from both the cleansers and the sealant can be dangerous.

After cleaning, let the surface dry completely but do not allow the surface to become overheated by the sun. During application, a heated surface can cause the solvent carrier to dry too rapidly, causing air bubbles in the sealant which can lead to future leaks.

Tank Seal can be applied in any one of three ways: by paintbrush, spraying or, in the case of gas tanks, sloshing. To slosh a tank, first plug any fittings or openings and protect threads with grease or oil. Then pour the fluid into the tank's filler neck and plug it up immediately. The tank can then be tipped, rotated and swung, forcing the fluid to

PHOTOS BY ERIC RICKMAN

coat the entire interior and seams. When fluid can no longer be felt sloshing around inside, carefully unplug the filler neck and pour in another container of fluid for another coating. For badly corroded surfaces, three coats should be enough. A 20-gal. tank should use about a pint per application.

Be careful when removing the plug, because the solvent (while drying) creates pressure, which could blow some compound out of the opening. Sealer also reacts very badly with paint, so keep clear of any painted surfaces.

Although Tank Seal virtually creates a bladder inside the gas tank, forget about using it for any fuel other than gasoline. Any fuel that includes methane, alcohol, nitro, etc., will destroy this compound, but, Tank Seal is completely inert to gasoline, diesel fuel and water.

For those of you who tow your restored automobile with a camper, motorhome, etc., Tank Seal also seals fiberglass or plastic tanks, but must not be stored in either. In large amounts, the solvent that is used as a carrier in the compound reacts badly with both plastic and fiberglass. However, the small amount used in coating dries so quickly it can't attack either the plastic or 'glass.

Tank Seal will normally set up (depending on weather) in 2 to 3 hours, but allow 6 hours for three coats. It can also be used as a contact cement for steel parts that is so strong it can only be removed by sandblasting or PVC solvent. Its uses are limited only by your imagination.

This sealer will retain resiliency indefinitely and is unaffected by vibration. Between competition dates you may wish to drain the tank to keep varnish from collecting in the fittings, but don't worry—with Tank Seal in place the interior metal will not rust and the sealant will not dry up and clog fuel lines. Bill Holiday adds a rust inhibitor to the compound which also turns the sealer white. This whiteness aids in seeing depth inside the tank.

Tank Seal has been successfully used to seal the tanks of offshore racing boats, seal rust patches in bait tanks attacked by salt water and to seal fresh-water tanks aboard sailing craft.

Tank Seal is priced at $4.75 per pint, $8.95 per quart and $26.00 per gal. and can be purchased through Bill Holiday, 180 N. Lewis Rd., Camarillo, Calif. 93010.

Those few extra points could make the winning difference.

1. Found in a wrecking yard, this 1934 Chevrolet pickup gas tank had been smashed flat before being rescued by its new owner.

2. The new owner removed the end piece and hammered the tank back into its original shape. But the solder failed to seal completely, and rust patches had caused pinhole leaks.

3. After protecting the threads with grease or oil, plug all openings.

4. Working in an open, well-ventilated area, pour Tank Seal into the large filler neck of the tank.

5. Using a rubber plug, plug the neck securely before sloshing.

6. Vigorously slosh the tank by tipping, rotating and jerking it around. This forces fluid into every nook and joint for better sealing.

7. Just one application of Tank Seal provides quite a thick coating.

2

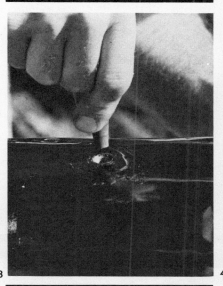

3

4

5

6

7

A STITCH IN TIME
UPHOLSTERY – CLASSIC TO CONTEMPORARY

BY RICK BUSENKELL

How many times have you seen a really spiffy car parked at curbside or even at a show, gone up to admire it and been turned off by a poor interior? It can happen with stock cars, restored classics or hot rods. It occurs fairly frequently, because reupholstering is the restoration chore usually saved for last, it is expensive, it is a black art even to most restorers and there appears to be a certain type of person who does not care what the inside of the car looks like as long as the outside is pretty.

This chapter is not a "how-to" so you can take your trusty needle in hand and do your own work; the variety of patterns and techniques is simply too great. We thought you'd like to know something of the history of the various upholstery materials, what age of vehicles each is properly used in and what can be done if you can't find the original material. There are a lot of terms which are perhaps unfamiliar to you now, and a knowledge of them will enable you to communicate better with the upholsterer when that great day dawns on which you will have your interior redone.

CLOTHS AND SYNTHETICS

The history of interior fabrics has been one of constant but gradual change. With the exception of leather, every material has enjoyed a decade or two of popularity and then been displaced by something else. The changes have been due to improvements in technology, better value for the money and the changing tastes of customers. Many auto buffs decry the changes, but the materials used in grandpa's 1920 Chevrolet would not be acceptable today, and the materials in today's Chevy did not exist in 1920. In the following discussion we'll omit leather, since it's treated separately later.

The classic cloth used in low-priced and mid-priced cars of the Twenties to the Forties was *mohair.* Originally meaning only the hair from the Angora goat, it came to be used for any wool cloth in a pile weave with a nap of medium length. Mohair was available in only a few colors; the universal favorite was gray, since it harmonized well with the common black exterior paint and didn't clash with any color. *Velour* was similar to mohair, but had a shorter nap. In expensive cars, the usual alternative to leather was *broadcloth,* a thick, closely woven wool fabric of conventional weave. It was a favorite of upholsterers, since it could be sewn into any pattern, was stretchable and easy to work, was stronger than mohair and wore very well. As with mohair, gray was the overwhelming color choice. *Bedford cord* was a variation of broadcloth which had cords running in one direction on the surface. It was named for New Bedford, Mass., the town where it was first woven.

For doors there was *sidewall material,* a combination of cotton and wool woven like broadcloth but thinner and lighter. And then there was *headliner,* again a cotton/wool combination (sometimes all cotton or all wool), but lighter than sidewall material.

All these fabrics were organic and had several advantages in common. They "breathed," so they were cool in summer and warm in winter; they stretched, so trimmers could fit them without difficulty; and they were relatively low in cost, though all-wool broadcloth was never really cheap. The disadvantages were that they were quite limited in color, were easily stained, absorbed water and were not resistant to bacterial attack, especially mildew. As the production of automobiles rose into the millions per year, this also made heavy demands upon the supply of these materials, especially wool. The suppliers responded by gradually

substituting more and more cotton, decreasing cloth thickness and raising prices. Therefore the synthetics had definite advantages to offer when they appeared.

The first synthetic was *pyroxylin,* introduced in the late Twenties as a substitute for leather. It was a coarse cloth coated with a nitrocellulose compound. It had a woven cotton backing and was known by the popular names of "leathercloth" and "leatherette." Though it looked quite like leather, it found favor chiefly as a substitute for sidewall material on doors, for it did not stretch at all and was prone to cracking if flexed too much. In the Forties pyroxylin with a stretchable knitted backing appeared, but it didn't work too well because of the inflexible coating.

In 1935 Du Pont first marketed *nylon,* setting off the greatest revolution in the textile industry since the invention of the automatic loom. Originally a trademark name and spelled with a capital "N," nylon became so famous it soon entered the lexicon as a common noun. It found uses everywhere, for it was much stronger than any natural fiber, immune to organic decay or bacterial attack, stretchable, nonabsorbent, could be dyed any color, did not burn, could be produced in massive quantities in filaments of

any size and was cheap. Despite these immense advantages, it did not immediately displace the organic fibers in the automotive industry, for there were a few drawbacks. Nylon felt clammy to sit on, since it did not absorb moisture or hold heat. It was nonflammable, but an open flame (or cigarette) would cause it to char and melt. Moreover, despite its hardness, it had poor abrasion resistance and could be cut rather easily.

It was not until after World War II that nylon began its all-conquering invasion of the auto industry. First to go was mohair, which disappeared in a few short years. Wool carpeting followed. Broadcloth put up a more stubborn fight, and it remains in favor today in limousines and limited-edition luxury cars. In the Fifties nylon was combined in varying proportions with cotton and *acetate,* another synthetic. The resulting cloth was warmer and cheaper than pure nylon. Gradually the cotton disappeared, and by 1960 there were no more organic fibers in American cars. Perhaps nylon's

greatest contribution to automotive upholstery was less noticeable—it replaced cotton as the stitching thread.

The rest of the synthetic revolution was carried out by *vinyl.* That word looks and sounds like one of those tricky trade names dreamed up by an imaginative advertising agency, but it isn't. Chemically, the vinyl group is a particular chemical series derived from ethylene. Vinyl is the general name given to any resin or plastic made by polymerization of compounds containing the vinyl group, even though such plastics may differ widely in their physical properties. For automobiles, the name denotes a flexible plastic coating on top of a cloth (usually nylon) backing.

Vinyl was another synthetic which owed much to wartime research. It first appeared in autos in 1947, replacing leatherette. It became quite successful, but what really sealed vinyl's destiny was its application on a stretchable knitted backing. The most famous of these was U.S. Rubber's *Naugahyde,* named for its

1. This 1932 Packard phaeton is typical of classic open cars in its lavish use of leather, even on the underside of the cowl. If your car is like this, it's going to cost a bundle to reupholster—but it will be worth a bundle, too.

2. More classic lavishness inside a 1939 Packard V-12 with a Rollston brougham body. Here the upholstery is cloth, but the material is just as costly and the craftsmanship just as exquisite. This particular pattern of tufted pleating, not a true diamond pleat, was quite popular during the classic era. There are only a handful of craftsmen capable of duplicating it today.

3. Mohair was the popular seat material in cheaper cars for a long time, but it was displaced by an inexpensive cotton/wool cloth. This 1941 Chevy ad shows that kind of cloth with the very thin pattern lines (usually blue) common to it at the time.

4. In 1950, Chevy's two-tone treatment used a band of dark cloth to accent the normal cloth, which by this time had acquired wider stripes and was available in a few more colors. The effect was lighter and airier, but interior designers of low-priced cars were still limited to a selection of only a few fabrics and colors.

3

4

plant in Naugatuck, Conn., on the river of the same name. Naugahyde was and remains a trade name used by U.S. Rubber (now UniRoyal) to denote all its coated fabrics, but like nylon before it, the name has so caught the public fancy that it is now commonly used to mean any vinyl from any manufacturer on a knit backing.

Finally upholsterers had the material which seemed perfect—cheap, stretchable, rotproof, fadeproof, stainproof, extremely flexible, available in any color or grain pattern, guaranteed not to check, crack or peel. Leatherette disappeared, and after its initial appearance around 1954, stretchable vinyl began competing with nylon as a seat covering material.

The Fifties saw a dazzling array of bright and often bizarre woven synthetic fabrics in automobiles. Vinyl replaced these in convertibles at first, then phased them out of closed cars in the early Sixties. The fabric of the Seventies appears to be *knit vinyl,* but it may be challenged by *breathable vinyl,* a new development which has thousands of tiny artificial pores and breathes like leather. Another recent development has been the strong return of cloth. This time it's nylon velour, and in the past several years it has become a very popular option in many cars.

What of modern replacements for all these older materials? Mohair is still available, though it is hard to find and now quite expensive. Only one mill in the U.S. and a few in Europe still make it, and they're getting astronomical prices: Expect to pay about $30 a yard at retail.

One of the new nylon velours might make an acceptable substitute for mohair if your car is intended only for street use and will never be entered in a show. However, nylon cannot replace wool where absolute authenticity is desired, because it has a characteristic sparkly glitter which betrays its synthetic origin.

Broadcloth, once more expensive than mohair, is now cheaper, because lighter grades of it are still in demand in the furniture and clothing industries, so mills are still set up to produce it. Connoisseurs insist on West of England brand, still the same superb stuff it was when supplied for the prewar classics. It now retails for about $27 per yard, but there is domestic wool broadcloth available which is almost as good and costs considerably less.

Classic cars often had splendid

custom interiors of linen, silk, satin and velvet, but these are such specialized and unusual fabrics for automobiles that we cannot discuss them in our limited space.

Incidentally, woven fabrics are priced and sold by the running yard, whereas leather is priced by the square foot. Cost comparisons between the two or between different fabrics would not be difficult if fabric *width* were constant; but it isn't. In the furniture trade a width of 54 ins. is standard, but in the auto industry it varies from 36 to 60 ins. or even wider.

The reason for the varying widths is that the auto manufacturers order the material from the mill with a particular car or cars in mind. For a small, sporty car with bucket seats, the width can be quite narrow, while a big car or pickup truck with a bench seat calls for a wide roll.

1

2

Keep this in mind when comparing different fabrics. If they come in different widths, the seemingly more expensive one may be wider and therefore actually cheaper to use, since fewer yards will be required for your car.

The most difficult materials to obtain now are those nylon-acetate cloths of the Fifties. They were in vogue for only a decade, meaning they aren't made any more, and they came in an enormous variety, meaning that the chances of your finding an upholstery shop with any leftover cloth which exactly matches your car are pretty slim.

If you have such a car which needs a new interior, you can look around thoroughly, but you'd better be prepared to accept the strong probability that you'll have to have it redone in something not quite original but still acceptable, like vinyl. Be sure to check the classified ads in publications such as *Hemmings Motor News,* which cater to owners of older cars. Occasionally rolls of material that a warehouse or shop wants to be rid of are advertised. Also, some reproduction material is now being made and advertised through enthusiast magazines. And don't forget your club, for clubs are still the very best way to learn about anything available for your particular car.

It must be noted that ArmorAll (and its similar competitor, RVL) is simply fantastic for vinyl and rubber. Not coatings, these liquids penetrate into the chemical structure of the synthetics and make them extremely resistant to deterioration. They can't cure cracked or split vinyl, but they can prevent it from getting that way.

LEATHER

Leather is the one constant in the ever-changing world of upholstery materials. It was used in the first cars (and even before, of course, in coaches), and it enjoys popularity today in expensive cars. It will probably always be used, something not true of any other material, since we don't know what synthetics of the future will be like.

The tanning of animal hides is older than recorded history. Primitive man wore animal skins as clothing, and by the time of the ancient Greeks, leatherworking was a highly developed art. All the tanning steps were known by then. Modern man has only been able to improve on them by more complete knowledge of chemistry and the substitution of accurate instruments, such as the thermometer, hydrometer, and Ph-meter, for the ancients' guesswork as to the speed and types of chemical reactions. Leather has historically been valued as much for its esthetic appeal as its usefulness, and it is this appeal which still makes genuine leather desirable today in spite of the invention of cheaper and more durable synthetic materials.

There is no shortage of leather. It is a by-product of the meat industry, and we consume a huge amount of meat. There are over 100 million cattle in the U.S. alone, or one for every two people. This does not include the other animals whose hides are tanned—horses, deer, pigs, goats, sheep, even buffalo—but since automotive leather comes from cattle, we'll concentrate on them.

There isn't space or necessity here to delve deeply into the fascinating leather industry, but some knowledge of the processes involved is helpful in determining what you want to buy. Briefly, then, cattle hides are packed in salt at the slaughterhouse and then shipped to the tannery. There, in a complex series of operations, they are thoroughly washed, defleshed, unhaired and *bated* (washed in chemicals which remove any remaining animal protein and the depilatory agents used in unhairing). Then they are *pickled* (washed in weak acid to prepare for tanning) and finally tanned.

The last step, tanning, is the process which converts leather from a perishable animal product into a stable, durable good with a very long life. Modern tanning, called *chrome tanning,* uses chromium sulfate as the tanning agent in place of the vegetable extracts of antiquity, which are saved for a later retanning step. Using this chemical and the two-step tanning sequence produces more durable and more uniform leather than previous processes.

One of the interesting side effects of tanning is that it enables leather to withstand boiling water without shrinking, whereas untanned leather will shrink markedly in water at 140°F. This is certainly a useful property; think what a disaster it would otherwise be if hot tea were spilled in a Rolls-Royce.

All the preceding work is done by the *tanner;* everything subsequent is properly the province of the *currier,* though often the two trades are combined in one company. After tanning, the hides are wrung through rollers to remove excess moisture; if they arrived in a dried state from a tanner at a separate location, they must first be soaked. Then they are split on a cutting machine to produce uniform thickness. The inner or next-to-the-flesh part is used to produce suede. The outer or *top grain* goes on for further treatment. The split can be of any thickness, depending upon the leather's use. Automotive leather is generally 1.3mm thick.

Next comes retanning, usually employing the oak extract *tannin,* also known as tannic acid—hence the process name. Color is added next if vat dyed, or added later if sprayed on.

Next is *fatliquoring,* another chemical bath which determines the leather's softness and varies with its intended use. Then it is dried, *staked* (mechanically softened by controlled stretching and flexing), and buffed (sanded to remove sur-

1. By 1952 Chevy was trying a more daring decor but still using conservative materials. Upholstery is a nylon and cotton combination in a herringbone weave. Salt-and-pepper carpeting is nylon in a tight loop weave, and wool sidewall material is still used on the doors and the seat back.

2. Noted for innovative ideas in interiors, Kaiser tried many unusual materials. In this '52 sedan, organic fibers are still much in evidence, from the terry cloth seats to the sidewall material that greatly resembles classical Bedford cord. Note armrests with matching terry cloth.

3. Howard "Dutch" Darrin, the Kaiser's noted designer, tried out those terry cloth-like seat covers in the '52 model. Materials like this were acceptable at a time when people wore conservative clothing, such as Dutch is wearing here.

4. One year later, the '53 Kaiser had succumbed to the lure of synthetics. Nylon and vinyl in stylized patterns had driven out the natural materials.

5. Recognize this car? It shows typical materials used in American cars of the mid-Fifties. The carpeting is cut-pile nylon, and everything else is an advanced form of leatherette, using vinyl instead of the earlier nitrocellulose coating. Award yourself a gold star if you spotted it as the rare Kaiser-Darrin.

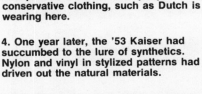
3

4

5

face imperfections) if necessary. Leather which is not buffed is called *full top grain,* and it is the best quality.

Then comes *finishing,* in which color is sprayed on if it has not already been added by vat dyeing. In either case, an additional transparent, film-forming liquid is sprayed on to protect the color from abrasion and staining.

Finally the leather is *plated,* a process in which heat and high pressure are applied to smooth the surface and seal the coatings. During the plating the leather may be embossed with an artificial grain or any other printed pattern. This is usually done to buffed leather, since buffing removes the natural grain. Then it is measured, graded and sent to the appropriate manufacturer. Whew! After all that, now at last we can make something with it.

The great bulk of leather is used for leather goods, especially shoes, a major product for which no synthetic material has yet equalled the natural one. And then there are handbags, luggage, wallets, gloves, belts, coats, furniture—the list is extensive. Only a small portion ends up as automotive upholstery, but that's where we come in.

Let's say that you've already determined that you want leather upholstery in your car. What should you look for?

The very best leather is full top grain which has been vat dyed. It can be identified immediately by looking at the back side. If the back is the same color as the grain side, it's been vat dyed; if the back is a natural tan, then the color has been sprayed on. Since the color goes all the way through on vat-dyed leather, it has superior resistance to finish cracking. It will generally endure from 200,000 to 300,000 flexings before cracking, whereas a surface-sprayed finish is good for only 60,000 to 100,000 flexings. Curriers say, though, that new synthetic finishes are closing that gap.

Vat-dyed leathers are very expensive. They currently run about $2.50/sq. ft. *wholesale;* you can expect to pay anywhere from that on up to about $5/sq. ft. retail, and the price is going up. This is the proper stuff to use on any American or European classic, since it's what they used originally. Several American companies can supply it, but the most famous brand is Bridge of Weir, a Scottish leather noted for its absence of barb scratches. Why?

Because cattle fences in Scotland do not use barbed wire.

If this is too much money, you can opt for full top grain with a surface-sprayed finish and save perhaps 15% of the retail cost. This is the leather typically supplied by American and European curriers. It is also the type used by all the high-quality European cars. Contrary to what you may have expected, Rolls-Royce does *not* use vat-dyed leather and hasn't since World War II, except in certain custom-built models.

Connolly Bros. of London, the largest supplier of upholstery leather in the world, is a familiar name for this product. Because of their huge volume (10,000 hides per week), they are, surprisingly, able to undersell most American curriers. Connolly has been around longer than the automobile—since 1878—and is famous for extremely good quality control. Their colors, thickness, texture and finishes are uniform, year after year; you can't buy a bad hide from Connolly.

Still too much? Well, now you can look at buffed leather, with or

without an embossed grain pattern. There is nothing wrong with this material. This was the type almost always used by Cadillac, Continental and Chrysler when leather interiors were ordered in their postwar cars, so it is actually correct for any postwar American car except the Continental Mark II (Bridge of Weir there, if you want absolute authenticity).

Be very careful when dealing with a company selling a lesser-known brand—or worse yet, *unbranded* leather. All the reputable American, European, Canadian and South American companies maintain high standards and stamp their company name on the back of each hide. But leather is a worldwide product, and there are some hides you would not want to put in a valuable old car no matter how cheaply you can obtain them.

Asian, Mexican, Central American and African hides are often tanned in a single step, using ureic acid rather than tannic acid or chromium sulfate, and they are not as durable. Staking is usually omitted

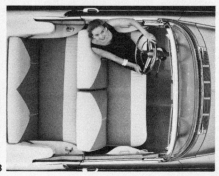

(which means less flexibility), a top finish is not applied over the color (early cracking, color rubs off, stains stay), and no plating is done (irregular surface, high porosity, low abrasion resistance). Take our word for it, you won't be happy with second-rate leather. As someone once said of another product, the pain of poor quality remains long after the thrill of low price is forgotten.

You can buy the leather yourself if you like; a good upholstery shop will not mind if you bring in your own material. Don't count on saving

---

1. In the late Fifties the synthetics ran riot. Vinyl was combined with nylon-acetate cloths with shiny threads in them, as shown in these seats carried by the young lady from a '56 Chevy Bel Air station wagon.

2. One of the great advantages of vinyl is that it can be embossed with any pattern. Kaiser used a special kind made to look like lizard skin which was called "Dragon Vinyl." Try finding some today. The great flexibility of vinyl pattern and color which made it so attractive to new car designers makes it a headache for restorers trying to match an obsolete pattern.

3. Seats covered entirely in vinyl, often combining the new stretchable kind with the older type in different patterns, started replacing the woven synthetics for seat coverings in the early Sixties. This trend was first evident in lower-priced convertibles, such as this '56 Chevy; high-priced convertibles still used leather.

4. During the decade 1955-65, the harsh glitter of nylon, in an ugly large-loop style, phased out the tight loops and pile weaves in the carpeting of cheaper cars such as this Chevy Impala. Pile weave, this time with nylon, made a return in the Seventies.

5. Leather, wool, broadcloth and pile carpeting continued to hold forth in expensive cars like this '60 Imperial LeBaron Southampton hardtop, even if they did look a trifle out of place with all that bright trimwork.

---

a bundle of money, however. You'll probably have to pay full retail price, which is what the upholsterer would charge if he had to order it for you.

Although it's priced by the square foot, you don't buy leather by specifying so many square feet. You buy either a full hide or a half hide. These are naturally irregular in shape and their areas vary, but you can figure on 45 sq. ft. for an average full hide.

Look especially for tiny holes, and reject the hide if there are several of them near the center. Such a hide cannot be used to cover large areas, since the upholsterer must cut around the holes. These holes (caused by the warble fly in the animal's lifetime) are tolerable if near the edge of the hide, but it's best if there are no holes at all. Reject also any hide which has unusual variation in thickness, does not flex or stretch well, or has large rough areas on the grain side.

How much do you need? That depends on the car. If it's a full-size car with front and rear seats, especially a prewar classic or one of several postwar cars (Rolls-Royce, Bentley, Continental II, high-level Mercedes) with leather on practically every surface, including the binding on the carpets, then six to eight full hides will be necessary. Postwar American cars, Jaguar sedans, middle-priced Mercedes sedans and most other cars which used leather, however, had it only on the wearing surfaces of the seats. The door panels and seat sides were of leathercloth or vinyl. For such a car, three to four full hides will suffice. And for a small, 2-seat sports car with leather only on the seat surfaces, one full hide would probably do the trick. Get a good estimate from a competent upholsterer, preferably the one who will do the job.

Perhaps you don't need the whole car done, just a part. The driver's seat usually shows wear faster than the others, and perhaps you want to redo just this seat. Examine the upholsterer's sample leather patches. Unlike vinyl, no upholsterer keeps leather hides on his premises, since the demand for them is so low. If he has no leather samples, find another upholsterer; don't let any upholsterer do your car who doesn't have experience with leather. If you can find a standard color offered by a currier which exactly matches what's already in your car, you're in business.

But let's suppose you can't match your car with a standard color. Then your hides are going to have to be custom dyed. The upholsterer will snip a little piece from the underside of the seat or some other inconspicuous place and send it to the currier, who will mix up a matching dye for your order. You'll have to wait about 3 weeks before the hides are ready, and they'll cost about 40¢/sq. ft. more than a standard, stock color. That's for a sprayed-on color; don't insist on a vat-dyed custom color for such a small order unless you are *really* prepared to pay through the nose.

If your leather is in pretty good shape but you don't like the color, it is possible to have the whole interior redyed. This is done with the leather in the car, and it costs several hundred dollars. That's a lot, but it's only about 10% of what a whole new leather interior would cost. The only trouble is that a redyeing job almost always *looks* like a redyeing job. A competent shop can also repair minor cracks or cuts with a vinyl process, but this is a bit tricky.

How about leather preservatives? There are quite a few on the market, including Connolly's own Hide Food; Lexol is probably the most fa-

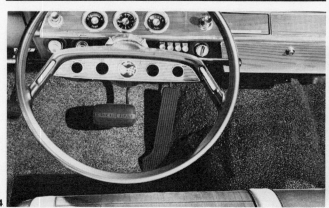

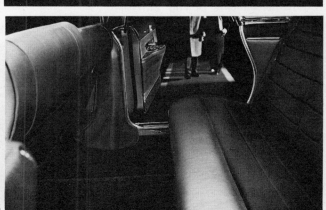

mous. Much is claimed for such preservatives, yet there is a problem here. The grain finish on good leather is designed to be nearly impenetrable. Leather breathes, but through such tiny pores that no liquid can enter through them.

These leather preparations, then, do little more than clean the surface, something as easily done with mild soap and water. Saddle soap is good for cleaning and beeswax adds a surface luster, but products that claim to soften leather can't do much of a job unless they can be used on the absorbent back side, where they can often work wonders with dried and stiffened leather. But since you can't get to the back side without tearing the whole car apart, treat the claims of these products with a certain skepticism. They help, but they are not wonder cures for leather which needs replacing.

Sunlight and mildew are great destroyers of upholstery leather. Avoiding prolonged exposure to a hot sun or a damp atmosphere are probably the most important precautions you can take to keep leather looking and smelling great for a long time.

CARPETING

As with so many other facets of interior restoration, the proper carpeting for expensive cars is easier to obtain (but not cheaper) than that for inexpensive cars. Almost all of the prewar classics and the best postwar cars used cut-pile wool. This is still available today from a variety of sources, though there has been a regrettable tendency in the last 15 years or so for the manufacturers to lessen the depth of the pile. Because of this, the best cut-pile wool carpeting still comes from the Wilton factory in England, an old-time supplier which has not changed its standards.

Low-priced cars of the Thirties had rubber mats in front and a sort of rubberized pile horsehair in the rear. The best modern replacement for the latter is a low-priced, short-nap, cut-pile wool in either charcoal or brown. Don't use nylon; it has a characteristic shine which instantly identifies it.

Nylon rather quickly phased out wool and other carpeting materials in the Forties and early Fifties. In the middle Fifties it was woven in very tight, compact loops, which gradually became larger and looser in succeeding years. Now in favor is

nylon in a cut-pile weave, bringing back some of the appearance of the classic cars.

Mouton is a special kind of wool. It is actually a sheepskin, since the fibers are still attached to the tanned hide, but they have been processed (often electrified) to make them stand straight up from the hide rather than lie in the characteristic woolen curls. This was originally done to make sheepskin resemble beaver and seal furs, once highly prized as material for lap robes and carpeting for the rear compartment in luxury cars.

For many years Rolls-Royce has offered optional mouton carpeting to snap over their standard carpeting, and several automakers offered a "nylon mouton." Both are still available, though again the natural product is easier to find but more expensive.

Materials for *binding* carpeting have varied. The most expensive cars always used leather; cheaper cars used cloth, then leatherette. Now vinyl is universal. Classic cars often used a different method of binding, too. Called *English roll binding,* the leather was first stitched to the carpeting edge with its grain side down, then pulled around the edge and stitched a second time (see illustration). The first stitching was hidden by the binding itself, while the second was hidden by the nap of the carpet, so the finished job presented a very neat appearance. The use of the best materials and attention to small details like this are what made the classics great; they're needed to make your restoration great, too.

Watch out for the method of attaching the carpeting to the floor, for even this has varied. Classic cars and the best postwar cars used something called an "invisible snap." It had two parts: a thin, tanged upper ring which was pushed into the carpeting until it was barely visible, and a lower piece which went on the underside of the carpeting and was held in position by the bent-over tangs of the upper ring. The lower piece then snapped over a stud screwed into the car floor.

These invisible snaps are all but impossible to obtain today. If your car has them, be sure to tell the upholsterer in no uncertain terms to reuse yours unless you are absolutely sure that he has a new supply.

Lesser cars used snap buttons, which are about ½-in. in diameter and quite visible. They became highly visible in the mid-Fifties, when it became common to chrome them, and that's the way they are supplied today to upholstery shops. If you are forced to use these snap buttons, you can render them less conspicuous by painting them the same color as the carpeting.

Some modern cars and upholstery shops get around the fastening problem rather forcefully by simply cementing the carpeting in place. This is acceptable in a street car but an absolute no-no in an authentic restoration. The only way to avoid

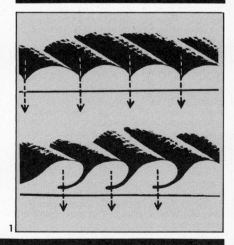

such situations is to know who you're dealing with and make very clear exactly what you want.

CONVERTIBLE TOPS

The production of the last Cadillac convertible focused a lot of attention in the popular press on that once-popular body style, but we auto nuts have known for a long time that old open cars are more valuable and more fun than closed cars. Tops varied a great deal from car to car, but there are certain points common to all old cars.

Probably the most common mistake made in connection with tops is the substitution of vinyl or vinyl-coated fabric in place of canvas on older cars. The synthetic fabrics were not used until the Fifties, and their use on any earlier car is incorrect. Be careful of details. We remember a shatteringly magnificent 1924 Rolls-Royce Phantom I tourer which missed getting a perfect 100-point score at a Classic Car Club of America concours because it had red vinyl trim on its top. The only correct trim on a canvas top is leather or more canvas.

On expensive cars the canvas was of a special type called *Burbank cloth,* very tightly woven and imported from England. This gave way to *Hartz cloth,* introduced in the late Forties, which had a canvas upper layer, a rubber center layer for waterproofing and a sateen backing. Burbank is no longer available, to our knowledge, but Hartz cloth can still be had in black or tan. Then came vinyl and vinyl-coated cloth. Those manufacturers—now solely European—still making ragtops continue to use vinyl.

GENERAL TIPS

A hundred things could be mentioned under this catchall heading, but we've only space for a few. Obviously the most important ingredient in a successful reupholstering job is the skill of the upholstery shop. Only you can determine its integrity and reputation. Ask around, talk to the shop owner and certainly examine previous jobs the shop has done. You can shop around and compare prices, but you'll probably find that there are very few places willing and able to work on an older car with the materials you want.

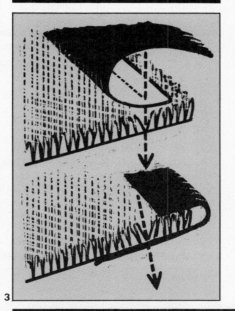

3

1. There are two basic ways of sewing pleats. The simple way (upper) is to stitch right through, which leaves the stitching exposed. A modern variation of this is to sew over preshaped lengths of foam which fill out the pleats. A better way is to sew through a double thickness from the back side, then roll the material over so that the stitching is invisible. This latter method has several names, the most picturesque of which is "tuck and roll." In either case, it's important to leave excess material between seams, so that seat can stretch.

2. Here's one reason you'd better think twice before trying to do your own reupholstering. Shops have some pretty specialized equipment, such as this air-operated, heavy-duty staple gun.

3. "Roll binding" is an elegant way to finish off the edges of carpeting in classic cars. The binding material (preferably leather) is first sewn from its back side to the top of the carpeting, then pulled around the edge and sewn a second time. Use of colored thread hides the second stitching.

4. This Bentley was reupholstered at a furniture shop instead of an auto upholstery shop. Result: a) There are seams at the seat corners where there were none originally; b) pleats were sewn so flat they are pulling apart; and c) original old leather beading was reused since the shop didn't have any, so now it's tearing away from the seat. Don't be penny wise and pound foolish.

You have probably noticed that we don't go into any real detail as to *how* upholstery is attached to the seat, nor shown any of the numerous possible pleating and folding patterns. This is because we believe that very few restorers do their own reupholstering. It requires specialized tools, including a heavy-duty sewing machine. More importantly, it also requires specialized knowledge, especially experience. It is one thing to tell someone to cut along a certain line, sew a certain type of seam, fold the material over and so on; it is something else to actually do it, especially if the material costs several dollars a square foot.

Upholstering is an art, not a science. Doing it well is not like disassembling and reassembling a mechanical part. A part goes together only one way and can be handled by anyone who carefully follows a step-by-step sequence. Your car has a particular pattern and material; we assume you are therefore more interested in duplicating it as closely as possible than in absorbing details about the dozens upon dozens of other patterns. If you are truly interested in learning enough about upholstering to do it yourself, a surprising number of adult education classes around the country are now offering such instruction. Check with your local high schools and colleges.

If you don't live close to a good auto upholstery shop, don't make the mistake of assuming that a furniture reupholstery shop can do an equally competent job. Auto upholstering uses techniques, fasteners and materials different from those in the furniture trade. Even if you have to ship the car into the next state and stay at your mother-in-law's (the one who thinks you're wasting her daughter's money on a stupid old car), have the job done right the first time and you'll be happy ever after. 🔱

4

GAUGES OF ALL AGES
SAGE STAGES TO SAVE RAGES AND WAGES
BY RICK BUSENKELL

The restoration of instruments is one of those jobs which the amateur restorer tends to put off till the end. It's much more exciting to see the engine go together and roar to life again, to see paint go on the straightened body, to smell that new leather and feel that new carpeting that's going to make the interior more opulent than a French bordello. This neglect of the instruments is even more pronounced if they actually work—sort of—but "merely" have the dial faces chewed up, with maybe a broken needle or two. By the time he gets around to it, the restorer may find he is facing a most frustrating and expensive job just when he thought everything was all downhill.

What do you do with damaged instruments? This is one area where it usually does not pay to go snooping around junkyards, especially if your car is relatively rare. Unless your instruments are actually missing, it's usually better to fix the ones you already have than to try to find better ones which will almost certainly need rebuilding anyway.

If you can buy brand-new duplicate instruments, fine, but these are available only for fairly recent cars. Many instrument repair shops (if you can find any) will not accept oddball instruments or ones with badly damaged faces. We sought out a man who does, Blair Davidson of Downey, Calif.

At his shop Blair explained that the cost of restoring a damaged instrument is about equally split between making it function properly and refinishing the dial face. If the instrument has not been hit, it can often be made to work properly by a complete disassembly and thorough cleaning. This requires the talents of a jeweler, for an instrument resembles nothing so much as a clock. Broken or missing springs are generally no problem, but a damaged gear can be; a new one may have to be made by hand.

Keep in mind that the instrument man has to be familiar with gauges which operate on quite different principles. He's expected to be able to repair both electric and mechanical speedometers and tachometers, as well as oil pressure gauges which work by Bourdon tube, diaphragm or electricity. All this requires a good grounding in electricity, mechanics and hydraulics. Unless you're awfully handy with those tiny wrenches and screwdrivers, you'd best leave instrument disassembly to a pro.

An even more specialized art is the refurbishing of the dial faces. At first you might think that putting back all those little numbers and letters is done with a teeny-tiny brush and a rock-steady hand. Theoretically it could be done that way, but the painter would need the talent of a Michaelangelo and it would still take forever. No, what is actually done is a more complicated but faster process. To understand it, let's take it from the top.

Let's assume that you have some damaged instruments with black numerals on a white or light-colored background, like the Pontiac instrument faces in these pictures. What is needed to duplicate these markings is a perfect stencil, much like the one the factory used in the first place. How do we get one? It's done with photography. A picture is taken of an original perfect gauge. Often this is not possible, in which case the picture is taken of the damaged gauge face.

The negative of this picture is

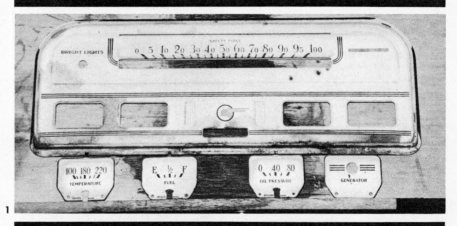

PHOTOS BY ERIC RICKMAN

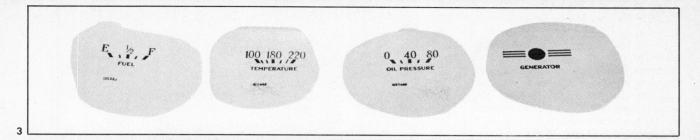

3

then enlarged and artwork is done on the enlarged negative to fill in the damaged areas. The enlargement is then photo-reduced back down to original size. The reason for this enlargement/reduction is that it's much easier to do touch-up artwork on a large negative, and any minor imperfections will disappear when the big, retouched negative is reduced.

Sometimes the dial face is so far gone that even this technique will not work, and then Blair and his fellow instrument specialists have to make an engineering drawing of the face—if they know what it was like.

4

1. This set of gauge faces for a '37 Pontiac is complete but in need of refinishing. However, the markings are plenty sharp enough to use for photographic reproduction.

2. The first step is to photograph the dial face and then enlarge the negative, as has been done with this speedometer from a '38 Ford Deluxe. Enlarging to twice full size allows room to carefully perform artwork on the negative until all scratches and blemishes have been corrected. It is then reduced back down to original size and used to make a silkscreen.

3. Background-color paint is applied to a strip of vinyl adhesive tape and silkscreened markings are laid on each patch of paint. Then the patches are cut out, stuck on the appropriate gauge and trimmed to fit. The cost per gauge is about $45.

4. The Pontiac gauge faces are crimped up at the edges, however, so the silkscreen cannot simply be laid over the surface. It wouldn't lie flat.

5. Here's the finished silkscreen for the '37 Pontiac gauges. Everything is included, even the serial numbers for the gauges and the Indian emblem. The speedo numbers at lower right are for a different car.

6. A lot trickier are instruments such as these from a '39 Chrysler Royal. Markings are done in outline letters on the reverse side of the glass, and they are really shot. At right is the background plate for the speedometer, which survived in excellent shape and will probably only need to be touched up around the edges.

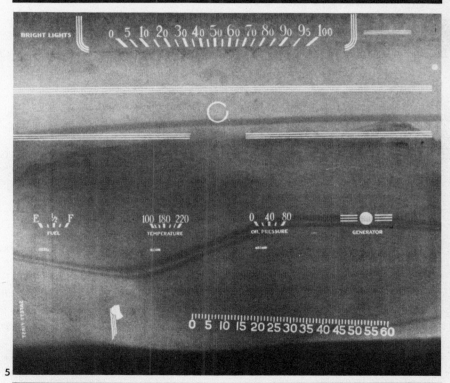

5

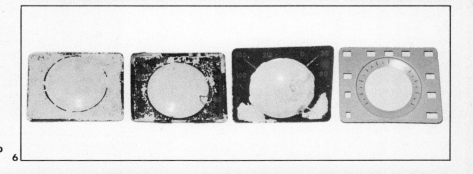

6

Then a photograph is taken of the drawing.

So, by one method or another, the specialist now has a photograph and its negative of the dial face. Now he proceeds to make a silkscreen. The negative (the 1:1-scale negative, not an enlargement) is placed on a sheet of photosensitive silkscreen material and exposed to light. When washed, those portions of the screen which were under the transparent areas of the negative disappear, leaving only the areas which were under the dark portions of the negative. This silkscreen is our stencil; it has holes where the negative was light, which is precisely where the dark markings were on the original gauge face (since a negative reverses light and dark areas). If the gauge had used white markings on a black background, we would have used a positive instead of a negative on the silkscreen to get our stencil.

With the silkscreen, we can now proceed to find matching colors for the dial face. White or black, the most common colors, are easy; but many gauges used oddball colors such as blue letters on a gray background. If true authenticity is desired, then custom colors will have to be mixed for such gauges. Once the colors are ready, the dial face can be stripped, sanded, primered and sprayed with the right background color. If the dial face is absolutely flat, the silkscreen can then be laid over it, the proper marking color sprayed or rolled on, and there you have it.

Suppose, however, that the dial faces are *not* flat, such as those of the '37 Pontiac shown here, which have crimped-up edges. Then the silkscreen won't lie down properly. For situations like this Blair uses a thin, sticky-back vinyl. A patch of the background color is put on the vinyl, and then the markings are silkscreened onto the patch. The patch is then cut out, stuck onto the dial face and the edges trimmed. Almost any irregular-shaped dial can be handled this way.

Incidentally, the process of printing with a stencil is called *xerography*. It was probably invented by the Chinese, although we Westerners have given it a Greek name. And you probably thought that big copy machine company dreamed up its corporate name just because it sounded funny.

The restoration process just described will suffice for most gauges. You can see that the restorer has to

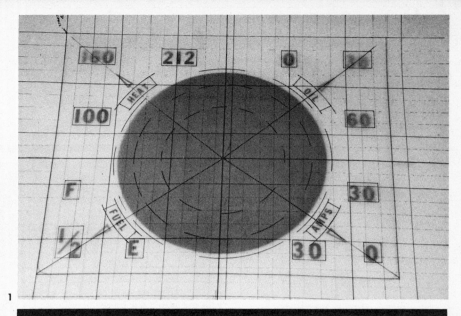

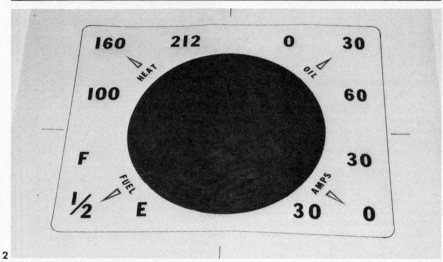

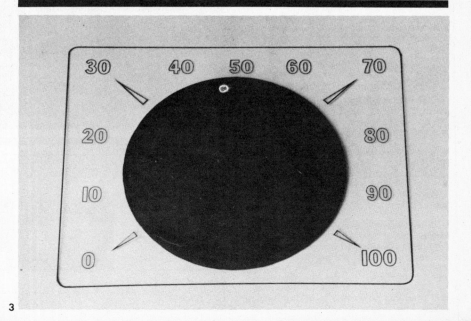

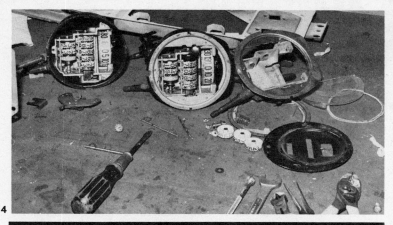

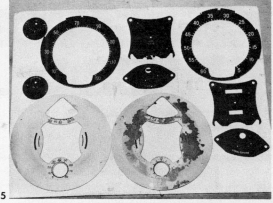

4

5

1. To redo the Chrysler faces, a scale drawing must be made. When done, a sheet of clear acetate is overlaid and the image drawn on it.

2. This acetate is then used to make the silkscreen, taking the place of the negative in the normal photographic reproduction process.

3. Speedometer numerals for the '39 Chrysler used outline lettering, which is time-consuming to duplicate photographically, since it involves a lot of negatives and positives overlaid to get the proper effect.

4. Lots of little pieces here. Better not get involved in speedometer repair like this unless you have lots of time, patience and skill.

5. Talk about rare—these gauges are from a 1938 Alfa Romeo 2900B Mille Miglia roadster, of which only four were made. But Blair knows what to do; he restored the instruments on one of the other ones!

6. Decals for your instruments are a good way to go if they're available and you're very careful.

7. Stick-on paper dial faces are not very satisfactory, but they're better than a damaged face. Such stick-ons can be made by a good amateur photographer. Just take a photo of a good dial, brush out the needle and print the result on high-contrast photographic paper.

6

7

be proficient in photography, painting, artwork, printing and drafting as well as the skills mentioned previously. But there's more. Many gauges are real demons of complexity and use a variety of plated parts. The restorer has to be able to recognize the difference between chrome plating, nickel plating, Butler finish and matte finish plating—when they're in a deteriorated condition—to be able to specify the proper replating.

Or how about those tricky numbers on the '39 Chrysler Royal shown here? They're printed on the back of the glass with a translucent paint. The speedometer numerals are outline or "skeleton" numbers, and to reproduce them requires more photographic hocus-pocus. A negative is made of the numerals to the outside dimensions, printed, and then photo-reduced to the inside dimensions. By overlaying the two sizes, the outline numerals are formed, if you get the proper sequence of positives and negatives in between.

Is there any way to shortcut all this work? If you have certain kinds of flat-faced dials, especially Fords, the answer is yes. You can get decals or thin cardboard "pasties" to stick over the dial faces. The former are not bad if they are applied *very* carefully, while the latter are generally unsatisfactory, as they don't look right and tend to become unstuck and warp in humid weather.

Other than a decal or pastie, there really isn't much you can do to cut corners. Either an instrument works properly and looks right or it doesn't; neither you nor the restorer is going to be happy with some sort of a quickie patch-up job. Take heart, however. If you go to an instrument man who's been doing this for awhile, he'll almost certainly have on file the silkscreens for your instruments, unless you have something really exotic. The file saves all that photography time. We strongly urge you to contact several instrument restorers before commiting your gauges to any of them, for if you can find one who already has the screens from a previous job, he'll be able to quote you a much lower price.

A PLATING PRIMER
ALL THAT GLITTERS IS NOT GOLD

Aside from poor bodywork and paint, poor plating will put black marks against your valuable restored car quicker than anything else. It's really amazing how flawless plating will make a car look so new and fresh; equally amazing is how quickly flaws can be spotted by anyone. That's because good plating is so mirror-bright and perfectly smooth that the eye is inevitably drawn to the slightest imperfection.

Now naturally we don't expect you to try plating in your own backyard or garage. But if you understand the principles of plating, and the problems faced by the plater, you'll be in a better position to intelligently discuss your pieces with him and perhaps even save some time, money and grief by doing some preparation yourself.

THE ELECTROLYTIC PROCESS

Almost all the common types of plating operate on the same general principle, the electrolytic process. It is basically simple. In a tank of a liquid which conducts electricity (called the *electrolyte)* are placed the piece or pieces to be plated and the plating material. All are parts of a DC electric circuit; the bar of plating material is the *anode,* or positive pole, while the piece to be plated is the *cathode,* or negative pole. When the current is switched on, current flows from the anode to the cathode, carrying along tiny amounts of the plating material and depositing it on the surface of the piece to be plated. The electrolyte varies with the plating material, and the amperage and time can be varied to control the thickness of the plating. Sounds pretty straightforward, right? Well, it isn't, so let's take a closer look at what goes on inside a plating shop when you take in some pieces from your pride and joy to be chrome plated.

CHROME PLATING

It's almost a shame that there's so much chrome on a car, because the time and complication spent in getting it there make chroming one of the most complicated and expensive processes in the whole plating field.

To begin with, there are no large deposits of chromium ore in the United States. Chromium is valuable; besides decorative plating, it is used in industrial hard chroming and is one of the principal alloying elements in stainless steel. Almost all that we use comes from Rhodesia or the Soviet Union, which makes it a politically sensitive material as well as an expensive one.

But it isn't the cost of chromium which makes chrome plating so expensive. As we will see, there is actually very little of it used on a typical plated piece. The real cost is for hand labor, and lots of it.

The first thing done to your parts is that they are chemically stripped down to the base metal. The basic material used in the stripping process is muriatic acid for stamped steel, forgings or fabricated pieces. In the case of die castings, which are susceptible to the errosive effects of muriatic acid, they are stripped electrically in a sulfuric

PHOTOS BY ERIC RICKMAN

2   3

1. Recognize these? They're from a classic '53 Studebaker coupe, and they're in the condition that just about everything is when it arrives at the plater's shop. With these pitted and weathered parts the plater is expected to work his usual miracles.

2. After stripping to remove all the grunge, repair work is the next step. Dents or even tears in the headlight shells of older cars are a common problem. This one required extensive welding, hammering and filing to get it right. Most platers will not do work like this anymore, so if you find one who is willing to do it, make him your friend for life.

3. Another common problem is rust pinholes in bumpers. These must be welded and then polished smooth.

4. The sequence of operations in chrome plating for all steel and die-cast parts is shown here.

5. Not every base metal needs the same sequence of operations to be chrome plated. Only steel, zinc and aluminum require all steps; different steps in the sequence can be eliminated for other metals, as shown.

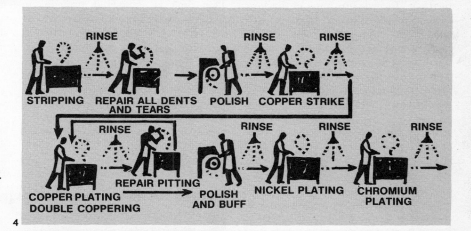

STRIPPING · REPAIR ALL DENTS AND TEARS · RINSE · POLISH · RINSE · COPPER STRIKE · RINSE

COPPER PLATING DOUBLE COPPERING · REPAIR PITTING · RINSE · POLISH AND BUFF · RINSE · NICKEL PLATING · RINSE · CHROMIUM PLATING · RINSE

CHROME PLATING	STRIP	POLISH	COPPER STRIKE	COPPER PLATE	POLISH	NICKEL PLATE	CHROME PLATE
STEEL	✔	✔	✔	✔	✔	✔	✔
COPPER	✔				✔	✔	✔
NICKEL	✔				✔		✔
ZINC ALLOY	✔	✔	✔	✔	✔	✔	✔
BRASS	✔	✔			✔	✔	✔
ALUMINUM	✔	✔	✔	✔	✔	✔	✔

acid bath. After stripping, any necessary repair work is done; we'll cover this in more detail later. The parts then go to the polishing room, where they are buffed and polished to a high luster: This is not just a precaution; it is absolutely necessary that the parts be as smooth as possible *before* any plating is done in order for the finished job to be right. After polishing, the parts are wired up and put through a series of rinses and cleaners to get rid of the polishing compound, and are then ready for their first pass through a plating tank.

"Chrome plating" is actually something of a misnomer, just as "tin can" is a rather misleading name for a steel can with a thin coating of tin. There are actually three plating layers involved—copper

over the base metal, followed by nickel, then chrome. This is the "triple chrome plating" process you may have heard or read about; that refers not to a triple thickness of chromium, but to this 3-metal plating sandwich. Why these three metals? Well, copper is soft and fills up tiny irregularities in the base metal extremely well. It can be polished to a fare-thee-well, and the brilliance

of the copper polishing is one of the key factors in the quality of the finished job. It is also a more compatible metal for the nickel to adhere to than steel or pot metal. Nickel adds its silvery color, and protects the copper and base metal from corrosion. However, it can oxidize (though more slowly than copper), and its yellowish tint is not generally considered highly attractive. So on top goes a very thin layer of chromium, which is quite resistant to oxidation and adds a bluish tint.

Is it theoretically possible to chrome plate directly on the base metal? Yes, it is. However, it would not have a high luster, because it is the polish given to the copper layer which determines the brilliance of the finished item. Also, chromium in the extremely thin layer used in plating is porous; it would allow the base metal to rust or corrode underneath it. In order to have chromium alone provide the corrosion protection of the copper and nickel layers (each about .002-in. thick) it would have to be of similar thickness. This would drive the cost of plating right out of sight, since chromium is a much more expensive metal than copper or nickel (which aren't exactly cheap themselves).

Now that you know *what* has to be done to your parts, let's return to the *how*. After cleaning, they are subjected to a copper "strike." The strike is nearly instantaneous and is similar to a prep coat in painting. Once the strike has struck, acting as a final cleaner should any residual material be left on the parent metal's surface, the parts are lowered into the copper bath. The bath is made up of a solution that contains copper cyanide, free sodium cyanide, caustic potash, brighteners and a wedding agent. Figured in amps per square foot of plated surface, it usually takes from 35 to 40 minutes at 40 amps to plate a layer .0015 to .002-in. thick. If a part is badly pitted and the plater knows there's going to be a lot of buffing and polishing involved, he can leave it in the tank for twice as long. This gives a copper layer about .004-in. thick, and is known as "double coppering."

From the copper tank, the parts return to the buffer/polisher where they are buffed and polished to an extremely high luster. Again we must stress that it is here where the real quality in chroming takes place. The thickness of the copper and nickel will give longevity, but the skilled craftsmanship of the polishers and buffers ensures the quality of the luster and the detail within the parts. With the buffing/polishing finished, the pieces go through another cleaning and rinsing opera-

tion as they did before, then they are placed into the nickel tank. The solution here is a combination of nickel chromide, nickel sulfate, boric acid, brighteners and a wedding agent. The nickel plating usually lasts from 35 to 40 minutes at 60 amps per square foot of plated surface. Build-up is generally kept at .002-in. thick. The nickel is *not* polished. After a cleaning rinse to remove the nickel solution, the parts are dunked into the chrome tank. This tank is somewhat unusual in that the chromium is not a solid bar at the anode, but is in solution in the combination of chromic and sulfuric acids which fill the tank. An extremely high current of 2000 amps per square foot forces the chromium out of solution and onto the nickelized surfaces. This current is maintained for just a very short time—45 seconds to 1 minute—and deposits only about .000050-in. of chrome. That's only 50 teensy-weensy mil-

lionths of an inch, about one-fortieth the thickness of the nickel, and can be really thought of as a "clear" protective coating to prevent the nickel from oxidizing and tarnishing. Now you know why there's not much chrome used in chrome plating. From the chrome tank the parts are given a final rinsing and cleaning, but not polished. Most good plating shops have a man with a soft cloth at the end of the line who wipes off all water marks, critically examines the pieces, and will send one back through for a complete redoing of the whole sequence if it is not up to par.

BASE METALS

The two most common metals you will want plated are undoubtedly *steel* (bumpers and wheel parts) and *pot* metal (trim). Grilles vary; some are assemblies of steel parts, others are castings, and some are combinations of the two. The plating tech-

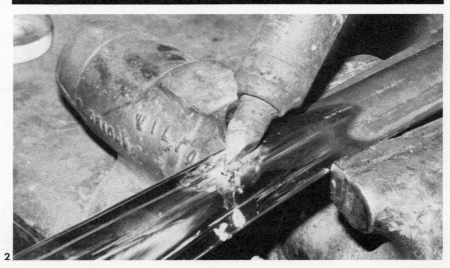

niques for both these metals are almost identical. It is in the repair of damaged parts that these metals differ widely, and we'll get into that a little later.

As you might expect from the description of the plating sequence, *nickel* is the easiest metal of all to chrome plate. It is simply polished and cleaned, and the chrome plated directly on it. However, you would probably never want to do this. If you have any solid nickel parts, for heaven's sake don't ruin their originality by chrome plating them. *Copper* is another metal easy to plate, as it naturally doesn't have to be copper plated before the nickel goes on. But again, you'll be destroying originality if you plate a copper part that was not plated when it left the factory, even if it is a pain to keep it polished. *Brass,* however, is a metal you will run into that you can plate, since it was used for a lot of trim pieces. Far stronger than pot metal but easier to work with than steel, you will commonly find it in the frames of windows and windshields and in the headlights of older cars. And of course in antique cars, brass in all its naked unplated glory is all over the place. Since brass is an alloy of copper and zinc, it takes plating almost as easily as pure copper. The

plater does not put on the copper layer, but does give it the copper strike before the nickel.

The only other bright metals you are likely to encounter are *aluminum* and *stainless steel.* Both can be plated, but it is pointless to do so. All stainless needs is an occasional polish to keep it looking spiffy, while plating aluminum can be disastrous. The coefficient of thermal expansion of aluminum is much higher than any of the plating metals, so if exposed to heating and cooling cycles aluminum can crack

and destroy plating. Like copper and brass, aluminum readily oxidizes, so keeping it polished can be something of a chore; but if you feel that you simply *have* to have something done to your aluminum, try anodizing. This is another electrolytic process, which deposits an incredibly thin 10 millionths of an inch of a copper-aluminum coating on the aluminum surface. That isn't much, but it's enough to stop the aluminum from oxidizing. Aluminum can be anodized in any color by the addition of dyes, but to keep things looking

1. By far the most difficult plating problem is corroded die castings, and unfortunately they're also quite common. Polishing will not remove these pits; the customer will have to get a new part, settle for pits in the final plating or have them filled by some very tedious work.

2. There's no getting around a badly pitted area; it simply has to be filled if there's no replacement. This is tricky business, since the zinc alloy melts at a low temperature. Heated with a soldering iron or a small torch, the pitted area is filled with zinc or a special low-temperature platable solder, then filed smooth.

3. Sometimes pitting can be in the darnedest places. Here's some right at the tip of the star in a Mercedes 300SL grille piece. The metal is very thin here, so it calls for special care during repair. Experts only!

4. After any necessary repair work, the parts are polished. The surface must be polished smooth *before* plating, because the plating will follow the surface contour and will never be shiny if it is irregular.

original tell the plater that you want *silver* anodize. Given proper care, the anodize coating lasts a long time, but it should never be polished, nicked, or scratched; just keep it wiped clean with a soft cloth.

OTHER PLATING PROCESSES

Nickel plating is like chrome plating without the last step. However, the nickel used today in chrome plating is not quite so pure as that used in the good old days as an exterior ornamental metal. This is due to the development of a modified nickel plating solution in the late 1920's. Several additional agents were added, notably nickel sulfate, which speeded up the plating time and also left a smoother and brighter surface; so smooth, in fact, that it did not have to be buffed and polished after plating, which previously had been necessary. However, the nickel deposited by this method was less pure, and it tarnished much more readily. It was to stop this tarnishing that the additional layer of chromium was added. But the combination of the faster nickel plating plus chromium plating still took less time and money than the old way of nickel plating, and that—aha!—was the real reason for the general industry-wide switch to chrome after 1927. So if you have nickel-plated parts that need redoing, what you must specify to the plater is *Watts nickel*. This requires use of that old-style bath, as well as subsequent buffing, and not every plater is equipped to do it. Search out one that is; you won't be happy with the improper type of nickel.

Plating with *copper* is straightforward, as you know by now. Copper and brass oxidize and tarnish readily, so most plating shops will spray on a coat of clear preservative (usually lacquer) over these metals if you want it. You will have to decide whether the reduced maintenance of this step is worth the lessened originality.

Satin chrome is a process in which the copper layer is polished with coarse cloths on the buffing wheel. This causes striations in the copper, which gives an interesting and attractive finish to the chrome when the plating is done. It is useful for plating underhood or interior body parts which look too garish if given the bright-chrome treatment. To put it another and sneakier way, satin chrome is a good way to plate something which was not originally plated, and where you want to avoid the obvious impression that you plated it. *Matte chrome* is similar. Here the copper is subjected to a vapor hone of water and glass beads under low pressure. The size of the beads, the pressure, and the length of time can all be varied to obtain the desired texture. The interior chrome parts of many older cars had a finish like this, so if you want it duplicated, take along a good sample piece to

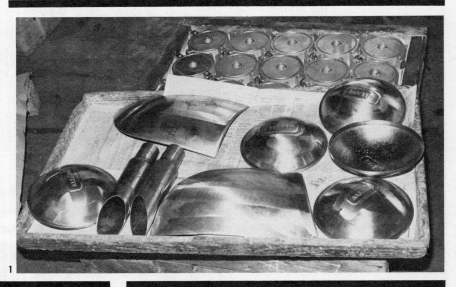

show the plater. A third variation is *Butler finish,* in which a slurry of pumice and water is used with the polishing wheel on the copper. This is followed by a plating with Watts nickel and polishing, rather than the normal nickel-chrome layers. This is another good finish on underhood parts, closely duplicating the original appearance of such parts which look all wrong if given the bright-chrome treatment.

You may have heard something recently about *black chrome.* It is gaining in vogue among certain restorers, especially Porsche owners. The process is the same as normal chrome plating, except that after the nickel layer the piece is submerged in a special chromic solution which has a catalyst and no sulfates. Left in for 6 to 10 minutes, chrome and oxides of chrome codeposit on the nickel to a depth of 30-50 millionths of an inch, leaving a smooth gloss black finish. It was originally developed for optical devices, and today has wide usage in cameras, computers, and aerospace equipment, any place where it contributes to control of light. Some restorers are substituting it for black paint. A prominent west coast plating shop notes that this is especially true for T-series MG's, where restorers are putting it on steering columns since it is relatively impervious to the gasoline dripped down on this item by the carburetors in these cars. But it is not really recommended for cars other than in a few isolated instances like these. In the first place, it wasn't original. In the second place, it's soft, much softer than bright chrome, and even heavy rubbing with ordinary chrome polish will go right through it. And it costs about 30% more than bright chrome. Attempting to put it on a part which normally gets very hot (exhaust manifold, exhaust pipe), creates an even worse problem, for as the copper layer underneath heats it tries to oxidize very rapidly, which makes the black chrome change colors. And if you leave off the copper, the black chrome isn't shiny. So black chrome has plenty of problems, and be prepared for them if you want this finish badly enough.

Believe it or not, *cadmium plating* is actually more expensive than chrome plating from a material cost standpoint. But because there is very little handwork involved, the total cost is less than half that of chrome. After cleaning and stripping in the same manner as the chrome-plating sequence, the parts are placed in a solution of cyanide, caustic soda, water and other additives. Pure cadmium is the anode. A current of 50 amps per square foot is then turned on for 15-30 minutes, depositing cadmium to a thickness of 10 to 70 millionths of an inch. If the plating is put on too fast or the amperage is too high, the plated metal will begin to take on a burned or milky cast and have too much buildup. Properly plated cadmium looks like satin finish silver paint.

If you're after authenticity, you'd stop right here; the parts would then be rinsed, dried and returned to you. However, you may want the additional protection of *gold iridit-ing,* a further plating step which gives the cadmium a bright golden or brassy appearance. Cad with gold iriditing is a very durable coating, and definitely outlasts chrome by a wide margin in adverse conditions such as salt air or heat. It is a fast process, with no under layers and no polishing necessary; parts can go through the whole plating sequence, including iriditing, in less than an hour. It is ideal for small engine and chassis parts, especially nuts and bolts, as it protects them and imparts a fresh and clean look, avoiding the overdone appearance of other forms of plating.

Don't forget that the plating shop can also remove unwanted plating.

4

1. These Allard parts have received the first polishing and are ready for the first plating step.

2. Before any plating is done, however, the parts must be cleaned again to remove polishing compound and grit. They are dunked briefly in a hot chemical bath which cleans without attacking the metal.

3. Sometimes the grit is stubborn, and then scrubbing is necessary to remove it. There's lots of handwork in the plating shop, even here.

4. Finally we're ready for some plating, and first is copper. The part is left in the copper tank about 40 minutes, then rinsed.

A PLATING PRIMER

If your car suffered through an improper restoration or was once a hot rod, it probably has a lot of chromed pieces on it (especially the engine) which were not originally chromed. We'll put in our plea for authenticity again, and urge you to have the offending parts stripped and given the proper finish. A plating shop charges practically nothing for stripping, since no hand labor is involved in the process.

HYDROGEN EMBRITTLEMENT

Normal chrome plating produces a loss in strength of the base metal. This is especially true of steel, where the loss of strength can be as high as 35%. This is due to the metal-absorbing hydrogen atoms from the acid baths, and is known as "hydrogen embrittlement." If the piece is merely decorative, this strength loss is not important. But if the part is stressed in normal operation, this factor can be critical. In a car being restored to original condition, probably the only parts you have that would possibly fit into this category are wheels, especially wire wheels. Hydrogen embrittlement can be cured by baking the parts in an oven at a time-temperature relationship ranging from 350° for 24 hours to 450° for 8 hours,

The parts should be baked after stripping and after the copper plating, but it is not necessary after the nickel and chromium plating, since the base metal is then protected by the copper. the hotter the temperature, the shorter the time. The sooner the parts go into the oven after plating the better, and on no account should they be kept waiting more than 2 hours. If you have any parts subjected to high stress, and particularly if they are made of a high-strength alloy steel rather than mild steel, think twice about having them chrome plated. If you still decide to go ahead, make absolutely sure the plating shop has the ovens—and uses them.

WHAT YOU CAN DO

Obviously you're not going to go out and buy your own plating tanks to set up a chrome shop in your backyard. From the foregoing, you can see what a specialized operation it is and how much skill and knowledge is required. But there are still certain things you can do to help the plater and reduce the total cost.

The first is to disassemble the parts as completely as possible. This may sound rather elementary, but platers insist there are a lot of customers who don't really understand that since the plated parts have to be immersed into a variety of chemical vats, they should not still be attached to other parts the customer doesn't want plated. If you don't do the disassembly the plating shop will have to do it for you, and you'll be charged about 20 bucks per hour for their labor. Door locks and trunk locks are a particular problem here, as many are not made to be taken apart without destroying them. If yours are like this, explain the situation to the plater and he can use special measures to protect the locking mechanism. Don't try to do this yourself with masking tape, electrical tape or other such materials, as these go away pronto when exposed to the stripping solutions. The plater uses a special flexible lead tape to wrap around the back of the lock, and plugs the keyhole with a special wax.

Another way to help is to specify exactly what you want to the plater. When you bring in an unidentifiable bracket, for example, the plater has no way of knowing which is the side exposed to view, and therefore the side which should be nice and shiny. So to be on the safe side he'll probably buff all the sides. You could have saved him the work—and yourself the cost—if you had specified which side was to have been shiny and which side could have been left unpolished. And in case you've been wondering what unbuffed and unpolished chrome plating looks like, peek at the back side of a new or newly replated bumper; it quite resembles freshly sprayed aluminum paint.

Be careful how you repair a damaged plated part. Above all, it must be stripped *before* you begin the repairs, not after. If you attempt to weld a damaged bumper before stripping, for example, you'll burn some of the plating metals right into the steel, and that's going to cause

1. For odd-shaped pieces, sometimes special electrodes must be devised. Model Plating Co. in Bell Gardens, Calif., kept getting wire wheels in for plating, so they made this circular electrode to pull current down into the hubs of these wheels.

2. If you think this looks like somebody's wash hung out to dry, you're almost right. These parts have been copper plated and are drying out preparatory to buffing.

3. The dirtiest and most demanding job in plating is the buffing, but it's here that the real brilliance of the finished job is determined.

4. Buffing wheels come in all sizes, with small ones used for tight curves such as those on this bracket.

problems at replating time. Sure, stripping the part first means two trips to the plating shop instead of one, but it's the only right way.

Don't expect broken metal parts that you carefully glued together to stay glued together in the plater's tanks, no matter what kind of super-duper ultra-strength adhesive you used. Repair of a die-cast part can indeed be a problem, but glue isn't the answer. We have an article covering repairs of this nature elsewhere in this book. If a damaged part cannot be repaired satisfactorily, it must be replaced with a part salvaged from a junkyard or a new reproduction part.

If you repair a part using a dissimilar metal, such as filling up drilled holes in a steel windshield frame with brass or lead, by all means tell the plater. These metals are softer than steel, and will form small depressions during that first pass under the buffing wheel unless the operator is being extra careful. If these depressions do form, then they have to be filled by extra time in the copper tank and a lot more buffing, perhaps even grinding, all of which costs time and money—your money.

Sometimes the quality of the finished plating job will depend on a decision by you. A perfect example is the die-cast script lettering trim found on many cars. Polishing the outer surface of the lettering is a straightforward task, but suppose you want the *edges* shiny, too? That's going to require some pretty careful work by a skilled buffer, and the use of some small-diameter buffing wheels. So you're going to pay a lot more for a difference that is noticeable only to someone looking for it. If your car is destined for show, of course you want the extra qual-

2

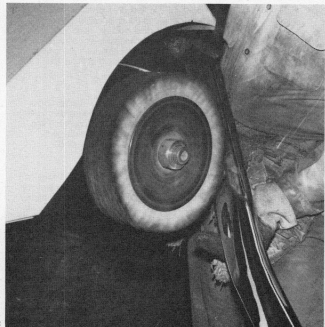

3

4

ity; but if it's going to be just a clean street car, well . . . only you can decide. But before that part disappears into the plating shop's interior, make sure the plater *knows* your decision.

There are quite a few repair tips, some of which are discussed in another article. One of the best we've heard concerns the reshaping of dented headlight shells, a common problem. Very few places will undertake to straighten these. Try a musical instrument shop. They get dented trombones and trumpets all the time, and have the necessary odd-shaped tools to put that sweet curve back into your old headlights.

PLATING DIE CASTINGS

Let's discuss one of the biggest headaches faced by both you and the plater, the plating of die-cast trim pieces.

1

Automotive trim was originally solid brass or nickel, as anyone familiar with horseless carriages knows. Though expensive today, these metals were much cheaper during the first decade of the 20th century, and well suited to the low-volume production processes in use at that time. Brass was much more widely used of the two, since it was cheaper and more easily machinable. But brass tarnishes rather quickly as it oxidizes, and to stop this the trim pieces were often nickel plated with the Watts nickel mentioned previously. In the late 1920's chrome plating was developed as an adjunct to a new nickel-plating process. At about the same time or a little earlier, die-cast trim pieces appeared. Die casting is a process greatly suited to high-volume production, and as American auto manufacturers developed their mass-production assembly-line techniques, the shift to die castings was natural. Brass was therefore superseded by zinc, a much better metal for die casting. By 1930, chrome-plated die castings were in common usage on almost all the low-priced high-volume cars, and by 1940, brass was still being used only by custom body builders.

There are only three principal zinc-based die-casting alloys used in the U.S. All three contain 4.1% aluminum, very small amounts of mag-

nesium, and differ primarily in their copper content, which ranges from 0 to 2.7%. These alloys have the popular name "pot metal" because of their rather low-melting points, around 730°F; they can be melted in an ordinary iron pot if you get a cracking good fire going under it, and such pots were originally used when making zinc castings. (Ceramic crucibles are used today.) They are so heavily used in die castings because they produce a smooth finish, accurately reproduce complex shapes, are easily plated, allow a long die life because of the low temperature, and are much cheaper than brass. They are usually sold under the commercial name "zamac," a foreign-sounding word which is actually an acronym simply meaning zinc, aluminum, magnesium, and copper. (Vuurry clever, these engineers.)

Zinc alloys of very high purity are used in die castings. The combined total of lead, iron, and cadmium impurities cannot exceed one one-hundredth of one percent, or one part in 10,000, yet even this rarefied level of impurities causes problems in automotive trim. Those pits and small raised areas you see on old trim pieces are caused by localized corrosion around tiny surface impurities.

No plating shop likes old die castings, and almost none will repair a

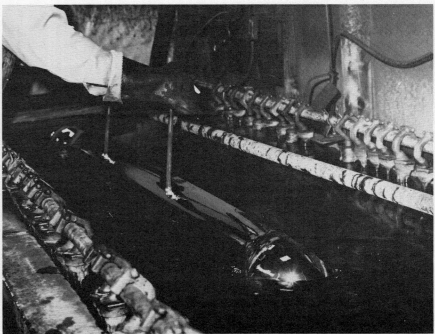

2

1. The difference that buffing makes is dramatic; the upper bumper here has been buffed, the bottom has not. It's too bad that copper tarnishes so quickly; the buffed copper parts are so pretty you're tempted to put them on the car as is.

2. Nickel plating takes its luster from the copper buffing, and chromium goes on to protect the nickel. Contrary to popular notion, the chrome is *not* buffed, merely rinsed and dried.

3. Finished parts are dried and laid out on clean cloths for examination before individual wrapping. Many shops today use a photographic record like this to keep track of parts as they are brought in, a more accurate way than the vague descriptions usually written on the receipt.

4. Any good plating shop will carefully wrap larger finished parts in paper to prevent scratching. Smaller parts are put in cardboard boxes; you'd be amazed at how many boxes a shop goes through in a month.

damaged one. If you have some damaged parts, read our articles on repair and repro parts and then decide what you want to do. But even if it isn't broken or damaged, an old and weathered die casting often stubbornly refuses to take new plating properly. And those pits won't magically disappear. The stripping, buffing, and plating operations will make them smoother, but the larger ones will still be visible when the parts are handed back to you. If you cannot stand this and insist on having the parts perfectly smooth, better talk it over with the plater. He can apply successive copper layers and buff them smooth, but that's going to be expensive because of all the buffing time. And the more plating layers and buffing that goes on, the more detail you're going to lose. This is not important with a headlight rim or trim strip, but it is with a hood ornament or escutcheon.

If the pitting is severe and there is no way to replace the part, you might try filling the pits with soft solder. Have the part stripped and then copper plated. From a welding supply house obtain some soldering flux and a few ounces of a platable soft solder, such as Sta-Brite 430. That number represents the melting temperature of the material in degrees F., about 300° less than the zinc alloy of the part. Handled carefully, this is a safe enough margin to enable you to heat the part with a torch and fill up the depressions with the solder. Don't use a soldering iron, as the heat is too localized, and don't put the solder directly on bare zinc. The copper plating spreads the heat, and the solder "takes" much better on copper. A useful tip is to use a hand drill with a countersink bit and actually enlarge the pits after the part is stripped but before it is copper plated; this opens up the pits and allows the solder to fill them more easily. When the soldering is done, file the part smooth and return it to the plater for buffing and final plating. If this sounds like a lot of work and running back and forth to the plating shop, it is. But you'll be very lucky to find a shop that will do this work, so if you want it done, better plan on learning how to operate that torch yourself. Incidentally, it doesn't have to be a fancy oxy-acetylene job; one of those small propane torches available at any hardware store will do.

POST-PLATING CARE

One of the best ways to avoid having to repeat all the headaches you've had getting the parts plated is to take proper care of them once they're done. Never, never, never—repeat, *never* —use a powerful abrasive such as rubbing compound or steel wool on chrome plating. Remember that 50 millionths of an inch! If the plating is so bad that ordinary chrome polish will not bring it back, it's time for replating.

Keep in mind that chromium, nickel, and copper do not rust; steel does. If you see rust splotches peeping through the plating, forget the polish and grab the wrenches; the part has got to come off. Few people bother to wax chrome, but that's a very good idea, especially in a damp climate. The backs of bumpers and other plated parts can be sprayed with silver epoxy paint to stop rust and corrosion from starting on the unpolished sides. If a plated part is to be taken off a car and stored for a while, spray it with WD-40 or equivalent and seal it in a plastic bag, if you can find one big enough. Ditto for newly plated parts which are going to hang around for weeks maybe months while the bodywork and painting are finished. Dirt holds moisture, so keep complex-plated assemblies (especially chrome wire wheels) clean by frequent washings. Anyone who has had chrome wire wheels knows what a pain they can be to keep shiny, but this chore can be eased by using a mild solution of phosphoric acid in water. Available under several trade names ("Sol-Brite" and "Taylor's Wire Wheel Cleaner" are two), this solution washes off dirt, grime and dulling surface film like magic, leaving a sparkling shine that doesn't need polishing and even repels water.

So there you have it. Good luck on your next trip to the dreaded plater. Keep your plating shiny and it will be a good reflection on you. 🚗

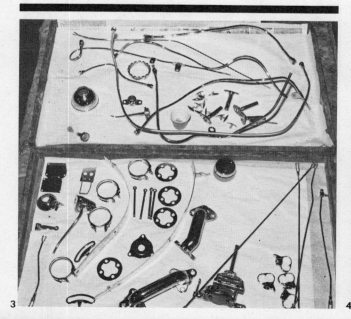

NEW METAL IN OLD SHAPES THE REPRO PARTS INDUSTRY AND HOW IT'S GROWING

BY RICK BUSENKELL

When the manufacturer of your pride and joy originally made it, parts for it were made by the hundreds of thousands, often literally by the millions. As long as it was fairly new, those parts were easy to obtain from the dealers or auto parts houses. But if you're reading this book, then the days when your little beauty was new are long behind it, right? And now you're probably having a little trouble finding parts for it. Well, join the crowd.

What became of all those parts? Most of them were used in making cars, which have gradually found their way into junkyards, where they were either destroyed or are presently being used as parts cars; junkyards are still the primary parts sources for most older cars. More new parts were designated as spares and sold to dealers, so most of those also ended up in cars which are now in junkyards. But of course there were a lot of parts the dealers never sold, and these parts form the NOS

(new old stock) supply so beloved by restorers.

What of the restorer who is enamored of a car which was not wildly popular when it was new, and for which there are now practically no NOS parts? He can live off junkyards for a while but he's still in trouble, especially for body parts. Junkyards typically yield much better mechanical parts than body parts, because the engine and chassis have been protected by the body, which has to endure the ravages of

weather. And usually the car was put in the junkyard in the first place because it was in an accident, which banged up part of the body badly but didn't do nearly so much damage to the mechanicals.

So we come to the repro part manufacturer, firms which make brand-new parts for old cars. Ford enthusiasts in particular are familiar with such firms, for surely a new Model A could be built entirely of repro parts now on the market. Such firms tend to concentrate on parts which are hardest to obtain but easiest to make, and small trim pieces fall right into that category. Often they are home workshop operations. Car club members find that there is a common shortage of some part such as a door handle, horn button or hood ornament, so one member sets up a mold at his home and makes the part for other club members. Since he's already got the mold, he scouts around for other problem parts, contacts other car clubs, and pretty soon there's a full-fledged business in operation.

Tasker Metal Products in Los Angeles started out in almost that way. From a small beginning with a few permanent molds for Model A parts, TMP has grown into a million-dollar-a-year business supplying repro parts for a wide variety of cars. In a cooperative venture with a lawn mower manufacturer, TMP makes stamped parts such as grilles and hoods as well as cast trim pieces. Tasker President Gene Golling has found rather surprisingly that the hottest market for his stamped parts is not old American cars, but certain European sports cars imported since World War II. The principal reason for this seeming paradox is that these cars were imported in moderate numbers; large enough to justify tooling to reproduce parts for, but not large enough so that junkyards are full of them. Sports cars of the early '50's have become legitimate restorers projects, and some of them,

3

4

5

1. Pride of Tasker Metal Products stamping operations is this replica grille for the MG TC and TD. Although these little roadsters are now classics among the sports car set, MG has been unable to supply this part for the last 20 years.

2. This 500-ton hydraulic press (that's the force it can exert, not its weight) is used to produce many repro sheetmetal parts. One of them is the MGB splash pan, which is visible in front with its white die.

3. Though it forms a part out of sheet steel, this die is made of phenolic resin supported by a welded steel framework. If chipped or damaged, it can easily be repaired. Since it is used for short production runs in which only a few hundred parts are made, its life is practically indefinite.

4. To make the MG TC-TD grille cap, several stamping steps are required. The sheet steel is first drawn into a tub-like shape, then the die at right stamps out the final shape.

5. Ye gods! Where are all those MG TC's? Here are two big boxes full of stampings for TC-TD bumper guards, with a finished one held above. TMP sells 1500 of these a year.

6. In the background are anodized aluminum MGB grille shells which are exact copies of factory originals, but TMP felt they weren't good enough. Now they make theirs out of brass. In the right foreground are brass shells awaiting plating; in the left foreground are plated ones.

6

NEW METAL IN OLD SHAPES

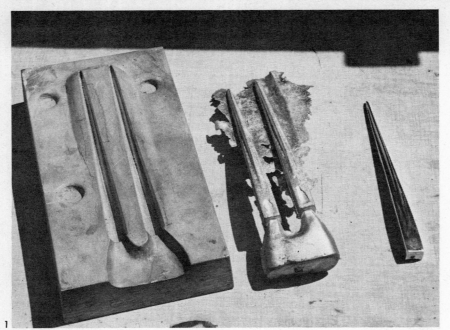

like the MG TC and TD and the Jaguar XK-120, are now considered classics; restorers are now willing to spend a lot of money on them. Being sports cars, however, they were usually driven vigorously, and often suffered front-end damage. Notable about TMP's line of repro body parts is that they are almost exclusively front-end parts, not rear-end parts.

The success of TMP in this market has an amusing sidelight. At first companies like British Leyland and Porsche were very happy to have TMP make parts for their older models, since they had long since ceased supplying spare parts for these cars. As TMP became more successful, however, it began to make repro parts for newer and newer cars, and now offers something as recent as a grille for a 1974 MGB. This places it in direct competition with British Leyland in sell-

ing spare parts to the factory's own dealers, and the giant British corporation is no longer quite so happy.

How can a little company compete with a huge corporation in making the same part? The answer lies in the type of tooling involved. A big factory engaged in mass production has high overhead costs, a

1. A permanent mold for headlight trim strips yields the casting at center, which, after the separation, cleaning and plating processes, becomes the finished article at right.

2. A permanent-mold operation is fascinating to watch. This one is used to make two Model A bumper medallions with attached bolts. (A) With the mold open, two bolts are inserted through holes in the cope (upper) half at left, one for each medallion. Finished casting is at right. (B) The mold is then closed and molten zinc poured into it. Mold must be kept hot enough so that it will not chill the zinc while it is being poured, but not so hot that it takes forever to solidify. (C) Only a few seconds later, retaining nuts holding bolts are removed, mold is opened and a light tap with hammer knocks casting free. Process is quick, taking only about 15 seconds from start to finish. (D) The result of a few hours work—hundreds of castings ready for trimming, plating and painting.

3. Some Old World handwork of a kind that's rare nowadays is done in the manufacture of these Jaguar XK-120 grilles. They are made the same way as the originals, with stamped brass strips soldered to a cast brass rim. The curved strips are cut to the proper length and held in a jig. A finished grille, ready for plating, is on the bench.

4. Triumph TR4 grilles are faithful replicas, made of extruded aluminum with heliarc-welded headlight circles.

lot of employees, and expensive "hard" tooling. It is like a musclebound giant; it can only make parts cheaply if it makes them in huge numbers, which requires a huge tooling investment. The spare parts were made during the production run which made the same parts for assembled cars; once that production run is ended, it is uneconomical for the factory to ever again make that part. (The only exception of which we are aware is that the Ford Motor Company, because of the exceptional historical interest of the 2-seat '55-'57 Thunderbird, is now offering spare body panels for those cars.)

The repro manufacturer is in a different boat. He has a small factory, a small number of employees, and knows that his total production run for any part will never be more than a few thousand pieces. He can thus use simple machinery and short-lived "soft" tooling, rather than high-volume automated machinery and expensive dies made out of hardened tool steel. For a trim piece, the original manufacturer used an automatic die-casting machine; the repro manufacturer can duplicate that piece with one man working part-time with a hand-operated permanent mold. He can even substitute a different material and an entirely different manufacturing process; in this article we show photos of cast aluminum parts sold as replacements for original ones made from stamped steel. An original manufacturer could not afford to do that, because casting is a much slower process than stamping; but a repro manufacturer can, since

he is not interested in the high volume allowed by stamping. And finally, a repro manufacturer knows he is making a part for which there is a proven demand among restorers, people who will pay extra to get good quality; thus it comes as no surprise that many repro parts are actually *better* than original. Tasker Metal Products, for example, makes their MGB grilles out of brass, having tried and discarded as inferior the steel 2nd aluminum used by the original factory part.

Let's take a closer look at this so-called "soft" tooling. Exactly what does that mean?

Actually, it has two meanings. The first is that such tooling is light and easily movable, as opposed to hard or "fixed" tooling. Thus it becomes a description of the size, weight and complexity of the machinery. Devices such as drill presses, small lathes, vises, table saws, belt sanders, grinding wheels and other small shop machinery are typical examples of soft tooling, while a Cincinnati stamping machine or a Bridgeport milling machine would be considered hard tooling. In casting, a good contrast has already been given in the use of a manually-operated permanent mold in place of an automatic die-casting machine.

In stamping, the name of the game in the big leagues is speed. Big stamping machines cost a bundle, and in order to justify their high price have to spew out parts at a tremendous rate. And this is exactly what the mass producers of autos need. There are problems, however. High machine speed means that the

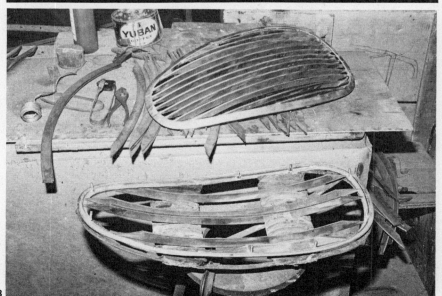

3

4

NEW METAL IN OLD SHAPES

die faces come together at a fast rate. Since the sheetmetal between those faces resists bending, it exerts a force against the faces which is proportional to the speed. This means rapid die wear unless the dies are extremely hard, much harder than the sheet steel being stamped. In practice these dies are very large and heavy, and usually made from a solid chunk of tool steel. When they start showing signs of wear they cannot be repaired, so they have to be replaced with new dies. The stamping machine itself is a Rube Goldberg mechanical wonder, usually employing an electric motor, a huge flywheel, many feet in diameter and a clutch. The inertia of the flywheel, which is kept rotating by the motor and is engaged by the clutch, provides the power for the sudden stroke of the movable part of the die (often called the *ram or punch)*. Engage the clutch, and whap! Out pops a Chevy hood.

The repro manufacturer doesn't need all that speed. Consequently he prefers to use a smaller hydraulic press, which squeezes just as powerfully but more slowly. Since the sheetmetal is bent more slowly, it doesn't "fight back" as much, so wear on the die faces is greatly reduced. Since the die wear is less per stamping and it will only be used for a few thousand stampings anyway, the dies can be made of lighter construction and softer material than tool steel, hence the name "soft" tooling. The dies can be made from a special metal alloy such as Kirksite, which is hard but has a low melting point. When such dies are worn they can be melted down and recast. Or they can be made of hard phenolic resin, laid over a fiberglass or metal form and supported by a steel framework. When worn or damaged, these dies can be repaired by simply adding more resin to the surface. So by accepting a slower production speed, the whole technology of metal stamping is changed and made much cheaper.

Let's say you've got this keen idea for a repro part you're sure there's a demand for, and no one is making it. Can you do something about it, even if you don't have a fancy workshop? Sure. Most small companies which do casting or stamping work will be happy to make a permanent mold or stamping die for you. Pay their price and you'll own the mold or dies, even if you leave them at the plant. Pay another fee and you can have a production run of the

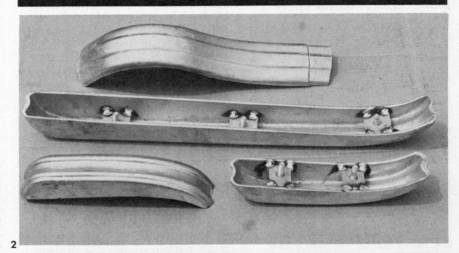

part, which you are then free to sell however you please. If you turn a profit, you can have another production run. This takes a little investment capital and faith, but if it works, you're sitting in the catbird seat with an exclusive market. Another arrangement might be made whereby the company foots the bill for the dies or mold, but you pay for the production run plus a fee for exclusive distribution. Talk the situation over with specialist companies in your area. Remember that if you've been looking hard for that certain part, then for sure some other people have too. There's no reason why you can't render a service to your fellow enthusiasts and reap a small reward for doing it.

To sum up, the repro manufacturer uses hand labor and simple machinery to substitute for the original manufacturer's expensive automatic machinery. And when you stop to think about it, that's really the way the antique and classic cars were built. So when you buy a repro part you're supporting a craft industry, a return to the good old days when men did fine work and were proud of it. Not a bad thought as you're bolting up that new part to your old bus, is it?

1. More Model A goodies—here's a whole boxful of instrument panels ready for the plater. Looking at quantities like this makes you realize how big the demand is for repro parts.

2. These unusual parts are (from top): an MGA front bumper, a Jaguar XK-120 front bumper and two XK-120 rear bumpers. But they are thick cast aluminum rather than stamped steel. Stiffer than the originals, they are cheaper to produce in small quantities and will be indistinguishable when plated and installed on a car.

3. Here's a repro right front fender for a Triumph TR3 and the die for making it. Low-pressure forming allows the use of a fiberglass-faced die supported by a steel framework.

4. Fenders and front aprons for the Triumph TR3 are stacked like so much cordwood. Tasker Metal Products is the only company in America making repro sheetmetal parts for sports cars.

5. Extruded aluminum channels fill the receiving yard at TMP. When bent to the proper shape and fitted with neoprene inserts, these become Porsche bumper strips.

6. "Little drops of water, little grains of sand,/Grilles of ev'ry shape and size clutter up the land."

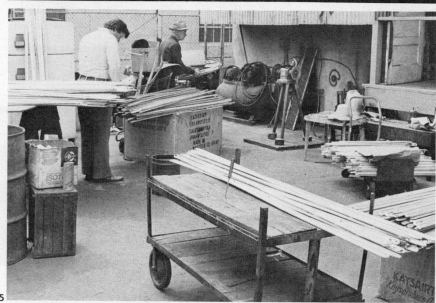

SWEET HEATERS FOR NEAT STREETERS HAVE A HOT TIME IN THE OLD TOWN CAR WITH AN ORIGINAL HEATER

If you're 15 or younger and an old car to you is a '65 model, the news that a car heater is not always built into a car might come as a revelation to you. During the '30's throughout the war years and well into the '50's, aftermarket car heaters sold rather well in hardware, auto parts and mail-order outlets. There were names like Chanson, Arvin, Red Head, HaDees, Tropic-Aire and South Wind. Places like West-

ern Auto, White Front, Sears and Montgomery Ward had their own brands of aftermarket heaters—and, of course, car dealers could install factory units in any of the popular cars of the day. But, by and large, the motoring public bought the heater and installed it themselves, or had the local service station or garage handle the simple task. Advertising claims aside, the heaters were just about alike—heater core,

small electric fan motor and an ingenious variety of flaps, doors and ducts to assist in routing the warm air throughout the interior.

In the early '30's Associated Parts in Toledo, Ohio, introduced an aftermarket hot water heater powered by "the force that stops freight trains" which, it turns out, was an air motor. Ah, what? Yup, seems instead of an electric motor to power the fan, AP came up with an air motor

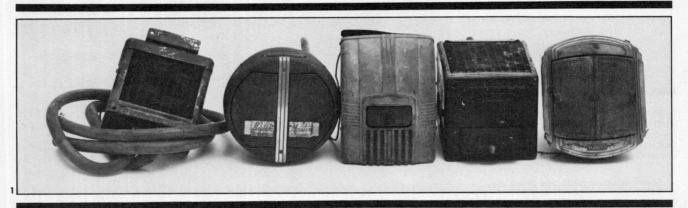

which drew vacuum from the intake manifold. Advertising copy appearing in November of 1932 would bring a man to tears or at least make him part with $9.50 for the Comet model by Associated Parts:

"Its speed is unusually steady because of its frictionless bearings and the centrifugal force of the driving wheel and fan. The air motor has no effect on the operation of the windshield wiper, clutch control or vacuum-operated spark control. It actually improves carburetion and gives greater fuel economy. It will soon be as universally accepted as 4-wheel brakes and balloon tires."

Unfortunately for AP, it didn't quite work out that way and the heater disappeared from the market shortly. Who knows, maybe the frictionless bearings had a bad habit of seizing.

If you'd like to have an early heater for your early-type car, the plan is to do a little shopping in the local wrecking yard or at the next swap meet. If you're shopping in a wrecking yard, don't pass up peering into early-type pickups in an effort to locate just the right size and shape for your particular application. Make sure the sheetmetal is as straight as you want it to be and that all chrome trim is intact. If the

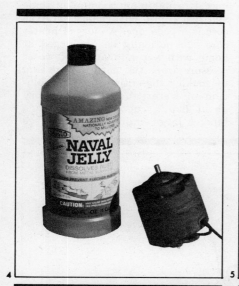

1. Here's a lineup of old beauties that could bring some warmth into your life. Properly restored, they would be a handsome asset to the right car.

2. This is a typical example of what you will probably find. It's an old Arvin that came from a swap meet and it's rough. You'll have to expect this from a 40-year-old heater.

3. Once this was great chrome. Doors still work, and with some imagination, "Arvin" can still be read. These pieces would be separated for chroming. Instead, gate plate was sanded, wrinkle painted for $2.

4. The exterior of the fan motor responded nicely to Naval Jelly. Motor must not be sandblasted but can be cleaned up some. Motor was checked with car battery, worked fine.

5. Next step for heater was to vapor blast internal sheet metal parts and spray on a liberal coat of primer.

6. Heater core was plugged, but the scale and dirt came loose in solution of Drano/water, flushed with garden hose. Do the Drano trick outdoors and wear goggles when sloshing that water around—avoid breathing fumes. Core after our boil out looks like new, doesn't leak and flows water like crazy.

heater is equipped with ducts, doors or shutters, make sure they are complete. At this point, don't be concerned if the heater works—just that it fits and looks good in your application.

There are only three parts of a hot water heater which can malfunction and all are easily repaired or replaced with modern mechanical components—which is why you should worry about appearance first, and function second. The first is the switch. Some early heaters had a switch located on the heater itself, while the majority had remote switches which clamped under the dash within easy reach of the driver. Two types of switches were common—one with off, high and low positions, and the other a straight rheostat type which varied the speed of the blower motor. Either type is readily available at automotive supply stores or radio supply houses. We had an old Arvin with an under-dash rheostat switch with a tiny light bulb contained in the knob. Recently we saw an entire display card in a small parts house contained several variations of this switch.

Second on the list of things to go wrong with an old heater is the blower motor. These are most always sealed, factory-lubed units which cannot be repaired once they fail. Before assuming the motor is no good, check out the switch and wiring—especially the ground. Do not assume that because the heater unit is hung from the firewall with a variety of brackets and bolts that the unit is grounded. If the motor is bad, a new one can be had through an automotive electrical shop or a wrecking yard. Keep in mind that all of the old stuff came with 6-volt motors. If your car has a 12-volt system, remedy this with a Volt-A-Drop. Or, since the common method of attaching motors to the heater frame was by two longish machine screws, 6-volt and 12-volt motors interchange easily enough for you to swap motors.

The third and final item to give problems in an old heater is the radiator. They can get clogged up and refuse to pass any water (in which case, you don't get any heat) or the radiator will leak and drip coolant all over your restored carpeting and white tennie runners. The clogged condition can easily be checked and normally remedied by turning a garden hose on with the end pressed into one of the two radiator openings. If a minimum amount of scale and rust comes out, chances are the core is a good one. A clogged heater core can normally be unplugged at home with a combination of water pressure from the garden hose and by soaking the entire core in a solution of water and Drano. Empty about half a cup of Drano into a bucket large enough to submerge

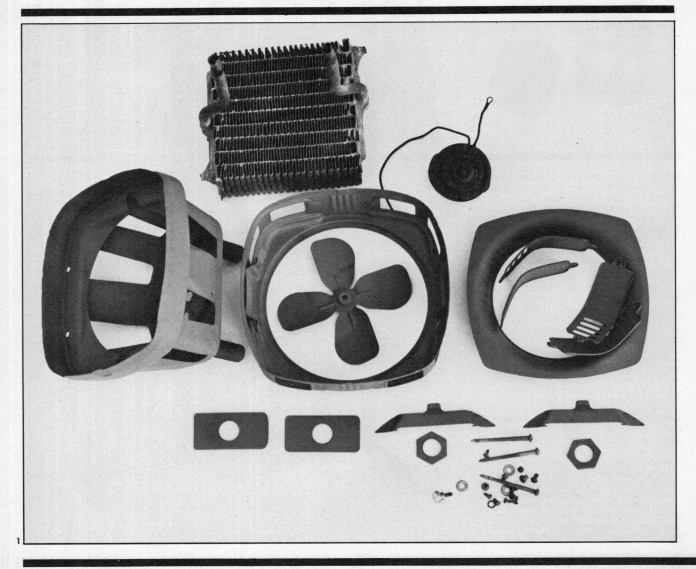

1

the entire heater core. Stir the mixture and then submerge the core for about an hour. If several applications of this and water pressure from the hose fail to free the clogged core, haul it to the nearest radiator shop where they can rod it out, pressure check it and solder up any tiny leaks, all for a very nominal sum.

If the core is not clogged, you can check it for leaks yourself by inserting a cork or rubber plug in one of the pipes and the hose in the other. You needn't turn the faucet on all the way, since a good cooling system doesn't operate over 14 psi and city water pressure is most always above 60 psi. If the core is leaking and you are good with a torch and a coil of solder, then you can repair the leak just as can be done with larger radiators. If you don't wish to tackle the job, the radiator shop is again the place to stop. There are several stock-size heater cores available through radiator shops onto which your fittings and tanks can be attached in case the core is not worth repairing.

The heater frame or exterior sheetmetal can be sandblasted and painted or simply sanded and painted while small trim pieces and name plates get sent out to be plated. Old heaters came in a variety of finishes—including wrinkle and woodgraining—pays your money and takes your choice, son!

Not surprisingly, many of the older heaters were (and still are) capable of pumping a lot of BTUs—and they are a welcome addition to an early car and an owner who likes a little comfort.

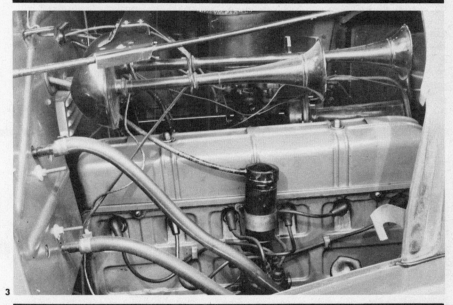

1. Here are the refurbished parts to our Arvin, ready to reassemble. Better make notes when you take it apart; it's not as easy to reassemble as it looks.

2. Our refurbished Arvin. It looks good as new, thanks to Illinois Bronze brand Wrinkle Finish paint. Color is Forest Green—brown, grey, black, silver, blue colors also available. Trick with this stuff is to heat parts (under lamp, in oven) after they're sprayed so wrinkles come on strong.

3. Plumbing from water pump (or block) is no different for old inline engines than modern V-8's. Core nozzles always poke through firewall, and hose clamps secure heater hose.

4. Here's a completed installation in a Pontiac where the owner stuck to the factory heater. It's a nice setup, with fresh wrinkle paint and stock knobs on the flap doors which match dash knobs. Foot room is lost, but comfort is gained.

DIE CASTING REPAIR
HOW TO SAVE BENT BEZELS AND GNARLED GRILLES

If you're like most people restoring an old car, the die-cast trim pieces can be your biggest problem. When faced with a damaged die-cast part, you have only five choices. If you belong to a well-organized club, you can perhaps locate an NOS (new-old stock) replacement; if your car is a Model A Ford or something similarly popular, someone is probably making a repro part; you can scour junkyards and pore over the classifieds in newspapers and enthusiast magazines hoping to find a used part in satisfacto-

ry condition; and as a last resort, you could have the part made. Short of that expensive last resort, however, you might try to have the part repaired.

Popular opinion has it that a die-cast part cannot be properly repaired. There is some foundation for this belief, since the high temperatures used in steel welding, brazing, and even some soldering will quickly turn a die casting into a glob of melted zinc. But by using extreme care and low temperatures, it is possible to repair a broken die-cast part.

To investigate this little-practiced art we sought out Louise Tasker Riggen at Automotive Brightwork in San Pedro, Calif. Louise, who learned her trade from her father, also repairs brass, aluminum, and some stamped steel parts, but die castings are her specialty. We took along a particularly nasty little piece of work, a 1953 Packard headlight rim which had been hit on the side with enough force to knock it out of round and tear apart its inside surface. On this particular rim that inner surface is visible when

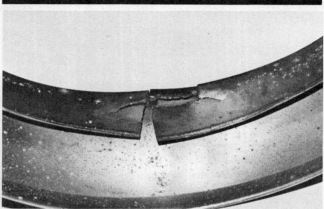

1. This was the damage we set out to repair. The headlight rim was pushed out of round and the inside surface torn. It was first chemically stripped at a plating shop.

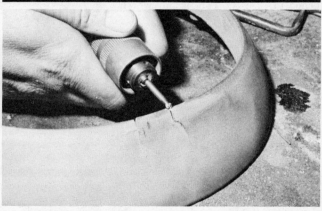

2. Louise begins by using a small rotary grinder to prepare edges of tear for tacking. Edges must be secured to rest of rim before reshaping can start.

3. Using a small oxyacetylene torch and a brass "puddling" rod, Louise tacks the edges of the tear. Not much heat needed; the alloy melts at 730°F.

4. To tap the rim back into shape, it must be heated. Louise moves it back and forth in the flame, heating about one-third of the rim to the right temperature.

the part is on the car, so the repair would have to be well-nigh perfect. Some readers may object by pointing out that this part is not particularly valuable, and could probably be replaced with another rim obtained at a swap meet for considerably less money than it cost to repair. Quite true, but the repair of this part demonstrates techniques which could be applied to any die-cast part, including an irreplaceable one or even a large grille.

To start, any die-cast part to be repaired has to be chemically stripped so that you're working with the bare zinc alloy. Your local plating shop is the place to do this, and the charge is very low. The techniques for repairing die castings are not difficult, but very tedious and exacting. If you can't find someone like Louise you can try it yourself, but you'd better practice on some disposable parts first before tackling something valuable.

The tools are not complicated.

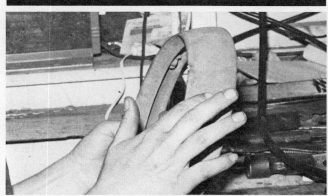

5. When is it hot enough? The metal should be about 350°, the temperature for frying pancakes. Louise uses the tried-and-true housewife method of a moistened finger.

6. Long-nose pliers are then used to bend the rim edge back where it belongs. This leaves dents in the surface, but they will be taken out later with a hammer.

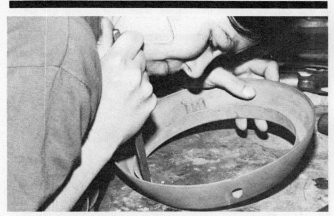

7. A blunt-edged chisel is used to push the leading edge of the rim back into position, since the part was deformed in this plane also. Hammer taps help.

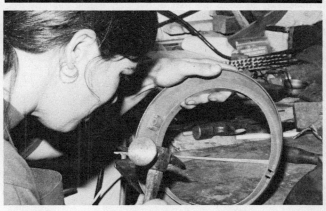

8. A pick hammer is now used on the back side to restore the proper contour to the rim and cure its out-of-roundness. Use many light blows, heating frequently.

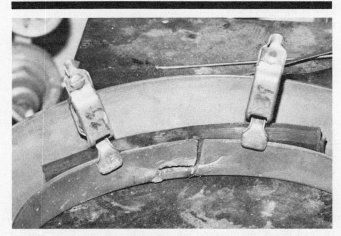

9. Now for that nasty torn section. Louise heats the area and bends the torn parts into proper position. A stainless steel strip is clipped on to form a dam.

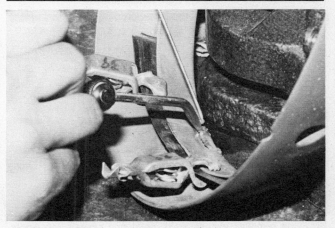

10. Alternating use of the brass puddling rod and zinc rods, Louise slowly adds material to the weld area. Dam keeps molten zinc in the weld.

DIE CASTING REPAIR

You'll need a small torch, some files, several sizes of automotive body hammers, and several types of dollies to hammer against. An old head from a claw hammer and some pipes would make satisfactory dollies, but the best would be a spoon dolly, available at most auto parts stores. Zinc welding rarely produces sparks, but goggles are still an advisable precaution. A thin brass or stainless steel rod is used to "puddle" the molten zinc during welding; these metals will not melt at zinc welding temperatures. A zinc rod is used to add material during welding. Louise makes her own by pouring molten zinc from a moving ladle onto a cool steel plate, which solidifies the zinc instantly into thin strips. Unless you have access to a crucible and ladle, however, you had better buy the rods at a materials supply house.

The general idea when straightening a bent area is to do a little at a time, keeping the area of the casting on which the work is being done at around 350°F. Any hotter and you run the risk of melting; any cooler and the alloy will not work well, probably cracking. Welding requires a localized temperature of around 750°, and great care must be taken during welding to keep this heat concentrated and prevent it from spreading. ✤

11. Welding heats the part up quickly. To prevent distortion it is necessary to keep the rest of the part below 300° by frequent brushings with water.

12. With rim now approximately in the right shape, front side of tear can be welded thoroughly. Note how closely the small flame is held to the work.

13. More hammering follows, seeking the perfect shape. A round pipe is used as the hammering dolly, and the rim is heated frequently to hold the right temperature.

14. No filing is done until the end is in sight. The workpiece should be cool, as filing it when still hot can cause distortion. Lots of patience here.

15. Filing removes excess weld metal and reveals low spots that need further heating and tapping. A bit more work and we'll be done here.

16. And this is the finished job, ready for plating. Total working time: 6 hours. All repair on the visible surfaces has been filed smooth. Nice work, Louise!

POUR A REPRO
THERE'S A POT OF ZINC AT THE RAINBOW'S END

So it's a bad day in Black Rock, your home town. Your obstreperous 10-year-old has just gone and broken the left front fender widget of your 1938 Maccolino-Rosetti X-32 Castagnabodied roadster. The child has been properly disciplined—sent to bed without hot fudge on his sundae, restricted to watching only the black-and-white TV set, and not allowed to ride his pet zebra for 3 days—but now what do you do? The widget cannot be repaired, since it shattered into 18 pieces, all of unweldable dolomite trincolenium alloy. And there's certainly no point in trying to locate a replica, since the world knows that yours is the only Maccolino-Rosetti ever built and none of its trim pieces ever graced a lesser car. Take heart! You need not hurl yourself into the fishpond with the sturgeon nor aim that engraved Webley-Fosbery .455 at your noggin. You can have the widget cast. Salvation!

Casting is an ancient art, the origins of which are lost in antiquity. The techniques vary only slightly, depending upon the metal being cast and the speed of the process. There are three main types: *sand casting,* a low-volume process in which the sand mold is destroyed in order to remove the casting; permanent-mold casting, a medium-volume process in which molten metal is poured by hand into a multi-part reusable mold, which is then opened up to remove the casting; and *die casting,* a high-volume automated process in which the molten casting metal is squirted into permanent molds under high pressure. What we are concerned with here is the use of sand casting by a specialist firm to replace an original die casting. Repro part manufacturers use permanent-mold casting. We'll use zinc alloy ("pot metal"), the same material used originally.

Knowledge of some casting terms will be helpful. A *pattern* is an exact duplicate of the part you want cast. It can be made of any material, but you will probably use a duplicate

1. Here's what we'll make, the headlight rim bezel found on many British cars of the '40's and '50's. Though once common, this item is no longer made. Sound familiar?

2. Steve starts by filling up the screw holes. He uses pure beeswax, which is more stable than paraffin wax and easily removed by heating when the job is done.

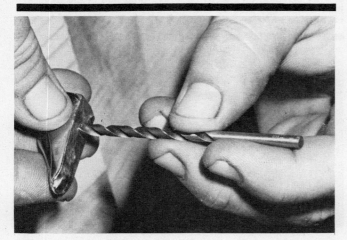

3. After scraping off the excess beeswax, the location of the holes is marked by slight indentations in the wax. They will be drilled and tapped in the new bezel.

4. The pattern is now laid on a heavy flat board and surrounded with fine-grained oil-based casting sand. A knife edge establishes the parting line.

PHOTOS BY ERIC RICKMAN

part taken from another car. The *mold* is the material which holds the pattern, while the *flask* is the structure which supports the mold. Molds and flasks must separate so that the pattern can be withdrawn; they generally do so in two pieces, the upper half being called the *cope* and the lower the *drag*. The *feeding system* consists of channels by which the molten metal can be poured through the mold into the cavity left by the pattern. The *sprue* or *gate* is the channel into which the molten metal is poured; it comes out of the *riser*, carrying any air bubbles or loose sand with it.

If we were making a precision casting, the shrinkage undergone by the casting as it cools would necessitate using an oversize pattern. But since the shrinkage rate of zinc alloys is approximately 0.1-in. per foot, we can safely neglect it for our small pieces, and use a full-size part for the pattern.

The pattern is extremely important. If your part is so rare that you must have a pattern made out of plastic, wood, or metal, it's going to cost plenty—$150 and up. So beg, borrow, or steal a duplicate part for the shop to use as a pattern. This will not damage the part, and it can be returned to its owner intact. We have illustrated such a procedure

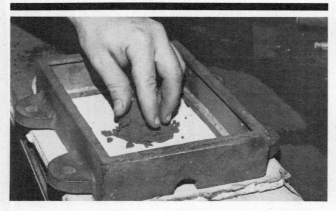

5. After dusting the board thoroughly with white parting compound, more casting sand is packed tightly around the pattern. The flask lower half is placed on the board.

6. The inverted flask drag is then filled with coarse foundry sand, which locates the pattern and will absorb heat during the casting.

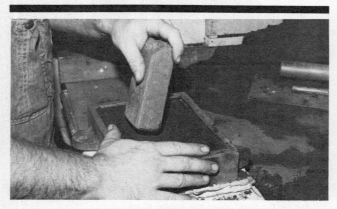

7. Steve uses a block of wood for the ramming, which packs the sand tightly. Ramming must be thorough to eliminate voids and the possibility of pattern shifting.

8. After scraping off excess sand, the drag half of the mold is then turned right side up and the board removed. The pattern cavity is carefully cleaned with a small brush.

9. After another generous dusting with parting compound, the cope half of the flask is placed on the drag and the process of sand packing and ramming repeated.

10. After ramming is completed, the two halves of the mold are separated and the pattern removed and set aside. Now we have an exact impression of the part we want.

A broken or damaged part can make an acceptable pattern. Broken pieces can be glued back on, and low areas filled with body putty and shaped.

How long does it take? From start to finish, the casting takes only about 3 hours, often less, so you will not be charged an arm and a leg unless the part is large or of such a complex shape that it presents casting difficulties. However, additional charges will naturally be made for any drilling, tapping, and plating, and most parts need all of these post-casting operations.

How about metals other than zinc? By far the principal cost a having a part sand cast is in the labor involved, so substituting a more expensive metal will not change the cost appreciably. However, labor costs increase because other familiar casting metals have much higher melting temperatures and are therefore more difficult to handle. Aluminum melts at around 1250°F, brass, 1750°, nickel, 2650°, and iron, 2800°. Brass has the best of properties and plates well; lead should never be used because of low strength and poor platability.

So let's follow Steve Riggen of Automotive Brightwork in San Pedro, Calif., as he casts a "widget."

11. To get metal into and out of this impression, we now have to cut a channel in the sand at each end of it. Steve uses a homemade U-shaped tool.

12. Another useful homemade tool cuts a hole for each channel to connect to the outside surface of the upper mold half. Steve made his from a shower curtain rod.

13. The mold halves are then clamped together, ready for casting. The molten zinc alloy, heated in a crucible, is poured down the sprue until it comes up the riser.

14. Since the metal was poured only a few degrees above its melting point, it solidifies rapidly. Only a minute later the mold is separated. Careful—it's still hot.

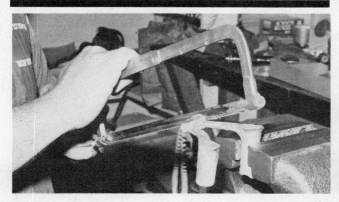

15. After cooling, the part is removed from the mold and trimmed by cutting off the sprue and riser, now simply unwanted flash. These go back to the pot.

16. A little work with hand files and the power rotary file removes the parting line and cleans up the shape. Now the new bezel is ready for drilling, tapping and plating.

MOLD YOUR OWN
USE PLASTIC POWER FOR NIFTY KNOBS

One of the more difficult steps in the restoration of an older auto interior is replacing those unusual, hard-to-find old plastic dash knobs and emblems. If you are like most old car buffs, time is more easily spent than money. After fruitless efforts scavenging the swap meets, there are three alternatives left for the ambitious collector. The first one can be overlooked by all but the larcenous. The second, is for those who don't really care what it looks like: Use old kitchen drawer pulls, screwdriver handles, assorted beer tap handles. All of these have some amount of class; unfortunately, it's all low. The third method is to make your own, of course!

There is only one prerequisite before tackling this adventure. You must be able to operate a lathe and milling machine (or know someone who can) if you do not have a good original pattern. Most of the operation is hand work. Take your time and the results will be realistic and rewarding.

If your only concern is doing one car and you have the necessary mechanical expertise, why not take a little extra time and make a few additional ones for those who don't have your skill? They'll be happy, you'll be happy and you can make a few bucks on the side. With the use of a flexible molding compound such as DuPont's RTV or Dow's Silastic, many exact duplicates can be produced.

MAKING THE PATTERN

First and most important is to use a good pattern. This can be either an original knob in good condition or one fabricated from any medium such as a close-grained wood, aluminum or plastic. It is important to remember that any imperfection in the master pattern will be faithfully reproduced in the RTV mold—and consequently in the molded part.

The author's ashtray pull knob for a 1940 Buick was beyond all repair, so a pattern was fabricated from both flat and round stock styrene. These pieces were cut to size and machined to fit. This particular knob consists of four separate pieces

and required only a few hours to complete. We won't go into the sordid details here, since they would be peculiar to this part, but it should be obvious that if you can locate a good original, either borrowed from a friend or bought at a swap meet, you can get down to the serious business of making duplicates right away. Even a damaged original is okay, as long as it can be repaired properly using plastic auto body filler (Bondo or equivalent).

MAKING THE MOLD

To make duplicates we'll need a mold. Now, the factory originally used metal molds for high-volume production, but we're going to try to do as good a job with a "soft tooling" rubber mold, since we're only interested in making a few parts.

The first step is to build a frame around the pattern. You can make a fancy permanent frame of wood, plastic or even metal, but a better idea is to make one which can be taken apart quickly to release the rubber mold once it has cured. After that, the frame is not necessary. A good method is to use four pieces of ⅛-in.-thick plastic (wood is fine) of a size sufficient to allow about 1 in. of clearance on all sides of the pattern; for our knob, this worked out to 3 ins. x 6 ins. To one edge of each side piece, attach (by screws or glue) a ½-in.-square block. These blocks will enable C-clamps to grip the sides and form the frame. Now assemble the frame with C-clamps and set it on a clean piece of glass. The glass plate forms the bottom of the frame.

To prevent any RTV from oozing out, it's advisable to run a strip of masking tape around the frame where it joins the glass.

To establish a parting line, buy about 1 lb. of modeling clay and use it to halfway fill up the frame. This clay will form the "dummy" half of the mold while you make the other half out of RTV. Next, take the pattern and press it firmly into the clay to a depth necessary to establish the parting line you have already decided upon. Now you're ready to pour some rubber.

The rubber molding compound consists of two parts, resin and catalyst, which are mixed together rather like the two-part epoxy glues with which you're probably more familiar. When mixed, the rubber sets or "vulcanizes" without any application of heat. Hence its general name, RTV, which stands for "Room-Temperature Vulcanizing." (Normal rubber requires a lot of heat to vulcanize, as the name indicates: Vulcan was the ancient Roman god of fire.)

Buy enough molding compound to fill the frame completely. Read the instructions carefully. Then thor-

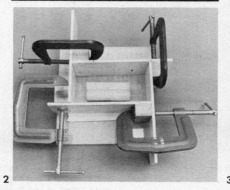

PHOTOS BY ERIC RICKMAN

oughly mix enough to half fill the frame; remember, the bottom half is filled with clay. With a small brush, "paint" the RTV onto the exposed part of the pattern and then slowly pour in the rest until the frame is filled. Don't worry about a mold release agent, as it's already mixed in with the resin. Set until the molding compound is thoroughly cured—about 12 hrs.

When cured, disassemble the frame and carefully remove the RTV. If all went well, you now have half the mold. Remove the pattern and discard the clay. Now repeat the pouring process, using the completed mold half as the base instead of the clay. Tip-cut two or more indentations in the parting line surface of the completed mold half. These will allow protrusions to form on the new mold half, which will locate and join the two halves to each other when you use them.

CASTING THE PART

You now have the completed mold, and the frame can be discarded. To make parts you now need casting resin, laminating resin or epoxy, all available from your local hobby shop or chemical supply store. You can buy dyes to make the part any color you wish, or you can paint it after it's finished. Mix the resin with the catalyst and pour it in the mold. A small weight on the upper mold half prevents flash (leakage) along the parting line; curing time is about 1 hr.

You can get fancy and cut in a sprue and riser in the upper mold half, like those used in metal casting, but you'll probably find that they are unnecessary. If you chose your parting line carefully, almost all the volume of your pattern will be in one half of the mold and only a small volume in the other half. Since casting resins and epoxies are extremely viscous—like honey—you can fill up both mold halves with the resin and then quickly place the low-volume half on top of the high-volume half without spilling the resin. That sounds a little tricky, but it really isn't. An hour later, pull the mold halves apart. There's a beautiful new knob, all ready for the final machining or tapping necessary to mount it on your car. ♟

1. Here's what we'll try to make: the ashtray pull knob for a 1940 Buick Roadmaster. This is not an original, but a pattern made up from machined pieces of polystyrene, since an original was not readily available. If you can get one, by all means use an original part as a pattern.

2. The pattern is placed inside a simple frame made of four sheets of plastic held together by C-clamps. This frame is taped to another sheet of plastic which forms the bottom.

3. The pattern bottom is covered with a layer of clay. Then RTV is poured into the frame, covering the pattern to a depth of about 1in. . When cured, the frame is taken apart and the mold and pattern are removed.

4. The clay is peeled off and out pops the pattern. Now half of our mold is done. Two depressions are cut into its parting line surface. When poured, the other mold half will fill these depressions and form locating points.

5. Now we reassemble the frame around the completed mold half, with the pattern in position, and we're ready to pour the other mold half.

6. Follow directions carefully and mix rubber ingredients thoroughly. Pour in enough to cover pattern to a depth of about 1 in. . RTV cures slowly; allow at least 12 hours.

7. When cured, open up the frame. Now we've got both halves of the completed mold. Remove the pattern, as its job is finished. Now we're ready to make duplicates.

8. This knob was made from epoxy with a black dye, but several different resin systems and any dye color can be used. Properly mixed epoxies cure in about 1 hour, so several parts per day could be made from this one mold.

4

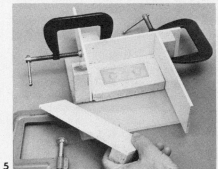

5

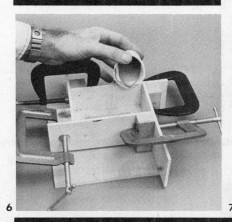

6

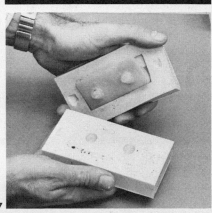

7

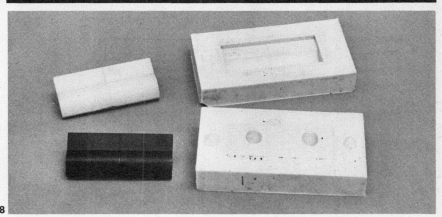

8

RUNNING BOARD REPAIR
RE-COVERING A WORN 'BOARD WITH REPRO MAT IS A SNAP IF YOU FOLLOW INSTRUCTIONS

More than just handy places to forget your toolbox, running boards are an important part of the overall appearance of your car. In the interests of originality, good used running boards should be wiped down with Armor All and left alone, although we've seen numerous attempts to regroove old board covers, seldom have these efforts met with good results. If yours are seriously worn or a chunk of the rubber is missing, you'll have to replace them entirely. Somehow a shiny, newly restored car doesn't look quite right with a pair of worn-out running board covers, even if they *are* "original." Various repro companies have new running board covers and complete running boards for the most popular cars. If your boards are at all repairable, save them by all means, since the repro steel running boarrds often aren't faithful duplicates of the originals, although they will work if you have nothing else. If yours are usable, the installation of new covers will bring them back to life.

PREPARING THE BOARDS

Getting the old rubber covers off isn't a quick operation. Two methods we've encountered include using solar heat or charcoal briquets. In the first method, lay the boards outside in hot sunlight and let the covers cook (if you have to work indoors, use a sunlamp). This softens the rubber enough that you can chisel it off, a slow process. If you can stand the smell, try dumping some hot charcoal briquets on the ground about the length of the running boards. Prop the boards up over the coals, rubber side up, and the heat will loosen the vulcanized grip of the covers enough so you can scrape them off. The best way to clean the boards, and make no mistake, they must be perfectly clean for the new covers to adhere, is to have them sandblasted on both sides. The undersides can be primed right away, but the top surface must remain clean metal. Gather a few helpers and a cover kit and you're ready to begin. The kits generally include the contact cement (often not enough), brush, and sandpaper to roughen up the backside of the covers, which are usually plastic.

INSTALLATION

At this point it will be very helpful if you make a dry run with your helpers to make sure they understand the *exact* positioning of the cover to the board. Close attention should be paid to the fit of the cover on each end, since this is your critical alignment area. Also notice how much material is supposed to hang over (about 1/16-in.) on the outside edge. Extreme care in applying the outside edge is necessary, as any jog in this bead will effect the appearance of all the horizontal lines on the upper edge. It will also be a very distracting, obvious mistake. If this happens, it'll take 25 of your biggest, meanest friends and a troop of Girl Scouts to pull that cover back off. The covers *are* removable, they just seem impossible.

With the board clamped to a table, clean the board and cover with

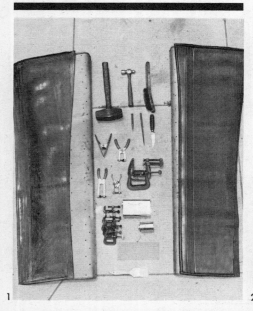

1

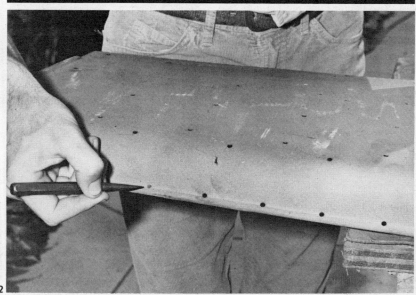

2

3

4

lacquer or enamel thinner, then set them in the sun to warm. Apply the cold cement in the *hot sun* and let it dry about 5 minutes. Remember, when applying the cover, to keep your fingers off the critical areas or they won't stick! As mentioned earlier, precise positioning of the corner is the trick. With one man on each corner of the cover holding it in a vertical position to the board—paral-

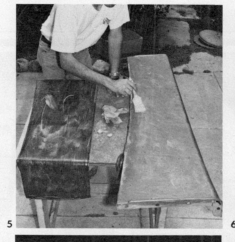

5

6

1. You won't need too many clamps for this operation since these plastic '33-'34 covers fit the boards, unlike the rubber '32 type. Note the hammers included in tools needed.

2. After the boards have been sandblasted, it may be necessary to clean out any old rubber left in the pinholes. These holes will assist in relieving any possible air pockets.

3. For better adhesion, sand the shiny side of the vinyl plastic cover. Use some good 40 or 60 grit paper.

4. To clean off any dirt or grease, use lacquer or enamel thinner on both the boards and the covers. You are then ready to apply the cement.

5. Plan to apply the contact cement in a well-vented room, or do it outside for faster drying. Brush on one good even coat, or cover will appear lumpy when job is finished.

6. This is what happens when the two cement-coated surfaces touch prematurely and you have to pull them apart. The only thing to do is apply more cement to that area.

7. Attach one corner first, exactly in the right spot—or you lose. Then run your hand along the bottom bead, pressing down to the other end.

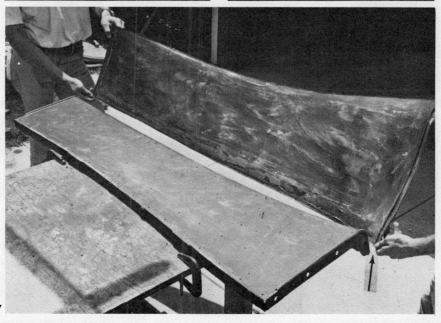

7

RUNNING BOARD REPAIR

lel to the outer edge—the third man should carefully press the bottom bead only, first from one end to the other and lastly, the other end. Once this bottom bead, on the outside edge, is in place, simply run your hand, end-to-end along the rail of the board, pressing carefully to prevent any air pockets. Work slowly toward the inside of the board, always watching the end alignment. Press the cover down with your hand. You might use some help from the end of a smooth box-end wrench in those hard-to-get corners. Work on the bottom bead by rolling the excess under to make sure it contacts. Trim later if it's desired.

Since the covers were made in a flat mold, the bend on each corner will have a bulge that must be cut with an X-acto knife or a razor blade. Loctite's Superbonder will bond the two pieces of plastic. The only other thing necessary is to cut some ⅛-in. thick rubber "gaskets" to fit on each end of the board before it's installed to each fender. You're simply taking up the slack where the cover laps over the edge. Otherwise the bolt holes will pull out of shape when tightening the bolts. The entire job shouldn't take more than a couple of hours. It's best if you have a work bench handy.

Hopefully this method of running board repair will prove an efficient one, and won't leave any substantial room for error. ⌘

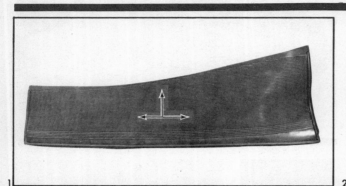

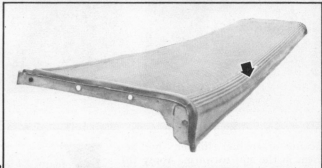

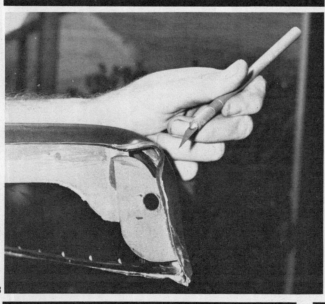

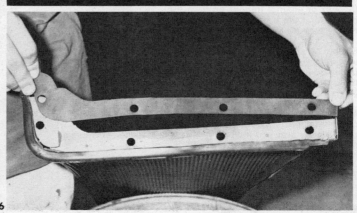

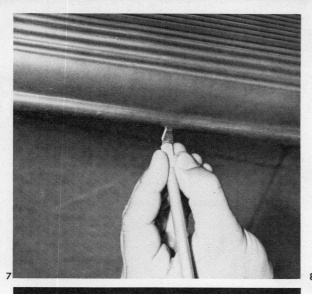

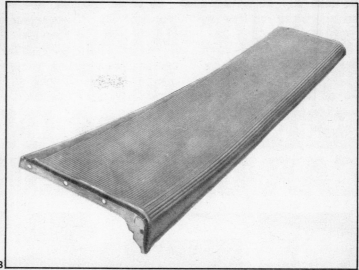

1. Once the bottom bead is properly aligned, the rest of the job is simply smoothing it down slowly to prevent air pockets (follow direction of arrows).

2. Arrow indicates a slight sag that can be detrimental to the appearance of the cover. Extreme care should be taken in aligning lower bead.

3. Bulge can easily be flattened by removing a V'd notch with sharp knife. More cement may be needed.

4. You may find it helpful to use a small piece of wood and a couple of clamps near the ends to hold the bead securely to the board.

5. Loctite's Superbonder will bond the corner notches permanently, preventing their causing trouble later.

6. Making a ⅛-in. rubber gasket to match the thickness of the cover will save your fenders when you come to bolt them to the boards.

7. If your lower bead has some excess, you may want to trim it even with the bottom edge of the board.

8. . . . and there you have it—a neat covered running board to make your '33-'34 look that much more real.

9. Though our how-to shows the installation of repro Ford covers, other makes of cars are not overlooked by a variety of suppliers. Chevrolet, Plymouth, Buick, even the mighty Duesenberg and the Auburn running boards can be recovered with authentic-looking material. Rubber floor mats are available, too.

10. Step plates were standard on some cars, options on others, or available from specialty suppliers. Many types are made in repro today. Maybe you can eliminate having to re-rubber your boards if they are worn in a single spot, by adding a step plate only.

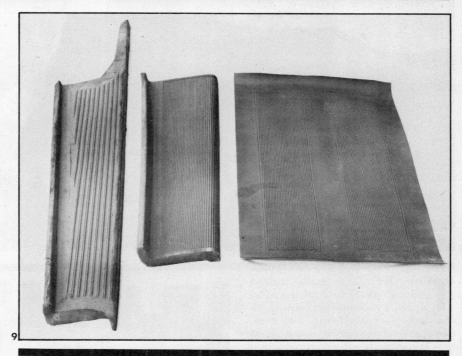

AN NOS AGENCY
WE'VE ALL SEEN OLD CAR PARTS. BUT HAVE YOU EVER SEEN THEM IN AN OLD CAR DEALERSHIP?

Throughout this book, indeed throughout almost all the literature available pertaining to the hobby of restoring old cars, there are references to many firms that specialize in either reproduction parts, NOS parts, or both. It's safe to assume that most are housed in modern buildings, well lighted, and many have such modern-day features as intercoms between the order desk and parts storerooms, conveyor systems between the packaging department and the shipping dock, and a computer to keep track of inventory, process the billing and tote up the payroll.

That's why there's so little resemblance between the "others" and Harold Looney's Vintage Auto Parts in Orange, Calif. For, you see, Harold conducts his business in a genuine automobile dealership building that originally opened back in the Thirties! Even some of the parts

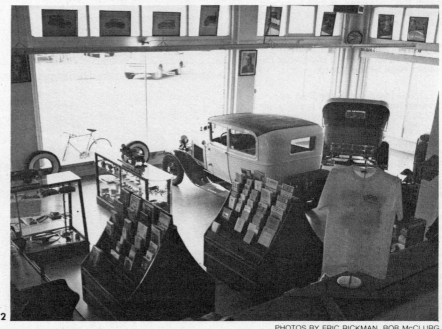

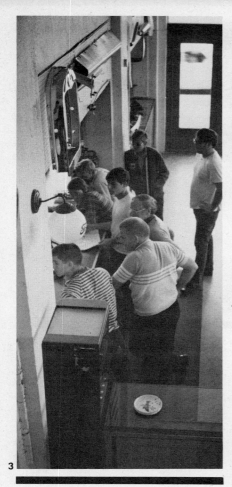

1. An agency showroom of the late Twenties? Not with that photo of Henry Ford II on the pillar. This is part of Vintage Auto Parts' display area, where restored cars are sold on consignment.

2. Center of showroom attraction at time of photo was two A's; a Tudor and a Phaeton. Anything of an early Ford nature may replace them by the time you read this article.

3. Parts counter entertains an array of customers almost without cessation. Buyers may want anything from NOS cotter key to a complete '32 roadster.

4. The inevitable agency parts counter—often found in the old days right off the new car showroom to stimulate foot traffic. Here's where the real action is, for both NOS and repro Ford parts are stocked.

5. If you bought a gennie old taillight lens from Vintage, but don't know where it goes, store has plenty of restorer's publications on hand.

6. Behind the parts counter are the bins and shelves (NOS themselves) that contain the goodies. Talk about a kid in a candy store, how'd you like to make a pass down these aisles with a shopping cart?

7. Another glimpse of the area that was formerly the service department. Most cars here are stored by owners not having garage space at home.

bins and shelving are original. The showroom is still that, a showroom where sellers can display cars for sale, on a consignment basis, of course. Because Vintage Auto Parts specializes in anything Ford, there are original signs and banners hanging from the walls, showcases, tire stands, and even a "There's a Ford in Your Future" neon sign.

Harold sells both new and used "gennies" and reproduction Ford parts to rodders and purists with equal enthusiasm. Vintage Auto is also in the mail order business, and is renowned for its fast service. Harold or one of his proteges can also be seen at nearly every major auto swap meet throughout the country.

Behind the showroom and parts counter, is a rather large garage area where customers can rent space to house their pride and joys. Vintage Auto doesn't get involved with the actual restoration of Ford products, but Harold is always more than willing to put the customer in touch with the proper parties.

Vintage Auto has become a local attraction around the area. The showroom is lighted in the evenings, and it's not uncommon to see a crowd poised in front, some reminiscing, others just plain admiring.

To some of the older residents of the area, Vintage Auto also has a humorous side effect. The building that now houses one of the finest vintage Ford parts houses in the country was originally a Chevrolet dealership!

6

1. Another display case, this one dating back to the agency's earlier days. Some of the parts on shelves are still in their FoMoCo boxes.

2. A rare item on display is this old salesman's pouch. Instead of catalogs or parts lists, salesmen of long ago carried samples of their wares with them. How would you like to have been an anvil salesman?

3. A rare item is this immediate postwar-era Ford neon sign.

4. A sign of the times are Model T shirts. Variations on the Ford dog ad theme are also available.

5. NOS and repro parts are displayed in an almost endless array.

6. New fenders line wall below that intriguing array of grille shells. Don't bother to wonder if Vintage has burglar alarm system. It does!

7. Reproduction convertible top header bows are available, as well as other wooden pieces for Fords.

8. Whatever rolls must have wheels, and here's the rubber to go around them. Most sizes are stocked for Model T's, A's and early V-8's.

9. Freshly rebuilt transmissions are a boon to the restorer since the agency will take his transmission in as partial trade.

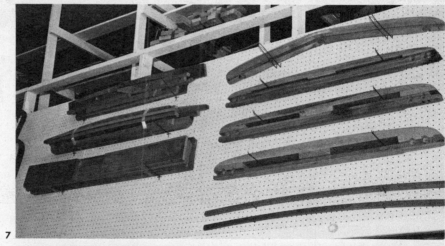

7

8

9

THE FIRST FORD RADIO
THE CHANCES ARE SLIM OF FINDING A 1932 FORD SCRIPT RADIO, BUT IF YOU DO, HERE'S HOW TO INSTALL IT

If there are more than a half dozen of our readers that find this story of an instructional nature, it will be since a minor miracle. This is true since the subject we'll be dealing with is one of the rarest Ford items of all. But we include it here for the simple reason that if you chance upon one at a swap meet, latch onto it. We guarantee you'll be the only restorer on your block with a genuine 1932 Ford radio.

The item pictured, or rather the assortment of items pictured, are the various components needed, back in the Depression years, to pluck words and music out of the air and play it for you as you motored down some country lane. But it's the Depression years themselves that make the unit so valuable since few people could scarcely afford anything as expensive as a new Ford (the Standard Roadster was the least expensive model that year at $410, while the highest was the B-400 Convertible Sedan at an even $600), much less one with an accessory that cost $49 as this radio did.

Ford did not install accessories at assembly plants. Of course there were accessories available in those days but they were sent directly to the dealerships for installation. This particular radio, belonging to a Frank Brown whose address, for obvious reasons, must remain a blank, somehow survived original installation and turned up, still boxed, at a swap meet where it was purchased for an undisclosed price. Luckily, all the necessary components were intact and still retained the Ford scripts, although they are affixed via stickers rather than being stamped into the metal.

MIND-STOPPER

The number of parts to this first radio is a mind-stopper. What's

more amazing, they're scattered throughout the entire car! The basic controls for the 6-volt radio are cable type with the control head mounted on the steering column just below the steering wheel. The off/on control switch is unique in the fact that it is nothing more

than a pin with a knob on the end of it. The entire pin can be removed—as it often was—and sometimes lost. The head also has a night light that shows the numbers in green. The cable controls run underneath the car to two remote boxes mounted under the feet of the

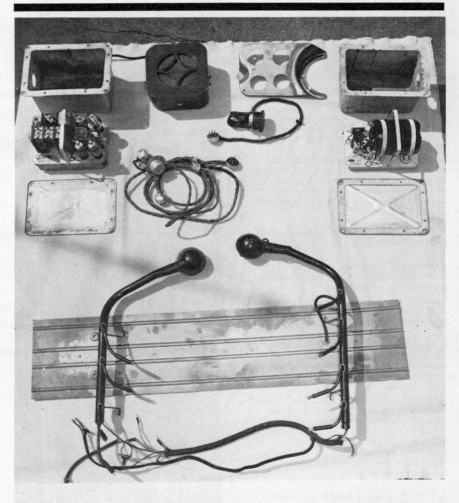

rumble seat passengers. Imagine cutting two 8x10 holes in a beautiful floor pan just behind the driver's seat. One box mounts the normal radio goodies like tubes, tuner, and condensers, while the other box has a two-brush motor/generator that served as a sort of vibrator, since vibrators as we know them now were non-existent in the early radios.

The two boxes are interesting. They were originally cadmium plated, and since they had to be watertight, their lids were mounted with white rubber gaskets. The contents of each box sat on a small platform and each was equipped with a strap-like handle over the top of the platform for easy removal.

The speaker was mounted on the firewall, directly in front of the driver's left knee. Frank comments about the radio's low-volume control and the fact that even on "low" the sound comes out quite loud. This is probably a compensation for possible loud road noises; and the radio's amplification more than makes up for it. The speaker had a special bracket which mounted on the firewall. The bracket mounting was curved to fit the gauge panel's firewall bolt pattern. The speaker box is stained wood with a cloth speaker cover.

The antenna for the radio was a

1. This 1932 Ford radio assembly is an item from the depression years and is extremely rare. The early Ford wire loom contains special spark plug wire suppressors for the radio.

2. This is one of the two boxes that mount under rumble seat passenger's feet. It contains tubes and tuner. Notice handle over top of assembly.

3. This motor/generator acted as the vibrator for radio system. All the Ford scripts were on paper seals as this one is, in lower left hand corner of motor platform.

4. This column-mounted radio head has a push/pull control switch in the silver band (arrow). Speaker and bracket mount on firewall with gauge panel support.

2

3

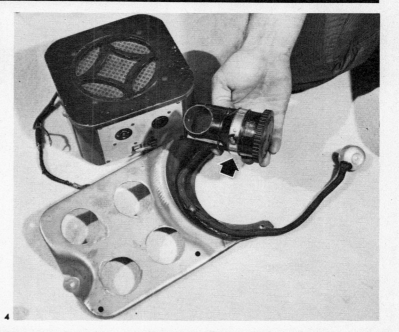

4

slightly corrugated piece of flat sheetmetal that mounted directly under the driver's running board by three countersunk oval-head screws (through the running board cover). It's a mind-blower to drill three ¼-in. holes in a new, original running board, as hard as they are to find. Along with the antenna assembly was a rubber/wire mesh sandwich—similar to a mud flap—that hung down from the intersection of the front left fender and the running board. Its actual purpose is not too clear, since they didn't last long, hanging in such an exposed position.

Suppression of the engine noise from the radio requires a special set of spark plug suppressors that attaches on the end of the plug wires where they connect to the plugs. Like today's installations, the '32 suppressors probably didn't last too long or were lost and forgotten, making them a super rare item today. The generator and distributor suppressors were the normal-appearing pigtail condenser type.

This original $49 beauty plays like you wouldn't believe. The sound has a rich bass tone as well as a treble and can be heard above the wind noises of the flapping side curtains. Back then—if you owned a radio, you weren't in very much of a depression.

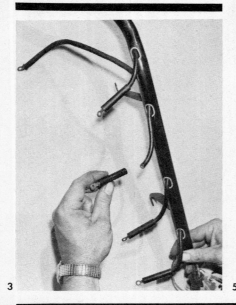

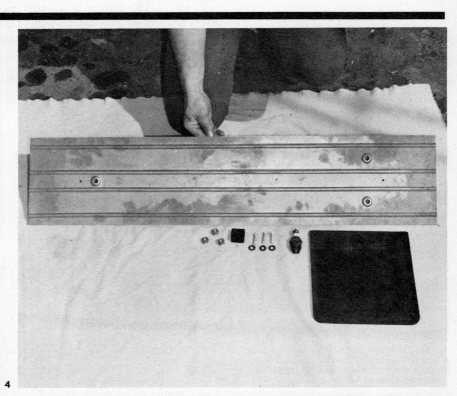

1. This control switch was probably designed to keep you from running the battery down when you forgot to turn the radio off. Entire end of head serves as tuner.

2. Looking into back side of speaker cabinet you can see the Ford script tag on lower left corner. Size of magnet was usually good indication of quality of speaker.

3. Spark plug suppressors simply fit on end of plug wire while other end fits on plug.

4. This is the antenna that belongs under driver's running board. Attaching bolts actually go through running board cover. Black portion of antenna hangs between the fender and the board.

5. Two holes must be cut in floor pan to house radio control boxes. They're directly behind driver's seat.

6. This should give a better indication of relationship between dash and speaker mount on firewall. Probably one of rarest oil check gauges is in this dash panel belonging to radio's owner, Frank Brown. Rare on/off oil check gauge is neighbor to a dual temp on right side of dash.

7. Speaker cabinet mounts on firewall with gauge panel. Even though speaker is mounted under dash, sound is still good on passenger's side.

8. Control head is in very handy spot for driver; entire head is tuner knob. This radio was available only up until late 1932.

9. This shot shows speaker and head in their natural environment, a deuce roadster. Large wires go behind kick panel, then are routed under car to control boxes.

10. This 1932 engine shows suppressors and plug wire assembly. Note tall coil on top of the distributor (lower right).

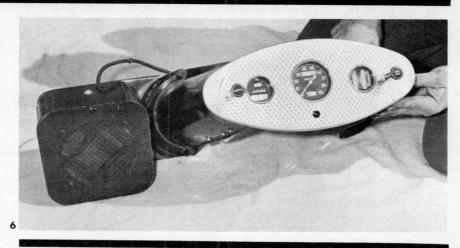

6

7

8

9

10

THE WOODEN WAY PUT YOUR CRATE IN A-1 SHAPE

BY BOB KOVACIK

When you own a woodie, you quickly learn that craftsmanship brings premium prices. So often the tendency is to lean upon your experience with bookshelves and cabinets and begin doing the work yourself. But hold it! It's true that there are portions of a wooden automobile body you can do yourself, but let's put automotive woodworking into a better perspective first.

Two basic types of wood are used in automobiles: ash (General Motors and Chrysler) and maple (Ford). Both are hardwoods, which means relatively long life and a natural resistance to wood-boring insects. Hardwoods, too, are surprisingly fire-resistant because of their density, except, of course, for any flammable coating you may use to preserve the finish. Another benefit of hardwoods is their ability to hold fasteners securely. Softwoods will soon work a bolt or screw loose, resulting in rattles and eventual breakage of the wooden body.

Of the two common hardwoods used in woodies, ash is the softer. It has wider bands of hard and soft veins and for the most part is better looking. Yet when it weathers, the softer veins are eaten away. Any dirt deposited on the surface penetrates into that softer portion, giving the wood a dirty appearance.

Maple, on the other hand, is a much denser, tighter-grained wood and more easily restored.

1. It may be necessary to completely dismantle the wooden body. Some of the earlier wagons used wood throughout, while the later versions use steel braces and supports to supplement the visible wooden structure.

2. Sometimes not evident on the surface, rotted, cracked or split pieces must be replaced. This portion of the work is best left to a man with the special knowledge and equipment needed.

3. If the woodie is disassembled, begin restoration of the wood by applying a stripper. Brush it on and let it set until it begins to bubble, or as long as the instructions call for.

4. Next, scrape off the old finish with a scraper or similar tool—but don't gouge the wood. Chances are it will take more than one coat of stripper to remove all or most of the original finish.

5. Use a jitterbug or sanding block to smooth out the wood after it has been stripped. Always sand along the grain with 220-grit or finer paper to keep from marking the wood.

6. If cross-grain sanding is required, use a very fine (600-grit) sandpaper to avoid damaging or scratching the grain. Use caution, because often any damaged grain won't be visible until after the final gloss coating is applied.

7. Be sure all the fine sanding dust is removed from the wood before continuing with the upcoming steps. The best bet is to use compressed air.

8. Apply a fairly liquid wood filler such as Tru-Test, which contains 75% linseed oil. Thicker filler may shrink. Then evenly sand it to blend the filler into the curvature of the wood.

Ash and maple are primarily used for the structural portion of wagon bodies. The accentuating panels are usually of darker-colored, ribbon-grain mahogany, although many early woodies used birch.

Before starting, determine the type or types of wood your car has; then decide whether new pieces are necessary. On cars that have been sitting a long while, it's usually necessary to dismantle the entire body. If you're going to rejuvenate the entire vehicle, it's best to do it now, before you get a new wooden body in place.

Refurbishing maple requires fewer steps than with ash, but the principles are basically the same. With maple it's not necessary to fill in, since you can sand away as much as 1/16-in. to get down to the new, clean wood.

With ash, the process is a bit more complicated. Whatever you do, don't try to bleach out the dirt. It's there to stay. Besides, you stand the chance of permanently damaging the appearance of the wood itself, because bleaching turns the wood white. When bleached wood is varnished, there will be little or no trace of grain.

To restore the dirty, blackened grain, the wood is first treated with a stripper. Zip-Strip is one of the more popular brands. It's available at most hardware stores, is non-flammable and doesn't eat up your hands as badly as many others. The stripper is usually just brush-painted on. Let it set for as long as the directions on the can indicate. It will lift and bubble the old finish, softening it sufficiently to allow you to scrape it off. A piece of glass, with one end taped as a handle, makes a good scraper. One coat is usually not enough to get off the finish. You may have to apply and scrape

off the stripper several times. Don't expect all the finish to come off easily even then—there are always a few stubborn spots that must be sanded away.

Hand sanding is without a doubt the most tedious part of the job. But be patient and meticulous, because any flaw you leave behind becomes pronounced when you finish off the job with a glossy coating.

Sanding should be done with the grain. Use No. 80 grit sandpaper on a jitterbug for starters. Coarser paper will leave jitterbug marks in the wood. You can hand sand as well, but you're risking severe hand cramps when dealing with a large surface. When cross-grain sanding, be very careful and use an even finer paper.

When the sanding chore is complete, be sure to remove all the fine wood dust from the surface. Blowing out all the crevices with compressed air is the best method.

On ash, the pithy, dirty wood will sand below the level of the harder layers of grain. In this case, a wood filler is necessary to build up these low areas. Be certain the filler you use is natural instead of colored, because the linseed oil base has a tendency to darken the wood slightly anyway.

Paint or wipe on the filler *across* the grain. This keeps the filled area level with the higher, hard grain. Let the filler set for about 15 minutes, until it loses its glossy finish. Then wipe it off. Again, wipe across the grain to keep from forming low spots.

Many fillers tend to shrink when they dry. If your brand does, be sure to follow directions carefully; otherwise you'll end up refilling and resanding numerous times. Tru-Test, used in the accompanying photo sequence, has a 75% linseed oil base

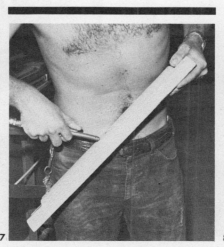

6   7   8

and shrinks very little. Curing time for the filler is about 24 hours. Don't try to hurry this step, because when you go to sand it down, any wet filler may chunk, leaving gaps. This means you'll have to go back and start all over.

When sanding the dried filler, use a hard rubber block with fine paper. Check constantly with your hand and eye to make sure the surface is smooth and even. Since the actual wood and the filler are of different hardnesses, it's easy to oversand an area. So be aware. Again, blow out the fine dust that accumulates.

Now the bare wood is ready to be treated. First, use a clear lacquer sanding sealer. Too many ambitious restorers eliminate this necessary step. The sealer prevents any varnish or stain you apply from soaking into the porous wood and permanently discoloring it.

Next comes the professional step. Aged wood has a yellowish tint, which allows the wood grain to show prominently. Without this, you've lost a lot of character. To achieve the aged look, use a high-quality spar varnish.

The final procedure affects durability. With today's modern chemistry, you can protect wood finishes almost indefinitely. One of the recommended protective coatings is Du Pont Imron, a clear, polyurethane finish. This is a two-part epoxy agent that dries extremely hard and gives a smooth, glossy finish. It's also available in colors for painting metal. Imron can be applied directly to the wood without a sealer if you don't plan to add a varnish. This is a method used by Frank Fowler at The Wood Guy, 15516 Vermont Ave., Paramount, Calif. 90723, who did the work on the 1948 Chevrolet wagon shown in the accompanying photos.

Finishing off the panels requires a bit of forethought, but only basic

1. After applying a clear lacquer sealer, varnish and/or epoxy finish, the various parts are reassembled, along with the darker mahogany or birch panels that highlight the car's appearance.

2. The difference between an old piece and a new one is evident here. The top piece is impregnated with dirt. The bottom piece is now nice and clean, requiring only the finish coats.

3. The use of T-nuts, depressed into the wood at locations where they'll not be visible, is the standard method used to hold the pieces together. Some wagon models used no glue whatsoever.

4. To join various pieces, finger grooves are necessary. These are individually cut and pieced together so that no gaps appear anywhere around the joints. Obviously, proper equipment is needed to do this.

5. Compound curves are best made from more than one piece of wood to cut down on waste and to get the proper grain effect. This particular piece is for the decklid of a Chrysler T&C.

6. Each newly made piece must be carefully sanded and shaped to fit each individual vehicle. Many woodies were made on a custom basis, though others went through mass production assembly.

7. The completed woodie is usually a joint effort between the owner and a professional restorer. Unless you're an expert woodworker, you'll need the services of a pro to get your vehicle into this kind of shape.

1

2

3

equipment. Plywood with a natural veneer is used for replacement. Wait until the structural pieces are together before beginning to assemble the panels. It's a good idea to make up a template of the panel area first. Then, using a bandsaw, cut a pattern about 1 in. larger than the actual size the panel should be. This is necessary so that if the very thin veneer splinters, cracks or chips, you won't end up with a damaged panel. The next step is to sand (that's right!) the plywood down to the proper size. When checking for fit, don't try to jam the plywood panel into place. Again, it could permanently damage the veneer.

It's best to use two ¼-in. plywood pieces instead of one thicker one. In this case, you'll be able to choose a piece where the veneer isn't seamed on either side. This also allows you to fill up the space between the two pieces with thinner plywood or masonite in case the paneling isn't wide enough.

Glue isn't recommended when installing the panels into their frames. Use the same type of screws that were removed. In some automobiles

the glue, oddly enough, creates rattles and squeaks, but the biggest reason for not using glue is that you'd have to break the panel out should you want to remove it again.

Panels are usually screwed into place from the inside of the vehicle, regardless of whether the body of the car is wood or metal.

Finishing the panel requires the same techniques as those used on the structural components, with one additional and seldom-followed procedure: Be sure to varnish the unseen edges of the plywood also. This not only protects the wood but helps seal the seams between structural wood and paneling.

Unless you're a highly skilled woodworker with the proper tools, chances are that this is about as far as you'll be able to go. You may be able to tackle some of the simple structural pieces that need to be remade, but those fascinating curves and joints that highlight your woodie's appearance require a lot of precision.

Finger joints, for example, must fit tight all around, so that no gaps exist at the sides and tips of the

fingers. Wood specialists usually use a single cutter and careful measurements to achieve this. It's easier, of course, to have a full set of cutters on a shaper for each type of job. But when you figure that one cutter alone costs more than $50, you can understand why any shop would be reluctant to have several specialized sets lying around that may be used only once a year. Consequently, each individual finger must be made separately.

Compound curves are particularly difficult, since the wood may curve in several directions at the same time, offering no flat plane on which to index the cutter. To further complicate the problem, finger joints are often angled as well. These curves are made of two or more pieces of wood finger-jointed together, then cut to the exact curve necessary and repeatedly hand sanded and shaped to an exact fit. The use of a single piece of wood for this procedure is not only extravagantly wasteful but would give you end grain. By piecing the wood together with finger joints, you can choose all side grain to give the proper effect. 🛠

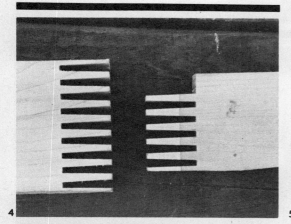

WAGON TIDBITS ODDS AND ENDS ON THE MODEL A AND TIPS ON WOOD REFINISHING

The use of wood in automobile manufacturing is a nearly lost art as you have by now learned elsewhere in this book. The crucible that is Detroit and from which cars pour forth faster than you can count, cannot slow down to match the necessary snail's pace of the master woodcraftsmen. Wood has to be worked by hand, especially where care and patience are exercised to prevent marring a panel that will later be finished to have its natural beauty showing through. In these days of spiraling labor costs and short-cut assembly techniques, there is simply no room for the infinite time required to hand-rub a birch or walnut surface unless, of course, you're involved with such luxuries as Rolls Royces or custom one-offs.

But even though wood was phased out of Detroit as long ago as our entrance into World War II, its laborious working is not an entirely dead art (as opposed to a science, since woodwork never became automated). If it was, there would be no auto restoration today, inasmuch as many cars of the Twenties and Thirties used it extensively.

On some of the foregoing pages we've seen some of the steps involved in bringing old wooden-bodied cars back to life. In some, the original wood was retained but it had to be completely refinished—a technique unto itself. In others, new wood replaced old deteriorated pieces, which were united to old but sound sections. Now, here's a rare look at a car being restored using *all* brand new pieces of wood, and the refinishing techniques are somewhat different where the wood has not become sun-bleached or dried out.

Our subject for this treatise is a 1930 Model A Ford station wagon, and its restorer, Harold Birchall, has some interesting tidbits on wood refinishing that we'd like to pass along, with a few hints to all Model A restorers along the way.

Harold, by way of introduction,

PHOTOS BY ERIC RICKMAN

has been a Ford mechanic, painter, bodyman and general enthusiast since the Model T days and, over the years, has probably performed every type of repair job on every type of Ford produced since 1927. Now retired, he still maintains regular working hours (and most evenings and weekends, too) doing private restoration work in the comfort of his sizeable and well-equipped home garage.

Harold's present project came his way via a Hollywood movie studio. Because early day moving picture moguls were not overly anxious to promote specific makes of cars, Ha-

rold's A had been fitted with a front end "mask" that extended from the base of the windshield forward, and terminated in a sharply Vee'd grille—all to fool theatre-goers into thinking this car wasn't just your everyday Ford station wagon. The mask had resulted in some prop department's butchery around the cowl, but Harold provided a "fix" and in so doing came up with an interesting bit of trivia.

Ford, you see, did not begin manufacturing its own station wagon bodies until 1929, at which time the sprawling Iron Mountain, Mich., facility opened for production. Thus,

of the Model A's short-lived four years of production, woodies were offered for only the final three. Now, as all 'A' buffs know, the 'A' passenger cars used a finely-threaded gasoline cap, with a peculiar hex shape, in '28 and '29, but switched to a round cap with a one-twist-and-it's-off thread for '30 and '31. Not so on the commercial cars, including the pickup trucks and station wagons, for the fine-thread, hex-head caps were used on all pickups from '28 through '31, and on the wagons from '29 to '31. When substituting a new cowl/tank unit on his '30 woodie, then, it didn't matter to Harold

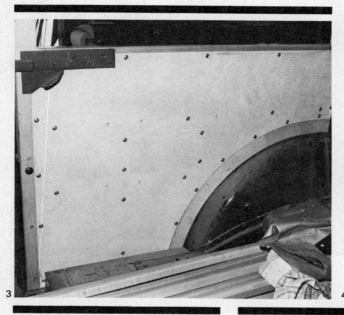

1. In the foreground is a 1930 Model A station wagon, or it will be when restorer Harold Birchall is through with it. On the wall are many A fenders, some welled and most NOS.

2. Birchall, left, was this far along on his current '30 wagon when editor Murray dropped by for a look-see. It's all downhill from here, but there is still much work ahead.

3. Some idea of the number of fasteners used by Ford is seen on the inside of the left rear panel. All the wood being used is new, faithfully duplicated and laboriously drilled.

4. The steps in varnishing the wood are explained in the text. After two brushed-on coats and several sprayed coats, Birchall begins the sanding sequence with automotive Wet-or-Dry paper with #600 grit, and water.

5. Power buffer with wool pad, and daubs of #00 enamel rubbing compound, are used to bring sheen back to the finish after hand-sanding. On another car he restored 8 years ago, the varnished wood has not discolored or otherwise deteriorated in the slightest.

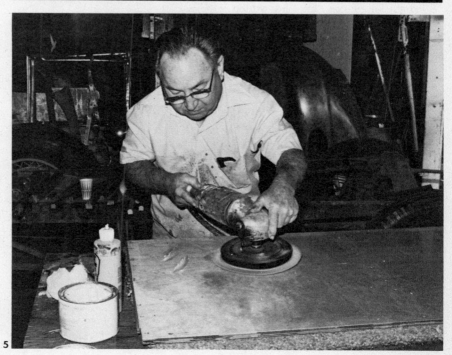

which year commercial cowl he used since they are all the same.

With the cowl fitted to his satisfaction, Harold turned to the chassis, engine and driveline, but we needn't go into that here since that sort of rejuvenation is on other pages.

When it came to the body, Harold knew he would have to replace all the wood, so this was discarded after all the myriad metal brackets, clamps, hinges, straps, gussets, etc., had been removed. Some of these would later be replaced with NOS or repro items, but others considered salvageable were cleaned, repaired (if needed), and painted.

From a private supplier with whom he worked to form the many templates required for the wooden body, Harold obtained special sheets of maple veneer plywood. Ford, you may not know, had used birch veneer plywood for 1929, but apparently it did not match well with the maple ribbing. So for 1930 (and 1931) both the paneling and the ribbing were maple. (The top slats, however, were basswood for the three years). Other than this, the 'A' wagon bodies are generally alike, except for some difference in wood cuts and attachment between '29, and '30—31.

From the same source Harold also received all the individual ribs, precut and formed to exact 'A' specifications, as well as the inner floor structure and assundry other wood parts. What he had, then, was a glorified station wagon "kit," but which he has yet to finish to perfection and assemble, obviously no simple task.

The wood supplier provided the panels and ribs with pin-pricks denoting the locations of all the screw and bolt holes, accomplished using extremely accurate templates. But it is up to the assembler to do the ac-

tual drilling and he must know the correct sizes and extent of the countersinking, where required, of the endless number of holes. To speed the task, Harold uses drill bits which, in silhouette, duplicate a specific screw, except for the threads and made slightly undersize. With one operation it taper-bores a hole, countersinks it, and stops at a pre-

set depth. Each rib in turn is clamped in proper position on a panel, then the boring tool is run through at each of the pricked locations. Because wood "gives", unlike steel, and drilling even with an accurate drill press means slight discrepancies in hole locations, each rib must be final-assembled in the same position where it was originally

drilled. To keep track of things, Harold stamps one end of each rib with a steel letter die, using the same die and location on the panel itself. A pencil or crayon mark wouldn't suffice, since sanding of the wood may obliterate such marks or the varnishing could smear them and make them illegible. This simple step obviously means a great saving of time.

Even though the wood pieces had been sanded by the supplier, Harold carefully dry-sanded each one again. The finishing steps then began, and Harold swears by Man 'O War marine quality spar varnish which is nearly colorless in the can but which turns the blanched-looking wood pieces to a satisfying light honey color—exactly like Ford's box works in Michigan had turned them out.

The first two coats are brushed on, with ample drying time of a few hours allowed between them. After the second coat, each piece is set aside for several days to thoroughly dry. Next comes light wet-sanding by hand, using #400 automotive type paper to eliminate the "nibs" caused by dust motes and to reduce the overly "wet" look that spar varnish usually has.

Now—and this is where a cabinetmaker will wince—Harold thins the spar varnish with ordinary automotive lacquer thinner, bringing it to spraying consistency. This thinner, he explains, speeds the drying time over that permitted by mineral spirits, yet there is still ample time for the coats to flow-out properly. Now, three or four spray coats are applied, again with drying time

allowed between each and, finally, another light wet-sanding, but this time using #600 Wet-Or-Dry automotive paper.

The last step in the finishing process is daubing a section of each panel with #00 grade enamel rubbing compound, then machine-buffing the surfaces to the final sheen. The thin ribs, of course, must be rubbed by hand, for the buffing pad would cut through the finish at the sharp corners in nothing flat.

Assembling all the bits and pieces is the last step, and here it's obvious that Harold won't have to face the cleaning of sanding dust or compound from the many cracks and crevices. He's also pretty well elimi-

nated the chances of sags or runs in the varnish since the pieces can be laid out horizontally when brushing and spraying them.

Assembly is the last and perhaps the most tedious operation, for the smallest goof with screwdriver or wrench could spell disaster and mean disassembly again, and refinishing from scratch (pardon the pun), if not total replacement of the piece.

The work is carried out on a large, flat-topped table covered with a piece of discarded carpeting—again in the interests of preventing scratches or mars.

Here's another tidbit that should be mentioned at this point. Ford did

1. Birchall begins assembly of the tailgate only after the primary panel and its many ribs have been buffed. Underneath is carpet for protection.

2. Before the pieces were varnished, each was clamped in place and drilled, then die-stamped to denote positioning to speed up assembly.

3. The literally hundreds of screws have to be carefully driven in to prevent marring the finish.

4. Upon assembly of the wood, the bracketing has to be installed.

5. Hinge bolts for the A are not available today except cad plated. Birchall has them unplated, then black-oxide treated to duplicate the original ones.

6. Here's a close look at the drill bit that speeds the work. It duplicates proper screw size in silhouette.

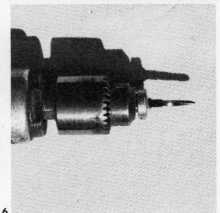

not use glue in Model A wagon assembly. Everything is held together by screws, bolts and other fasteners. Harold discovered this some years ago while restoring yet another '30 woodie and without thinking, glued, *then* screwed the pieces together. The final car was as clean a restoration as you'd care to see, but it squawked and groaned at every dip in the road. The glue did not permit the wood to "work" as originally engineered, and Harold reports you could hear his 'A' coming down the lane even above the familar poketa-poketa of his engine.

Harold found some peculiar wide-headed carriage bolts used in his 'A' to securely hold the tailgate hinges and some other pieces. Many were badly deteriorated so he went searching for more. Trouble was, the Ford bolts were black and all that are available today in the specific size are cadmium-plated—and paint won't stick to them. The answer was to have the cad-plated items unplated, then black oxide treated. The result is indistinguishable from the original Ford product.

Because of the resurgence of in-terest in cars of the Twenties and Thirties, especially in the wooden-bodied variety, complete Model A wooding *may* someday become available on the general market. It may also follow that the special metal bracketry—seat hold-downs, and so forth—will be offered in reproduction form. The non-deteriorated metal pieces from Harold's Model A have already been used as patterns for sand-casting new ones. If and when that day arrives, you can start with virtually any body style Model A and end up with a woodie—if one other little-known fact is kept in mind. You see, the cowl posts that form the sides of the windshield are the same for both the pickup and station wagon, at least Ford stamped the blanks the same. Those slated for the pickup were then notched for attachment of the door hinges. The woodie, though, using special piano hinges for its doors, does not have the cowl post notches. By finding, then, the more common pickup posts and filling in the hinge notches by welding, one can reproduce his own proper wagon posts. From there, it's all downhill—*if* the "kit" sees the light of day.

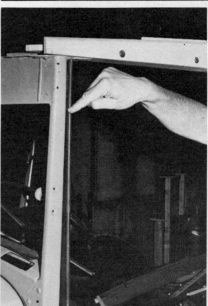

1. Birchall explains the difference between commercial Ford cowls and the passenger versions.

2. Model A wagon parts may become available in repro with exception of the cowl posts. Commercial A posts are notched for the hinges on all but the wagons. But they can be filled in to duplicate the wagon posts.

3. Hand indicates where the hinge notches used to be. Original wagon posts are in truly short supply, but the pickup and other models are not.

4. Another look at the '30 undergoing restoration. Patience is the prime ingredient on a project like this, but it's worth it.

WRITERS' CHOICES

WITH COST NO OBJECT, HERE ARE OUR PERSONAL DRUTHERS

BY SPENCE MURRAY

The editor is to be blamed for the idea of having this book's staff members list the restored cars they'd most like to have, with cost no object. It seemed like a fun project at first, but it was yours truly that had the most trouble reaching a decision. My colleagues reasoned that I'd put the 1936 Ford Roadster at the top of my selection, because I've been a fan of this model since virtually the day they were announced. But I felt this wouldn't be fair, since I already have one! (It's a labor of love, over 8 years abuilding.) To include another in my list would be akin to hoarding. My choices, then, must omit this most desirable (to me) car of all time. After deliberation, I decided to opt for the following:

1. 1946 MERCURY SPORTS-MAN. The Ford Division built 3392 "convertible station wagons" for the immediate postwar market, but delivered only 197 additional bodies to the Lincoln-Mercury Division, which united them with Merc sheetmetal and chassis. Until recently it was thought that none of the latter had survived, but two have reportedly surfaced recently. My first choice, then, is based primarily on rarity, although open cars are my favorites and I love the natural beauty of wood.

2. 1941 CHEVROLET CABRIO-LET. When my high school chums were driving Fords, I had a Chevy just to be different. It was a 2-year-old (then) '41 Chevy ragtop, and I literally drove the wheels off it for the rest of the war years. The very sight of one of these cars today brings back fond memories of those halcyon days, though faithful restorations are few and far between. My color choice would be maroon, and the car must have the factory fender skirts, twin Appleton spotlights and a pair of Guide foglamps.

3. 1936 FORD TUG. This choice is just to one-up the legions of Ford

lovers, who as a group have restored virtually every kind of Ford car and truck from '03 to the near present. I've yet to see one of these—but one would sure wow 'em at a Ford-only concours. The Tug was, of course, a product of Ford of England, and was offered from October 1935 until the end of '37. Today its streetability might be questionable, but its three wheels would qualify it in current legal eyes as a motorcycle, so the single headlight would probably pass inspection. NOS parts are probably scarce and repro goodies are nonexistent, so when I get my Tug, it had better be a 100-pointer.

Here's the rest of my list without further expounding:

4. 1959 Chevrolet El Camino. Black, 283 V-8, automatic.

5. 1936 Jensen-Ford Roadster. Baby blue.

6. 1903 "curved dash" Oldsmobile Runabout.

7. 1932 Ford station wagon. Black, V-8.

JAY STORER

1. 1932 DUESENBERG MODEL SJ DUAL-COWL. First and foremost, I would cast my vote for this car, one of the recognized "heavies." No one would deny that this is one of the most desirable (hence highest priced) of all American cars. I love exotic engines, and the SJ's 420-cu.-in. straight-8 (a copy of half a Bugatti 16 aircraft engine) amounts to a heart-starter for me. The idea of ordinary gasoline combining with air in huge carburetors, being force-fed into hemispherical combustion chambers, burning to produce 265 hp, controlled by four valves per cylinder prodded by a pair of overhead cams, and exiting through those racy, bright pipes would excite me whether at 10 mph or 100 mph. And a Duesey could span those speeds in top gear with nary a shudder.

Laughing in the face of the De-

pression, the Duesenberg incorporated the finest components possible, from the chassis engineering to the custom coachwork that graced it, as if the economic spasms of the mortal world around it were of no consideration. I want this proud thoroughbred because most of them are in the clutches of "investors," who pass these cars from cold auction hand to cold auction hand without ever slicing a highway wind with that rapier-like hood ornament. I would drive mine, and give it a loving home. And if the day ever came when I lost my passion for automobiles, I suppose I would locate an appreciator of such heavy metal, sell the car and buy the Caribbean Ocean.

2. 1934 FORD ROADSTER. My second choice may seem to be at the other end of a spectrum of wishful thinking, but I'd almost give up my present cars to have one of these, with radio, wind wings, luggage rack and cigar lighter. My automania is Ford-based, and the '34 represents to me the pinnacle of Henry Ford's achievements. Not only was it the best-looking Ford ever produced, but it was quick enough to be sporty and reliable enough to depend on. I can think of only two improvements of later years that would add anything to this car's desirability: hydraulic brakes and a Columbia 2-speed rear end. Its improved V-8 could run circles around other production cars of the period, and under my TLC would probably outlast the pyramids. The scoop of the front fenders, the ice-cutter grille, the raked windshield, comfortable seating and peppy flathead V-8 will always grace the garage of my dreams.

3. 1966 SHELBY COBRA ROADSTER. My third choice doesn't quite fall within the vintages covered by this book, but no one can argue with its desirability. From the day a Texan began combining British bodies/chassis with Yankee

horsepower and dependability, I've always lusted after a Cobra roadster. Now rare and expensive, they were the most successful limited-production sports cars ever built. Drop by my house with a blue '66 with 289 engine, and if you can throw in a California blonde and four Weber carbs, I'll trade you my mortgage for the keys to the Cobra.

ERIC RICKMAN

1. 1932 PLYMOUTH CABRIOLET. For sentimental reasons, I'd choose this car for restoration. My very first car (back in 1937) was one of these jewels, although it had the Business Coupe body. The basic lines, however, were identical. I kept that car for over 9 years, tearing it down every 3 years or so for valves, rings and bearings. My first fling into hot rodding was to invert the side-mounted intake manifold and install a downdraft carburetor. The frequent teardowns were necessary, since I literally drove the wheels off it—flat-out most of the time. This Plymouth had the famed Floating Power and freewheel, combined with a vacuum-controlled clutch that was actuated when you lifted up on the throttle and came in when you applied the gas pedal. It was almost an automatic clutch that allowed you to shift without using the left foot.

The neighbors didn't appreciate the 4-pipe exhaust whistle I installed. It made a raucous, train-like sound when cut in at about 80 mph on a country road late at night. A quick shift into 2nd and a blast when passing an unsuspecting motorist was always good for a laugh.

2. 1954 CHEVROLET CORVETTE. This is my second choice, having owned one when it was new. I deep-sixed the 6-cyl. engine, though, and inserted an Oldsmobile V-8 with triple progressive carburetion. Full throttle opened all three carbs, a rare situation, since half throttle on just one carb was good for 80 mph.

1946 MERCURY SPORTSMAN

1941 CHEVROLET CABRIOLET

1936 FORD TUG

The car pictured here was seen at a recent racing event, and it was for sale... for $15,000 (with the 6-cyl. engine, yet).

These early 'Vettes really turned me on, starting with the model shown at the first GM Motorama show: the original Nomad, which was nothing less than a 'Vette station wagon!

3. 1935 810 CORD. The famed coffin-nose Cord, which came on the scene in 1935, was, to me, the ultimate macho machine. Of course, I was only sweet 16 and had just discovered there was more fun to be had after you'd traded your track shoes for dancing slippers. This probably had a lot to do with my selection of this tiger as the last word in masculinity.

Powered by a Lycoming water-cooled L-head V-8 delivering 195 supercharged horsepower, the Cord was one of the best performing cars of that era, an early-day muscle car.

Front-wheel drive was a curiosity at the time, rumor having it that you had to be a real he-man to handle one of these beauties. The styling is ageless, and it still turns heads when one drives down Hollywood's Sunset Boulevard—which one occasionally does. It has the subtlety of design that radiates strength and brute horsepower, but without being as blatant as some of today's attempts at macho styling. No wonder it was the ultimate dream of boys back in the Thirties. I admit to wanting one desperately, but today's prices are as far out of my reach as they were when I was a lad in high school.

JIM NORRIS

1. 1948 LINCOLN CONTINENTAL. Black exterior with maroon leather interior. This car is king of the modern classics—maybe of all classics, because it can be more readily made into a luxury speed-burner. When it comes to me restoring one of these in my own way, I'd

1932 DUESENBERG MODEL SJ DUAL-COWL

1934 FORD ROADSTER

1966 SHELBY COBRA ROADSTER

go the Chrysler Hemi engine route, installed correctly, of course, and blueprinted. This would also call for extensive suspension snubbing and more sound insulation. The basic integrity of the Lincoln chassis will take care of holding all that beef in check, as will the most beautiful of automotive designs, to any taste.

2. 1957 FORD THUNDERBIRD. Black or dark green. Stick shift with overdrive. Here's the personal 2-seat convertible par excellence. Small. Fast. Maneuverable. With AM/FM stereo set to full vibes, a straight road at evening and a member of the opposite gender, this little number at max growl can make good music. One of the sexiest of designs, the little 'Bird is more a lover than a racer, although with not all that much folding green, nice things can happen on straight roads.

3. 1947 FORD CONVERTIBLE. Dark blue or beige. The fiend of Flathead City. I'd want Heddman headers, 2-in. longer shackles at the rear springs, ripple disc hubcaps and lots of bobby soxers in the back seat, then go lay 10-in. strips of rubber under the principal's window. This car is a must for every restorer, and they're still around if you look.

Space eliminates discussion of the rest of my selections, but in order of preference I'd like to have:

4. 1946 Ford station wagon. Light blue.

5. 1952 Hudson Hornet.

6. 1934 Ford Deluxe Phaeton. Black with Tacoma Cream stripes.

7. 1933 Pierce Silver Arrow. V-12. Silver.

8. 1938 Cadillac Series 90 V-16. Black.

9. 1933 Mercedes-Benz 540K convertible. Black.

10. 1927 Ford Model T Touring. Any color, as long as it's black.

RICK BUSENKELL

1. 1933 PACKARD DIETRICH-BODIED V-12 SEDAN. "Pick any number of cars," the editor said.

1932 PLYMOUTH CABRIOLET

1954 CHEVROLET CORVETTE

1935 810 CORD

"Cost no object." Oh, my. How often have we all played that game? What an enormous wealth to choose from! Well, I followed the classical wisdom and for the top three picked one open, one closed and one sports car. Actually, I must break down and confess that if it had to be only *one* car, that one would be Packard's "Car of the Dome," that incredible Dietrich-bodied V-12 sedan exhibited at the 1933 Chicago World's Fair. With its bronze paint, gold-plated interior fittings, lavish appointments (including a bar) and Packard quality at its finest, this huge but rakish sedan was a monument to Splendid Excess, the most shatteringly impressive car ever built. You may keep such commonplaces as Bugatti Royales. It would arouse monarchical impulses in the meekest schoolmarm, and anyone with a sense of propriety would certainly throw gold-tipped pink cigarettes to the prostrate masses from it. But only one was built, and presumably no one but the Grim Reaper could pry it from its present owner. So I must look elsewhere.

2. 1932 PACKARD DIETRICH-BODIED 904 SPORT PHAETON. Who can resist the allure of a dual-cowl phaeton? Not I. For grand touring in benevolent weather, this is the way civilized man was meant to travel. And of all such machines, the 1932 Packard model 904 Dietrich-bodied sport phaeton was as fine as they came. Noble of line, regal in deportment, powered by a very quiet engine of generous dimensions, this land yacht afforded the pinnacle of open motoring.

3. 1939 4¼-LITER JAMES YOUNG-BODIED BENTLEY COUPE. Among closed cars, I've always been reduced to a gibbering idiot by the exquisite perfection of this model Bentley. All 4¼-liter Bentleys had the sweet controls, beautiful appointments and faultless craftsmanship expected of any Rolls-built product, but in addition

1948 LINCOLN CONTINENTAL

1957 FORD THUNDERBIRD

1947 FORD CONVERTIBLE

1933 PACKARD DIETRICH-BODIED V-12 SEDAN

offered a handier size, more spirited performance and much handsomer bodies than the contemporary Rolls-Royces to which they were so closely related. Most smashing of all was the James Young coupe, of which about six were built. It was the ultimate expression of English "razor-edge" styling, the perfect car with which to pick up Ingrid Bergman of a foggy night under a gaslight, as we rush to meet Humphrey Bogart, due in at midnight on the Orient Express.

·4. 289 SHELBY COBRA. A sports car should go like the hammers of hell, stop on a dime, stick like glue and look like a jillion dollars, but be easy to drive, untemperamental and serviceable by anybody at the corner gas station. Carroll Shelby's 289 Cobra filled these conflicting requirements better than anything else ever bolted together, and he did it for a reasonable price to boot. Cobras won races everywhere, but you could trickle one down a country lane without the slightest fear that it would boil its head off or blow some $50 gasket not available until next Bastille Day. A classic.

Here are the rest of my top 10, without comment:

5. '52-'54 Bentley Continental.
6. '53-'57 Mercedes-Benz 300S, Sc.
7. '65 Ferrari 275LM.
8. '55-'57 Continental Mark II.
9. '32 Lincoln KB.
10. '52-'53 Jaguar C-type.

1932 PACKARD DIETRICH-BODIED 904 SPORT PHAETON

1939 4¼-LITER JAMES YOUNG-BODIED BENTLEY COUPE

AL HALL

1. 1925 DOBLE MODEL E 5-PASSENGER PHAETON. When the editor asked me how I would fill a 10-car garage with American iron if cost were no object, this was my reply. I beg you to forgive my colleagues their ignorance in matters of automotive superiority. They prattle on about rarity, exotic engines,

1925 DOBLE MODEL E 5-PASSENGER PHAETON

1913 MERCER MODEL 35-J RACEABOUT

horsepower, classic lines or quality without realizing that they are not describing individual choices, but merely the vehicle I have chosen.

The Doble is as different from the cars they selected as night is from day, skiing from walking, gliding from flying and sailing from motor boating. You see, the Doble automobile was propelled rather swiftly by powerful, silent, non-polluting, economical steam! It is the Rolls-Royce of steam cars, and only 25 samples of the magnificent Model E were produced. I was fortunate enough to sample the pleasures of steam car motoring in 1968 via a test of the car I selected here. It resides in Harrah's Automobile Collection, Reno, Nev. I've driven quite a variety of exotic machinery, but I'll never forget one moment of that memorable August when three road testers and two Harrah's Automobile Collection representatives cruised the highways, byways and freeways in a swift, silent, powerful American classic.

2. 1914 MERCER RACEABOUT. I suppose the Doble would be rather lonely in that big 10-car garage, so a racy 2-seater would make a fitting companion. I'll choose the Mercer Raceabout in bright yellow with black striping. But only for companionship!

COMPENDIUM

SERVICES

AUCTIONS

Brooks Motors Auction Co.
921 S. Seguin
New Braunfels, Tex. 78130

C&S Investments, Inc.
P.O. Box 1184
San Bernardino, Calif. 92402

Christie, Manson & Woods
U.S.A. Ltd.
867 Madison Ave.
New York, N.Y. 10021
(212) 744-4017

Hudson and Marshall, Inc.
2683 Houston Ave.
Macon, Ga. 31206
(912) 781-2601

Kruse Classic Auction Co., Inc.
300 S. Union St.
Auburn, Ind. 46706

McLeod's Auctions
7808 123rd Ave. N.E.
Kirkland, Wash. 98033

John Ritchie & Son
1658 Pandosy St.
Kelowna, B.C., Canada

Sotheby Parke-Benet, Inc.
980 Madison Ave.
New York, N.Y. 10021

Von Reece Auctioneers
5000 E. Ben White Blvd.
Austin, Tex. 78741
(512) 441-8171

BABBITTING AND RODS

The Babbit Pot
52 Harrison Ave.
Glen Falls, N.Y. 12801
(518) 793-5411

Nelkco Bearing & Machine
8101 Allport Ave.
Santa Fe Springs, Calif. 90670
(213) 698-6625

BRASS RESTORATION

Chris' Music
957 Riverside
Fort Collins, Colo. 80521

Darold Wellbaum
5302 Grantland Dr.
Covina, Calif. 91722

CARBURETOR REPAIR

J.R.R. Company
P.O. Box 2220
Alderwood Manor, Wis. 98036

CAR COVERS

Beverly Hills Motor Parts
200 S. Robertson Blvd.
Beverly Hills, Calif. 90211
(213) 657-0200

Covercraft Industries Inc.
20447 Nordhoff St.
Chatsworth, Calif. 91311

Warren Cox
P.O. Box 216
Lakewood, Calif. 90713
(213) 421-2882

CASTINGS

Atkinson and Co.
P.O. Box 871
Greenwich, Conn. 06830

Automotive Brightwork
318 S. Pacific Ave.
San Pedro, Calif. 90731

Lynn Bell
550 Weaver
Chambersburg, Pa. 17201

Burbank Foundry
3083 N. California St.
Burbank, Calif. 91504

T.E. Dobbins
Golf Course Specialties
P.O. Box 988
Huntington Park, Calif. 90255

CHROME PLATING

Bill's Metal Polishing
David Rd. & Camden Ave.
Magnolia, N.J. 08049
(609) 784-4019

Christensen Plating
2455 E. 52nd St.
Los Angeles, Calif. 90058
(213) 585-8730

Classic Custom Plating
N. Western at 71st
Oklahoma City, Okla. 73116
(405) 818-5717

Father & Son Plating
6252 San Fernando Rd.
Glendale, Calif. 91201
(213) 245-5451

High-Grade Plating Co.
1245 W. 2nd St.
Pomona, Calif. 91766

Hygrade Polishing & Plating Co.
2207 41st Ave.
L.I. City, N.Y. 11101
(212) 392-4082

Model Plating
6709 E. Florence Ave.
Bell Gardens, Calif. 90201
(213) 773-3506

O'Donnell Plating Shop, Inc.
41 A Mill St.
P.O. Box 33, Forest Park Sta.
Springfield, Mass. 01108

R&S Chrome Plating
1933 Forster St.
Harrisburg, Pa. 17103
(717) 236-5693

Watervliet Plating Co.
911 11th St.
Watervliet, N.Y. 12189

CLUTCHES

A-1 Clutch Co.
6910 Aragon Cir.
Buena Park, Calif. 90620
(714) 994-4210

Precision Clutch
6393 E. Washington Blvd.
Los Angeles, Calif. 90040
(213) 728-2112

DRIVESHAFT REPAIRS

Cannon Engineering Co.
10921 Chandler Blvd.
North Hollywood, Calif. 91601

Drive Line Service
11840 E. Washington Blvd.
Whittier, Calif. 90606

ELECTRICAL

Harnesses Unlimited
P.O. Box 140
Plymouth Meeting, Pa. 19462

Hollywood Generator Exchange
5255 Santa Monica Blvd.
Los Angeles, Calif. 90046
(213) 663-9316

George Pounden (magnetos)
1520 High School Rd.
Sebastopol, Calif. 94572
(707) 823-3824

Wayne Schlotthauer (diagrams)
5815 Nielsen Dr.
Paradise, Calif. 95969

The Wire King
P.O. Box 222
North Olmsted, Ohio 44070

Y 'n' Z's Yesterday's Parts
18263 Seville
Fontana, Calif. 92335

ENGINE REPAIR

Ace Gasket Co.
244 W. Lincoln Ave.
Mt. Vernon, N.Y. 10550
(914) 664-3710

California Engine Co.
14928 Oxnard St.
Van Nuys, Calif. 91411

Drake's Engine Shop
15 Evelyn St.
Rochester, N.Y. 14606
(716) 458-0217

Egge Machine Co. (pistons)
8403 Allport Ave.
Santa Fe Springs, Calif. 90670
(213) 945-3419

Joe Gemsa (manifolds)
2004 Seaman Ave.
El Monte, Calif.
(213) 448-2704

Head Gasket Co.
c/o Fred Stelling
164 S. Park
San Francisco, Calif. 94107

H.R. Hendrix
Ford A & B
Rt. 1
Gray Court, S.C. 29645

Jahn's Pistons
2662 Lacy St.
Los Angeles, Calif. 90031
(213) 225-8177

Judson Mfg. Co., Inc.
1345 Byberry Rd.
Cornwells Heights, Pa. 19020

Kelly's Block Welding
12910 W. Washington Blvd.
Los Angeles, Calif. 90066
(213) 870-6795

1953 PACKARD

Gerald J. Lettieri
132 Old Main St.
Rocky Hill, Conn. 06067
(203) 529-7177

Motor Mart
1733 S. Zeyn St.
Anaheim, Calif. 92802

Ramsey Products Corp.
(timing chains)
724 Gesco St.
Charlotte, N.C. 28208
(704) 376-6477

The Restoration Engine Shop
R.D. 1, P.O. Box 223
Jamesburg, N.J. 08831
(201) 521-1123

Reynolds Head & Block Repair
2318 Charles Page Blvd.
Tulsa, Okla. 74127

Speedwin Automotive
Engineering
945 Motor Pkwy.
Hauppauge, N.Y. 11787
(516) 234-2409

West Coast Porcelain Co.
(manifolds, gaskets)
12512 E. Orange Dr.
Whittier, Calif. 90601
(213) 695-9978

INSTRUMENTS

Blair Davidson
9949 Tecum Rd.
Downey, Calif. 90240
(213) 927-8440

Tom Johns
8618 Dent Dr.
San Diego, Calif. 92119

Paul C. Sullivan
4311 Sunset Blvd.
Los Angeles, Calif. 90029

The Temperature Gauge Guy
45 Prospect St.
Essex Junction, Vt. 05452

INSURANCE, TITLES AND RELATED

M. Charlson
113 Hinsdale
Mattydale, N.Y. 13211

Condon & Skelly
P.O. Box 1000
Willingboro, N.J. 08046
(609) 871-1212

James A. Grundy Insurance
308 York Rd.
Jenkintown, Pa. 19046
(215) 885-4400

Specialty Title
P.O. Box 850
Brookline Village, Mass. 02147
(617) 734-5400

J.C. Taylor
8701 W. Chester Pike
Upper Darby, Pa. 19082
(215) 853-1300

INVESTMENTS

Classic Car Investments
3130 Rosewell Rd.
Atlanta, Ga. 30305
(404) 261-8037

LATCHES, FASTENERS

Guy Close, Jr.
13426 Valna Dr.
Whittier, Calif.
(213) 696-3307

LEATHER AND RELATED

The Clausen Co.
1055 King George Rd.
Fords, N.J. 08863

Connolly Bros., Ltd.
39-43 Chalton St.
London, N.W.1, England

Hides, Inc.
P.O. Box 30
Hackettstown, N.J. 07840

Imendo Mfg. Co. (straps,
hardware)
P.O. Box 452
Dover, Del. 19901

Lexol Corp. (preservatives)
West Caldwell, N.J. 07006

McPherson's House of Leather
200 S. Los Angeles St.
Los Angeles, Calif. 90012
(213) 626-4831

Pacific Hide
14000 S. Broadway
Los Angeles, Calif. 90061
(213) 321-6730

LOCK AND KEY SERVICE

The Antique Key
P.O. Box 443
Los Angeles, Calif. 90048

ORNAMENTS AND RELATED

Greenland Co.
3761 Hillway Dr.
Glendale, Calif.
(213) 249-1439

Harry Pulfer
P.O. Box 8526
La Crescenta, Calif. 91214
(213) 249-3555

Vintage Auto Parts
402 W. Chapman Ave.
Orange, Calif. 92666
(714) 538-1130

Bill Williams
5059 Washburn Ave. South
Minneapolis, Minn. 55410

RADIATOR REPAIRS

Continental Radiator
10511 Beach Blvd.
Stanton, Calif. 90680

Feich's Antique & Classic
Columbiana, Ohio 44408

Pacific Metal Stamping
11489 Vanowen St.
North Hollywood, Calif. 91605
(213) 875-0807

RADIO REPAIRS

Carl Heuther (pre-1957)
Hobbs Rd.
Pelham, N.H. 03076
(603) 635-3048

McMahon's Vintage Radio
(diagrams)
P.O. Box 2045
Palos Verdes Peninsula
Calif. 90274

Dan Packard
8 Florence Rd.
Marblehead, Mass. 01945
(617) 631-2449

RUBBER MOLDINGS

The Complete Automobilist Ltd.
39 Main St.
Baston
Peterborough, PE6 9NX
England
Telephone: Greatford 312

Bob Drake (Ford)
23032 Hatteras
Woodland Hills, Calif.
(213) 346-6199

Metro Moulded Parts
P.O. Box 33098
Minneapolis, Minn. 55433

Lynn Steele
21144 Robinwood
Farmington, Mich. 48024

SEAT SPRINGS

Snyder's Antique Autos, Inc.
New Springfield, Ohio 44443

SHEETMETAL AND BODY WELDING

Burbank Foundry
3083 N. California St.
Burbank, Calif. 91504

California Metal Shaping
1704 Hooper Ave.
Los Angeles, Calif. 90021
(213) 749-5542, 749-4078

Die Cast Products, Inc.
821 W. Rosecrans Ave.
Gardena, Calif. 92633
(213) 324-6615

H-M Mould Welding, Inc.
16833 S. Broadway
Carson, Calif. 90248

Metal Fabrication
Chester Auto Restoration Service
Perry St.
Chester, N.J. 07930
(201) 879-5941

SHOCK ABSORBERS

Classic Auto Shocks
17121 Palmdale
Huntington Beach, Calif. 92647
(714) 842-0707

M&S Hydraulics
P.O. Box 461
Oak Harbor, Wash. 98277

Floyd Metson
4705 Howard
Ontario, Calif. 91761

SPRINGS

Hollywood Spring & Axle
6009 W. Sunset Blvd.
Los Angeles, Calif. 90028
(213) 464-4051

Paramount Spring Engineering
12337 E. Telegraph Rd.
Santa Fe Springs, Calif. 90670
(213) 944-7907

Vanowen Brake & Wheel
11576 Vanowen St.
North Hollywood, Calif. 91605
(213) 765-4893

STEERING WHEEL REPAIR

Jim Ellis
P.O. Box 4633
Long Beach, Calif. 90804

Steering Wheel Exchange
14214 E. Rosecrans Ave.
La Mirada, Calif. 90638
(213) 944-8549

Byrd W. Wing
12726 Magnolia Blvd.
Chino, Calif.
(714) 628-4818

STRIPPING AND RUST REMOVAL

Auto Strippers & Restorers, Inc.
900 W. Commerce St.
Cambria, Wis. 53923
K.C. Metal Strippers
8th & Mulberry
Kansas City, Mo. 64101

Lehman General Sales Co.
Sand Blast Unit
1835 Stelzer Rd.
Columbus, Ohio 43219

Los Angeles Metal Stripping
4520 Brazil St.

Los Angeles, Calif. 90039
(213) 243-9111

Redi-Strip, Inc.
2528 Merced Ave.
South El Monte, Calif. 91733
(213) 443-6918

Other Redi-Strip locations:

1732 Armitage Ct.
Addison, Ill. 60101

13841 Redskin Dr.
Herndon, Va. 22070

SERVICES

3530 S. Meridian Ave.
Oklahoma City, Okla. 73119

9125 10th Ave. South
Seattle, Wash. 98108

91-291 Kalaeloa Blvd.
Ewa Beach, Oahu
Hawaii 96706

"EZ" Truman
Sandblasters
1330 Market St.
Youngstown, Ohio 44507
(216) 743-9733

W.T. Tyrrel
Dept. H
P.O. Box 98
East Northport, N.Y. 11731

TRAILERS

AMR Co.
P.O. Box 824
Kearney, Neb. 68847
(308) 234-1939

Bowsman Trailers
R.R. 4, Box 410
Three Rivers, Mich. 49093
(616) 279-5908

C&C Mfg. Co.
300 S. Church St.
Hazletown, Pa. 18201
(717) 454-0819

Thomas O. Hudson
Tommy's Trailers
P.O. Box 71
Ada, Okla. 74802
(405) 332-7785

Don Jensen Enterprises
411 4th Ave. North
Humboldt, Iowa 50548

Passport Transport, Ltd.
9479 Aero Space Dr.
St. Louis, Mo. 63134
(314) 426-6777

G. Sturgeon
3209 Erie Dr.
Orchard Lake, Mich. 48033

Trailex, Inc.
120 Industrial Park Dr.
Canfield, Ohio 44406
(216) 533-6814

Wells Cargo
1503 W. McNaughton St.
Elkhart, Ind. 46514

TRANSMISSION

Lucas Transmission
1623 Compton Blvd.
Los Angeles, Calif. 90021
(213) 749-5491

UPHOLSTERY & TOPS

Antique Fabric and Trim Co.
Rt. 2, Box 870
Cambridge, Minn. 55008
(612) 742-4025

Julius Burgeson
Rt. 1, Box 1820
Meadow Vista, Calif. 95722

Carter's Cut and Cover Shop
P.O. Box 80
800 E. 6th St.
Beardstown, Ill. 62618

Cover Up
34 Secord Dr.
St. Catherines, Ont.
Canada

Bill Hirsch
396 Littleton Ave.
Newark, N.J. 07103
(201) 243-2858

Jack's Auto Interiors
18309 Ventura Blvd.
Tarzana, Calif.
(213) 344-9752

LeBaron Bonney Co.
14 Washington St.
Amesbury, Mass. 01913

Wes Salyer
P.O. Box 237
Kearney, Mo. 64060
(816) 676-2571

Stitt's
2771 U.S. Hwy. 1
Trenton, N.J. 08638

The Trim Shop
South Amboy, N.J. 08879
(201) 721-2260

Van Waters & Rogers (vinyl)
620 E. Slauson Ave.
Los Angeles, Calif. 90011
(213) 265-8123

WHEELS

Borrani Wheel Service
(wire wheels)
328 Lincoln Blvd.
Venice, Calif. 90291
(213) 399-9492

Buchanan's Frame Shop
629 E. Garvey
Monterey Park, Calif. 91754
(213) 280-4003

Dayton Wheel Products, Inc.
2326 E. River Rd.
Dayton, Ohio 45439
(513) 294-7565

Hanmar Corp.
520 State St.
Glendale, Calif. 91203
(213) 240-0170

Meinzer (wooden, respoked)
23459 Mobile St.
Canoga Park, Calif. 91304
(213) 347-3627

Norbit Reischl (wood)
13759 Mar Vista
Whittier, Calif. 90602

Pico Wheel & Tire Inc.
(wire wheels)
2761 W. Pico Blvd.
Los Angeles, Calif. 90006
(213) 735-1294

Riggs Rim & Wheel
5916 Compton Ave.
Los Angeles, Calif. 90001
(213) 583-2366

Taylor Made Wheels
9020 S. Atlantic
South Gate, Calif. 90280
(213) 567-3998

Valley Wire Wheel Service
14725 Bessemer St.
Van Nuys, Calif. 91411
(213) 997-7000

Wheel Repair Service of
New England
176 Grove St.
Paxton, Mass. 01612

1955 KAISER

WOOD AND RELATED

Amsley Antique Auto Body
78 W. South St.
Chambersburg, Pa. 17201

Bob Betsch
2343 W. Swift
Fresno, Calif. 93705

Bradley Brown
7821 Alabama Ave., Unit 14
Canoga Park, Calif. 91304

James F. Cecil
906 Forest
Morristown, Tenn. 37814

Chalmer's Coach Works
24415 Highway 74
Perris, Calif. 92370

Frank Fowler
15516 Vermont Ave.
Paramount, Calif. 90723

John R. Guerin
221 Herbert Ave.
Fanwood, N.J. 07023
(201) 889-6863

Hall of Restoration
3151 21st Ave.
Sacramento, Calif. 95820
(916) 452-6126

Jim Howell
719 Springfield Ave.
Ventura, Calif. 93003

Gene Irving Auto Woodworking
1778 Emrick Rd.
New Madison, Ohio 45346

Oak Bows
122 Ramsey Ave.
Chambersburg, Pa. 17201
(717) 264-2602

James M. Rodman
P.O. Box 735
Westville, Ind. 46391

WOODGRAINING

Don Benson
P.O. Box 213
Etiwanda, Calif. 91739

Bob Kennedy
8609 Ocean View
Whittier, Calif. 90605

Monterey Finishing
4653 Druid St.
Los Angeles, Calif. 90032

Spectrum
P.O. Box 621
Auburn, Wash. 98002

COMPLETE RESTORATIONS

ALABAMA

Lonsdale & Young
2323 W. Fairview Ave.
Montgomery, Ala. 36108
(205) 263-2498

ARIZONA

Franklin Service Co.
1405 E. Kleindale Rd.
Tucson, Ariz. 85719
(602) 326-8038

CALIFORNIA

Adair's Early Iron
1000 S. East End Ave.
Pomona, Calif. 91766

Andrews Auto Restoration
4921 Folsom Blvd.
Sacramento, Calif. 95819
(916) 452-8127

Antique-Classic
7341 Orangethorpe Ave.
Buena Park, Calif. 90621

Bill's Antique Body Works
908 9th St.
Turlock, Calif. 95380
(209) 634-7996

Chuck Peters Restorations
12205 C E. Whittier Blvd.
Whittier, Calif. 90602

Coachcraft
1144 N. La Brea Blvd.
Los Angeles, Calif. 90069
(213) 465-2350

Custom Auto Service
302 French St.
Santa Ana, Calif. 92701
(714) 543-2980
Specialty: Packards

Doug's Auto Body
37 Duffy Pl.
San Rafael, Calif. 94901
Specialty: Antiques & Classics

Franklin Auto Restorations
2993 Las Vellis Dr.
Thousand Oaks, Calif. 91360
(805) 497-4417
Specialty: Classics

Graber & Sons Wheelwrights
2136 Magnolia Ave.
Petaluma, Calif. 94952
(707) 763-6217

Grand Era Motorcars
853 Production Pl.
Newport Beach, Calif. 92663

Hill & Vaughn
1428 2nd St.
Santa Monica, Calif. 90401
(213) 395-1785

Dale Hughes
11576 Vanowen St.
North Hollywood, Calif. 91605

Sparks Automotive
1065 Gower St.
Los Angeles, Calif. 90038
(213) 464-3208

COLORADO

Antique Auto House, Inc.
3329 N. Garfield
Loveland, Colo. 80537

CONNECTICUT

Fine Car Engineering Studios
801 N. Main St. Ext.
Wallingford, Conn.
(203) 265-2808

Reuter's Coachworks, Inc.
27R Catoonah St.
Ridgefield, Conn. 06877
(203) 438-6417

Vintage Auto Restorations
P.O. Box 83
Ridgefield, Conn. 06877
(203) 438-4949
Specialty: High-perf. cars.

FLORIDA

Belote's Antique & Classics
949 Broadway
Dunedin, Fla. 33528
(813) 733-7350

Hayden's Auto Service
4824 Kennedy Rd.
Tampa, Fla. 33609
(813) 884-3312
Specialty: Classics

Horseless Carriage Shop
1881 Main St.
P.O. Box 898
Dunedin, Fla.
(813) 733-9340

KANSAS

Pearson Restorations
1511 S. 25th St.
Kansas City, Kans. 66106
Specialty: Rolls & Cadillacs

KENTUCKY

Motor Parts Depot, Inc.
211 E. College
Louisville, Ky. 40204

Pearson & Marzian, Inc.
501 E. St. Catherine St.
Louisville, Ky. 40204

MARYLAND

Doug Heinmuller
P.O. Box 565
McDonogh Rd.
Baltimore, Md. 21208
(301) 363-2442

MASSACHUSETTS

Antique Auto House
P.O. Box 79
Hanover, Mass. 02339

Vetco
East & Warwick
Northfield, Mass. 01360

MICHIGAN

Clark-Patton, Inc.
4775 Curtis
Plymouth, Mich. 48170
(313) 662-9033

Leonard A. Davis
1345 Whitney Dr.
Watkins Lake
Pontiac, Mich. 48054
Specialty: Early antiques

Fleet Supply Co.
2896 Central Ave.
Detroit, Mich. 48209
(313) 843-2200
Specialty: Antiques

Hotton Associates
510 Savage Rd.
Belleville, Mich. 48111
(313) 697-7129
Specialty: Ford products

Restoration Service
37040 Huron River Dr.
New Boston, Mich. 48164

MINNESOTA

Johnson Iron & Machine Co.
P.O. Box 435
1201 De Mers Ave.
East Grand Forks, Minn. 56721
(218) 773-0525
Specialty: Antiques

MISSOURI

Auto of Yesteryear
Interstate 44 & U.S. 63
Rolla, Mo. 65401
(314) 364-1810

NEVADA

Adams Custom Engines, Inc.
806 Glendale Ave.
Sparks, Nev. 89431
(702) 358-8070

Ken Gooding
1150 Marietta Wy.
Sparks, Nev. 89431

Harrah's Automobile Collection
P.O. Box 10
Reno, Nev. 89504
(702) 786-3232
Advice only for a fee.
Ask for Mike Moore.

NEW JERSEY

Robert J. Gassaway, Inc.
519 Main St.
South Amboy, N.J. 08231
(609) 641-5873

Hibernia Auto Restorations, Inc.
Maple Terrace
Hibernia, N.J. 07960
(201) 627-1882

The Restoration Shop
R.D. 1, Box 228
Jamesburg, N.J. 08831
(201) 521-1128

NEW YORK

Buffalo Motor Car
24 Myrtle Ave.
Buffalo, N.Y. 14204
(716) 855-1931
Specialty: Model A

Del's Auto Body
112 Glen St.
Glen Cove, N.Y. 11542
(516) 671-3130
Specialty: Vintage sport cars

OHIO

Budley & Sons
5599 Highland Rd.
Cleveland, Ohio 44143

Cobb's Antique Auto
717 Western Ave.
Washington C.H., Ohio 43160

Joseph R. McNutt
4228 State Rd.
Akron, Ohio 44119
Specialty: Early Packards

OKLAHOMA

Classic Motors, Inc.
1046 N.W. 71st St.
Oklahoma City, Okla. 73116
(405) 848-2456

PENNSYLVANIA

Durland Edwards
350 Slocum St.
Swoyersville, Pa. 18704

Richard's Auto Restoration
R.D. 3, Box 83A
Wyoming, Pa. 18644
(717) 333-4191

TEXAS

Classic Automobile Service
2810 Live Oak
Dallas, Tex. 75226
(214) 826-7188

Coleman & Oquin
1569 Sheffield
Houston, Tex. 77015
(713) 455-2355

Jack Hildreth
7305 Lakehurst Ave.
Dallas, Tex. 75230
(214) 369-2748

WISCONSIN

Dick's Autobody
Marshfield, Wis. 54449

CANADA

J. Brown Motors
Gorric, Ontario, Canada
(519) 335-3325
Specialty: Antique Fords

W.J. Oatman
75 Bartley Dr.
Toronto, 16, Ontario, Canada

PARTS

NEW OLD STOCK (NOS)

Antique Ford Supply
3040 W. McDowell Rd.
Phoenix, Ariz. 85009

Automotive Obsolete
1023 E. 4th St.
Santa Ana, Calif. 92701
(714) 541-5167
Specialty: Chevrolet

Bob Burchill
Antique Auto Parts
4150 24th Ave.
Port Huron, Mich. 48024

Frost & French
838 S. Alvarado St.
Los Angeles, Calif. 90057
(213) 387-6171
Specialty: Packards, Studebakers

Lester J. Harris
1823 W. 9th St.
Upland, Calif. 91786
Specialty: Gaskets, engine
and chassis parts

Kwik-Teck, Inc.
6640 W. Buckeye Rd.
Phoenix, Ariz. 85031
Specialty: Chevrolet

Dean McDonald
R.R. 3, Box 61
Rockport, Ind. 47635

P.R. O'Connor & Co.
290 S. Elm St.
Windsor Locks, Conn. 06096

Pat Day Co.
310 Rigsbee Ave.
Durham, N.C. 27702
(704) 688-2620
Specialty: Ford

John Philo
P.O. Box 16313
Seattle, Wash. 98116

John Pinizzotto
68 Angola Rd.
Cornwall, N.Y. 12518
(914) 534-2014

Jim Tygart
P.O. Box 497
Nashville, Ga. 31639
Specialty: Chevrolet

Valley Obsolete
11604 Vanowen St.
North Hollywood, Calif. 91605
(213) 765-9266
Specialty: Ford

Vintage Auto Parts
402 W. Chapman Ave.
Orange, Calif. 92666
(213) 538-1130, 538-1139
Specialty: Ford

REPRODUCTION (REPRO) PARTS

ACCESSORIES

Bill Hirsch
396 Littleton Ave.
Newark, N.J. 07103

PARTS

Jim's Auto Parts
P.O. Box 69
Sharon, Mass. 02067

Bill Lester
5610 Bellefontaine Rd.
Dayton, Ohio 45424

Bill McDowell
Packard Farm
Rt. 6, Box 152
Greenfield, Ind. 48170

Roger Mitchell
8361 Louise Dr.
Denver, Colo. 80221

AIR CLEANER DECALS

Lou MacMillan
1339 McGee St.
Berkeley, Calif. 94703

ALUMINUM SILL MOLDINGS

Lewis Clark
10401 Lloyd St.
Portage, Mich. 49081

BATTERIES

Keystone Battery Corp.
35 Holton St.
Winchester, Mass. 01890

BOOKS AND MAGAZINES

American Cars of the 1930s
Bart Vanderveen—$7.95

Auto Enthusiasts Directory
P.O. Box 24308-H8
Speedway, Ind. 46224

Automobile Quarterly
245 W. Main St.
Kutztown, Pa. 19530

Classic Car Magazine
P.O. Box 978
6226 Vineland Ave.
North Hollywood, Calif. 91603

Complete Encyclopedia of Motorcars
from 1895 to the Present
G.N. Georgano—$30.00

Hemmings Motor News
P.O. Box 380
Bennington, Vt. 05201

Old Cars Magazine
Iola, Wis. 54945

Old Car Value Guide
P.O. Box 681
El Paso, Tex. 79944

Olyslager Auto Library
American Cars of the 1930s
American Cars of the 1940s
American Cars of the 1950s

Petersen Publishing Co.
6725 Sunset Blvd.
Los Angeles, Calif. 90028
(Send for catalog)
Attn. Customer Service Dept.

E.S. Schecter & Co.
181 Glen Ave.
Sea Cliff, N.Y. 11579

Special Interest Autos
P.O. Box 196-B
Bennington, Vt. 05201

J.C. Whitney & Co.
1917 Archer Ave.
Chicago, Ill. 60616

BRASS

Monty Holmes Brass
3653 Commodore Wy.
Seattle, Wash. 98199
(206) 282-4934

CARPETS

Carpetex International
8th Floor
5 W. 9th St.
New York, N.Y. 10011

Bill Hirsch
396 Littleton Ave.
Newark, N.J. 07103

Fred Kanter
P.O. Box 33R
Morris Plains, N.J. 07950

DASH PARTS

Jack Miles
P.O. Box 228
Woodland Hills, Calif. 91365

ENGINE PAINT

Egge Machine Co.
8403 Allport Ave.
Santa Fe Springs, Calif. 90670

Lawrence Kessler
216 N. Lincoln
Olney, Ill. 62450

EXHAUST SYSTEMS

Burton Waldron
P.O. Box C
Nottawa, Mich. 49075

FAN BELTS (Also hoses)

Gates Rubber Co.
Product Application Dept.
999 S. Broadway
Denver, Colo. 80217
Catalog: Attn. Darrell Balm

FLOOR PANS

John Bradley
4200 South 1-85
Charlotte, N.C. 28214
(704) 392-3206

FUEL TANKS

Syverson Co.
Palatine, Ill. 60067

FUEL TANK SEALER

Bill Hirsch
396 Littleton Ave.
Newark, N.J. 07103
(201) 243-2858

Pro-Tech Products Co.
8846 Alondra Blvd.
Bellflower, Calif. 90706

HANDLES, LATCHES

Dayton Carrier Co. (Luggage trunk latches)
6161 Rip Rap Rd.
Dayton, Ohio 45424

Mark Auto Co., Inc.
Layton, N.J. 07851

HEADLIGHTS, SPOTLIGHTS

Packard Industries
610 Cedar St.
Boonton, N.J. 07005
(201) 334-9575

Don Sommer
625 Redwood
Troy, Mich. 48084

Dick Williams
P.O. Box 2003
Westminster, Calif. 92683

HUBCAPS, COVERS

James McConville
4205 W. 129th St.
Hawthorne, Calif. 90205

Jim Tygart
P.O. Box 497
Nashville, Ga. 31639

Vintage Auto Parts
402 W. Chapman Ave.
Orange, Calif. 92666

INSTRUMENTS, GAUGES

Jim Tygart
P.O. Box 497
Nashville, Ga. 31639

INTERCHANGEABLE PARTS LIST (Between makes)

J. Hartley
17 Fox Meadow Ln.
West Hartford, Conn. 06107
(203) 523-0056

JUTE BACKING FOR FIREWALL, FLOOR MATS

Don Snyder
Antique Auto Parts
New Springfield, Ohio 44443

KNOBS (See Ornaments)

LAMP REPAIRS (BRASS)

Chris' Music
Fort Collins, Colo. 80521

LEATHER

Eagle Ottawa Leather Co.
Grand Haven, Mich. 49417

Fred Kanter
601 Cedar St.
Boonton, N.J. 07005

Vince Martino
3160 Draper St.
Philadelphia, Pa. 19136

LITERATURE, ORIGINAL CATALOGS, MANUALS

Nat Adelstein
102 Farnsworth
Bordentown, N.J. 08505
(609) 888-1000

Antique-Classic Restorations
7341 Orangethorpe Ave.
Buena Park, Calif. 90621
(714) 523-8852

Autobooks
2900 Magnolia Blvd.
Burbank, Calif. 91505
(213) 849-1294

Automotive Memorables
114 Portage Trail
Cuyahoga Falls, Ohio 44221

Tom Bonsall
P.O. Box 7298
Arlington, Va. 22207

Crank'en Hope Publications
450 Maple Ave.
Blairsville, Pa. 15715

Bill Lester
5610 Bellefontaine Rd.
Dayton, Ohio 45424

Duane Steele
Automotive Obsolete
1023 E. 4th St.
Santa Ana, Calif. 92701
(714) 541-5167

Vintage Auto Parts
402 W. Chapman Ave.
Orange, Calif. 92666

NAME PLATES

Pulfer & Williams
5059 Washburn Ave. South
Minneapolis, Minn. 55410

ORNAMENTS, CAPS, MASCOTS, EMBLEMS, ETC.

Bob Aker
56410 Eastlea Dr.
South Bend, Ind. 46619

Dennis Carpenter
9832 Pinewood Ln.
Charlotte, N.C. 28213

Originals IV, Inc.
P.O. Box 986
Dayton, Ohio 45401
(513) 258-1381

Pulfer & Williams
5059 Washburn Ave. South
Minneapolis, Minn. 55410

Reizer Restorations
12 Circle Dr.
Caseyville, Ill. 62232
(618) 398-1721

Duane Steele
Automotive Obsolete
1023 E. 4th St.
Santa Ana, Calif. 92701

Tag Co.
P.O. Box 19968
Kansas City, Mo. 64141

Jim Tygart
P.O. Box 497
Nashville, Ga. 31639

The Ultimate Buckle Co.
554 C St.
Hayward, Calif. 94541

Vintage Auto Parts
402 W. Chapman Ave.
Orange, Calif. 92666

PAINT & PAINT INFORMATION

Auto Body Color Supply
15311 6th Ave. S.W.
Burien, Wash. 98166

Jud Irish (Ditzler products)
30 Old Mill Rd.
Chappaqua, N.Y. 10514

Nyquist, Inc. (Ditzler)
George Nyquist
2821 Cresmont Ave.
Baltimore, Md. 21211

Pioneer Chemical & Mfg. Co.
West Point, Ohio 44492

RADIATORS

Walker Radiator Works
694 Marshall Ave.
Memphis, Tenn. 38103

RADIATOR HOSES

Bob Drake
P.O. Box 642
Woodland Hills, Calif. 91365

RADIATOR REPAIRS

Feich's Antique Repair
Columbiana, Ohio 44408

RADIO TUBES

Barry Electronics
512 Broadway
New York, N.Y. 10012

REAR END GEARS

Diverco
138 Windmill Rd.
W. Seneca, N.Y. 14218
(716) 674-8333

RUBBER PARTS, GROMMETS, MATS

Ford Rubber Reproductions
9109 E. Garvey Ave.
Rosemead, Calif. 91770
(213) 288-2127

Duane Steele
Automotive Obsolete
1023 E. 4th St.
Santa Ana, Calif. 92701

Ed Still
6 Dogwood Ln.
Clarksboro, N.J. 08020

Vintage Auto Parts
402 W. Chapman Ave.
Orange, Calif. 92666

Wesco Rubber Mfg.
1655 Euclid Ave.
Santa Monica, Calif. 90404
(213) 393-0303

SEAT SPRINGS

Roger Mitchell
8361 Louise Dr.
Denver, Colo. 80221

Specialized Distributing
7130 Capital St.
Houston, Tex. 77011

SHOCKS

M&S Hydraulics
P.O. Box 461
Oak Harbor, Wash. 98277

STAINLESS STEEL REPAIRS

John Young
Christian St.
New Preston, Conn. 06777

**STAINLESS STEEL RUNNING
BOARDS, RACKS, INCL.
TRUNK RACKS**

Roger Abbott
1199 S. El Molino
Pasadena, Calif. 91106

Lynn H. Steele
21144 Robinwood
Farmington, Mich. 48024

STEERING WHEEL REPAIRS

Steering Wheel Exchange
14214 E. Rosecrans Ave.
La Mirada, Calif. 90638

STEP PLATES

Courtney Cook
5240 W. Brown Pl.
Denver, Colo. 80227

Duane Steele
Automotive Obsolete
1023 E. 4th St.
Santa Ana, Calif. 92701

Jim Tygart
P.O. Box 497
Nashville, Ga. 31639

TAILLIGHT LENSES

Duane Steele
Automotive Obsolete
1023 E. 4th St.
Santa Ana, Calif. 92701

Vintage Auto Parts
402 W. Chapman Ave.
Orange, Calif. 92666

TANK SEALER

Bill Hirsch
396 Littleton Ave.
Newark, N.J. 07103
(201) 243-2858

P.J. Downing
P.O. Box 3068
West Station
Newark, N.J. 07103

TIRES, TUBES, FLAPS

Bill's Antique Tires
P.O. Box 176
7526 Lay Lynn St.
Stanley, Kans. 66223
(913) 897-2685

Coker Tire Co.
5100 Brainerd Rd.
Chattanooga, Tenn. 37411

John Kelsey
Kelsey Tire Co., Inc.
P.O. Box 564
Camdenton, Mo. 65020
(314) 346-2506

Lester Tire Co.
828 N. 6th St.
St. Louis, Mo. 63101

Lester Tire Co.
26881 Cannon Rd.
Bedford Heights, Ohio 44146
(216) 232-9030

Lucas Automotive
11848 W. Jefferson Blvd.
Culver City, Calif. 90230
(213) 397-3732

Universal Tire Co.
2650 Columbia Ave.
Lancaster, Pa. 17603

Willie's Antique Tires
7227 W. Diversey Ave.
Chicago, Ill. 60639
(312) 622-4037

TOP SOCKETS

Ron Brown
P.O. Box 1516
Auburn, Calif. 95603

TOPS (CONVERTIBLES)

Stan Coleman
P.O. Box 1002R
Morristown, N.J. 07960
(201) 539-8317

TRUNK PARTS (Early Thirties)

Warren C. Christensen
30 Pomeroy St.
Wilbraham, Mass. 01095

Varco Vintage Accessory
Reproduction Co.
621 Proctor Pl.
Midwest City, Okla. 73110
(405) 732-1637

UPHOLSTERY MATERIALS

Certified Upholstery
1120 S. Victory Blvd.
Burbank, Calif.
(213) 849-5859

Eagle Ottawa Leather Co.
Grand Haven, Mich. 49417

William Fessler
4509 Fairmont
Kansas City, Mo. 64111

LeBaron Bonney Co.
14 Washington St.
Amesbury, Mass. 01913

Stitts
2771 Brunswick Pike
Trenton, N.J. 08638

**REPRO PARTS—
GENERAL**

Antique Auto & Parts by Pete
2144 W. Superior St.
Chicago, Ill. 60612
(312) 486-1910

Antique Auto Parts, Inc.
9113 E. Garvey Ave.
Rosemead, Calif. 91770
(213) 288-2121

Arthur Howell Co.
P.O. Box 7513
Beaumont, Tex. 77706
(713) 769-7704

Bill Hirsch Co.
396 Littleton Ave.
Newark, N.J. 07103
(201) 243-2858

Bob Drake Co.
P.O. Box 642
Woodland Hills, Calif. 91365
(213) 346-6199

Dennis Carpenter
9835 Pinewood Ln.
Charlotte, N.C. 28213

The Craftsman Guild
P.O. Box 105
Palo Verde, Ariz. 85343

Dean McDonald Co.
R.R. 3, Box 61
Rockport, Ind. 47635
(812) 359-4965

Diverco
138 Windmill Rd.
West Seneca, N.Y. 14218

Paul Ellis
Rt. 28
Knoxville, Tenn. 37920
(615) 577-9729

Gene Scott Co.
P.O. Box 213
El Monte, Calif. 91734
(213) 288-2127

James Rice Co.
4404 44th Ave. South
Minneapolis, Minn. 55406
(612) 729-9270

John Bradley Co.
4200 S. I-85
Charlotte, N.C. 28214

Fred Kanter
P.O. Box 33
Morris Plains, N.J. 07950
(212) 866-4605

Lucas Engineering
11848 Jefferson Blvd.
Culver City, Calif. 90230
(213) 397-3732

Luxury Motor Cars, Inc.
P.O. Box 1326
Portsmouth, Ohio 45662

Lynn H. Steele Co.
21144 Robinwood
Farmington, Mich. 48024

M&S Hydraulics
P.O. Box 461
Oak Harbor, Wash. 98277
(206) 675-1707

Mack Products
P.O. Box 278
Moberly, Mo. 65270
(816) 263-7442

Mark Auto Co., Inc.
Layton, N.J. 07851
(201) 948-4157

MiniWoodie, Div. of Ol'
Chicago Auto Museum
2455 N. Sheffield Ave.
Chicago, Ill. 60614
(312) 477-3334

Owen Higgs Co.
3532 Pringle Cir.
Ogden, Utah 84403

Paul Ezra Co.
Rt. 2 Winamac, Ind. 46996
(219) 278-7219

Rick's Antique Auto Parts
P.O. Box 662
Shawnee Mission, Kans. 66208
(913) 722-5252

Syverson Cabinet Co.
2301 Rand Rd.
Palatine, Ill. 60067
(312) 358-8428

Tasker Metal Products
611 E. Washington Blvd.
Los Angeles, Calif. 90015
(213) 748-1328

Varco Vintage Accessory
Reproduction Co.
621 Proctor Pl.
Midwest City, Okla. 73110
(405) 732-1637

Wagman-Wolf, Inc.
4920 N. 20th St.
Philadelphia, Pa. 19144
(215) 457-7777

J.C. Whitney & Co.
1917 Archer Ave.
Chicago, Ill. 60616

**NEW OLD STOCK AND
REPRO PARTS—
FORD ONLY**

ARIZONA

Vintage Ford Parts
4257 E. Thomas Rd.
Phoenix, Ariz. 85018

CALIFORNIA

All Ford Parts
701-18B Kings Row
San Jose, Calif. 95112

Antique Automotive
4124 Poplar
San Diego, Calif. 92105

Antique Auto Parts
9101 E. Garvey Blvd.
Rosemead, Calif. 91770

Bob Drake
23032 Hatteras Ave.
Woodland Hills, Calif. 91364

Ford Parts Obsolete
1320 W. Willow St.
Long Beach, Calif. 90810

Larry Grider
632 W. Berkeley Ct.
Ontario, Calif. 91762

Homer Kacy
1326 E. Workman Ave.
West Covina, Calif. 91790

Ragnar Lindman
500 S. Illinois
Anaheim, Calif. 92805

Mal's "A" Sales
4968 S. Pacheco Blvd.
Martinez, Calif. 94553

Rootlieb T Hood Works
545 S. Center St.
Turlock, Calif. 95380

Sacramento Ford Parts
5919 Palm Dr., Bldg. E
Carmichael, Calif. 95608

Valley Obsolete
11604 Vanowen St.
North Hollywood, Calif. 91605

Vintage Authentic Reproductions
10015 Long Beach Blvd.
Lynwood, Calif. 90262

Vintage Auto Parts
402 W. Chapman Ave.
Orange, Calif. 92666

PARTS

Vintage Ford Center
1589 Laurelwood Rd.
Santa Clara, Calif. 95050

COLORADO
Sam's Vintage Parts
2025 E. 44th Ave.
Denver, Colo. 80216

CONNECTICUT
Ford Parts Specialties
P.O. Box 301
Canton, Conn. 06019

ILLINOIS
Antique Auto & Parts by Pete
2144 W. Superior St.
Chicago, Ill. 60612

Antique Auto Specialties Co.
3803 15th St. "A"
Moline, Ill. 61265

Bob's Antique Auto Parts
P.O. Box 1856
7826 Forrest Hills Rd.
Rockford, Ill. 61110

Midwest Auto Parts Co.
P.O. Box 1081
Galesburg, Ill. 61401

Rock Valley Antique
122 S. Pine St.
Stillman Valley, Ill. 61084

Syverson Cabinet Co.
2301 Rand Rd.
Palatine, Ill. 60067

INDIANA
Paul Ezra
R.R. 2
Winamac, Ind. 46996

Girtz Welding & Machine
R.R. 3
Monticello, Ind. 47960

IOWA
Early V-8 Store
P.O. Box 66
Walker, Iowa 52352

KANSAS
Rick's Antique Auto
P.O. Box 662
Shawnee Mission, Kans. 66201

MICHIGAN
Motor City Auto
24440 Harper Ave.
St. Clair Shores, Mich. 48080

MINNESOTA
Little Dearborn Parts
2424 University Ave., S.E.
Minneapolis, Minn. 55414

NEBRASKA
Model A Service
4727 S. 24th
Omaha, Neb. 68107

NEW HAMPSHIRE
Page's Model A Garage
Main St.
Haverhill, N.H. 03765

NEW JERSEY
Mark Auto Co., Inc.
Layton, N.J. 07851

NEW YORK
Antique Auto Parts
Model T Specialist
173 Hotchkiss St.
Jamestown, N.Y. 14701

Joblot Automotive
98-11 211th St.
Queens Village,
L.I., N.Y. 11429

Walter Trautwein
725 Old Kensico Rd.
Thornwood, N.Y. 10594

NORTH CAROLINA
Beam Distributors
Davidson, N.C. 28036

Dennis Carpenter
9835 Pinewood Ln.
Charlotte, N.C. 28213

Pat Day Co.
310 Rigsbee Ave.
Durham, N.C. 27702

OHIO
The Early Ford Store
2141 W. Main St.
Springfield, Ohio 45505

Gaslight Auto Parts
P.O. Box 291
Urbana, Ohio 43078

Snyder's Antique Auto Parts
12925 Woodworth Rd.
New Springfield, Ohio 44443

V-8 Shop
8464 Riverview Rd.
Brecksville, Ohio 44141

OREGON
Antique Car Parts
9400 S.E. 41st St.
Portland, Ore. 97222

The Craftsman's Guild
Wood Parts
Rt. 1, Box 146D
Cornelius, Ore. 97113

Jim Davis
4219 Ross Ave.
Portland, Ore. 97220

Mike McKennett
1250 N.W. Bella Vista Ave.
Gresham, Ore. 97030

John Wagers
1901 Brandon, N.E.
Salem, Ore. 97303

TEXAS
Jim's New Parts
4219 Ross Ave.
Dallas, Tex. 75204

Specialized Auto Parts, Inc.
301 Adams
Houston, Tex. 77011

Specialized Distributing
7130 Capitol St.
Houston, Tex. 77011

WASHINGTON
Early Ford Parts
124 Canyon View Dr.
Longview, Wash. 98632

WISCONSIN
Old Time Auto Parts, Inc.
Rt. 2, Box 24
Oregon, Wis. 53575

FORD THUNDERBIRD
Tee Bird Products
Exton, Pa. 19341
(Including fiberglass replica parts)

T-Bird Sanctuary
15055 Weststate
Westminster, Calif. 92683
(714) 531-8850

NOS AND REPRO PARTS—OTHER MAKES

CHEVROLET
Hubert Friend
Kwik-Teck
6640 W. Buckeye Rd.
Phoenix, Ariz. 85031

Don Rossi
16522 E. Easter Wy.
Denver, Colo. 80232

Duane Steele
Automotive Obsolete
1023 E. 4th St.
Santa Ana, Calif. 92701

Jim Tygart
Obsolete Chevrolet Parts Co.
P.O. Box 497
Nashville, Ga. 31639

CHEVROLET CORVETTE
T. Michaelis Corvette Supplies
Rt. 1, 424 East
Napoleon, Ohio 43545

CHRYSLER PRODUCTS
Antique Autos
P.O. Box 65
Prentice, Wis. 54556

Atkinson & Co.
P.O. Box 871
Greenwich, Conn. 06830

Bennett's Antique Auto Parts
Rt. 5, Hardin Pike
Wapakoneta, Ohio 45895

Burchill Antique Auto Parts
4150 24th Ave. (U.S. 25 North)
Port Huron, Mich. 48060

Garton's Auto Parts
5th & Vine
Millville, N.J. 08332

Robert N. Long
203 Nancy Ln.
Punxsutawney, Pa. 15767

John Pinizzotto, Jr.
24-32 21st St.
Astoria, N.Y. 11102

CONTINENTAL MARK II
Holiday Special Interest Autos
3621 Burbank Blvd.
Burbank, Calif. 91505

CORD
Erie S. Cain
The Cord Shop
9375 E. 12th
Tulsa, Okla. 74112

HUDSON
Bill Albright
16581 Arrow
Fontana, Calif. 92335

KAISER-FRAZER, WILLYS, HENRY J
John Parker
828-E E. Walnut
Fullerton, Calif. 92631

OTHER GM CARS
Warner Antique Car Parts Co.
4592 Warner Rd.
Cleveland, Ohio 44105

PACKARD
Classic Packards
10353 Otis St.
South Gate, Calif. 90280

Bill Hirsch
396 Littleton Ave.
Newark, N.J. 07103

Kanter Packard Industries
610 Cedar St.
Boonton, N.J. 07005

Packard Parts Unlimited
P.O. Box 823
Groveland, Mass. 01834

MUSEUMS

A NOTE ABOUT MUSEUMS

Call or write to learn the correct hours of operation and the amount of the entrance fee, if any. In this list, some of the highlights of the museums' contents are noted under the various entries.

ARKANSAS
Max Shaw's Car Barn
Highway 70 West
Hot Springs, Ark. 71901

The Museum of Automobiles
Petit Jean Mountain
Rt. 3
Morrilton, Ark. 72110
(501) 727-5427
42 cars, incl. 1905 Ford
Model B

CALIFORNIA
Automotive Collection
Los Angeles County Museum
900 Exposition Blvd.
Los Angeles, Calif. 90007
(213) 746-0410
39 cars, many vintage

Briggs Cunningham
Automotive Museum
250 Baker St.
Costa Mesa, Calif. 92627
(714) 546-7660
80 cars, many imports

Movieland Cars of the Stars
6920 Orangethorpe Ave.
Buena Park, Calif. 90620
(714) 523-1520
80 cars, many from movies

Pierce A. Miller Transportation
Museum
9425 Yosemite Blvd.
Modesto, Calif. 95351

Schlotthauer's Museum
and Sales
7400 Skyway
Paradise, Calif. 95969
45 cars, all years, many Thirties

COLORADO

Colorado Car Museum
Highway 24 West
Manitou Springs, Colo. 80829

Forney Transportation
Museum
1416 Platte
Denver, Colo. 80202

The House of Cars
1102 S. 21st St.
Colorado Springs, Colo. 80904
'30 Duesenberg Sport Sedan,
other classics

Lookout Mountain
Rt. 3, Box 667-F
Golden, Colo. 80401

Neibling's Auto Museum
Highway 7 South
Estes Park, Colo. 80517

The Ray Dougherty Collection
Rt. 2, Box 253-A
Longmont, Colo. 80501
(303) 776-2520
35 cars, many antique

CONNECTICUT

Museum of Transportation
Rt. 95, R.D.
Groton, Conn. 06340

DELAWARE

Magic Age of Steam
Rt. 82
Yorklyn, Del. 19736
(302) 239-4410
24 cars, incl. 15 Stanleys

DISTRICT OF COLUMBIA

National Museum of History &
Technology
Smithsonian Institution
Washington, D.C. 20560
(202) 381-5939
40 cars, many important

FLORIDA

Bellm's Cars & Music of
Yesterday
5500 N. Tamiami Trail
Sarasota, Fla. 33580
(813) 355-6228
90 cars, 600 music boxes

Early American Museum
P.O. Box 188
Silver Springs, Fla. 32688
(904) 236-2404
50 cars, 50 horse-drawn

Elliott Museum
A1A on Hutchinson Island
Stuart, Fla. 33494
(305) 287-4256
36 cars, incl. dual-control
Anderson Electric

Hialeah Fire Engine Museum
E. 10th Ave. & 27th St.
Hialeah, Fla. 33010

Museum of Speed
U.S. 1 South Daytona
P.O. Box 4170
Daytona Beach, Fla. 32021
(904) 767-0181
12 cars, record holders.
Also boats and motorcycles

GEORGIA

Antique Auto Museum
U.S. 78, Memorial Park
Stone Mountain, Ga. 30083
(404) 482-2259
32 cars, incl. curved-dash
Olds pie wagon

Tom Protsman Collection
2045 Robson Place, N.E.
Atlanta, Ga. 30317

ILLINOIS

Automotive Exhibit
Museum of Science and
Industry
57th St. & S. Lake Shore Dr.
Chicago, Ill. 60637
(312) 684-1414
30 cars, many rare

Bureau County Museum of
Historic Automobiles
Princeton, Ill. 61356

Chicago Historical Antique
Auto Museum
3160 Skokie Valley Rd.
Highland Park, Ill. 60035

INDIANA

Auto Repository
Cedar and Third Sts.
Auburn, Ind. 46706

Brown's Antique Auto Museum
315 N. Fifth St.
Zionsville, Ind. 46077

Hubbard Hill Museum
State Rd. 19
Elkhart, Ind. 46514

Indianapolis Motor
Speedway Museum
4790 W. 16th St.
Speedway, Ind. 46224
(312) 241-2501
18 cars—11 "500" winners

KANSAS

King's Antique Car Museum
U.S. 81
Hesston, Kans. 67062
(316) 327-4458
50 cars, many Model T
& A Fords

L.L. Lacer Collection
219 N. Jefferson
Junction City, Kans. 66441

Thierolf Collection
East Beloit, Kans. 67420

MARYLAND

The Ordnance Museum
Oberdeen Proving Ground
Aberdeen, Md. 21001

MASSACHUSETTS

Museum of Antique Autos
Princeton, Mass. 01541

Museum of Transportation
Lars Anderson Park
15 Newton St.
Brookline, Mass. 02146
(617) 524-6630
Many types of vehicles

Salem Auto Museum &
Americana
19½ Washington Sq.
Salem, Mass. 01970

Wolfpen Automotive Museum
Rt. 30 & Sears Rd.
Southborough, Mass. 01772

MICHIGAN

Detroit Historical Museum
Woodward & Kirby Cultural
Center
5401 Woodward Ave.
Detroit, Mich. 48202
(313) 321-1701
26 cars on rotating exhibit

Gilmore Car Museum
Rt. 1, Box 99
Hickory Corners, Mich. 49060
(616) 671-5089
65 cars, many vintage

Henry Ford Museum
Greenfield Village
Oakwood Blvd.
Dearborn, Mich. 48214
(313) 271-1620
200 cars, huge Americana
section

Poll Museum
353 E. 6th St.
Holland, Mich. 49423
(616) 392-8727
25 cars, other vehicles

B.J. Pollard Collection
14300 Prairie Ave.
Detroit, Mich. 48221

MINNESOTA

Hemp Antique Vehicle
Museum
Country Club Rd.
Rochester, Minn. 55901
(507) 282-7788
60 cars, many very early

MISSOURI

Kelsey's Antique Cars
U.S. 54
P.O. Box 564
Camdenton, Mo. 65020
(314) 346-2506
44 cars, incl. '33 Auburn V-12

Lowell F.F. Rei Museum
Clayton Rd. at Kehr Mills
Ballwin, Mo. 63011

NEBRASKA

Chevyland USA
Elm Creek Exit, I-80
Elm Creek, Nebr. 68836
Over 50 cars. Most Chevys,
incl. '14 Royal Mail roadster

Harold Warp Pioneer Village
U.S. 6, 34 & Nebraska 10
Minden, Neb. 68959
(308) 832-1181
250 cars, historical buildings

House of Yesterday
14th and Burlington Ave.
Hastings, Neb. 68901

Sandhills Museum
Valentine, Neb. 69201

NEVADA

Harrah's Automobile Collection
P.O. Box 10
Reno, Nev. 89504
(702) 786-3232
1500 cars; world's largest
collection

NEW HAMPSHIRE

Meredith Auto Museum
Rt. 3
Meredith, N.H. 03253

NEW JERSEY

DeLaplaine Collection
125 Georges Rd.
P.O. Box 861
New Brunswick, N.J. 08902

Frontier Village
Cape May County Airport
Wildwood, N.J. 08260

Museum of Knight Engine
20 Old Army Rd.
Bernardsville, N.J. 07924

Roaring 20's Autos
Highway 34
Wall Township, N.J. 07719
(201) 681-8844
80 cars, many classics

NEW YORK

The Carriage House
Stony Brook
Long Island, N.Y. 11790
Pre-automotive carriages

Gaslight Village
Lake George, N.Y. 12845

Horseless Carriage Museum
Centershore & Westfield Dr.
Centerport, L.I., N.Y. 11721

Long Island Automotive
Museum
Rt. 27, Southampton
Long Island, N.Y. 11968
(516) 676-0845
60 cars, Henry Clark
collection

Myron Miller Antique Car
Museum
N. Franklin St.
Watkins Glen, N.Y. 14891

Scher Collection
7-11 North St.
Larchmont, N.Y. 10538

Upstate Auto Museum
U.S. Rt. 20
Bridgewater, N.Y. 13313

NORTH CAROLINA

Antique Auto Museum
P.O. Box 154
Wilkesboro, N.C. 28697

OHIO

Antique Automobile Museum
Etna, Ohio 43018

Frederick C. Crawford
Museum
10825 East Blvd.
Cleveland, Ohio 44106
150 cars, many antiques

OREGON

The Antique Auto-torium
Highway South 97
Bend, Ore. 97701

PENNSYLVANIA

Automobilorama
U.S. 15 at Pa. Turnpike
P.O. Box 1855
Harrisburg, Pa. 17105
(717) 766-4792
200 cars, incl. '33 Packard
Boattail

Boyertown Museum of
Historic Vehicles
Warwick St.
P.O. Box 30
Boyertown, Pa. 19512
(215) 367-2146
80 cars, some rare

COMPENDIUM

MUSEUMS

Carnegie Library of Pittsburgh
4400 Forbes Ave.
Pittsburgh, Pa. 15213

Museum of Mack Trucks
2100 Mack Blvd.
Allentown, Pa. 18103
(215) 439-3011

Pollock Automotive Museum
70 S. Franklin St.
Pottstown, Pa. 19464
(215) 323-7108
55 cars, other early vehicles

Swigart Museum
Museum Park
Rt. 22 East
Huntingdon, Pa. 16652
(814) 643-0885, 643-3000
50 cars on rotation;
world's largest collection
of license plates

Thomas McKean Automobile
Reference Collection
Free Library
Logan Sq.
Philadelphia, Pa. 19141

SOUTH DAKOTA

Horseless Carriage Museum
Keystone Rt.
Rapid City, S.D. 57701
(605) 342-2279
100 vehicles, incl. 1905 Orient
buckboard

Pioneer Auto Museum
Highways 16 & 33
Murdo, S.D. 97559

Swenson Car Museum
Alcester, S.D. 57001

TENNESSEE

Smokey Mountain Car Museum
U.S. 441
Pigeon Forge, Tenn. 37863
30 cars, incl. James Bond
Aston Martin

TEXAS

Classic Car Showcase
3009 S. Post Oak Rd.
Houston, Tex. 77027
(713) 621-2281
26 cars, many big classics

Witte Memorial Museum
3801 Broadway
San Antonio, Tex. 78209
(512) 826-0647

VERMONT

Bomoseen Auto Museum
Rts. 4 & 30
Castleton Corners, Vt. 05735

VIRGINIA

Car and Carriage Caravan
P.O. Box 748
Luray, Va. 22835
(703) 743-6552
75 cars, incl. Valentino's
'24 Rolls

Petit's Museum of Motoring
Memories
P.O. Box 445
Louisa, Va. 23093
(703) 967-0444
75 cars, incl. '47 Tucker

Roaring Twenties Antique
Car Museum
Rt. 230 West
Hood, Va. 22723
(703) 948-5214
25 cars; engines also

WISCONSIN

Brooks Stevens Automotive
Museum
10325 N. Port Washington Rd. 13W
Mequon, Wis. 53092
(414) 241-4185
75 cars, many owned
by royalty

FWD Museum (4-Wheel Drive)
Clintonville, Wis. 54929

Sunflower Museum of
Antique Cars
Lake Tomahawk, Wis. 54539

CANADA

Canadian Automotive Museum
99 Simcoe St. South
Oshawa, Ontario
Canada

CLUBS

A NOTE ON CLUBS

The clubs included in the following list are the largest and best-known ones. We're sorry that space limitations precluded our listing them all.

In addition to club names and addresses by individual marque, we have included a "General" clubs listing comprised of organizations dealing with multiple makes, historical cars, classical cars, antiques, specialty groups, etc. These clubs may be able to help you find a lead to a group not listed here.

GENERAL CLUBS

American Automobile Club
of America
1712 G. St., N.W.
Washington, D.C. 20006

Antique and Classic Car
Club of Canada
Box 1304, Postal Terminal A
Toronto 1, Ontario
Canada

Antique Automobile Club
of America
501 W. Governor Rd.
Hershey, Pa. 17033

Antique Race Car Club
8321 S. Highway 100
Franklin, Wis. 53132

Ass'n. of California Car
Clubs, Inc.
P.O. Box 96
Fullerton, Calif. 92632

Auto Enthusiasts International
P.O. Box 2379
Dearborn, Mich. 48123

Automotive Old Timers
P.O. Box 62
Warrenton, Va. 22186

Classic Car Club of America
P.O. Box 443
Madison, N.J. 07940

Contemporary Historical
Vehicles
71 Lucky Rd.
Severn, Md. 21144

Forties Limited, Inc.
3941 W. 117th St.
Hawthorne, Calif. 90250

Front-Wheel Drive Auto Club
P.O. Box 22
San Marcos, Calif. 92069

GM Cars
General Motors Restorers Club
P.O. Box 307
Highland Station
Springfield, Mass. 01109

Historical Automobile Society
of Canada
72 South St. West
Dundas, Ontario
Canada

Horseless Carriage Club
of America
9031 E. Florence Ave.
Downey, Calif. 90240

International Truck
Restorers Assn.
2026 Bayer Ave.
Fort Wayne, Ind. 46805

Mid-America Old Time
Automobile Assn.
1799 Mignon Ave.
Memphis, Tenn. 38107

Midwestern Council of
Sports Car Clubs
1812-R N. Kennicott Ave.
Arlington Heights, Ill. 60004

Milestone Car Society
P.O. Box 1166-L
Pacific Palisades, Calif. 90272

The Motor Bus Society
767 Valley Rd.
Upper Montclair, N.J. 07043

Pioneer Automobile Assn.
17445 Battles Ln.
South Bend, Ind. 46614

The Society of Automotive
Historians
P.O. Box 24
Edinboro, Pa. 16412

Society for the Preservation
and Appreciation of Antique
Motor Fire Apparatus in America
184 Jasper St.
Syracuse, N.Y. 13203

Southern California Classic
Club
13234 Lake St.
Los Angeles, Calif. 90066

Sports Car Collectors Society
of America, Inc.
P.O. Box 1855
Quantico, Va. 22134

Sports Car Club of America
(SCCA)
P.O. Box 22576
Denver, Colo. 80222

Steam Automobile Club
of America
1937 E. 71st St.
Chicago, Ill. 60649

United States Auto Club
(USAC)
P.O. Box 24001
Indianapolis, Ind. 46224

United Truckers of Southern
California
264 E. 18th
Costa Mesa, Calif. 92627

Vehicle Restorers Assn.
Box 761
Regina, Saskatchewan
Canada

Veteran Motor Car Club
of America
17 Pond St.
Hingham, Mass. 02043

Vintage Car Club of Canada
Box 2070
Vancouver, British Columbia
Canada

Vintage Sports Car Club
4350 N. Knox Ave.
Chicago, Ill. 60641

Vintage Sports Car Club
of America
170 Wetherill Rd.
Garden City, N.Y. 11530

Woody Wagon Club
P.O. Box 641
Franklin, Mich. 48025

CLUBS BY MARQUE

AC
AC Owners Club
American Centre
Vinemont Rd. No. 6
Sinking Springs, Pa. 19608

ALFA ROMEO
Alfa Romeo Owners Club
P.O. Box 331
Northbrook, Ill. 60062

Vintage Alfa Romeo
International
900 N. College
Fort Collins, Colo. 80521

ASTON-MARTIN
Aston-Martin Owners Club
195 Mount Paran Rd., N.W.
Atlanta, Ga. 30327

AUBURN
Auburn-Cord-Duesenberg
Club, Inc.
P.O. Box 11635
Palo Alto, Calif. 14306

AUSTIN-HEALEY
Austin-Healey Club
557 Canton Dr.
San Jose, Calif. 95125

AVANTI
Avanti Owners Assn. Intl.
21A Carney St.
Uxbridge, Mass. 01569

BENTLEY
Bentley Owners Club
c/o Klein Kars
Elizabethtown, Pa. 17022

The Bentley Drivers Club
76A High St.
Long Crendon
Aylesbury, Bucks, England

BMW
BMW Car Club of America
800 Boylston St., Box 96
Boston, Mass. 02199

BMW 507 Owners Club
2815 Philmont Ave.
Huntingdon Valley, Pa. 19006

Int'l. Assn. of BMW Clubs
P.O. Box 1312
Garden Grove, Calif. 92642

BUGATTI
American Bugatti Club
8724 E. Garvey Ave.
Rosemead, Calif. 91770

BUICK
Buick Collectors Club
of America
4730 Centre Ave.
Pittsburgh, Pa. 15213

McLaughlin Buick Club
of Canada
409 Tecumseh St.
Newmarket, Ontario, Canada

CADILLAC
Cadillac Automobile Club
P.O. Box 2842
Pasadena, Calif. 91105

Cadillac-LaSalle Club
3340 Poplar Dr.
Warren, Mich. 48091

CHEVROLET
Corvair Society of America
145 Ivywood Ln.
Radnor, Pa. 19087

National Chevrolet Restorers
Club
P.O. Box 311
La Mirada, Calif. 90638

National Council of
Corvette Clubs
3044 W. Grand Blvd.
Detroit, Mich. 48202

National Council of
Corvette Clubs
6672 Balsam Dr.
Reynoldsburg, Ohio 43608

National Nomad Club
P.O. Box 606
Arvada, Colo. 80001

Nifty Fifties
227 S. Grove St.
Denver, Colo. 80219

Vintage Chevrolet Club
1 Beechwood Ave.
Crescent Trailer Park
Gloucester, N.J. 08030

The Vintage Chevrolet Club
of America
P.O. Box 1135
Bellflower, Calif. 90706

Vintage Corvette Club
of America
2259 W. Adams
Fresno, Calif. 93706

CHRYSLER
Airflow Club of America
1475 President St.
Yellow Springs, Ohio 45387

Chrysler & DeSoto
Airflow Club
2750 E. Spring St.
Long Beach, Calif. 90306

Chrysler Products
Restorers Club
542 Regent St.
Houston, Pa. 15342

Chrysler 300 Club
(Eastern Div.)
3033 Durran Rd.
Louisville, Ky. 40205

Chrysler 300 Club
(Western Div.)
4614 32nd Ave. S.E.
Portland, Ore. 97202

Golden Lions
909 Edgewood Terrace
Wilmington, Del. 19809

National Chrysler Restorers
Club
P.O. Box 311
La Mirada, Calif. 90638

W.P.C. Club (Eastern Div.)
5986 Irishtown Rd.
Bethel Park, Pa. 15102

W.P.C. Club (Western Div.)
17916 Trenton Dr.
Castro Valley, Calif. 94546

CITROEN
Citroen Car Club
P.O. Box 743
Hollywood, Calif. 90028

COBRA
The Cobra Club
833 Lakeshore Rd.
Grosse Point Shores
Mich. 48236

CORD
See AUBURN

CROSLEY
Crosley Automobile Club
200 Ridge Road East
Williamson, N.Y. 14589

DAIMLER
Daimler Club
1500 Story Rd.
San Jose, Calif. 95122

DESOTO
Airflow Club of America
1475 President St.
Yellow Springs, Ohio 45387

DeSoto & Chrysler Airflow Club
2750 E. Spring St.
Long Beach, Calif. 90806

DeSoto Club of America
P.O. Box 4912
Columbus, Ohio 43202

DODGE
Dodge, Chrysler, Plymouth,
DeSoto, Maxwell Club
982 E. 81st St.
Brooklyn, N.Y. 11239

DUESENBERG
Auburn-Cord-Duesenberg
Club, Inc.
P.O. Box 11635
Palo Alto, Calif. 94306

DURANT
Durant Owners Club
7614 Langdon St.
Philadelphia, Pa. 19111

EDSEL
Edsel Owners Club, Inc.
Rt. 1, Box 206
Jacksonville, Tex. 75766

Edsel Owners Club of America
P.O. Box 7
West Liberty, Ill. 62475

International Edsel Club
P.O. Box 304
Bellevue, Ohio 44811

ESSEX
Hudson-Essex-Terraplane
Club
7522 Canby, No. 5
Reseda, Calif. 91335

FACEL-VEGA
Facel-Vega Club
34585 Quaker Valley Rd.
Farmington, Mich. 48024

FERRARI
Ferrari Club of America
520 S. Second St., Apt. 1510
Springfield, Ill. 62701

Ferrari Owners Club
3460 Wilshire Blvd., Suite 1007
Los Angeles, Calif. 90010

FIAT
Fiat Club of America, Inc.
P.O. Box 192
Somerville, Mass. 02143

FORD
Classic Thunderbird Club Int'l.
48 Second St.
San Francisco, Calif. 94105

The Early Ford V-8 Club
of America
P.O. Box 2122
San Leandro, Calif. 94577

Ford-Mercury Club of America
P.O. Box 3551
Hayward, Calif. 94544

Ford & Mercury Restorers Club
P.O. Box 2133
Dearborn, Mich. 48125

Ford Motorsports Assn.
12263 Market St.
Livonia, Mich. 48150

Model A Ford Club of America
P.O. Box 2564
Pomona, Calif. 91766

Model A Restorers Club, Inc.
P.O. Box 1930A
Dearborn, Mich. 48121

The Model T Ford Club
of America
P.O. Box 711
Tarzana, Calif. 91356

Model T Ford Club Int'l.
c/o The Allerton
701 N. Michigan Ave.
Chicago, Ill. 60611

National Ford Restorers Club
P.O. Box 311
La Mirada, Calif. 90638

National Woodie Club
5522 W. 140th St.
Hawthorne, Calif. 90250

Retractable Ford Club
1761 National Rd.
Dayton, Ohio 45414

The Shelby Owners Assn.
28 Union Ave.
Hempstead, N.Y. 11550

Vintage Thunderbird Club
of America
26056 Deerfield
Dearborn Heights, Mich. 48127

FRANKLIN
The H.H. Franklin Club
P.O. Box 66
Syracuse, N.Y. 13215

FRAZER
Kaiser-Frazer Owners Club
8013 Glenhaven Rd.
Soquel, Calif. 95073

Kaiser-Frazer Owners
Club Int'l.
705 N. Lillian St.
McHenry, Ill. 60050

Kaiser-Frazer Owners
Club of America, Inc.
4015 S. Forest
Independence, Mo. 64052

FRONTENAC
Frontenac Club
45 Greenwood St.
Tamaqua, Pa. 18252

GRAHAM
Graham & Graham-Paige
Registry
30 N. Broadway, Apt. 5E
White Plains, N.Y. 10601

Hupmobile-Graham Club
of America
P.O. Box 215
Glenview, Ill. 60025

HUDSON
Greater Super Six Club
1118 N. Alton Ave.
Indianapolis, Ind. 46222

Also see ESSEX

HUPMOBILE
Hupmobile Club
150 Bradley St.
Chagrin Falls, Ohio 44022

CLUBS

The Hupmobile Club
P.O. Box AA
Rosemead, Calif. 91770

Hupmobile-Graham Club
of America
P.O. Box 215
Glenview, Ill. 60025

ISOTTA-FRASCHINI
Isotta-Fraschini Owners Assn.
9704 Illinois St.
Hebron, Ill. 60034

JAGUAR
Classic Jaguar Association
1450 Boeger Ave.
Westchester, Ill. 60153

Jaguar Affiliates
6974 Mohican Ln.
Westland, Mich. 48185

Jaguar Clubs of North America
600 Willow Tree Rd.
Leonia, N.J. 07605

Jaguar Owners Club
2707 Granville Ave.
Los Angeles, Calif. 90064

JAVELIN-AMX
AMX of America, Ltd.
1029 LaPorte Ave.
Fort Collins, Colo. 80521

JEEPSTER
Jeepster Club, Inc.
P.O. Box 281
Cuyahoga Falls, Ohio 44221

Midstates Jeepster Association
222 W. Wood St.
Brookfield, Mo. 64628

Willys-Overland Jeepster Club
395 Dumbarton Blvd.
Cleveland, Ohio 44143

KAISER
See FRAZER

KISSEL
Kissel Kar Club
R.D. 2, Box 92A
Hartford, Wis. 53027

KNIGHT
The Willys-Overland-Knight
Registry
2754 Lullington Dr.
Winston-Salem, N.C. 27103

LAGONDA
The Lagonda Club
10 Crestwood Trail
Lake Mohawk
Sparta, N.J. 07871

LAMBORGHINI
Lamborghini Club of America
c/o G.T. Cars
3054 N. Lake Terrace
Glenview, Ill. 60025

LANCIA
American Lancia Club
50 Mansion Rd.
Springfield, Pa. 19064

LA SALLE
See CADILLAC

LINCOLN
Lincoln Continental Owners
Club
P.O. Box 549
Nogales, Ariz. 85621

Lincoln Continental Owners
Club
National Headquarters
28 Harmony Ln.
Westbury, N.Y. 12993

Lincoln Owners Club
P.O. Box 189
Algonquin, Ill. 60102

Lincoln Zephyr Owners Club
6628 Verna St.
Library, Pa. 15129

LOTUS
Club Elite of North America
P.O. Box 351
Clarksville, Tenn. 37040

Lotus Elite Owners Club
140 The Post Road, Apt. A
Springfield, Ohio 45503

MARMON
Marmon Owners Club
5364 Stuart Ave., S.E.
Grand Rapids, Mich. 49508

MASERATI
Maserati Club
The Filberts, 39 Aylesbury Rd.
Wendover, Bucks, England

MAXWELL
See DODGE

MERCEDES-BENZ
Gull Wing Group
P.O. Box 2093
Sunnyvale, Calif. 94087

Mercedes-Benz Club
P.O. Box 2111
San Fernando, Calif. 91343

MERCER
Mercer Associates
MGT Dept., Texas Tech
Lubbock, Tex. 79409

MERCURY
See FORD

MG
Classic MG Club
6449 Arundel Dr.
Orlando, Fla. 32808

MGA Register
P.O. Box 13, Annex Station
Providence, R.I. 02903

MGA Twin-Cam Register
256 Galaxy Dr.
Pine Circle, Minn. 55014

New England MG "T"
Register
Drawer No. 220
Oneonta, N.Y. 13820

T.C. Motoring Club
4105 Leamington Ave.
Chicago, Ill. 60641

MORGAN
Morgan Car Club
8600 16th St.
Silver Spring, Md. 20910

Morgan Owners Group
40-01 Little Neck Pkwy.
Little Neck, N.Y. 11363

Morgan Plus Four Club
3402 S. Walker Ave.
San Pedro, Calif. 90731

NASH
Nash Car Club of America
Elvira Rd., R.R. 1
Clinton, Iowa 52732

Nash Car Club of America
635 Lloyd St.
Hubbard, Ohio 44425

Nash-Healey Car Club
R.D. 2
Corning, N.Y. 14830

OLDSMOBILE
Curved Dash Olds Club
7 Kiltie Dr.
New Hope, Pa. 18938

Oldsmobile Club of America
P.O. Box 1498, Samp Mortar Sta.
Fairfield, Conn. 06432

The Oldsmobile Club of Canada
117 Hespeler Ave.
Winnipeg, Manitoba R2L 015
Canada

OVERLAND
See KNIGHT

PACKARD
Eastern Packard Club, Inc.
P.O. Box 672
Bridgeport, Conn. 06608

Packard Automobile Classics
P.O. Box 2808
Oakland, Calif. 94618

Packard International Motor
Car Club
P.O. Box 1347
Costa Mesa, Calif. 92626

PEUGEOT
Peugeot Owners Club
P.O. Box 7363
Columbus, Ohio 43209

PIERCE-ARROW
Pierce-Arrow Society
135 Edgerton St.
Rochester, N.Y. 14607

PLYMOUTH
Early Plymouth Club
128 Crain Rd.
Paramus, N.J. 07652

Plymouth 4- and 6-Cylinder
Owners Club
87-30 Little Neck Pkwy.
Floral Park, N.Y. 11001

Plymouth Owners Club
R.D. 1, Box 306
Jeannette, Pa. 15644

PONTIAC
Oakland-Pontiac Enthusiasts
Organization
P.O. Box 518
Keego Harbor, Mich. 48033

Pontiac-Oakland Club
International
P.O. Box 612
Escondido, Calif. 92025

Safari Club of America
220 17th Ave. South
Seattle, Wash. 98144

PORSCHE
Porsche Club of America
5616 Clermont Dr.
Alexandria, Va. 23310

Porsche Four Cam Register
P.O. Box 1027, Station Q
Toronto, Ontario
Canada

Porsche Owners Club
6229 Outlook Ave.
Los Angeles, Calif. 90042

Porsche Register
6243 N. Oak Ave.
Temple City, Calif. 91780

RENAULT
Team Renault
100 Sylvan Ave.
Englewood Cliffs, N.J. 07632

REO
The Reo Club of America
113 Gillin Rd.
Ambler, Pa. 19002

The Reo Club of Canada
117 Hespeler Ave.
Winnipeg, Manitoba R2L 0L5
Canada

RICKENBACKER
Rickenbacker Club
13572 Appoline
Detroit, Mich. 48227

ROLLS-ROYCE
Rolls-Royce Owners Club
1822 N. Second St.
Harrisburg, Pa. 17108

SHELBY
See FORD

SIMPLEX
Simplex Automobile Club
Meadow Spring
Glen Cove, N.Y. 11542

STEVENS-DURYEA
Stevens-Duryea Associates
3565 New Haven Rd.
Pasadena, Calif. 91107

STUDEBAKER
Antique Studebaker Club
175 May Ave.
Monrovia, Calif. 91016

Studebaker Automobile
Society
50 Hickory Dr.
East Hartford, Conn. 06118

Studebaker Drivers Club
P.O. Box 3044
South Bend, Ind. 46619

The Studebaker Driver's
Club, Inc.
3328 Shorewood Dr.
Mesquite, Tex. 75149

Studebaker Owners Club
P.O. Box 5294
Pasadena, Calif. 91107

STUTZ
Stutz Nuts
3856 Arthington Blvd.
Indianapolis, Ind. 46226

SUNBEAM
Sunbeam Tiger Owners Assn.
638 Cornell Ave.
Albany, Calif. 94706

TRIUMPH
Triumph Sports Owners Assn.
c/o British Leyland Motors
600 Willow Tree Rd.
Leonia, N.J. 07605

TUCKER
Tucker Register
229 E. Rosewood Ct.
Ontario, Calif. 91764

VOLKSWAGEN
Volkswagen Club of America
P.O. Box 5357, Station E
Atlanta, Ga. 30307

WILLYS
See KNIGHT